Yale Egyptological Studies 8

The Mortuary Papyrus of Padikakem

Walters Art Museum 551

Yekaterina Barbash

Yale Egyptological Seminar · New Haven, CT

Yale Egyptological Studies 8

ISBN 978-0-9740-0255-2

Library of Congress Cataloging-in-Publication Data

Barbash, Yekaterina.
The mortuary papyrus of Padikakem : Walters Art Museum 551 / Yekaterina Barbash.
p. cm. -- (Yale Egyptological studies ; 8)
Revision of the author's doctoral thesis--Johns Hopkins University, 2005.
Includes bibliographical references and indexes.
ISBN 978-0-9740025-5-2 (alk. paper)
1. Egyptian language--Papyri, Hieratic. 2. Egyptian language--Writing, Hieratic. I. Title.
PJ1661.W35B37 2011
299'.31388--dc22
2011008885

The drawing of the *Akh*-bird is adapted by Elena Sakevich.

Typeset in Minion Pro and Warnock Pro,
Transliterations in Transliteration v. 2.0,
Hieroglyphics in JSesh (v. 4.3).

Printed in the United States of America on acid-free paper.

Contents

List of Plates and Hieroglyphic Transcriptions

List of Tables

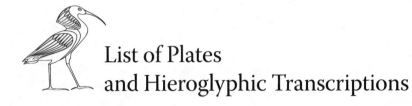

Preface and Acknowledgments

The present work is a revision of my doctoral dissertation, submitted to the Department of Near Eastern Studies at Johns Hopkins University in 2005. The original commentary, interpretative texts, and bibliography have been expanded considerably, and I have made a number of changes and corrections. I am sincerely grateful to many who have helped me in the course of this effort. I wish to express my gratitude to Dr. Regine Schulz, Curator of Ancient Art at the Walters Art Museum, for granting me the permission to study and publish papyrus W551. I also thank Dr. Richard Parkinson, Assistant Keeper at the Department of Ancient Egypt and Sudan at the British Museum, for allowing me to study and make reference to the photographs of the unpublished papyrus BM 10081.

This work would not have been possible without the guidance, patience, and wisdom of my advisor, Dr. Richard Jasnow, who oversaw the initial stages of the dissertation and offered numerous significant insights during the revision process. I am also deeply indebted to Dr. Betsy Bryan for the invaluable education and advice she afforded me. To Dr. Colleen Manassa and Dr. John Coleman Darnell, whose revisions and suggestions of further bibliography greatly enhanced the present manuscript, I owe a special debt of gratitude. I thank Dr. Hans Fischer-Elfert for his indispensable comments on this work. In addition, I thank the William K. and Marilyn M. Simpson Egyptology Endowment Fund of the Department of Near Eastern Languages and Civilizations, Yale University, for making this publication possible.

I am forever indebted to my parents Natasha and Vitaly Barbash for their sincere encouragement and support. I am profoundly grateful to Maxim Fortun for his thoughtful comments, assistance, and devotion throughout the entire process. I thank Prof. Ogden Goelet for introducing me to Egyptology and offering his support and friendship as I pursued the journey of exploring ancient Egypt. This work would not be possible without the numerous people who have assisted my study and research. I express my sincere gratitude to everyone at Johns Hopkins University and my Brooklyn Museum family.

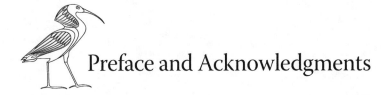

Abbreviations

The abbreviations are divided into two sections: Bibliographic Abbreviations and Designations of Texts and Terms. The full references are listed in the Bibliography and Indexes.

BIBLIOGRAPHIC ABBREVIATIONS

ÄAT	Ägypten und Altes Testament
AegLeo	Aegyptiaca Leodiensia
AEPHE	*Annuaire de l'École Pratique des Hautes Études*
ÄgAb	Ägyptologische Abhandlungen
AH	Aegyptiaca Helvetica
AnOr	Analecta Orientalia
ASAE	*Annales du Service des Antiquités de l'Égypte*
AT	Aegyptiaca Treverensia
AV	Archäologische Veröffentlichungen, Deutsches Archäologisches Institut, Abteilung Kairo
BAe	Bibliotheca Aegyptiaca
BdE	Bibliothèque d'Étude
BIFAO	*Bulletin de l'Institut Français d'Archéologie Orientale*
BSFE	*Bulletin de la Société Française d'Égyptologie*
CDD	*Chicago Demotic Dictionary*, Oriental Institute, University of Chicago http://oi.uchicago.edu/OI/DEPT/PUB/SRC/CDD/CDD.html
CdE	*Chronique d'Égypte. Bulletin Périodique de la Fondation Égyptologique Reine Élisabeth*
DAIK	Deutsches Archäologisches Institut, Abteilung Kairo
DAWW	Denkschriften der Kaiserlichen Akademie der Wissenschaften in Wien, Philosophisch-Historische Klasse
DiscEg	*Discussions in Egyptology*
EEF	Egypt Exploration Fund
EgUit	Egyptologische Uitgaven
ÉPRO	Études Préliminaires aux Religions Orientales dans l'Empire Romain
EVO	*Egitto e Vicino Oriente*
HÄB	Hildesheimer Ägyptologische Beiträge
HP	Möller, Georg. *Hieratische Paläographie,* vol. III (Osnabrück: Zeller, 1965)
GM	*Göttinger Miszellen*
GOF	Göttinger Orientforschungen

IFAO	L'Institut Français d'Archéologie Orientale du Caire
JEOL	Jaarbericht van het Vooraziatisch-Egyptisch Genootschap Ex Oriente Lux
JARCE	*Journal of the American Research Center in Egypt*
JEA	*Journal of Egyptian Archaeology*
JNES	*Journal of Near Eastern Studies*
LÄ	Helck, Wolfgang and Otto, Eberhard. *Lexikon der Ägyptologie*, 7 vols. (Wiesbaden: Harrassowitz, 1975–89)
LÄS	Leipziger Ägyptologische Studien
MÄS	Münchner Ägyptologische Studien
MDAIK	*Mitteilungen des Deutsches Archäologisches Institut, Abteilung Kairo*
MIFAO	Mémoires Publiés par les Membres de l'IFAO
MonAeg	Monumenta Aegyptiaca
MRE	Monographies Reine Élisabeth
MVAG	*Mitteilungen der Vorderasiatischen-Aegyptischen Gesellschaft*
OBO	Orbis Biblicus et Orientalis
OIP	Oriental Institute Publications
OLA	Orientalia Lovaniensia Analecta
PAe	Probleme der Ägyptologie
RdT	*Recueil des Travaux relatifs à la Philologie et à l'Archéologie Égyptiennes et Assyriennes*
SAK	*Studien zur Altägyptischen Kultur*
SAOC	Studies in Ancient Oriental Civilization
SAT	Studien zum altägyptischen Totenbuch
SIE	Studies in Egyptology
StudAeg	Studia Aegyptiaca
SSEA	Society for the Study of Egyptian Antiquities
TSBA	*Transactions of the Society of Biblical Archaeology*
UGAÄ	Untersuchungen zur Geschichte und Altertumskunde Ägyptens
Urk.	Urkunden des ägyptischen Altertums, founded by G. Steindorff.
Urk. I	Sethe, Kurt. *Urkunden des Alten Reichs*. Urk.1. (Leipzig: Hinrichs, 1933)
Urk. IV	Sethe, Kurt. *Urkunden der 18. Dynasty. Historisch-biographische Urkunden von Zeitgenossen der Hatschepsowet*. Urk. 4/7 (Leipzig: Hinrichs, 1906)
Urk. V	Grapow, Hermann. *Religiöse Urkunden: ausgewählte Texte des Totenbuches*. Urk. 5 (Leipzig: Hinrichs, 1915–17)
Urk. VI	Schott, Siegfried. *Urkunden Mythologischen Inhalts*. Urk. 6 (Leipzig: Hinrichs, 1929)
USE	Uppsala Studies in Egyptology
Wb.	Erman, Adolf, and Grapow, Hermann. *Wörterbuch der ägyptischen Sprache*. 6 vols. (Berlin: Akademie Verlag, 1971)
WdO	*Die Welt des Orient: Wissenschaftliche Beiträge zur Kunde des Morgenlandes*
YES	Yale Egyptological Studies
ZÄS	*Zeitschrift für ägyptische Sprache und Altertumskunde*

DESIGNATION OF TEXTS AND TERMS

All transliterations of PT and CT spells are based on the hieroglyphic transcriptions of Sethe, *Die altägyptischen Pyramidentexte*, 2 vols., and De Buck, *Egyptian Coffin Texts*, 7 vols., respectively. The PT are designated with spell and paragraph numbers based on Faulkner, *Ancient Egyptian Pyramid Texts*. In referring to publications, the author's last name and title of the publication or part thereof are used. Full details of all publications cited are provided in the Bibliography.

B	Papyrus Berlin 3057
BM	Papyrus British Museum 10081
BMI	Papyri British Museum 102524 and 102525
BMII	Papyrus Salt 1821 (A)
BMIII	Papyrus British Museum 10317
BD	Book of the Dead
ca.	circa
cf.	compare
ch.	chapter
col(s).	column(s)
CT	Coffin Texts
ed(s).	editor(s)
fig.	figure
GR	Greco-Roman period
LP	Late Period
MK	Middle Kingdom
MMA	Papyrus Metropolitan Museum of Art 35.9.21
n(n).	note(s)
NK	New Kingdom
N(N)	personal name
OK	Old Kingdom
OM	Opening of the Mouth
P.	Papyrus
p(p).	page(s)
pl	plural
pl.	plate
PT	Pyramid Text(s)
P.W551	Papyrus Walters Art Museum 551
SIP	Second Intermediate Period
TT	Theban Tomb
TIP	Third Intermediate Period
var.	variant
vol(s).	volume(s)

1
The Papyrus Walters Art Museum 551

1.1 INTRODUCTION

1.1.1. PRELIMINARY REMARKS

The subject of this volume is the papyrus W551 of the Walters Art Museum in Baltimore. The scroll was acquired by Mr. Henry Walters before 1931. Unfortunately, the date and place of the purchase are not documented in the records. The manuscript records a series of hieratic mortuary texts for a man named Padikakem, whose name was inserted in the blank spaces provided for this purpose. As the composition is comparable to numerous Late Period (LP) and Greco-Roman (GR) papyri, it offers insights into Egyptian mortuary texts of that era. Some texts in this manuscript originate as early as the Old Kingdom (OK). Others bring to mind various genres of Egyptian literature, illuminating the homogeneity, as well as the "evolution," of scribal traditions throughout Egyptian history. The good preservation of this papyrus allows a broader understanding of the orthography and paleography of the LP and GR eras.

1.1.2. DESCRIPTION OF THE PAPYRUS

P.W551 is described in the museum records as an Egyptian "Funerary Papyrus" of the "Ptolemaic period, Dynasty XXX."[1] The unrolled manuscript is light beige in color and measures 168 cm in length and 41 cm in height. The papyrus is made of five sheets of an average length of 31.5 cm, except for the first sheet on the right, which is 20.5 cm long, and the last sheet, which is only 18 cm long. The five joins are visible at the beginning of col. 1, down the middle of col. 4, at the end of col. 6, down the middle of col. 8, and at the end of col. 9. Each right-hand sheet overlaps the left-hand one, as is typical in scrolls.[2] The fact that col. 1 is preceded by 20.5 cm of uninscribed papyrus indicates that it is the beginning of the scroll.[3]

1 Papyrus W551 has not been published previously, but was briefly described by Coenen and Verrept, *GM* 202 (2004): 97–102.

2 Cf. P.BM 10209, Haikal, *Nesmin* I, p. 18.

3 This is characteristic of books or lengthy documents on papyri, see Černý, *Paper & Books*, p. 19. For example, MMA similarly begins with 26 cm of blank papyrus, see Goyon, *Imouthès*, pp. 7 and 9, fig. 1.

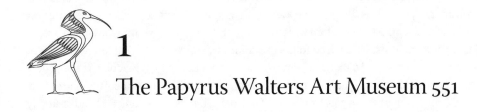

The text comprises ten columns of text, ranging from 21 to 55 lines. The first five columns are considerably narrower than the rest and have an uneven left edge. Col. 1 measures 6.5 cm at its widest, col. 2 is 8 cm at its widest, cols. 3 and 4 range in width from 3.7 to 7.5 cm, and col. 5 is 8 cm at its widest. The following columns, which record a different text, have even edges on both sides.[4] Col. 6 is 14 cm wide, cols. 7 and 8 are 19.5 cm, col. 9 is the widest, measuring 21.5 cm, and the last col. 10 is about 10 cm wide. The texts of cols. 1–9 are fairly even, ranging in length from 34.5 to 35.5 cm. The final col. 10 is 18 cm long and ends roughly in the middle of the papyrus sheet, leaving the bottom portion un-inscribed, which suggests that the manuscript is complete. It is overall in good condition, with the exception of some damage to col. 1 and through the middle of the scroll on cols. 1–9. Judging by the improving condition of the papyrus towards the final column, we can assume that the papyrus was rolled up in a manner where the final column was on the inside of the scroll.[5]

The upper and lower margins of the papyrus were not demarcated by the scribe. The side margins, however, are indicated by a double vertical line drawn in red ink.[6] The papyrus seems to have been inscribed on one side parallel to the fibers.[7] The body of the text is written in black ink, with red ink used for rubrics and names of certain deities.

1.2. PALEOGRAPHY AND DATE

Papyrus W551 is for the most part written by one scribe, except for ten lines of col. 9,[8] where the handwriting drastically changes to a much more cursive script, indicating that this section was written by a different scribe. Following a line gap, the handwriting resembles the rest of the manuscript, suggesting that the first scribe finished the text. Remarkably, the same spell is continued by the separate hands. This feature is rare in funerary texts that are generally written by one scribe.[9] One example of a change in handwriting is found in the Ptolemaic papyrus of Nesmin (P.BM 10209).[10] There, however, the shift takes place gradually, as the text becomes slightly more cursive in col. 3 and yet broader and more cursive in cols. 4 and 5.[11]

---

4 The two texts in P.W551 are described in detail in section 1.7, below.

5 This is typical of Egyptian papyri, see Černý, *Paper & Books*, p. 19.

6 The use of vertical framing lines to separate columns is characteristic of hieroglyphic texts and hieratic books of certain kinds, see Tait, in M. Bierbrier, ed., *Papyrus, Structure and Usage*, pp. 72 and 75. MMA exhibits the same practice, see Goyon, *Imouthès*, pp. 13–14.

7 For a brief discussion of the preference for writing texts on the horizontal fibers of papyrus, see Černý, *Paper & Books*, p. 17, nn. 92–93.

8 Lines 22–32.

9 This phenomenon may be compared with the tradition of inserting an individual's name by a different hand in various Book of the Dead (BD) papyri, such as the papyrus of Ani; see Goelet, *Egyptian Book of the Dead*, p. 142.

10 Haikal, *Nesmin* I, p. 18, and pls. 8–9.

11 Due to this, Haikal, *Nesmin* I, p. 18, attributes the change to "obvious fatigue" on the part of the scribe. On the contrary, since each "new" handwriting corresponds with a different part of the composition in the papyrus of Nesmin, both papyri were most likely written by more than one scribe.

Unfortunately, Greco-Roman (GR) hands are rather difficult to date definitively, partly due to their characteristic neatness and regularity.[12] Because of their religious nature, late hieratic papyri were generally not dated by the scribes.[13] Furthermore, many late manuscripts do not have an established archeological context, exacerbating the problem of their date. As a result, many late manuscripts must be dated on the basis of paleography. The difficulty of dating LP and GR hieratic is made worse by the frequent similarity between scribal hands dated centuries apart.[14]

Although the text of P.W551 does not contain clear dating criteria, such as a royal name or an event, it may be dated to the Ptolemaic period. Its paleography resembles such early Ptolemaic texts as P.Bremner-Rhind,[15] the papyri of Nesmin,[16] P.BM 10252[17] and P.BM 10288.[18] A comparison with Möller's *Hieratische Paläographie*, vol. III (HP)[19] and Verhoeven's *Untersuchungen zur späthieratischen Buchschrift*[20] supports this date.

Table 1 presents a selection of signs characteristic to the scribe of P.W551 and/or resembling those in the above-mentioned late papyri, which support a date in the Ptolemaic period. According to the paleographical works of Möller and Verhoeven, the following signs are similar to P.Bremner-Rhind: D36, D40, D41, D55, E17, F18, F26, F36, G14, G24, G32, V29 and V36. A53, G1 and L2 are reminiscent of the early or mid-Ptolemaic mummy bandages, Berlin 3073.[21] D3 and T7 are similar to those in the GR papyrus fragments of Bakakhuiu, P.Berlin 7809–7810.[22] D32 is written by the scribe of P.W551 in two different ways, resembling P.Bremner-Rhind and P.Berlin 7809–7810. The horizontality of K1 is paralleled in the Saite papyrus of Iahtesnakht, P.Colon.Aeg. 10207.[23] R11 resembles the GR mortuary papyrus Leiden J32,[24] while W1 is similar to the late papyri Berlin 13242 and P.Bremner-Rhind.[25]

The scribe of P.W551 has a few distinguishing features, such as the tendency of placing a dot next to the weary man (A7)[26] and below the man with stick (A24), although this is

12 Tait, in M. Bierbrier, ed., *Papyrus, Structure and Usage*, p. 75, alludes to the problems of dating LP hieratic during the entire 1st millennium BCE.

13 Verhoeven, *Untersuchungen zur späthieratischen Buchschrift*, p. 6.

14 Möller, *Hieratische Paläographie* III, p. *1.

15 P.BM 10188, see Faulkner, *Bremner-Rhind*.

16 P.BM 10208 and P.BM10209, see Haikal, *Nesmin* II.

17 Verhoeven, *Untersuchungen zur späthieratischen Buchschrift*, pp. 75–81, points out that P.BM 10252 corresponds to P.Bremner-Rhind and should be dated to 306 BCE; see *ibid.*, 80.

18 Caminos, *JEA* 58 (1972): 205–24.

19 Möller, *Hieratische Paläographie* III.

20 Verhoeven, *Untersuchungen zur späthieratischen Buchschrift*.

21 Möller, *Hieratische Paläographie* III, p. *9; Kockelmann, *Untersuchungen*, pp. 25–47.

22 Möller, *Hieratische Paläographie* III, p. *12.

23 Verhoeven, *Untersuchungen zur späthieratischen Buchschrift*, pp. 72 and 151.

24 Möller, *Hieratische Paläographie* III, p. *11.

25 For the former, see Möller, *Hieratische Paläographie* III, p. *11. For the latter, see Verhoeven, *Untersuchungen zur späthieratischen Buchschrift*, pp. 75–80 and 201.

26 This feature also occurs in the Ptolemaic papyrus Berlin 3030, see Möller, *Hieratische Paläographie* III, pp. *14–15 and 8.

not always the case.[27] The conical loaf (X8) has a distinctive slant to it,[28] while the lung and windpipe sign (F36) shows an unusually pronounced stroke beneath it.[29] B1, G53, G54, F27, and F40 are also distinctive for this scribe.

Table 2 presents seven hieroglyphic-like signs that appear in the text. Both tables incorporate the sign number, according to Gardiner's sign list (#) and according to Möller's *Hieratische Paläographie* (HP), the hieroglyphic sign (Sign), its hieratic version in P.W551 (Hieratic), and a parallel hieratic sign from another text (Comparanda).

1.3. GRAMMAR

Although a number of the spells in P.W551 closely parallel the Pyramid Texts (PT), the grammar of this text is mostly proper Middle Egyptian.[30] Collections of mortuary spells similar to those in papyrus W551 appear to have been continuously altered and expanded throughout Egyptian history.[31] The differences in grammar of the various spells in the same compilation testify to this phenomenon.[32] The small number of obvious grammatical errors, as well as the careful handwriting, demonstrate the scribe's competence. Nevertheless, some grammatical and orthographic peculiarities of this scribe deserve mention. Notably, these are seldom paralleled by the corresponding texts. The following presents a list of features peculiar to P.W551 and other late papyri.

PRONOUNS

a. The 1st person plural suffix pronoun *n* is indicated with .[33]

b. The 1st person plural suffix pronoun is written .[34]

c.  is used for the 2nd person singular dependent pronoun *ṯw* in many instances, but not always.[35]

---

27 The scribes of the Ptolemaic P.Bremner-Rhind and P.Berlin 3008 also point this sign, see Möller, *Hieratische Paläographie* III, pp. *9–10 and 2.

28 The slant is comparable to the GR P.Berlin 13242, see Möller, *Hieratische Paläographie* III, pp. *11 and 55.

29 Although this stroke occurs in most late hands, its size may compare to P.Bremner-Rhind and the GR fragments P.Berlin 7809–7810; see Möller, *Hieratische Paläographie* III, pp. *12 and 16.

30 For a detailed discussion of the parallels see section 1.7.3, below.

31 For a discussion of the verbal system used in various texts of the GR period and the modification of certain 'classical' Egyptian texts over time, see Engsheden, *La reconstitution du verbe*; Lustman, *Étude Grammaticale du Papyrus Bremner-Rhind.*

32 For the history and likely modes of transmission of glorification spells, in particular, see section 2.3, below.

33 Line 2, 8.

34 Line 1, 35.

35 See for instance, line 1, 4.

TABLE 1 Selection of Signs from P.W551.

#	HP	SIGN	HIERATIC	COMPARANDA	
A7	32				P.Berlin 3030
A24	15				P.Berlin 3008 P.Bremner-Rhind
A53	10				P.Berlin 3073
B1	61				
D3	81				P.Berlin 7809–7810
D32	110				P.Berlin 3030 P.Bremner-Rhind
D36	99				P.Bremner-Rhind
D40	105				P.Bremner-Rhind
D41	101				P.Bremner-Rhind
D55	121				P.Bremner-Rhind
E17	128				P.Bremner-Rhind
F18	160				P.Bremner-Rhind
F26	165				P.Bremner-Rhind
F27	166				
F36	181				P.Bremner-Rhind P.Berlin 3030

TABLE 1 Selection of Signs from P.W551 (continued).

#	HP	SIGN	HIERATIC	COMPARANDA	
F40	173				
G1	192				Berlin 3073
G14	193				P.Bremner-Rhind
G24	201				P.Bremner-Rhind
G32	203				P.Bremner-Rhind
G53a	230				
G54	227				
K1	253				P.Colon.Aeg. 10207
L2	260				P.Berlin 3073
R11	541				P.Leiden J32
T7*3	548				P.Berlin 7809–7810
V29	398				P.Bremner-Rhind
V36	590				P.Bremner-Rhind
W1	493				P.Berlin 13242 P.Bremner-Rhind
X8	569				P.Berlin 13242

TABLE 2 Hieroglyphic-like Signs in P.W551.

SIGN	#	HIERATIC	COLUMN, LINE
	E1		9, 10; 9, 18; 10, 4; 10, 7; 10, 8
	E31		9, 6; 9, 10
	G17		8, 16
	G38		9, 7; 9, 10
	G43		5, 44; 5, 52
	L1		7, 9
	P1		6, 15

d. The 2nd person plural suffix pronoun *ṯn* is written in many instances.[36]

e. The 2nd person singular dependent pronoun *ṯw* appears interchangeably as *tw* and *kw* throughout the manuscript. The choice of either of the two variants does not appear to be conditioned syntactically, as they occur with both the *sḏm=f* and *sḏm.n=f* forms, not depending on whether the subject is nominal or pronominal.[37]
Since the variation occurs in P.W551 as well as in such parallels as the PT,[38] it may not be viewed as a dating criterion.

f. The 2nd person singular independent pronoun *ṯwt* is characteristic of the PT.[39]

g. *sw* is used in place of the 3rd person singular feminine suffix pronoun *s*.[40]

36 For an example, see line 8, 14. For this reading of (G4), see Daumas, *Valeurs phonétiques* II, p. 312; Fairman, *ASAE* 43 (1943): 226. For the reading of (G4) as *tw*, see Edel, *Neue Deutungen*, pp. 46–48.

37 For an overview of interpretations of the *kw* and *tw* variation, see Vernus, in H. Willems, ed., *The World of the Coffin Texts*, Annex D, pp. 192 and 194, who shows that the variation is not determined syntactically, grammatically, or phonetically.

38 Allen, *Inflection of the Verb*, p. 202.

39 Line 8, 5. This pronoun survives in Middle Egyptian as an archaism, see Gardiner, *Egyptian Grammar*, §64.

40 Line 3, 48.

h. *s* stands for the 3rd person singular feminine dependent pronoun *st*.[41]

i. *s* also stands for the 3rd person singular masculine dependent pronoun *sw*.[42]

k. The 3rd person plural suffix pronoun *sn* is written in a variety of ways:
1. Likely due to the close similarity of the horizontals, 𓊃 and 𓈖, it frequently appears as 𓈖𓈖.[43]
2. For the same reason it appears as 𓊃𓊃.[44]
3. The 𓈖 is omitted.[45]
4. The 𓈖 and 𓊃 are frequently reversed throughout the manuscript.[46]

ARTICLES

Definite articles, typical of Late Egyptian texts, are practically absent from P.W551.[47]

DEMONSTRATIVES

a. The demonstratives *iptn* and *ipw* are an archaic form of *pw*.[48]

b. The demonstratives *pfy* and *pwy* appear to be used interchangeably, although *pfy* is preferred.[49]

c. The plural demonstrative *nwy* is used nominally.[50]

PREPOSITIONS

a. 𓇋𓂋 often stands for the preposition *r* throughout the manuscript.[51]

b. *ḥnʿ* is written in a variety of ways, omitting the phonetic ʿ [52] or both ʿ and *n*.[53]

---

41 Lines 4, 3 and 6, 42; see Gardiner, *Egyptian Grammar*, §§43 and 46.

42 Line 8, 10.

43 Lines 6, 5, etc.

44 Line 6, 5.

45 Line 7, 15.

46 Lines. 7, 22; 8, 33; 8, 34; 8, 37; and 9, 16.

47 They do, however, occur occasionally, see for example lines 2, 14 and 4, 26.

48 Lines 6, 4 and 8, 14, for example. See Gardiner, *Egyptian Grammar*, §110; *Wb.* I 69, 6–7.

49 *pwy* appears in lines 6, 19; 8, 16; 8, 39; 9, 18; 9, 20; 9, 22; 9, 27; 9, 31. For the variation between the demonstratives *pwy* and *pfy*, see Lustman, *Étude Grammaticale du Papyrus Bremner-Rhind*, p. 8.

50 Line 8, 2; *Wb.* II 216, 2–17; Wilson, *Ptolemaic Lexikon*, p. 498.

51 This is a typical feature of Late Egyptian orthography, see Lustman, *Étude Grammaticale du Papyrus Bremner-Rhind*, p. 23.

52 Line 7, 45. For this spelling, see *Wb.* III 110.

53 Lines 7, 19 and 7, 44.

c. The construction *r-iw* stands for the preposition *r-ir*.[54]

GENITIVE ADJECTIVES

a. *nty* stands for the genitive adjective *nt*.[55]

NEGATIVES

a. The negatives *n* and *nn* are seemingly interchangeable.[56]

b. 𓈖 is written in place of 𓂜.[57]

c. *im* negates imperatives.[58]

INTERROGATIVES

a. The Late Egyptian interrogative *ny-m* is used in one instance.[59]

VERBAL FORMS

a. The frequent confusion of the *sḏm=f* and *sḏm.n=f* forms is a noteworthy feature of the text.[60]

b. The *i*-prefix rarely appears with the emphatic form.[61]

---

54 Line 8, 4. It should perhaps be understood as a mistake.

55 Lines 2, 11 and 5, 32.

56 For example, see lines 5, 2 and 3, 14. For the confusion between *nn* and *n* in the *n sḏm=f* construction, see Gardiner, *Egyptian Grammar*, §455.5. For the rare use of *n* expressing non-existence, see Gardiner, *Egyptian Grammar*, §108.3, n. 7. Lustman, *Étude Grammaticale du Papyrus Bremner-Rhind*, p. 164, proposes that the differentiation between *nn* and *n* is not made in late texts, such as P.Bremner-Rhind.

57 Line 1, 3. For an example of 𓂜 (D35) used as the phonetic *n* of *ꜥnḫ*, see line 3, 28. The confusion likely stems from the frequently interchangeable use of 𓈖 (N35) and 𓂜 (D35) as phonetic negation *n*; see Gardiner, *Egyptian Grammar*, p. 490.

58 Line 7, 16. For the Old Egyptian negative subjunctive/imperative *im+sḏm* construction, see Allen, *Inflection of the Verb*, p. 13; Gardiner, *Egyptian Grammar*, §342.

59 Line 4, 14; Gardiner, *Egyptian Grammar*, §496.

60 For a brief discussion of the meanings of the *sḏm=f* form in late texts, such as the Book of Traversing Eternity, see Herbin, *Le livre de parcourir l'éternité*, p. 45. For a summary of the reasons for the variation of the two forms in late texts, see Lustman, *Étude Grammaticale du Papyrus Bremner-Rhind*, p. 116, n. 9 and p. 137; Engsheden, *La reconstitution du verbe*, pp. 158–76. Servajean, *Les formules des transformations du Livre des Morts*, pp. 34–38 and 41, especially §40, offers a comprehensive overview of the arguments, and varying opinions regarding the present or the 'performative' sense of the *sḏm.n=f* form in ritual contexts.

61 The particle *iw* stands for this prefix in line 8, 4. For the use of the *i*-prefix with the emphatic form, see Edel, *Altägyptische Grammatik*, §449.

c. The *i*-prefix is used in the 2nd tense initial prospective *ḫpr*.[62]

d. The passive is expressed with the insertion of *tw*, and in the *sḏmw=f* construction.[63]

PARTICIPLES AND RELATIVE FORMS

a. *iw* is used in the *iw+sḏm=f* past relative construction.[64]

b. The participial prefix *i.ir* is spelled as *iw*.[65]

c. The relative past perfect is expressed with a *wn=f (ḥr) sḏm* construction.[66]

ERRORS [67]

a. The 1st person singular suffix pronoun is erroneously written with  and .[68]

b. The 1st person singular suffix pronoun, written below *n* looks like  (X1), and may stem from the frequently occurring genitive group .[69]

c. The 2nd person singular masculine suffix pronoun *k* is placed before the determinative.[70]

d. The 2nd person singular masculine suffix pronoun *k* is a scribal mistake, as the dependent pronoun *tw* follows immediately.[71]

e.  appears as a corrupt writing of , standing for the 2nd person singular dependent pronoun *ṯw*.[72]

---

62 Line 3, 2; Černý and Groll, *Late Egyptian Grammar*, p. 382, 26.18.6.

63 Line 6, 11, for example.

64 Line 1, 11. Černý and Groll, *Late Egyptian Grammar*, p. 510, 54.4.1; Johnson, *The Demotic Verbal System*, p. 182.

65 Line 5, 10 and 5, 26. For the spelling of *i* as *iw* in this prefix, see Junge, *Einführung in die Grammatik des Neuägyptischen*, p. 68, 2.1.

66 Line 8, 3. Here, *wn* is a relative form and the following verb is an infinitive, see Černý and Groll, *Late Egyptian Grammar*, p. 488, 51.6.7.

67 Černý, *Paper & Books*, p. 28, suggests that some errors may be explained as arising from dictation, however, stressing the lack of proof for the employment of dictation before the Roman era.

68 Line 3, 12.

69 Line 1, 7. Its position at the end of the line and the parallel MMA 40, 7 indicate that the group must be read as *n=i*.

70 Line 1, 4.

71 Lines 6, 7 and 7, 44.

72 Line 8, 1. For the occasional similarity of the two signs in hieratic, see Verhoeven, *Untersuchungen zur späthieratischen Buchschrift*, pp. 192 and 194.

f. stands for the 2nd person independent pronoun *ntwṯ*.[73]

g. *r* stands for the genitive *n*.[74]

h. The unusual spelling of Isis, , points to the confusion between her name and that of Osiris.[75]

i. *iw*, "to detach, separate," is written with (A1).[76]

j. The words *iwꜥ=f di ꜥ=f*, "his heir. His arm is given" are written .[77]

k. *imnt* and (G4) are frequently omitted from the epithet of Osiris, *ḫnty-imntyw*, "Foremost of the Westerners."[78]

l. stands in place of in the name of Mehenyt.[79]

m. The *n* of the common epithet *wsir ḫnty-imntyw wsir n NN* is written after the first *wsir*.[80]

n. *sꜥḥꜥ* "to lift up" is written with the (A7) determinative.[81]

o. The *k* under *ḏ* of *sḏr*, , is erroneous.[82]

p. *ḏfꜣw* , "provisions" is written with the (G7) determinative.[83]

---

73 Line 8, 3. Edel, *Altägyptische Grammatik*, p. 79. The reading is supported by the parallel of PT 365 (§623a): . For this reading, see Gardiner, *Egyptian Grammar*, § 62.3.

74 Line 7, 42. The genitive *n* is used in the parallel of PT 677 (§2026b).

75 Line 6, 13. The spelling may simply be an error.

76 Line 4, 12.

77 Line 8, 12. The scribe may have easily confused the common writing of *iwꜥ=f ꜥꜣ*, "his eldest heir," with *iwꜥ=f dit ꜥ=f*, "his arm is given." Either reading points to a scribal mistake (the extra suffix pronoun for *ꜥꜣ*, or the erroneous spelling of *dit*). The much more clearly written parallels of BM 26, 8 and P.Sekowski 12, 5 have the phonetic *iwf=f dit ꜥ=f*.

78 Lines 6, 50 and 7, 31, for example.

79 Col 3, 45. The close similarity of (D26) and (Q7) in hieratic may have caused confusion for the copyist, see Verhoeven, *Untersuchungen zur spähieratischen Buchschrift*, pp. 116 and 174, respectively. The parallel MMA 49, 9 and BM 12, 15 have (Q7). Nevertheless, (D26) logically occurs as one of the determinatives in the name of Mehenyt, who may literally spit fire against enemies.

80 Line 8, 37.

81 Line 8, 11. This reading is supported by the phonetic complements *s* and *ꜥ*, and the determinative (A21) in the parallel BM 26, 5.

82 Line 6, 6.

83 Line 3, 2. The determinative most likely stems from the confusion with (T14), seen in the parallel MMA 46, 9.

CORRECTIONS AND ADDITIONS[84]

a.  is inserted above the line.[85]

b. The enclitic particle  is inserted above the line.[86]

c.  of the 1st person singular suffix pronoun is inserted above the line.[87]

d.  is inserted above the line.[88]

e.  is often omitted and inserted above the line.[89]

f. *w* and the 3rd person singular masculine suffix pronoun  are inserted above the line.[90]

g. The phonetic complement  of *sḫm* is inserted above the line.[91]

1.4. ORTHOGRAPHY

Although the grammar of this text is basically Middle Egyptian, persistent superfluous *ws* and *ts* in the spelling of many words and the occasional irregular determinatives are typical of Late Egyptian orthography. Dots are an interesting feature of the papyrus W551. In many instances they act as verse points, indicating the end of a clause[92] or a continuation of a word on the following line.[93] In other cases, these dots represent a small sign, such as a phonetic complement *r* (D21) in the preposition *ḥr*.[94] Yet some occurrences of dots do not appear to carry any grammatical significance.[95]

84 Listed in order of appearance.

85 Line 1, 17.

86 Line 2, 13.

87 Line 5, 7.

88 Line 6, 31.

89 Lines 7, 12; 7, 14; 7, 15 and 7, 16.

90 Line 8, 14.

91 Line 9, 3.

92 See for example line 1, 49, where a dot is placed at the beginning of the 2nd stanza, after the phrase "said by Nut." Černý, *Paper & Books*, p. 24, suggests that verse-points were added later, during the reading of the text. According to Parkinson and Quirke, *Papyrus*, p. 46, these marks were generally written in red ink, which is not the case in P.W551. Red dots in the *s3ḫw snty* liturgy in P.Carlsberg 589 are interpreted as musical notation, which may have accompanied the performance of such texts, see von Lieven, in S. Lippert and M. Schentuleit, eds., *Tebtynis und Soknopaiu Nesos*, p. 61, n. 13, and von Lieven, in K. Ryholt, ed., *Carlsberg Papyri 7*, pp. 19–22.

93 Line 7, 42 and 5, 48. Tait, in M. Bierbrier, ed., *Papyrus, Structure and Usage*, p. 66, points out that the practice of dividing a single word between two lines frequently occurs on Demotic papyri.

94 Line 2, 5.

95 See Table 1, above. For instance, the  determinative (A24) of *nḥm* in line 7, 18 has a dot below it, while it is not written in A24 of *ḫsf* in line 4, 7. This feature is typical to the Ptolemaic period, as is clearly seen in the BD dated to the reign of Ptolemy III, P.BM 10037; Verhoeven, *Untersuchungen zur späthieratischen Buchschrift*, pp. 82 and 107. See section 1.2, above.

A selection of other orthographic peculiarities of P.W551 that may be considered characteristic of the GR period is presented below:

a.  for *iwn*, "color."[96]

b. The adverb *im* is frequently written with  throughout P.W551.[97]

c. The pupil ○ stands for the phonetic *ir*, while two pupils are used for *m33*, "to see."[98]

d. The demonstrative *pfy* is most often spelled .[99]

e. *f3w* appears as , often replacing the  determinative (Y1) with  (F7) in LP and GR texts.[100]

f.  stands for *mn*.[101]

g. The group *mḥ*, "to fill" is spelled with .[102]

h. The preposition *m-ẖnw* is spelled .[103]

i. , as the determiner "every" and the noun "lord," is usually written with the feminine *t*.[104]
In a number of instances, the noun *nb* exhibits a stroke or a *n* above  as a phonetic complement.[105]

j. The abbreviated spelling of Nedit, , is typically late.[106]

k. The verb *rdi* frequently shows a phonetic *t*.[107]

l.  is a typically late spelling of Hapy.[108]

96 Line 2, 2; *Wb.* I 52, 10–17. This spelling is paralleled by MMA 43, 7 and BM 9, 18.

97 See line 1, 19. For an example of this spelling, see Fairman, *BIFAO* 43 (1945): 110; *Wb.* I 72.

98 For example, see lines 5, 10 and 1, 20, respectively. Daumas, *Valeurs phonétiques* I, p. 154. For the use of the two pupils (D12) for the verb *m33* in P.Bremner-Rhind, see Lustman, *Étude Grammaticale du Papyrus Bremner-Rhind*, p. 51.

99 Line 5, 3, for example.

100 Line 5, 41; *Wb.* I 575, 3–12. For a brief discussion of this term see Wilson, *Ptolemaic Lexikon*, p. 388.

101 Line 3, 7. For this reading, see *Wb.* II 60, 6–11.

102 Line 1, 7; *Wb.* II, 116; Goyon, *Imouthès*, p. 85, n. 6.

103 Line 1, 18; *Wb.* III 368, 17.

104 For an example, see lines 7, 9 and 3, 3, respectively. For this late spelling of *nb*, see *Wb.* II 234 and 227; Herbin, *Le livre de parcourir l'éternité*, p. 39.

105 Line 3, 8. This spelling of *nb*, "lord," occurs mostly in the first composition of P.W551 and is frequently paralleled in MMA. For the phonetic complement of *nb*, "lord," typical to the PT, see *Wb.* II 227.

106 Line 8, 11, see *Wb.* II 367, 15.

107 Line 7, 8. Notably, the parallels in PT 593 (§1632b) and the tomb of Mutirdis have *di*. For this late spelling of the *sḏm=f* form of the verb *rdi*, see *Wb.* II 464; Herbin, *Le livre de parcourir l'éternité*, p. 39.

108 Line 3, 24; *Wb.* III 42.

m. (A32) or (T30) over (O26) for *ḫbt*, "place of punishment, execution" appears in the LP.[109]

n. stands for the phonetic *ḥ* in the name of Horus: .[110]

o. is a typically GR spelling of *sꜣṯ.w*, "ground."[111]

p. The phonetic change from *š* to *ḫ* and vice versa appears throughout the text.[112]

q. *tp*, "head," is written with in the GR period.[113]

r. is a GR spelling of *ky ḏd*, "another reading."[114]

s. Geb is frequently spelled .[115]

t. The distinction between *d* and *t* is not made in various words throughout the papyrus.[116]

u. The distinction between *ḏ* and *d* is similarly not made in various words throughout the papyrus.[117]

v. The group *ḏd* stands for the phonetic *ḏ* in the name of Thoth .[118]

1.5. VOCABULARY

The vocabulary of papyrus W551 is essentially that of Middle Egyptian mixed with Old and Late Egyptian terminology. The abundant parallels with the PT add a considerable number of older words,[119] while the late date of the texts accounts for a number of typically late ex-

109 For the determinative (A32), see line 5, 27. This determinative likely originates from *ḫbb*, "to dance," see *Wb.* III 252, 9–14. For , see line 9, 7; *Wb.* III 252, 9–14.

110 Line 6, 10, for example. Daumas, *Valeurs phonétiques* I, p. 264.

111 Lines 2, 5 and 9, 1. See *Wb.* III 423, 8–12. This spelling is paralleled by MMA 43, 11and BM 9, 21. (M17) is likely a phonetic complement, which may be supported by the Coptic ⲉⲥⲏⲧ, "ground," see Crum, *Coptic Dictionary*, p. 60.

112 This is evident in such words as *ḫnw*, "child," in line 2, 2. For the wide-spread phonetic change between *š* and *ḫ* in LP texts, see Fairman, *BIFAO* 43 (1945): 64 and 77. See also *sḫr(w)*, "state, condition," in line 3, 26, the reading of which is supported by the gloss *sḫr=k* in BM 11, 27; see Goyon, *Imouthès*, p. 89, n. 35.

113 Line 2, 2. For this spelling, paralleled in BM 9, 18, see *Wb.* V 263.

114 Line 5, 22. For this spelling, see *Wb.* V 111, 11.

115 Lines 5, 55 and 6, 19, for example. For the spelling of the name of Geb with *Δ*, which appears as early as Dynasty 21, see Bedier, *Die Rolle des Gottes Geb*, p. 163, and n. 55; *Wb.* V 164, 6–11.

116 *it*, "father," is spelled with a phonetic *d* in line 7, 8.

117 See the phonetic complement *d* for *nḏ* in line 7, 12 and the phonetic complement *d* for *wḏb* in 5, 14.

118 Line 6, 12. This writing may point to the vocalization of the group prevalent at the time.

119 See for example the 2nd person independent pronoun *ṯwt* in line 6, 47, which commonly occurs in Old Egyptian, Gardiner, *Egyptian Grammar*, §64.

pressions.[120] The later date, supported paleographically, is further confirmed by numerous words and epithets characteristic of the Late and GR periods.[121] The following terms and expressions may be noted:

a. *ꜣb*, "to stop, finish; stopping," is used with the preposition *n*.[122]

b. *imim* is a late term for "lamentation" and variant of *im*.[123]

c. *ꜥnḫw*, "stars."[124]

d. *wꜥbt*, "heaven."[125]

e. The standard preposition *m/r hꜣw* is frequently written without the first component, *m/r*, but with the preposition *ḥr* at the end.[126]

f. The construction *m r-ꜥwy*, "in the hands" may mean "work, action" in the GR period.[127]

g. *ns*, "to go, travel."[128]

h. *ḥꜥ*, "palace (to which tribute is brought)."[129]

i. *sꜣw ḥꜣ*, "to protect (someone/something)."[130]

j. *siwꜥ*, "to cause to inherit."[131]

k. *tštš*, "to crush, cut up."[132]

l. *kkw*, "to make dark (of face; i.e., make blind)" is used transitively in the GR period.[133]

m. *m nw r nw*, "always."[134]

n. *biꜣ*, "sky."[135]

---

120 For a discussion of the typical variation of vocabulary in later copies of PT, see Patane, *DiscEg* 24 (1992): 43–46.

121 The epithets of Osiris and other deities in P.W551 that are attested only in the LP or GR times are listed in the Appendix: Index of Epithets. Most of these are paralleled by the corresponding late papyri and post-NK tombs. Additional examples of the epithets appear in Leitz, et al., eds., *Lexikon*.

122 Line 1, 26; *Wb.* I 6, 6.

123 Line 8, 16; *Wb.* I 82, 22.

124 Line 8, 20; *Wb.* I 204, 6.

125 Line 8, 16; *Wb.* I 284, 10.

126 Line 2, 3; *Wb.* II 477, 12–14.

127 Line 3, 3; *Wb.* II 395, 13–18 and *Wb.* II 396, 1–3, respectively.

128 Line 2, 4; *Wb.* II 321, 1–3; Wilson, *Ptolemaic Lexikon*, p. 544.

129 Line 10, 20; *Wb.* III 39, 17.

130 Line 3, 44; *Wb.* III 416, 12; Wilson, *Ptolemaic Lexikon*, p. 782.

131 Line 6, 40, *Wb.* IV 34, 8.

132 Line 4, 21; *Wb.* V 330, 5–10.

133 Line 2, 8; *Wb.* V 144, 12.

134 Line 8, 32; *Wb.* II 219, 15.

135 Line 8, 40; *Wb.* I 439, 9; Wilson, *Ptolemaic Lexikon*, p. 306.

1.5.1. WORD PLAY

Egyptian scribes employed a variety of word plays, including paronomasia, homophony and alliteration as a common literary device[136] in order to introduce nuances, metaphors and levels of symbolism to the text.[137] Although the phrase "word play" may carry a frivolous connotation, exploring the connection between sounds, roots, words, phrases, as well as appearances of writing was clearly a serious and scholarly matter for the authors and copyists of Egyptian texts.[138] The use of word play spans a broad range of genres of Egyptian literature, including love songs, tales and hymns, among others.[139] However, the clear preference for punning and alliteration in religious texts likely stems from the belief in the magical properties of writing and utterance.[140]

The Egyptians perceived associations among words with apparent etymological or visual connections and different meanings to be divinely inspired.[141] Illuminating these connections was, thus, an act of religious scholarship, as well as a style of writing.[142] In other words, word play pointed to the multifaceted quality of Egyptian religion and the complexity of each specific religious text. The corresponding roots or initial sounds of words and the duality of their meaning implied the harmony of *maat,* verifying the significance and authenticity of a text.[143]

Due to a lack of precise understanding of certain vocabulary and the principles of pronunciation of the Egyptian language, most instances of word play will remain hidden from

136 The phenomenon of word play in Egyptian texts is attested as early as the OK PT and gained increasing popularity into the GR period, see Morenz, in *Festschrift Johannes Jahn*, p. 24; Watterson, in J. Ruffle, G. Gaballa, and K. Kitchen, eds., *Glimpses of Ancient Egypt*, pp. 167–69; Guglielmi, in F. Junge, ed., *Studien zu Sprache und Religion*, p. 493. For a discussion of GR word plays in Edfu and Dendera, see Derchain-Urtel, in *Mélanges Adolph Gutbub*, pp. 55–61.

137 Morenz, in *Festschrift Johannes Jahn*, pp. 23–24 and *passim*; Guglielmi, in F. Junge, ed., *Studien zu Sprache und Religion*, p. 492. For a definition of Egyptian paronomasia, as well as phonetic, semantic and graphic punning, see Loprieno, in S. Noegel, ed., *Puns and Pundits*, pp. 4–6 and 13.

138 Jasnow and Zauzich, *The Ancient Egyptian Book of Thoth*, pp. 114–17, describe the considerable use of word play in the Book of Thoth and its scholarly implications.

139 Morenz, in *Festschrift Johannes Jahn*, p. 24. For instance, see the discussion of word play and alliteration in the Eloquent Peasant, in Foster, *BES* 10 (1989–90): 65 and *passim*.

140 For example, a detailed linguistic analysis of word play and alliteration in PT is presented by Hodge, in S. Noegel and A. Kaye, eds., *Afroasiatic Linguistics, Semitics, and Egyptology*, pp. 203–5. See also Manassa, *Late Egyptian Underworld*, p. 312, n. 158, who highlights examples of alliteration in the Seventh hour of the Amduat; Morenz, in *Festschrift Johannes Jahn*, pp. 24–26, points to the extensive use of alliteration in dream interpretation texts. For a discussion of the role of utterance in creation, see Zandee, in T. van Baaren et al, eds., *Verbum*, pp. 33–66.

141 Guglielmi, in F. Junge, ed., *Studien zu Sprache und Religion*, pp. 493–94, points to the frequent use of alliteration in Ptolemaic offering formulae.

142 Morenz, in *Festschrift Johannes Jahn*, pp. 25–27; Derchain-Urtel, in *Mélanges Adolph Gutbub*, pp. 55 and 59–60. Loprieno, in S. Noegel, ed., *Puns and Pundits*, pp. 8–9 and 13, suggests that word play involved a "scientific classification of the world and its entities."

143 Derchain-Urtel, in *Mélanges Adolph Gutbub*, p. 60; Foster, *BES* 10 (1989–90): 61–76.

modern translators.[144] Nevertheless, a considerable number of examples occur in P.W551. All of these are cited in the text notes, but a number of illustrative examples is discussed below.

The most frequently detected type of word play in the present manuscript is paronomasia, or punning, in which the deliberate use of common sounding words suggests an intentional ambiguity of meaning. This type of punning was often achieved by the addition of determinatives not expected in a given context, but suggesting the possibility of alternate readings for a word. For instance, Isis says to Osiris: *rm=i ḥr ꜣw n mḥw=k*, "I weep as long as (I am) grieving you."[145] The unexpected determinative of , *mḥ*, "to worry, grieve," which is omitted in the parallel texts, alludes to a pun on *mḥ*, "to flood, overflow."[146] Nevertheless, the application of either word is appropriate in the context of grief over the murdered Osiris, whose efflux was often recognized as the source of the Nile's inundation.[147]

In other cases, the absence of determinatives similarly created a dual meaning. Isis finds Osiris being "very black" (*km.ti wr.ti*) in his "name of '*km-wr*' (=Great Black One)."[148] The epithet *km-wr* is commonly translated as a geographical designation Athribis, "Bitter Lakes," or "Great Black Wall," due to the determinative (O36) of *km-wr*, which occurs in the PT source of this line. However, the choice of this geographical location is likely attributed to the similarity of the locality's name, *km-wr*, with the phrase *km wr*, "very black,"[149] which associates Osiris with the regenerative qualities of soil in the Nile valley. The lack of a determinative for the term *km-wr* in P.W551 emphasizes word play between the characterizations of Osiris in the previous phrase and his epithet. Notably, *km.ti wr.ti* also carries another meaning, offering the possibility of understanding the phrase as "complete and great."

In addition to single word punning, Egyptian scribes explored the aural ambiguity of phrases. Isis addresses Osiris: ⌜*in*⌝*k imw n sšr=k*, "⌜I⌝ am the one who grieves over your condition."[150] The latter part of the phrase presents a word play with *imn-sḫrw*, "One Hidden of Forms," an attested epithet of Isis.[151]

While some paronomasia can reveal nuances of meaning or a possible etymology, other examples of word play introduce new levels of textual interpretation by alluding to a similar sounding, yet unrelated term. For instance, in the request for Osiris' quick return, *wn*, , is translated as "to hurry" because of the determinative (D54).[152] However, the

144 Loprieno, in S. Noegel, ed., *Puns and Pundits*, p. 7.

145 Line 5, 17.

146 For further discussion of this and the following examples, see the text notes for the appropriate lines.

147 For further discussion of Osiris' association with the Inundation, see text notes for Stanzas 2 and 4.

148 Line 7, 6.

149 For a discussion of the use of paronomasia in place names, as well as personal names of deities, see Morenz, in *Festschrift Johannes Jahn*, p. 24.

150 Line 3, 26.

151 Note the varying interpretations in the parallel texts: BM P11, 27 adds a gloss *sḫr=k*, , next to *sšt=k*, , while the scribe of B writes *sš=i*(!), . MMA 48, 3, in turn offers a different reading: *ink wꜥt im n sš=k*, "I am alone, grieving over your condition."

spelling of *wn*, , in the otherwise exact parallel of MMA 43, 13 suggests a pun on the very different "to neglect, be careless." Although the notions of rushing and being careless may carry a logical correlation in the context, these two terms with a similar root do not likely share the same etymology.

Another common form of word play in P.W551 is alliteration, demonstrating a deliberate choice of words that repeat the initial sound throughout the phrase. Since alliteration frequently occurs in temple inscriptions, which were presumably recited, this type of word play may have been used to facilitate the continuity of recitation and memorization.[153] An example of alliteration in P.W551 is *nṯrw nṯrwt ib=sn nḏm*, "The gods and goddesses, their hearts are cheerful."[154] The scribe of the parallel MMA 55, 13 overlooked the opportunity for alliteration, while presenting a synonymous statement: *nṯrw nṯrwt ibw=sn ꜣw*, "The gods and goddesses, their hearts are rejoicing." Similarly, the Late Egyptian possessive article *pꜣy*, which is otherwise unusual for P.W551, appears almost certainly for the sake of alliteration with the b/p sound: ⸢*pꜣy=ỉ*⸣ *bnw bnbn=k ỉw pr=k*, ⸢My⸣ *Benu* bird, may you return to your house!"[155]

The Egyptian belief in the divinely inspired connections among phonetically or visually similar hieroglyphic words is well attested.[156] However, the extension of visual or graphic punning to hieratic, evident in P.W551, deserves more attention. The scribe of the present manuscript appears to intentionally use signs with an ambiguous cursive form that may be interpreted as different hieroglyphs, each with a distinct sound and reading. An example is the Osirian epithet *šps prw m ḏfꜣw*, "One with whose Provisions the Temples are Made Splendid."[157] Interestingly, the similarity of (A52) for *šps* and (U39) for *wṯs* in hieratic, , presents a visual pun with *ṯs-prt*, "to plant seeds." The phrase *ṯs-prt* is in turn associated with the act of creation and fertility, essential to the Osirian myth.[158] The dichotomy of meaning was occasionally evoked by an unusual choice of signs and their grouping. While the scribes of the parallel texts wrote *snsn*, "to be brotherly," in a more typical manner—with phonetic complements (and), the scribe of the present manuscript employed the unusual , alluding to the *snwt* shrines: .[159]

It should be noted, however, that it is at times difficult to differentiate scribal errors and word play for the modern translator. What a later reader may interpret as intentional word play could in fact be the scribe's misunderstanding of a dictated text. For instance, PT 364 (§611b) reads: *sḏm n ḥr n sww n=k rdi.n=f šms kw nṯrw*, "Listen to Horus: it will not be dangerous for you, for he has made the gods follow you." The parallels of this spell in P.W551 and the Saite tomb of Mutirdis replace *n sww n=k* with *nis.n=k*, resulting in *sḏm n ḥr nis.*

---

152 Line 2, 7.

153 Watterson, in J. Ruffle, G. Gaballa, and K. Kitchen, eds., *Glimpses of Ancient Egypt*, p. 168; Eyre, *The Cannibal Hymn*, pp. 32–33; Loprieno, in S. Noegel, ed., *Puns and Pundits*, pp. 15–16.

154 Line 5, 29.

155 Line 1, 45.

156 Goldwasser, *GM* 123 (1991): 37–50; Vernus, *Littoral* 7/8 (1983): 27–32.

157 Line 3, 4.

158 Wilson, *Ptolemaic Lexikon*, pp. 1173–74.

159 Line 7, 16.

n=k..., "Listen to Horus, whom you have summoned...."[160] The later scribes may have noticed the similarity of sounds of the two phrases and applied them, intentionally altering the text. At the same time, the possibility that the later authors simply misunderstood what they were hearing when the text was recited should also be considered.

1.6. OWNER'S NAME AND PROVENANCE

The name of the original owner of this manuscript, Padikakem, appears to have been added in the blank spaces after the papyrus was written.[161] Thus, the papyrus was likely not inscribed to order, but rather purchased ready-made.[162] Unlike P.W551, most late mortuary papyri containing glorification spells are either inscribed for a particular individual[163] or do not record any names at all.[164] The practice of inscribing the name of the owner after the papyrus is completed is a more common feature of the Book of the Dead (BD).[165]

The "*pꜣ-di* + deity" construction, which became popular in LP Egypt, supports the proposed date of this manuscript.[166] All instances of the name are preceded by the usual formula *wsir ḫnty-imntyw wsir n NN*, "Osiris, Foremost of the Westerners, Osiris of NN."[167] Such invocations generally indicate discrete sections of a text. However, as Smith has pointed out, "the reasons for its (=invocation) insertion at the points where it occurs are not always obvious."[168]

Somewhat unusually, the titles, names of the parents, and provenance are not provided in the manuscript.[169] The Lower Egyptian town of Athribis has been suggested in the museum records as a possible place of origin based on two factors. First, *km-wr*, a designation of

160 Line 7, 23.

161 The name of Padikakem first occurs in line 6, 20.

162 Rössler-Köhler, *ASAE* 70 (1984–55): 383–408, especially 389. Cf. P.Berlin 8351 in Smith, *Liturgy of Opening the Mouth for Breathing*, p. 2.

163 See for example MMA, Goyon, *Imouthès*.

164 Such as the unpublished papyrus BM 10081.

165 Goelet, *Egyptian Book of the Dead*, p. 142.

166 Ranke, *Personennamen* I, pp. 121–26.

167 For the identification of the deceased with Osiris, especially in LP Egypt, see Morenz, in P. Derchain, ed., *Religions en Égypte*, p. 78; Smith, in B. Backes, I. Munro, S, Stöhr, eds., *Totenbuch-Forschungen*, p. 337. Cf. the same invocation in P.Berlin 8351, see Smith, *Liturgy of Opening the Mouth for Breathing*, p. 11. The genitival adjective *n* in this designation began to replace the direct genitive (Osiris NN) in Dynasty 21, and became increasingly common in the GR period. For a detailed overview of the various theories on the formula "*wsir n* NN" and its seeming equivalence with "*wsir* NN," see Smith, *Mortuary Texts of Papyrus BM 10507*, pp. 75–79. Smith interprets this designation as referring to a "particular form or aspect of Osiris to which there has been assimilated ... a particular deceased person NN. It is distinct from the god Osiris."

168 Smith, *Liturgy of Opening the Mouth for Breathing*, p. 11, n. 56.

169 Normally, LP mortuary papyri which name the owner tend to provide the titles and names of parents. The most abbreviated of these state the names of the owner and his father. For an example of the former, see P.Louvre 3079, Goyon, *BIFAO* 65 (1967): 89–156; for the latter, see P.BM 10507, Smith, *Mortuary Texts of Papyrus BM 10507*.

Athribis, is mentioned several times in the papyrus.[170] However, this theory is not well-supported, since *km-wr* occurs in numerous parallel passages, such as the PT, as a place-name. The second factor concerns the name, Padikakem, which was added in the blank spaces by a different hand with ⊗ (O49) at the end. This spelling may support Athribis as the provenance of the papyrus only if one assumes that the name of the original owner was, in fact, Padika. Then ⊗, the crocodile skin (I6), and the village determinative (O49) may represent Athribis, his place of origin. However, due to the lack of a preposition preceding the assumed place-name and the omission of the titles and parents' names, which generally occur with the provenance, the name should be read as Padikakem. The well-attested epithet *kꜣ-km*, "The Bull of Egypt," frequently refers to Amun and Amun-Re.[171]

The rare name Padikakem appears in a Demotic document from Tuna El-Gebel, dated to the reign of Ptolemy VI Philometor.[172] *Pꜣ-ti-kꜣ-km* (whose name is written in two ways:), who is otherwise unattested in Demotic, is listed as the father of the woman *tꜣ-rt*, the second party in the annuity contract. A GR man with a similar name, Padikem (), is listed as the grandson of Petosiris, and is claimed to have lived during the reign of Ptolemy III Euergetes.[173] Since the name Padikem appears only rarely, the possibility of this being a variant spelling of Padikakem, or the Demotic *pꜣ-ti-kꜣ-km*, should be considered. Also noteworthy are two matching female names, Tadikem () and Tadipakakem (), attested in the family of Petosiris.[174] The examples of a name comparable to Padikakem, the owner of this manuscript, may not all belong to the same individual. However, in view of the possible correspondence of the two above examples, as well as the instances of GR orthography and terminology in this papyrus, this correlation should be kept in mind until further evidence may arise.

The spelling of the owner's name varies, perhaps depending on the amount of space provided.[175] The variant spellings of the name Padikakem are listed in Table 3 according to the order of their frequency.

---

170 *km-wr* designates Athribis from the reign of Sahure to Roman times, see Vernus, *Athribis*, *passim*.

171 Leitz, et al., eds., *Lexikon* VII, p. 274. Gabra, *Rapport*, p. 12, suggests that *kꜣ-km*, "Black Bull," was worshipped in Athribis, pointing to a Delta origin of this name.

172 Farid, in S. Bedier, K. Daoud, Z. Hawass, eds., *Studies in Honor of Ali Radwan*, pp. 323–46, equates this date to 176–75 BCE.

173 Lefebvre, *Petosiris* I, pp. 5 and 12, reads the name as Petoukem. This name is mentioned in inscription 61 in the tomb of Petosiris; see Lefebvre, *Petosiris* II, pp. 36–38. See also, Ranke, *Personennamen* I, p. 126, 11. The funerary monument and equipment of a certain Padikem, whose titles include Royal Scribe, Accountant of all Property within the Borders of Khemenu, Priest of Thoth, Sobek, and the Living Cat of the Temple of Pakhet, was excavated in Tuna el-Gebel in the vicinity of the tomb of Petosiris; see Gabra, *Rapport*, pp. 11–37.

174 The female names, likely belonging to the grandmother and niece (or granddaughter) of Petosiris, respectively, are mentioned in a number of inscriptions in his tomb; see Lefebvre, *Petosiris* I, pp. 3, n. 3 and 6, n. 1. However, according to Smith, *Papyrus Harkness*, p. 130, n. 732, the two may in fact be variants of the same name. The coffin of Tadipakakem, JE 43098 (CG 29316), is published in Lefebvre, *ASAE* 23 (1923): 230; Maspero, *Sarcophages des époques persane et ptolémaïque* II, pp. 101ff.; Porter and Moss, *Topographical Bibliography* IV, p. 175.

175 Cf. the various spellings of Pawerem in P.BM 10288, where the name appears to have been written simultaneously with the text, however; Caminos, *JEA* 58 (1972): 208.

TABLE 3 Variant Spellings of the Name Padikakem.

HIEROGLYPHIC	HIERATIC	COMMENTS
	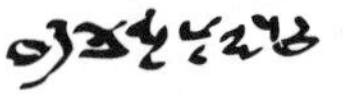	The most frequent spelling, occurring 42 times.[a]
	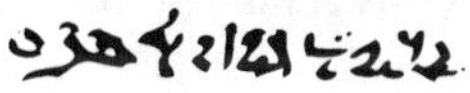	This spelling occurs 8 times.[b]
		This spelling occurs 3 times.[c] The hieroglyphic writing of the 1st bull is notable.
		This spelling occurs once. Note the Demotic form of the crocodile skin (I6).[d]

a Lines 7, 3; 7, 4; 7, 14; 7, 16; 7, 20; 7, 21; 7, 23; 7, 31(?); 7, 39; 7, 41; 7, 42-3; 7, 44; 8, 1; 8, 2; 8, 5; 8, 6; 8, 7; 8, 13; 8, 15; 8, 19; 8, 22; 8, 28(?); 8, 31; 8, 32; 8, 34; 8, 36; 8, 37; 8, 38; 8, 39; 8, 40; 9, 1; 9, 3; 9, 4 (twice); 9, 5; 9, 8; 9, 9; 9, 15; 9, 16; 10, 2; 10, 10–11; 10, 12.

b Lines 6, 20–21; 6, 26; 6, 48; 6, 49; 6, 51; 7, 12; 7, 36; 7, 37-8.

c Lines 10, 4–5; 10, 7; 10, 8–9.

d Line 6, 36. The same example probably also occurs in line 6, 37, where it is partially damaged. There,  (I6) is more typical. For the Demotic *km*, "black," see *CDD*, k, 21.

1.7. DESCRIPTION OF THE TEXT

1.7.1. PARALLELS AND THEMES

P.W551 consists of two mortuary texts. The "Ritual of Introducing the Multitude on the Last Day of *Tekh*" is the initial text in the papyrus and does not name the owner. This section ends on line 36 of col. 5 with the familiar formula *iw=f pw nfr*, "it has come (to an end) well."[176] The five columns of this ritual are considerably narrower than the rest, setting it apart from the subsequent text. Following a small gap, the second section begins on line 37, comprising a collection of glorification spells (*s3ḫw*) for Padikakem. Each glorification spell opens with a short title written in red ink. This section ends with the same formula, *iw=f pw nfr*.

The entire manuscript is paralleled by the unpublished Ptolemaic papyrus BM 10081, also known as P.Malcolm.[177] Dr. Richard Parkinson kindly provided permission to examine

176 *Wb.* I 45, 1–4.

177 This text was described by Le Page Renouf, *TSBA* 9 (1893): 298, and is pending publication by François Herbin.

its photographs and to ascertain that it contains the same texts. It should be noted that P.Malcolm opens and closes with compositions not paralleled by papyrus W551.[178]

1.7.2. SECTION 1 OF P.W551

The first column of P.W551 begins the "Ritual of Introducing the Multitude on the Last Day of *Tekh*," as is indicated by the rubric title in line 1. It ends on line 36 of col. 5. The arrangement of the text in narrow columns results in the separation of some clauses into multiple lines.[179] The single line structure is characteristic of LP ritual texts[180] and appears to be connected with the division of the text into stanzas. This section closely corresponds to cols. 40–56 of the papyrus of Imouthès (MMA), published by Goyon,[181] a portion of P.Schmitt (B),[182] and a section of P.Malcolm (BM).[183] The narrow size of the columns is echoed in the parallel manuscripts. The edition of MMA was instrumental in reconstructing several damaged lines in papyrus W551. However, minor but notable differences are found among the texts, demonstrating that they are not exact parallels.[184] Some lines present in P.W551 are omitted in the parallel texts and vice versa.[185] Virtually every line exhibits variations in orthography and/or vocabulary from the other texts. Frequent divergences in grammar among the parallels point to different interpretations of the composition made by the scribe.[186] Furthermore, the numerous discrepancies in voice significantly alter the sense of otherwise similar phrases.[187]

Section 1 is written in Middle Egyptian with only a few examples of "Late-Egyptianisms." Among these, especially common are the phonetic changes between the letters *d* and *t*, *ḫ*

178 Bellion, *Egypte ancienne*, p. 59, lists two other mortuary texts in P.BM 10081. For the most extensive description of this manuscript, see Le Page Renouf, *TSBA* 9 (1893): 295–306. The parallel of P.W551 to P.BM10081 is also mentioned by Coenen and Verrept, *GM* 202 (2004): 97–102.

179 See, for example, lines 5, 21–22.

180 For instance, the ritual of the Procession of Ptah-Sokar-Osiris in the Ptolemaic papyrus Louvre 3176; see Barguet, *Papyrus N. 3176*, pp. 3–14 and pl. 1.

181 P.MMA 35.9.21 (MMA) is now in the Metropolitan Museum of Art. The *sꜥr ꜥšꜣ* ritual of MMA is also translated and edited in detail in the forthcoming publication of Andrea Kucharek, *Die Klagelieder von Isis und Nephthys*, Text und Kommentar, pp. 251–92.

182 P.Schmitt is accessioned as papyrus Berlin 3057. The ritual is recorded in lines 23a, 1–28 and 23.

183 P.Malcolm is accessioned as papyrus BM 10081, see lines 8, 1–15, 20. These three texts will only be cited in the case of variants or inconsistencies and referred to as MMA, B and BM, respectively.

184 Cf. line 1, 14: *nḏm.wy ḥḥ n=f kꜣp=k*, the parallel MMA 40, 14: *iw n=f kꜣp=k*, and the versions of B and BM 8, 15: *nḏm.wy ḥḥ n=f*.

185 For example, MMA 46, 15 and the corresponding lines of B and BM have a clause which is omitted from P.W551 lines 3, 8–9, while MMA 50 omits the line present in line 4, 5 of P.W551.

186 For instance, the *nn sḏm=f* construction of P.W551 2, 2: *nn wiꜣ iwn=f*, has future sense, while the *n sḏm.n=f* of MMA 43, 7: *n wiꜣ.n inm=f* represents the negative present, significantly altering the sense of the clause.

187 See, for example, the variation between the 2nd and 3rd person suffix pronouns in line 5, 20.

and *š*, and the seemingly interchangeable negatives *n* and *nn*,[188] which are rarely mirrored by the parallels of MMA, BM, and B. Although the corresponding manuscripts also contain examples of Late Egyptian orthography and vocabulary, these occur in different instances than in P.W551. Subsequently, while these papyri contain parallel texts, they are certainly not copies.

Unlike the composition of the following cols. 5 through 10 (=*s3ḫw*), the text of this ritual is not personalized for the original owner of the papyrus. Rather, it comprises seven stanzas of incantation spoken by Isis, Nephthys, and Nut, addressing Osiris.[189]

The intended speakers of each stanza are as follows:

Stanza 1 – Isis and Nephthys.[190]

Stanza 2 – Nut.[191]

Stanza 3 – Isis.[192]

Stanza 4 – Isis (possibly with Nephthys),[193] quoting "men and women."

Stanza 5 – Isis.[194]

Stanza 6 – possibly Isis.[195]

Stanza 7 – Isis.[196]

The poetic beauty of their words, as well as the direct first person speech, is reminiscent of love poetry.[197] They combine the primal and human feelings of love and sadness with rituals

188 This is discussed in further detail in sections 1.3 and 1.4, above. Although Late Egyptian uses *bw* or *bn* for negation, this phenomenon is a common example of modified late Middle Egyptian, or "Neo-Mittelägyptisch," according to Junge, *Einführung in die Grammatik des Neuägyptischen*, pp. 21 and 164.

189 For the term *ḥwt*, "chapter, stanza," see Goyon, *Imouthès*, p. 8, n. 27; Schott and Schott, *Bücher und Bibliotheken*, pp. 289–90.

190 Although the two goddesses are not named in the text, the use of the 1st person pronouns, addressing Osiris, suggests that one sister recites the beginning of the text. The identification of this sister with Isis is based upon the similarity of this stanza with the genre of love poetry that generally records the discourse of a lover or a wife; see Mathieu, *La poésie amoureuse de l'Égypte ancienne*, pp. 133 and 144–45.

191 Nut is named in the first line of the stanza, see line 1, 49.

192 This stanza is said to be recited by "Isis, the mother of Horus."

193 The specific speaker is not made explicit. Such phrases as "Come my sister, let us mourn him" in line 3, 15 imply that it is one of the lamenting sisters, Isis or Nephthys.

194 Isis is not named, but rather refers to herself, when addressing Osiris, as "the wife of my brother, of your mother."

195 Here again, no speaker is provided by the text. Most likely Isis is meant to continue her speech from the previous stanza.

196 Line 5, 1 continues the somewhat damaged stanza 7 from the previous column with the words "you have fertilized and I became pregnant," clearly referring to the conception of Horus. Thus, Isis must be the intended speaker.

197 Lichtheim, *Ancient Egyptian Literature* II, p. 181. For the connection between lamentations and love poetry, see Vernus, *Chants d'amour*, p. 41; Guglielmi, in A. Loprieno, ed., *Ancient Egyptian Literature*, p. 338.

recited in cult by the priests.[198] Isis says: "My limbs are torn up in suffering because of the great crime against you and towards me … Shentayt mourns him, she has remembered keenly regarding it. I weep for you. My heart, it is suffering at the extent of your love for me!"[199]

Although this ritual is not personalized for Padikakem, it is an integral part of a complete mortuary manuscript. As such, the text recorded here was likely intended to assist the deceased in his transition to the hereafter. The presence of this ritual on papyrus allowed Padikakem to "virtually" participate in an Osirian temple celebration. Moreover, as the deceased Padikakem became associated with Osiris, he benefited from the speech of the goddesses and the men and women addressed to this god.[200]

The title "Introducing the Multitude on the Last Day of *Tekh*" raises two questions. First, the meaning of the term "the multitude" is not entirely clear. Secondly, the term *tḫ* is made obscure by the range of meanings of its determinatives (𓏏𓐍𓏊𓏤𓎰𓇳). Since this ritual is not well-attested outside of the above-mentioned sources,[201] its sense remains to be derived from the context. *ꜥšꜣt*, "the multitude," appears to refer to the crowd of men and women whose speech appears in much of the fourth stanza.[202] Two epithets of Osiris from earlier columns of the MMA manuscript—*mr ꜥšꜣt/msꜥ*, "(Golden Youth) who Loves the Multitude/Company,"[203] and *ꜥšꜣ ꜥšꜣt /msꜥ*, "Rich of Multitude" or "One with Innumerable Subjects"—support this interpretation.[204] Thus, "the multitude," also described as the *rḫyt pꜥt*, "commoners and mankind,"[205] specifies the subjects of Osiris, the ruler of the Netherworld.

The second enigmatic feature in the title of this ritual is the term *tḫ*, 𓏏𓐍𓏊𓏤𓎰𓇳, which may be rendered *tḫ ḥb*, "Festival of Drunkenness," or simply *tḫ*, "the month of *Tekh*."[206] The first translation results from the 𓏊 (W22) and 𓎰 (W3) determinatives that follow the phonetic *tḫ*. This hieroglyphic group may be transliterated *ḥb-tḫ* and refer to the Festival of Drunkenness.[207] Although this festival was held on a number of occasions, the 20th of the first month of inundation (*Tekh*) appears to be the principal celebration of the Festival of Drunkenness, primarily honoring Hathor.[208] For example, this occasion is recorded in an

---

198 For the "distinctive emotional coloring" in the lamentations, see Smith, *Mortuary Texts of Papyrus BM 10507*, p. 21.

199 Lines 5, 21–24.

200 For further discussion of the benefits of both compositions for the deceased, see section 1.7.4, below.

201 Cols. 40, 1–56, 5 of MMA; cols. 23a, 1–28 and 23 of B; cols. 8, 1–15, 20 of BM, see above.

202 The fourth stanza begins on line 2, 49 and ends on line 3, 25 of P.W551. See Goyon, *Imouthès*, p. 83.

203 MMA lines 5, 4–5; Goyon, *Imouthès*, pp. 31 and 84, n. 11.

204 MMA line 18, 8; Goyon, *Imouthès*, pp. 51 and 84, n. 12.

205 Line 3, 21 of P.W551.

206 *Wb.* V 325, 18–20.

207 Wilson, *Ptolemaic Lexikon*, p. 1150. For the Ptolemaic Festival of Drunkenness held at Dendera, see Parker, *Calendars*, pp. 31 and 37; Spalinger, in P. der Manuelian, ed., *Studies in Honor of William Kelly Simpson*, pp. 756 and 758–59; and Spalinger, *SAK* 20 (1993): 299–301.

208 Depauw and Smith, in F. Hoffmann and H. Thissen, eds., *Res Severa verum gaudium*, p. 87; el Sabban, *Temple Festival Calendars*, pp. 181–82; Spalinger, *RdE* 44 (1993): 166–67; Spalinger, *SAK* 20 (1993): 297–98. According to Cauville, *Dendara: les fêtes d'Hathor*, p. 50, this date is attested from the Middle Kingdom (MK) to Ptolemaic times. Darnell, *SAK* 22 (1995): 47, also suggests that the festival held on the 20th of *Tekh* described in the Hymn to Hathor in Medamud likely dates back to the late MK.

inscription in Room 9 as well as the hypostyle hall in the temple of Dendera.[209] Festivals of Drunkenness are also attested on the 1st of *Tekh*, as well as the 5th of the second month of inundation (*Paophi*).[210] Festivals of Drunkenness were held in honor of various Egyptian goddesses connected with the myth of the wandering eye of the sun, such as Hathor, Mut, Bastet, and others.[211] For instance, the celebration of Bastet's homecoming is described by Herodotus as festivities of excessive wine-drinking which attracted "huge crowds … of men and women together." [212] Similarly, inscriptions in the temple of Dendera indicate that the image of Hathor was presented to the crowds on the 1st of *Tekh*, coinciding with the procession to the roof of the grand hall and union with her father.[213] Such crowds may explain the *ꜥšꜣt*, "multitude," in the ritual's title. The main reason for reading the term as a name of a festival lies in the  alabaster basin determinative (W3). However, since this determinative was also frequently used in month names, the translation must depend on the context.[214] In view of the strictly Osirian nature of the text, the second interpretation of *tḫ* as a month name, during which the Hathoric Festival of Drunkenness took place, seems more likely.[215]

Notably, a clear, although at times implicit connection between Hathor and Osiris undoubtedly existed.[216] "Hathor" or "Hathor-Osiris" was prefixed to the name of the female deceased instead of "Osiris," from about 400 BCE.[217] Love and sexuality, which were major aspects of Hathoric mythology, were also essential to Osirian rebirth. These themes are illuminated in this ritual's sexually charged descriptions of Osiris, such as *bꜣ-nk*, "Copulating Ba." [218] Furthermore, numerous myths associate the goddess of the solar eye, Hathor, with Sokar or depict her in a function paralleling Isis.[219] Despite the above associations, the con-

---

209 Alliot, *Culte d'Horus*, pp. 239, n. 6 and 244, n. 3, respectively.

210 Cauville, *Dendara: les fêtes d'Hathor*, p. 51.

211 Spalinger, *RdE* 44 (1993): 166–67; DuQuesne, *DiscEg* 61 (2005): 11–12; Darnell, *SAK* 22 (1995): 47–48, who suggests that Hathor became most prominent in connection with this festival in the Ptolemaic period. For further discussion of Festivals of Drunkenness, which played an important role in the Feast of the Valley, among others, see Gutbub, in *Mélanges Maspero* I, pp. 46–70.

212 Depauw and Smith, in F. Hoffmann and H. Thissen, eds., *Res Severa verum gaudium*, p. 87; Herodotus II, chapter 60, see Waterfield, *The Histories. Herodotus*, p. 119.

213 For a discussion of these inscriptions, see Cauville, *Dendara: les fêtes d'Hathor*, p. 56, who points out that no specific circumstances or place for the presentation of Hathor to the population is described.

214 Van Walsem, in R. Demarée and J. Janssen, eds., *Gleanings from Deir el Medina*, pp. 215–27. For the connection of the festival names with month names from the original lunar calendar, see Spalinger, in P. der Manuelian, ed., *Studies in Honor of William Kelly Simpson*, p. 757.

215 For *tḫ*, "the month of *Tekh* (*Thoth*)," see *Wb.* V 325, 18–20.

216 Hathor's connection with the West, or the funerary realm, is made explicit by her epithet *nbt imntt*, "Mistress of the West," see Leitz, et al., eds., *Lexikon* IV, p. 17; Riggs, *The beautiful burial in Roman Egypt*, p. 44.

217 For a list of the instances in which the female deceased is designated Hathor NN, Hathor of NN, and Osiris-Hathor of NN, see Smith, *Mortuary Texts of Papyrus BM 10507*, p. 75. See also Riggs, *The beautiful burial in Roman Egypt*, pp. 43–45.

218 Col. 2, 18. See Manassa, *Late Egyptian Underworld*, p. 252, n. 230; Riggs, *The beautiful burial in Roman Egypt*, pp. 43 and 47.

219 Manassa, *Late Egyptian Underworld*, p. 252; Yoyotte, *AEPHE* 87: 167–69. Sexuality and inebriation are explicitly connected in the festivals of drunkenness; see DuQuesne, *DiscEg* 61 (2005): 8–14; Darnell

nection between Hathoric drunkenness (*ḥb-tḫ*) and Osirian festivals of the LP is not apparent,[220] especially when the simpler explanation points to the Abydene ceremonies in honor of Osiris, which were held in the month of *Tekh* (*tḫ*).[221] Nevertheless, the identical name of the festival and the month cannot be merely coincidental. The Festivals of Drunkenness held for Hathor, and other goddesses, during the month of *Tekh* were likely meant to also benefit Osiris by celebrating sexuality and (pro)creation, essential to both deities. Thus, while the last word in the title of this ritual is interpreted as a month name, its association with festivities for Hathor should not be disregarded. This interpretation is further supported by the record of a festival for Osiris on the last day of *Tekh* in the NK Cairo Calendar.[222] Unfortunately, there seems to be no evidence for the persistence of this festival in GR times. Osirian celebrations during *Tekh* include the Great Procession (*prt ꜥ3t*) of Osiris, fixed to the 22nd day of this month in the Medinet Habu calendar.[223] The presence of an Osirian festival at the end of *Tekh* is further supported by the suggestion that Osiris' death coincided with the end of the *Wag* feast, which was held on the 18th–19th of this month.[224]

Considering the selection of texts in the MMA manuscript, Goyon proposes that the ritual of "Introducing the Multitude," originally executed for the festival of Abydos, was adopted for the *Khoiak* festival of the "reliquary-temples of Osiris" in LP Egypt.[225] Osiris was undoubtedly celebrated during the month of *Khoiak*, based on the abundant evidence for the so-called mysteries of Osiris held in this month.[226] The beginning of the inundation

---

SAK 22 (1995): 52–57, who quotes the Address to the Living over the entrances to the chapels of the divine adoratrices in Medinet Habu: … *ir ḥmwt=tn n ḥwt-ḥr ḥnwt imntt di=s ms=sn n=tn ṯ3w ḥmwt*, "… may your wives celebrate for Hathor, Mistress of the West, with the result that she cause that they bear for you men and women;" Daressy, *RdT* 20 (1898): 74.

220 The connection between Hathoric-related drinking and Osiris was suggested by Kuentz and Desroches-Noblecourt, *Le petit temple d'Abou Simbel*, p. 224, n. 535. This connection is doubted by Goyon, *Imouthès*, p. 84, n. 7.

221 See P.Salt 825, Derchain, *Papyrus Salt 825* I, pp. 62–64.

222 For P.Cairo JE 86637, verso col. XXIII, 8, see Leitz, *Taglewählerei*, p. 441; Bakir, *Cairo Calendar*, p. 588; pls. LIII–LIIIA; el Sabban, *Temple Festival Calendars*, p. 58.

223 Spalinger, in C. Berger, G. Clerc and N. Grimal, eds., *Hommages à Jean Leclant*, p. 375; el Sabban, *Temple Festival Calendars*, p. 91.

224 Kuentz and Desroches-Noblecourt, *Le petit temple d'Abou Simbel*, p. 116; Spalinger, in C. Berger, G. Clerc and N. Grimal, eds., *Hommages à Jean Leclant*, p. 375, bases his view on the consideration of the calendar in the tomb of Neferhotep (TT 50) by Winter, *ZÄS* 96 (1970): 151–52.

225 Col. 1 of MMA takes place on *grḥ nṯry*, the night of the 24th–25th of the fourth month of *Akhet*, i.e., *Khoiak*. The ceremony is opened by the prophet of Osiris in line 1, 7 marking the beginning of a long celebration, in the course of which various rituals, including glorifications (col. 18), are performed; see Goyon, *Imouthès*, pp. 21 and 83–84; Goyon, *BIFAO* 78 (1978): 418. For further discussion of Osirian mysteries during the month of *Khoiak*, see Chassinat, *Le mystère d'Osiris au mois de Khoiak*, p. 9–23; Cauville, *Le temple de Dendara* I, *passim.*; *ibid.*, II, pp. 17–19 and 220–24.

226 For instance, the Abydos calendar of Ramses II describes Osirian celebrations in the month of *Khoiak*; see el Sabban, *Temple Festival Calendars*, p. 41; Kitchen, in G. Posener, ed., *Actes XXIXe Congrès des Orientalistes*, pp. 68–69. For further discussion of Osirian festivals held at numerous cult centers during the month of *Khoiak*, see Yoyotte, *AEPHE* 86 (1977–78): 164–69; Yoyotte, *AEPHE* 88 (1979–80): 194–97; Herbin, *RdE* 54 (2003): 67–127; Manassa, *Late Egyptian Underworld*, pp. 417–18. For the mysteries of *Khoiak*, see Cauville, *BSFE* 112 (1988): 23–36; Cauville, *Le temple de Dendara* I, pp. 13–28; *ibid.*, II, pp. 17–19.

season in the month of *Tekh* marked the birth of Re-Horakhty, whose creation was similarly celebrated three months later, during *Khoiak*.[227] In support of this, Osirian celebrations may have occurred almost identically during the months of *Tekh* and *Khoiak* of the same year.[228] Notwithstanding, the above indicates that the first section of P.W551 contains an Osirian ritual held on the last day of the month *Tekh*.

1.7.3. SECTION 2 — *s3ḫw*[229]

The second section begins on line 37 of col. 5 and runs until the end of the papyrus on line 10, 21. A title marks the second composition of the papyrus, comprising a collection of glorification spells (*s3ḫw*): *s3ḫ ir m ḥwt-nṯr nty wsir ḫnty-imntyw i in ḫry-ḥbt ḥr tp n pr tn ḏdw m h3-snḏ m ḥb nb n imntt*, "Glorification which is to be performed in the temple of Osiris, Foremost of the Westerners, by the lector priest and chief of this temple. To be spoken in jubilation at every festival of the West."

The recorded spells are for the benefit of a man named Padikakem, whose name is inserted by a different hand in the blank spaces.[230] Typical to LP tradition, the deceased is associated with Osiris through the epithet *wsir ḫnty-imntyw wsir n …*, "Osiris Foremost of the Westerners, Osiris of …," which appears to have been written by the principal scribe of the papyrus.

This section contains sixteen glorification spells, which belong to the category of *s3ḫw* III, according to Assmann's and Goyon's classification of mortuary liturgies.[231] These spells are described in detail in Table 4 at the end of this chapter. Each spell begins with a rubric *s3ḫw*, "Glorification spell." Small gaps throughout the papyrus further indicate the beginning of some of the spells.[232] In most cases, the spell is introduced by the conventional heading *ḏd mdw in ḫry-ḥbt*, "words spoken by the lector priest."[233] However, five of the spells do not mention the intended speaker.[234] Within each spell, the vocative *ḥy*, "O!" is written in red

227 Graindorge, *JEA* 82 (1996): 97–101.

228 Spalinger, in C. Berger, G. Clerc and N. Grimal, eds., *Hommages à Jean Leclant*, pp. 375–76. For an overview of the later fusion of Osirian festivals with those of Sokar, see Spalinger, in C. Berger, G. Clerc and N. Grimal, eds., *Hommages à Jean Leclant*, p. 373; Cauville, *Le temple de Dendara*, pp. 245 and 254. Graindorge, *JEA* 82 (1996): 102, provides a table with corresponding days in the months of *Tekh* and *Khoiak*.

229 For a more detailed discussion of *s3ḫw*, see chapter 2.

230 See section 1.6, above.

231 Assmann, in S. Groll, ed., *Studies in Egyptology*, pp. 11–12 and 38, fig. 8; Goyon, in *Textes et Langages*, p. 79. This division was the result of a collaboration of Goyon and Assmann. For further information of the categorization of the books of *s3ḫw*, see chapter 2.

232 It should be noted that some gaps do not seem to carry any meaning, as the same spell is continued following the gap between lines 9, 32–33.

233 For the use of *ḏd mdw*, as well as other indications of the beginning or the end of a spell, see Gestermann, *Die Überlieferung ausgewählter Texte*, pp. 392–93.

234 Spells 6–10.

ink. Red ink is also preferred for further important instructions, such as the specific actions which are to accompany a spell,[235] or *grḥ*, "pause."[236]

A matching title begins a compilation of *s3ḫw* in the aforementioned P.Malcolm (BM), cols. 16–32, which, until recently, was the only known copy of *s3ḫw* III.[237] The papyrus W551 is the second attested example of this category. The sixteen spells are recorded in the same order on both papyri. A number of spells in col. 7 correspond to inscriptions from the 26th-Dynasty tomb of Mutirdis.[238] However, the inscriptions in this tomb generally relate more closely to the PT parallels. Interestingly, the parallel text 104a in the tomb of Mutirdis spans spells 7 and 8 of *s3ḫw* III. Notably, the PT comprising the entire spell 7, as well as portions of spells 6 and 8, of *s3ḫw* III are recorded in the same order in the tomb of Psametik at Saqqara.[239] Much of col. 8 and partly col. 9 of P.W551 are paralleled by a portion of P.Sekowski, published by Szczudlowska.[240] Strikingly, the separate spells are arranged in an entirely different order in the P.Sekowski parallel. This liturgy also occurs in parts of the *Stundenwachen* ritual[241] and a number of such unpublished papyri as P.Schmitt (B),[242] portions of P.Salt 1821 B27, P.BM 102525 and P.BM 102524,[243] and P.BM 10317.[244]

As discussed in chapter 2, glorification spells occur in various periods of Egyptian history and were being altered and expanded continuously in the LP. Although a number of CT are copied in papyrus W551, the PT present the principal source of glorifications in the manuscript. More specifically, cols. 6 to 8 closely replicate eleven PT spells. The orthography of specific words in P.W551 generally resembles the PT from the pyramids of Merenre (Nemtyemsaf) and Pepi II (Neferkare) of Dynasty 6.[245] Some spells show various modifications, such as a less frequent phonetic spelling of words and the use of simpler phrases than the PT originals.[246] The replacement of royal attributes by those appropriate to a private individual mark the adaptation of Pyramid spells for private use. While the PT address the

235 See spell 4 in line 6, 25: *ḏd mdw sp 4*, "Words spoken four times," and spell 12 in line 9, 1: *ḏd mdw is in n=k srt p3 4 rdi šm=sn iw=sn m m3ʿw tpw=sn*, "Words spoken. Now, the 4 geese are brought to you, in order to be caused to go as they are sacrificing their heads."

236 See, for example, line 7, 34, where *grḥ* separates spells 7 and 8. For a brief discussion of *grḥ*, see Grapow, *Sprachliche und schriftliche Formung*, p. 53; Parkinson and Quirke, *Papyrus*, p. 46.

237 Papyrus W551 is not included in Assmann's studies of *s3ḫw* spells; see Assmann, in S. Groll, ed., *Studies in Egyptology*, pp. 1–45 and *Totenliturgien* I.

238 Gestermann, *Die Überlieferung ausgewählter Texte*, p. 376. For the tomb of Mutirdis (TT 410), see Assmann, *Mutirdis*.

239 For the tomb of Psametik, see Daressy, *RdT* 17 (1895): 17–25.

240 P.Sekowski=P.Cracovie 03.03.1992, see Szczudlowska, *ZÄS* 98 (1970): 50–80. The Sekowski manuscript corresponds to lines 8, 9–15; 24–40 and 9, 1 of P.W551.

241 Junker, *Stundenwachen*, pp. 108 and 113ff. For an overview of the *Stundenwachen* ritual, see Altenmüller, *LÄ* IV (1986): cols. 104–6.

242 Cols. 1–3 of P.Berlin 3057 (P.Schmitt).

243 Cols. 4–5.

244 Cols. 12–22, see Szczudlowska, *ZÄS* 98 (1970): 52, n. 11.

245 For example, line 7, 6 has *3st pw ḥnʿ nbt-ḥwt*. PT 364 (§609c) from the pyramid of Neferkare reads *3st ḥnʿ nbt-ḥwt*, while *ḥnʿ* is omitted in the same spell in other pyramids.

246 See notes for lines 6, 15–17 and 7, 10.

deceased king only, associated with Horus, in later funerary texts the deceased becomes one with Osiris. This adaptation is extended to the "genealogy" of the gods. Thus, an OK pyramid spell, which reads "you are on the throne of Osiris (the father of Horus)," is emended in the later papyrus W551 to "you are on the throne of Geb (the father of Osiris)."[247]

1.7.4. COMPILATION OF TWO MORTUARY RITUALS

The two compositions of papyrus W551 are different in many respects. Section 1 is laid out in narrow, uneven columns, while section 2 is written in considerably wider columns with even edges on each side. Section 1 is a ritual addressed to Osiris and said to be recited by Isis, Nut, Nephthys, and a crowd of "men and women." Section 2 is a compilation of glorification spells to be spoken by the lector priest for the deceased Padikakem, the assumed owner of this manuscript. Moreover, unlike the ritual, glorification spells contain detailed instructions for recitation.

Nevertheless, the two compositions of P.W551 have more in common than it may seem at first glance and should be viewed as a unity.[248] The fact that they are recorded continuously, with only a blank line separating section 1 from section 2 in the same col. 5, supports this notion.[249] This is further confirmed by the use of the same hand,[250] with blank spaces provided for the name throughout the apparently complete manuscript.[251]

Both compositions of papyrus W551 are mortuary in character and address Osiris or the deceased associated with him. As such, the texts represent two aspects of dealing with death—secular and divine. Thus, while section 1 contains earthly expressions of love and mourning for the deceased, section 2 deals with his transition to a new state of being in the hereafter. The sequence of the texts corresponds with the Egyptian perception of death, i.e., the deceased is gradually transformed after death, from this world to the sphere of the divine.

Furthermore, the nature of both texts is ritualistic. The identity of the speakers in the ritual of section 1 suggests its origin in temple performances.[252] Similarly, the instructions included in section 2 indicate that the spells were, at least at some point, meant to be recited in Osirian temple celebrations.[253] Unfortunately, there is no evidence for or against the reci-

247 Line 7, 37; and PT 677 (§2021a).

248 Compiling various rituals and spells on one manuscript is a common feature of LP mortuary papyri containing *s3ḫw* spells. For example, P.BM 10252 contains *s3ḫw* I and such rituals as the Great Ceremony of Geb, and Bringing in Sokar; see Assmann, in S. Groll, ed., *Studies in Egyptology*, p. 31, fig. 1; Schott, *Mythe und Mythenbildung*, pp. 8–10. P.Louvre 3079 records *s3ḫw* IV, the ritual of Bringing in Sokar, and a number of BD spells; see Goyon, *BIFAO* 65 (1967): 89; Assmann, in S. Groll, ed., *Studies in Egyptology*, p. 31, fig. 1. Similarly, Goyon, *Imouthès*, p. 15, suggests that the six texts of MMA, which include a Ceremony for the Glorification of Osiris, are a coherent ensemble adopted for private use from temple library archives.

249 For a description of the layout of P.W551, see section 1.2, above.

250 Except for 10 lines in col. 9, see section 1.2, above.

251 For a physical description of the papyrus, see section 1.2, above.

252 For a list of the intended speakers of the ritual, see section 1.7.2, above.

253 For a discussion of the use of glorification spells, see section 2.5.

tation of the spells in P.W551 in temple contexts in the GR era. Nevertheless, both texts of this manuscript should be interpreted as rituals that were likely recited in conjunction with the funeral.[254] Their existence in written form was believed to be beneficial to the owner of this mortuary papyrus.[255] More specifically, the mere presence and/or recitation of the rituals in P.W551 allowed the deceased to participate in Osirian ceremonies, whether or not they were being performed at this time.[256] Moreover, having been equated with Osiris, the deceased owner of the papyrus also benefited from each ritual for the "rejuvenated god." In light of the above similarities of the two sections of P.W551, the papyrus should be viewed as a coherent whole, without denying the possibility that the distinct sections may have been used independently as well.[257]

254 See section 2.5.

255 Similarly, the various ritualistic texts of MMA benefit *Imouthès*, the owner of the manuscript, see Goyon, *Imouthès*, p. 15. For further remarks regarding the benefits of the spells in written form, see section 1.7.2, above, and section 2.5.

256 See section 2.5.

257 The same may be said of the mortuary composition of P.Harkness; see Smith, *Papyrus Harkness*, p. 37.

Table 4 Order of the Spells in P.W551 and their Parallels.

Spell	Col.	Lines	Parallels[1]	Instructions
1	5	37–55		
2	6	2–20	PT 670 (§§1972–86), var. PT 482 (§§1004b–10c) CT 754, VI 383–84[2]	To be recited in the evening.[3]
3		20–30	Opening of the Mouth (OM), scene 55A[4] Coffin of Ankhhophi, 2–12[5]	
4		31–39	CT 363, V 23b–24c CT 429, V 275a–76d[6]	
5		39–46	PT 368 (§638), var. PT 588 (§§1607–08)[7]	
6		47–7, 2	PT 426 (§776a–b)[8] PT 357 (§590b–c) PT 367 (§634a–b)[9] PT 677 (§2020a–b)[10] PT 593 (§§1627–37) var. PT 366 (§§626–33)[11] Tomb of Bakenrenef[12]	

1 This table excludes P.Malcolm (BM), which parallels the entire manuscript, and such unpublished papyri as P.Schmitt (B), P.Salt 1821 B27, P.BM 102525 and P.BM 102524, P.BM 10317, and parts of the *Stundenwachen* ritual, which are occasionally mentioned in the text notes. Cf. the table of *s3ḫw* III of P.Malcolm in Assmann, in S. Groll, ed., *Studies in Egyptology*, p. 38, fig. 8.

2 CT 754 corresponds with lines 6, 10–15 of P.W551.

3 The end of this spell instructs: "The lector (priest) says this on the evening, as Re is setting," see lines 6, 19–20.

4 See Otto, *Mundöffnungsritual* I, pp. 124ff. This spell contains two rubric titles, *s3ḫw ḏd mdw in ḫry-ḥbt*, "Glorification spell. Words spoken by the lector priest," which may suggest that they are, in effect, two separate spells. This concept is supported by the fact that they are recorded in separate columns 18–19 of P.Malcolm, which reserves one column for each spell in every other case. However, I follow Assmann in interpreting the two glorifications as spell 3 of *s3ḫw* III, since both spells continuously reproduce OM, scene 55A.

5 Maspero, *Sarcophages des époques persane et ptolémaïque* II, p. 59.

6 CT 363 corresponds with lines 6, 31–34, while CT 429 corresponds with lines 6, 34–39.

7 Lines 6, 42–44. Assmann, in S. Groll, ed., *Studies in Egyptology*, p. 38, fig. 8, does not explain his comparison of this spell with PT 33 (§25).

8 Line 6, 48.

9 Lines 6, 49–51.

10 Assmann, in S. Groll, ed., *Studies in Egyptology*, p. 38, fig. 8, lists only PT 367 (§634) as a parallel for spell 6.

11 PT 593 corresponds with lines 7, 1–2.

12 The inscription from the ceiling vault in the tomb of Bakenrenef (L24) parallels lines 6, 51–7, 1, see El-Naggar, *EVO* 9 (1986): 28.

TABLE 4 Order of the Spells in P.W551 and their Parallels (cont.).

SPELL	COL.	LINES	PARALLELS	INSTRUCTIONS
7	7	2–34	PT 593 (§§1627b–37a), var. PT 366 (§§626b–33a)[13] PT 356 (§§575–77)[14] PT 370 (§645)[15] PT 357 (§§590–92)[16] PT 367 (§§634c–35)[17] PT 364 (§§609–21)[18] Tomb of Mutirdis[19]	
8		34–45	PT 677 (§§2018–28c)[20] Tomb of Mutirdis[21] This text is adopted as spell 12a of *s3ḫw* I.[22]	
9	8	1–9	PT 365 (§§622–25) PT 373 (§§654–55)[23] This text is adopted as spell 12b of *s3ḫw* I.[24]	
10		9–21	PT 247 (§260)[25] CT 349, IV 383[26] P.Sekowski 12, 2–13, 3[27] This text is adopted as spell 2 of *s3ḫw* I.	To be recited at night.[28]

13 Lines 2–11.

14 Lines 12–15.

15 Line 7, 15.

16 Lines 16–19.

17 Line 7, 16.

18 This lengthy spell does not have a *s3ḫw* title, but begins simply with the instruction *grḥ*, "pause." This is paralleled by P.Malcolm 23, which records this spell in one of the widest separate columns. Lines 20–34 parallel PT 364.

19 Texts 91 and 92 in the tomb of Mutirdis also record PT 593 and echo lines 20–38 of P.W551; see Assmann, *Mutirdis*, pp. 94ff. Text 104a from this tomb parallels lines 7, 20–34; see Assmann, *Mutirdis*, pp. 84–85. The latter text also occurs in the tomb of Psametik; see Daressy, *RdT* 17 (1895): 17–25.

20 Lines 34–45.

21 Text 104a from the tomb of Mutirdis; see Assmann, *Mutirdis*, pp. 94ff. Further examples of this spell are found in P.Louvre 2129, N 38–42; Assmann, *Mutirdis*, p. 94, n. 100.

22 Assmann, in S. Groll, ed., *Studies in Egyptology*, p. 34, fig. 4.

23 PT 365 parallels lines 1–6; PT 373 parallels lines 7–9.

24 Assmann, in S. Groll, ed., *Studies in Egyptology*, p. 34, fig. 4.

25 Lines 8, 9–11.

26 Lines 8, 9–11.

TABLE 4 Order of the Spells in P.W551 and their Parallels (cont.).

SPELL	COL.	LINES	PARALLELS	INSTRUCTIONS
11		21–30	P.Sekowski 19, 6–20, 5[29] This text is adopted as spell 2 of *s3ḫw* I.	To be recited while slaughtering 4 geese.[30]
12		31–9, 1	P.Sekowski 18, 8–19, 4[31] P.Sekowski 18, 2–6[32] This text is adopted as spell 2 of *s3ḫw* I.	To be recited while slaughtering 4 geese.[33]
13	9	2–11		The end of this spell indicates that it should be performed during sacrifice.[34]
14		11–19	CT 839, VII 42–43f. This text is adopted as spell 25b of *s3ḫw* II.	
15		19–44	*Stundenwachen* type.[35]	
16	10	1–21		Instructions for recitation and action.[36]

27 Lines 9–15. For P.Sekowski, see Szczudlowska, *ZÄS* 98 (1970): 50–74. For the parallels of P.Berlin 3057 (=P.Schmitt) 1 (B); P.BM 102525 and P.BM 102524 (BMI) 4–5; P.Salt 1821 (A) (BMII), P.BM 10317, B27 (BMIII) and parts of the *Stundenwachen* ritual, XVII–XVIII (S), see Szczudlowska, *ZÄS* 98 (1970): 52, n. 12.

28 The end of this spell suggests that it should be recited at night: "This is a glorification for every star of the night who comes forth as Re," see lines 8, 20–21.

29 Lines 24–30. For the parallels of P.Berlin 3057 (=P.Schmitt) (B) 1; P.BM 102525 and P.BM 102524 (BMI) 4–5; P.Salt 1821 (A) (BMII), P.BM 10317, B27 (BMIII) and parts of the *Stundenwachen* ritual, see Szczudlowska, *ZÄS* 98 (1970): 50–80.

30 The instruction is given at the end of this spell in line 8, 29.

31 Lines 31–36. For the parallels of P.Berlin 3057 (=P.Schmitt) (B) 1; P.BM 102525 and P.BM 102524 (BMI) 4–5; P.Salt 1821 (A) (BMII), P.BM 10317, B27 (BMIII) and parts of the *Stundenwachen* ritual, see Szczudlowska, *ZÄS* 98 (1970): 50–80.

32 Lines 38–40.

33 See the end of this spell in line 9, 1.

34 "Words spoken. Now, bound are the offering bull, goat, and fowl, which were presented to the slaughtering place," see line 9, 10.

35 Assmann, in S. Groll, ed., *Studies in Egyptology*, p. 38, fig. 8.

36 Assmann, in S. Groll, ed., *Studies in Egyptology*, p. 38, fig. 8.

2
sꜣḫw Glorification Spells

2.1. INTRODUCTION

LP funerary-religious literature and, specifically, glorification spells are largely based on texts from the OK. Numerous spells in LP papyri reproduce the originals exactly. Some spells show various modifications, while others do not appear to have any parallels from earlier times. Much like the selection of tomb equipment, the choice in mortuary literature was likely determined not only by the preferences of the deceased, but also by the literary and religious trends that existed during his or her lifetime.[1] Thus, it is important to consider the specific spells chosen for each compilation within their larger social, historical, and religious context. An analysis of this corpus can better elucidate the religious traditions that remained for centuries, as well as those that were altered and expanded upon.

Glorification spells of the category *sꜣḫw* III comprise the largest part of papyrus W551.[2] In order to better understand what *sꜣḫw* spells are, their content, history, and function will be further examined.[3] The meaning of the term *sꜣḫw* and the apparent purpose of the texts headed by this title can significantly clarify these spells. A survey of the history of *sꜣḫw* offers insights into their original use and meaning. In the course of several millennia, the corpus of texts belonging to this genre accumulated portions of the PT, CT, and the BD, as

---

1 This is evidenced by the frequently occurring practice of annexing glorification spells to various other liturgies in the Ptolemaic period, see section 1.7.3, above; Assmann, in S. Groll, ed., *Studies in Egyptology*, pp. 3–4. For a brief discussion of the tomb owner's role in his own funeral and mortuary cult, see Roth, in S. D'Auria, P. Lacovara, and C. Roehrig, eds., *Mummies and Magic*, pp. 52–53.

2 Assmann, in S. Groll, ed., *Studies in Egyptology*, pp. 1–13, has divided the corpus of glorification spells into four categories according to their frequency in LP papyri. *sꜣḫw* I contains 18 spells originating in the PT, CT, and the *Stundenwachen* ritual and is attested on 7 papyri and numerous LP sarcophagi. *sꜣḫw* II is found on 4 LP papyri. Its 25 spells parallel the PT and CT and occur in the same order in Theban tombs of the Saite period and on a number of MK coffins (see Altenmüller, *Texte zum Begräbnisritual*, pp. 49–51 and 62). *sꜣḫw* III includes 16 spells paralleling the PT, CT, portions of the Opening of the Mouth (OM), and the *Stundenwachen* rituals. Papyrus W551 is the second attested example of this category, discussed in section 1.7.3, above. *sꜣḫw* IV occurs in 6 copies and echoes the Lamentations of Isis and Nephthys; see Assmann, in S. Groll, ed., *Studies in Egyptology*, p. 5, n. 6; Coenen and Verrept, *GM* 202 (2004): 101, n. 19.

3 An overview of these factors was presented in section 1.7.3, above.

well as other compositions.[4] Although the broad spectrum of their sources may suggest that this designation was used for mortuary literature in general, the following analysis will illustrate a more specific meaning of the term.[5] Moreover, it is important to review the specific rituals and/or cultic acts associated with glorification spells in various sources. The broad range of use of these spells throughout Egyptian history is indicated by their attestation as both mortuary and temple liturgies. As such, the function of glorification spells as oral utterances or written spells may be better analyzed.

2.2. DEFINITION

The Egyptians used the word *sꜣḫw* as a name of a ritual and as the title of specific spells. *sꜣḫw* is generally translated as "glorification spells," "spells for the dead (or) Osiris," and, more broadly, as "hymns and prayers."[6] The latter reading stems from *ꜣḫ*, "spell," or, literally, "effective thing."[7] In light of this, *ꜣḫ* is interpreted as an expression of effectiveness, which is an "attribute of magical speech."[8] Nevertheless, *sꜣḫw* should primarily be understood as a causative form of *ꜣḫ*, "to be a spirit."[9] In order to better understand the nuances of this word, the root *ꜣḫ* must be investigated further.

The notion of *ꜣḫ*-effectiveness is connected with *ꜣḫt*, "horizon," as it is the place from which the sun effectively emanates light, while remaining invisible at dusk and dawn. Accordingly, *ꜣḫt* is a 'transitional area,' perceived as a 'border' between night and day, as well as the meeting point of the earth and the sky.[10] The rarely encountered *ꜣḫt*-eye of the sun, which illuminates the inhabitants of the Netherworld, supports this notion with its as-

4 See section 1.7.4, above.

5 Assmann, *LÄ* II (1975): col. 999, nn. 4–5. Barta, *Bedeutung der Pyramidentexte*, p. 62, views the entire corpus of the PT as *sꜣḫw*. However, an examination of the themes in some PT, in addition to the evidence from later compilations of *sꜣḫw*, which include only specific PT and CT spells, suggests otherwise; see sections 2.3 and 2.4, below.

6 *Wb.* IV 24, 1–10.

7 *Wb.* I 15, 7–8. In this sense *ꜣḫ* is used almost interchangeably with *ḥkꜣ*, "magic;" see Ritner, *The Mechanics of Ancient Egyptian Magical Practice*, pp. 30–32 and 34. He cites text A of the Cippus of Horus (CG 9401) 2–3: *šd.n=i m ḥkꜣw=k ḏd.n=i m ꜣḫw=k*, "I have recited by means of your magic (*ḥkꜣ*). I have spoken by means of your spells (*ꜣḫw*);" see Daressy, *Textes et dessins magiques*, p. 2. This notion is further illustrated by an inscription in the tomb of Ramses IX (KV 6), which addresses the king as, …*wꜥ pn ḥnꜥ ḥkꜣ ḫsf=f ḏw-ḳd m ꜣḫ.w=f*, "…this singular one, together with Heka, who defeats the evil-of-character with his *ꜣḫ*-spells;" see Darnell, *Enigmatic Netherworld Books of the Solar-Osirian Unity*, pp. 364 and 368 [c]. On the contrary, Ogdon, *DiscEg* 40 (1998): 141, suggests that the reading of *ꜣḫ* as "spell" derives from the term *sꜣḫ*, "the specific name of the funerary ritual by which a dead person became an *ꜣḫw*, 'radiant dead spirit.'"

8 Ritner, *The Mechanics of Ancient Egyptian Magical Practice*, p. 34.

9 *Wb.* I 15, 3. For the belief in the supernatural power of the *ꜣḫ*-bird, representing the dead, see Kees, *Totenglauben*, p. 37. For a general discussion of *ꜣḫw*, see Darnell, *Enigmatic Netherworld Books of the Solar-Osirian Unity*, pp. 364–68.

10 Jansen-Winkeln, *SAK* 23 (1996): 207–8. The term *ꜣḫt*, "horizon," connects the *ꜣḫ* with the notion of the "unseen power of the sun as it enters the horizon at dawn." DuQuesne, in J. Assmann and M. Bommas, eds., *Ägyptische Mysterien*, p. 38.

sociation with the unified Re-Osiris and, thus, with rebirth.[11] The term *3ḫ* also refers to the "blessed dead," who are associated with the king[12] and the gods (*nṯrw*) and are partaking in their power.[13] Spell 1 in P.W551 addresses the deceased Osiris: "You have appeared as the king of Upper and Lower Egypt, you have power over the Ennead."[14] Numerous scholars derive the concept *3ḫ* from the idea of luminosity, basing this claim on an etymological connection of *3ḫ* with *i͗3ḫw,* "light, to be brilliant, luminous."[15] However, considering the contexts of use and the predominance of the  (N8) determinative for *i͗3ḫw,* but never *3ḫ,* this theory should be reconsidered.[16] The more secular translation of *3ḫ* as "effectiveness," which is employed in both daily life and the sphere of the divine, is a more fitting interpretation.[17] Spell 7 of P.W551 commands the deceased to be both spiritual and physically strong: "Be strong, be effective, be a *ba,* be glorified, be powerful of body, forever."[18]

According to the CT, the so-called 'Letters to the Dead,' and other texts, the *akh* is said to occur as a form of one's *ba,* when it affects or communicates with the world of the living.[19] Since the *akh* enjoyed a certain influence over the dead and the living, controlling issues ranging from health to wealth, it was frequently called to action or appeased with rituals and offerings.[20] Jansen-Winkeln argues that just as the sun's effectiveness is hidden in the *3ḫt,* "horizon," the cause of effectiveness of magic or the deities, ascribed with *akh*-power, is concealed.[21] Since the diverse uses of the word *3ḫ* in contexts of everyday life, magic, and the sphere of the divine include a certain obscurity of cause and/or function,[22] the difficult

---

11 Darnell, *Enigmatic Netherworld Books of the Solar-Osirian Unity,* pp. 87–88, nn. 240–43. For the significance of the *3ḫt*-eye to the "solarization" of Osiris-Sokar, see Graindorge, *JEA* 82 (1996): 99.

12 Lloyd, *JEA* 68 (1982): 172, points to such phrases as *nsw mnḫ i͗rw 3ḫt n i͗t=f,* see *Wb.* Belegstellen II 85, 6. Brand, *GM* 168 (1999): 23–33, argues that in reference to the king the term *3ḫ* should generally be understood as "beneficial, useful, effective," rather than "glorious."

13 Demarée, *The 3ḫ i͗ḳr n rꜥ- Stelae,* pp. 194 and 262–63. For the hierarchical connection between *3ḫ, b3,* and the gods, see Gee, in Z. Hawass, ed., *Egyptology at the Dawn,* p. 231.

14 Lines 5, 44–45.

15 For an overview of the theories of various scholars regarding the notion of *3ḫ,* see Englund, *Akh,* pp. 17–19 and 190; Demarée, *The 3ḫ i͗ḳr n rꜥ- Stelae,* p. 191, n. 11.

16 Jansen-Winkeln, *SAK* 23 (1996): 205–7, points out that the  (N8) determinative does appear in both terms during the LP when spelling is largely based on the phonemes of the spoken language.

17 Friedman, *JARCE* 19 (1982): 145–46, points to the "Letters to the Dead," which refer to the *akh* as an able and effective being, without any insinuation of luminous glory. Nevertheless, Friedman maintains that the reading of *3ḫ* as "luminosity" is secondary and stems from its use in the mortuary context, since the *3ḫ*-spirit of the deceased was believed to not only participate in divine life, but also to exist in a physical form. See also *Wb.* I 13, 7–14, 25. For a similar translation of *3ḫ* as "beneficial power" and its correlation with *mnḫ,* see Lloyd, *JEA* 68 (1982): 169, n. 10.

18 Line 7, 34.

19 Gee, in Z. Hawass, ed., *Egyptology at the Dawn,* pp. 231–32, who points to CT spells 99 and 103; The Bentresh Stela 11, 20–21, etc. The *3ḫ* not only refers to the transfigured spirit of the deceased, but also to the "entities who occupy an intermediate position between members of the pantheon and humans;" DuQuesne, in J. Assmann and M. Bommas, eds., *Ägyptische Mysterien,* p. 37.

20 Gee, in Z. Hawass, ed., *Egyptology at the Dawn,* p. 532.

21 Jansen-Winkeln, *SAK* 23 (1996): 208–11, refers primarily to gods such as Atum, Re, and Osiris.

22 Jansen-Winkeln *ibid.,* 213–15.

term *3ḫ* must encompass both the notion of effective ability and the mystery of the divine. The dual nature of an *akh* is also illuminated in a portion of spell 3 of P.W551: "(O, Osiris of Padikakem.) Awaken, that you may do that which those who know you and those who are ignorant of you did."[23] Here, the glorified deceased is expected to be as effective as the blessed dead (those who know Osiris) and as the living (those who do not know Osiris).

The identification of the deceased with his or her *akh*, and the numerous references to the *3ḫ* situated in front of, behind, as well as within the individual, suggest that it may be viewed as a distinct entity.[24] Nevertheless, the idea of divine effectiveness must not be underestimated.[25] The nuances of "creative power"[26] and "artistic creativity"[27] in the term *3ḫ* demonstrate that the *3ḫ* was an integral part of the deceased, rather than an entirely separate entity. The notion of creativity supports the term's secular interpretation without denying its supernatural aspects. Borghouts sums up the concept *3ḫ* well: "It (*akh*) has substantiality, a form-like quality, but one of an immaterial nature."[28]

The word *3ḫ* does not only describe an abstract concept or an element of a person, but also refers to a blessed or beatified state of being.[29] In view of this, Westendorf interprets the root *3ḫ* as "(Wieder)-Erstandener."[30] Consequently, it is important to consider how this state may have been reached.[31] Englund proposes that the notion *3ḫ* represents an immutable element or state that could be achieved after death,[32] but does not reject the possibility of attaining this quality during life, through the recitation of proper spells.[33] In addition, the *3ḫ*-status was at times granted by the gods, such as Atum, Re, Osiris, and Anubis.[34] The *3ḫ* condition, which permits life in the hereafter, may be achieved upon the union of the

23 Line 6, 21.

24 Barta, *Bedeutung der Pyramidentexte*, p. 105; Demarée, *The 3ḫ ỉḳr n rʿ- Stelae*, p. 192. See for example PT 581 (§1557c): *šm=k m-ḫt 3ḫ=k*, "You will go after your *akh*;" PT 612 (§1731a): *3ḫ=k ḥ3=k*, "Your *akh* is about you;" and PT 717 (§2228): "[You have your *ba*] around you, you have your *akh* within you [and you have your] heart [of] your body;" see Allen, *The Ancient Egyptian Pyramid Texts*, pp. 185, 195, and 247, respectively.

25 Borghouts, in A. Roccati and A. Siliotti, eds., *Magia in Egitto ai Tempi dei Faraoni*, p. 38, is perhaps overly restrictive in limiting the notion of *3ḫ*, "power," strictly to the world of the gods.

26 Ritner, *The Mechanics of Ancient Egyptian Magical Practice*, p. 30. The text of the Seventh Hour of the Amduat supports this notion: "It is by means of the magic (*ḥk3*) of Isis and the Elder magician and by the spells (*3ḫw*) on the mouth of this god (Re) himself that he travels;" see Ritner *ibid.*, p. 31; Hornung, *Das Amduat*, p. 118 and *ibid.*, II, p. 125.

27 This notion is alluded to in the Instructions of Ptahhotep, P.Prisse, 56: *nn ḥmww ʿpr 3ḫw=f*, "No artist's skills are perfect;" see Lichtheim, *Ancient Egyptian Literature* I, p. 63.

28 Borghouts, in A. Roccati and A. Siliotti, eds., *Magia in Egitto ai Tempi dei Faraoni*, pp. 35–36.

29 Otto, *LÄ* I (1975): col. 51. Demarée, *The 3ḫ ỉḳr n rʿ- Stelae*, p. 194, points out that this concept evolved into the Coptic "demon;" see Crum, *Coptic Dictionary*, p. 89.

30 Westendorf, *ZÄS* 92 (1966): 147, n. 4. Demarée, *The 3ḫ ỉḳr n rʿ- Stelae*, p. 191, notes that a number of scholars have taken the word to mean "enlightened" or even "initiated."

31 For an overview of the various means of achieving the state of *akh*, see Englund, *Akh*, pp. 201–5.

32 Englund, *Akh*, p. 206.

33 Englund, *Akh*, pp. 19–20, 102, and 172.

34 Englund, *Akh*, p. 105–6.

deceased's *ba* and *ka*,[35] or the joining of the corpse with the *ba*.[36] Nevertheless, the term *3ḫ* is at times applied to the living as well.[37] Admittance to the hereafter required certain knowledge[38] and possibly certain moral standards.[39] Consequently, these factors, as well as the transformation into an *akh*, were believed to be brought about by ritual acts, such as the recitation of *s3ḫw*, in conjunction with a proper burial.[40]

In summary, the literal rendering of *s3ḫ*, "to make someone an *3ḫ*-spirit," not only carries with it divine connotations of mystery, but also the secular notions of ability and effectiveness, all of which ultimately describe the desired qualities of "the blessed dead."[41] The corpus of *s3ḫw* spells was concerned with elevating Osiris and/or the deceased to a new state of existence and should be understood as a category of Egyptian mortuary literature. As Smith has put it: "Important features of this elevation are the complete restoration of mental and physical faculties and integration within the hierarchy of gods and blessed spirits. *s3ḫw* are not descriptions of this state. Rather, they are concerned with the deceased's transition to it."[42]

35 Allen, in S. D'Auria, P. Lacovara and C. Roehrig, eds., *Mummies and Magic*, p. 45, argues that this union is the only requirement for attaining the *3ḫ*-status.

36 Žabkar, *A Study of the Ba Concept*, p. 106; Barta, *Bedeutung der Pyramidentexte*, p. 63. In support of this notion, see the title of spell 15 of *s3ḫw* I=BD 191: "Spell for Bringing the *Ba* to the Body;" see Schneider, in C. Berger, G. Clerc and N. Grimal, eds., *Hommages à Jean Leclant*, p. 356. This notion also appears in a Theban liturgy, which was likely meant to be recited on the 26th of *Khoiak*; see Herbin, *RdE* 54 (2003): 68–69.

37 PT 457 (§859d) refers to the deceased king and his survivor as an *3ḫ*: *hy NN 3ḫ.ti 3ḫ tpy-t3*, "Ho, NN! You have become *akh*, and your survivor has become *akh*;" see Allen, *Ancient Egyptian Pyramid Texts*, p. 119. See also DuQuesne, in J. Assmann and M. Bommas, eds., *Ägyptische Mysterien* pp. 38–42, who also points to passages from the BD, the Solar Litany, and the Amduat, among others, that demonstrate the *akh's* place upon earth.

38 Englund, *Akh*, p. 20. The necessity of knowledge for the integration among divinities is illustrated in CT 1131, VII 474a–e: *ir s nb rḫt=f mdt=sn sw3=f im ḥms=f r gs nṯr ꜥ3 m bw nb ntf im iw=f snḏ=f n=f ꜥpr 3ḫ pw mi ḳd*, "As for anyone who shall know what they speak, he shall pass by, and he shall sit beside the Great God wherever he may be, and he shall give respect to him, for he is one wholly equipped and spiritualized (*3ḫ*);" see Faulkner, *Ancient Egyptian Coffin Texts* III, p. 170.

39 Englund, *Akh*, p. 204; Demarée, *The 3ḫ iḳr n rꜥ- Stelae*, p. 277.

40 A "proper burial" would include embalming and presentation of offerings; see Kees, *Totenglauben*, p. 37; Demarée, *The 3ḫ iḳr n rꜥ- Stelae*, p. 193.

41 Wilson, *JNES* 3 (1944): 209–10.

42 Smith, *Mortuary Texts of Papyrus BM 10507*, p. 20. In CT 96, II 89c, the deceased declares: *ḥk3=i m s3ḫw=i*, "My magic is in my ritual incantations;" see Faulkner, *Ancient Egyptian Coffin Texts* I, p. 95.

2.3. SOURCES AND HISTORY

In order to ascertain the role of *s3ḫw* in ancient Egyptian mortuary literature, one must look into the origins of these spells.[43] *s3ḫw* are attested in most periods of Egyptian history, from the OK[44] to Demotic examples.[45] Their sources occur in tombs, coffins, and stelae.[46] However, the PT present the principal source of *s3ḫw,* frequently copied almost *verbatim* in later texts.[47] The only substantial difference with later copies is marked by the addressee of the spells. While the PT were directed only to the deceased king, the later copies generally addressed a private individual and were altered accordingly.[48] Certain Harper's Songs, dating as far back as the MK, are yet another source of glorification spells.[49] Furthermore, utterances from the corpus of CT and the BD, some of which were originally titled *s3ḫw,* frequently occur in later collections of glorifications.[50]

The so-called "Lamentations of Isis and Nephthys" belong to the same mortuary genre and are often included in compilation with glorification spells.[51] Both the lamentations and

---

43 Goyon, *Rituels funéraires*, p. 169, n. 4, describes glorification spells as a collection of very different texts alluding to the Osirian cycle for the benefit of the deceased.

44 The rite of "reciting many *s3ḫw*" is attested as a title of a spell in the mortuary cult of the OK; see Assmann, in S. Groll, ed., *Studies in Egyptology*, p. 4; Barta, *Aufbau und Bedeutung*, p. 29.

45 Such as P.BM 10507, see Smith, *Mortuary Texts of Papyrus BM 10507*.

46 See for example the list of sources of *s3ḫw* I in Goyon, in *Textes et Langages*, p. 80.

47 Assmann, in S. Groll, ed., *Studies in Egyptology,* p. 3, states that 33% of PT have an affinity with our genre, while the CT amount to only 8%. For a list of PT paralleled by P.W551, see section 1.7.3, table 4. For a list of PT utilized in other mortuary texts, see Allen, *Occurrence of Pyramid Texts.* According to Gestermann, *Die Überlieferung ausgewählter Texte,* pp. 127, nn. 752–53, and 374, most PT spells occurring in LP tombs parallel the pyramid of Unas. Nevertheless, the PT in P.W551 most resemble spells in the pyramids of Merenre and Pepi II; see section 1.7.3, above.

48 Assmann, *LÄ* II (1975): col. 999. For the adaptation of royal mortuary spells for private use, see Goyon, in *Textes et Langages*, p. 79. Breasted, *Development of Religion and Thought*, p. 257, referred to this adaptation as the "democratization of the hereafter." However, see Smith in J. Dieleman and W. Wendrich, eds., *UCLA Encyclopedia of Egyptology,* pp. 1–11, who disputes the use of the terms "democratization or demotization (of the afterlife)." Smith demonstrates on pp. 4 and 9–10 that the appearance of the CT does not mark a change in belief that the *akh*-status may be attained only by the royal deceased, but rather a change in practice, whereas non-royal individuals begin to gain access to transfiguration through texts inscribed on coffins and perhaps papyri, as well as through recited spells. See also section 1.7.3, above.

49 Assmann, *JEA* 65 (1979): 56–58. Assmann, *Totenliturgien* II, p. 583, proposes that the Harper's Songs that belong to the genre of glorifications were most likely recited by harpers, rather than mortuary priests.

50 CT spells 754; 363, var. 429; and 839 occur in P.W551, see section 1.7.3, table 4. For example, CT I, 1 is introduced with the phrase *ḏd mdw s3ḫw,* "Words spoken: *s3ḫw*;" see de Buck, *Egyptian Coffin Texts* I, p. 1. Similarly, a NK papyrus begins the BD chapter 17 with *ḥ3 m sṯsw s3ḫw,* "Beginning of exaltations and *s3ḫw*;" see Urk. V, 4, 5. Furthermore, a number of glorification spells are annexed to the BD in P.Louvre 3129; see Urk. VI.

51 As mentioned earlier, the category of *s3ḫw* IV includes texts comparable to the lamentations; see Assmann, in S. Groll, ed., *Studies in Egyptology,* p. 5, n. 6. Cf. the Demotic texts of P.BM 10507 in Smith, *Mortuary Texts of Papyrus BM 10507*, pp. 20–22, and P.Harkness in Smith, *Papyrus Harkness,* p. 27, both of which contain a mixture of lamentations and glorifications. For a discussion of corresponding motifs in the lamentations and glorifications, especially those belonging to *s3ḫw* IV, see the forthcoming publication of Andrea Kucharek, *Die Klagelieder von Isis und Nephthys,* ch. 1; ch. 2, pp. 9–11, and ch. 8.

glorification spells contain instructions connecting them to Osirian temple celebrations[52] and address the deceased (whether it is the god Osiris or the private individual associated with him). Both texts are related to the *Stundenwachen* ritual and dwell on such significant mortuary themes as protection, resurrection, and Horus' vindication of Osiris.[53] Notably, however, the lamentations show a considerable difference in presentation and attitude from the *sꜣḫw*.[54] A significant dissimilarity may be observed in the intended speaker of the text. While lamentations identify the speakers as Isis and Nephthys, glorification spells generally do not.[55] Here, the title of the priest who is to recite the spells is stated, while the role he has to assume is not explicitly indicated.[56]

The attitude towards death presents another discrepancy between the lamentations and glorifications. The lamentations bring about the revitalization of Osiris by means of mourning itself.[57] The two goddesses, Isis and Nephthys, refer to death from the viewpoint of the living, uncovering their human emotions, as they recall their love for Osiris and grieve for

52 The Lamentations of Isis and Nephthys in P.Berlin 3008, 1, 1–5 begin with the instruction: *nis sꜣḫw iry.n snty n pr wsir ḫnty-imntt nṯr ꜥꜣ nb ꜣbḏw m spr 4 šmw 25 iry mitt m st nbt n wsir m ḥb=f nb*, "Recitation of glorifications, which is made by the two sisters in the temple of Osiris, Foremost of the Westerners, the Great God, lord of Abydos, in the fourth month of Inundation, day 25, which is done similarly in every temple of Osiris, and his every festival;" Faulkner, in *Mélanges Maspero* I, pl. 1; cf. Lichtheim, *Ancient Egyptian Literature* III, p. 116. *sꜣḫw* III of P.W551 5, 37–38 commence with the statement: "Glorification spell which is made in the temple of Osiris, Foremost of the Westerners, said by the chief lector (priest) of this temple, spoken in jubilation in every festival of the West." For a more detailed discussion of the connection of these texts to the temples of Osiris, see section 2.4, below.

53 Lichtheim, *Ancient Egyptian Literature* III, p. 116. The *Stundenwachen* was published by Junker, *Stundenwachen*. For the themes of glorification spells, see section 2.4, below.

54 Smith, *Mortuary Texts of Papyrus BM 10507*, p. 21.

55 Smith, *Mortuary Texts of Papyrus BM 10507*, p. 21; Assmann, *JEA* 65 (1979): 64–65; Assmann, in J. Assmann, E. Feucht, and R. Grieshammer, eds., *Fragen an die ältagyptische Literatur*, pp. 66–67.

56 In most cases, P.W551 instructs that spells should be spoken by the lector priest, *ḫry-ḥbt*. Notably, *sꜣḫw* IV of Assmann's classification is instructed to be recited as lamentations by priestesses playing the roles of Isis and Nephthys; see Assmann, in S. Groll, ed., *Studies in Egyptology*, p. 4, n. 6. For the instruction for reciting *sꜣḫw* IV in P.Louvre 3079, line 1, 4, see Goyon, *BIFAO* 65 (1967): 95. See also Assmann, *Totenliturgien* I, pp. 29–33.

57 For a discussion of the revival of the deceased by means of mourning, see Smith, *Mortuary Texts of Papyrus BM 10507*, p. 21, nn. 52 and 53. He points to an inscription on col. 2 of the back pillar of a LP statuette, addressing the deceased person: *sꜣḫ tw sn.ty m i(ꜣ)kb=sn*, "The two sisters will glorify you as they lament;" see Bakry, *ASAE* 60 (1968): 2 and pl. IV. The Liturgy of Opening the Mouth for Breathing (P.Berlin 8351 I, 10–11) depicts the same concept: *pꜥy=k m [r sṯꜣw] m hrw m sꜣt ir rꜥ nby nm ṱ=k r tꜣ m ḫr hrw ḥs ṱ=k ꜣst ḥnꜥ nbt-ḥ(t)*, "You (Osiris) will rise up from [Rostau] diurnally in exultation every day. Betake yourself to earth daily. Isis and Nephthys will favor you;" see Smith, *Liturgy of Opening the Mouth for Breathing*, pp. 23 and 30. Thus, Osiris is enabled to rise up from the underworld and travel to earth daily by the praises/songs (*ḥs*) of Isis and Nephthys; see Smith, *Liturgy of Opening the Mouth for Breathing*, pp. 7, n. 38, and 38, n. a, for line 11. See also Darnell, *Enigmatic Netherworld Books of the Solar-Osirian Unity*, pp. 182–84 and 368, who points to a parallel notion of speech "assisting in the manifestations of Re's *ḫprw*" in corridor G of the tomb of Ramses VI: *mdw=sn m ḫtw rꜥ h<ꜣ=sn m> ḫprw=f*, "When they speak in the following of Re, <they descend by means> of his realization." See also the Great Litany of Re in Hornung, *Das Buch der Anbetung des Re im Westen* I, pp. 223–24; Hornung *ibid.* II, pp. 90 and 145–46, n. 505.

him.[58] On the contrary, glorifications tend to deal with death from a more mythological perspective of the hereafter. Thus, unlike the earthly pleas of Isis and Nephthys, the myth of Osiris, Horus, and Seth is evoked in spell 10 of P.W551: "The Great One (=Osiris) awakens, the Great One wakes up. Osiris raised himself on his side, the One who Hates Sleep (i.e., death), One who does not Love Weariness. The god stands, being powerful of his body. Horus has lifted him up, he raised him in Nedit. His son protects him from Seth. Horus protects him, he repels his enemies. He cures the mourning in his heir. His arm is given by Horus, his two legs are given to him by Geb."[59] In the *s3ḫw,* as well as in other mortuary texts such as the BD, the transformation into an *akh* occurs by means of association of the deceased with the god Osiris and his incorporation into the sphere of the divine.[60] Here, gods such as Nut, Geb, Horus, Isis, Nephthys, Khnum, and others bring about the revitalization of the deceased Osiris.[61]

Collections of glorifications appear to have been continuously altered and expanded in the LP and thus should be viewed as compilations.[62] Assmann rejects the ideas of Möller,[63] Altenmüller,[64] and Silverman,[65] among others, who interpret the appearance of PT in LP and Ptolemaic sources as an "archaistic revival."[66] As an alternative, he proposes that these texts were not copies of ancient sources but rather of contemporary "manuscripts of mortuary service," having been used continually throughout Egyptian history.[67] Following the Second Intermediate Period (SIP), most funerary literature was collected in a series of "books" used by private individuals,[68] as is evidenced by the ritual books and funerary scrolls occasionally found in private archives.[69] However, the principal mode of transmission of glorification spells was likely, through the House of Life (*pr-ʿnḫ*).[70] This is supported by the numerous references to the recording and recitation of *s3ḫw* in the *pr-ʿnḫ*.[71] Such

58 Faulkner, in *Mélanges Maspero* I, pp. 337–48.

59 Lines 8, 9–12.

60 Altenmüller, *Texte zum Begräbnisritual*, p. 62.

61 For a detailed description of the role of various deities in Osiris' revitalization, see section 2.4, below.

62 Barta, *Bedeutung der Pyramidentexte*, pp. 63 and 67; Goyon, in *Textes et Langages*, pp. 78–79.

63 Möller, *Ueber die in einem späthieratischen Papyrus*, p. 7.

64 Altenmüller, *Texte zum Begräbnisritual*, pp. 40 and 279.

65 Silverman, in *L'Égyptologie en 1979*, p. 69, n. 16.

66 For an overview of the opinions regarding the "archaistic revival" vs. the tradition of continuity, see Kahl, *Siut-Theben*, pp. 349–55.

67 Assmann, in S. Groll, ed., *Studies in Egyptology*, p. 24.

68 Allen, in S. D'Auria, P. Lacovara and C. Roehrig, eds., *Mummies and Magic*, p. 41.

69 Parkinson and Quirke, *Papyrus*, p. 62.

70 Smith, in J. Dieleman and W. Wendrich, eds., *UCLA Encyclopedia of Egyptology*, pp. 7–8, points to OK evidence of the existence of archives where glorification spells were stored and were perhaps available for use with limited access. For a possible reconstruction of the origins and transmission of mortuary texts and tomb plans in Asyut, see Kahl, *Siut-Theben*, p. 355, fig. 61. For the function of the *pr-ʿnḫ* at the Ramesseum and its relationship with similar institutions, such as the *pr-md3t,* see LeBlanc, *Memnonia* 15 (2005): 93–101.

71 Gardiner, *JEA* 24 (1938): 169 and 178. Parkinson and Quirke, *Papyrus*, p. 60, point out that BD papyri were stored and compiled in the House of Life. Morenz, *GM* 181 (2001): 81, corroborates that manuscripts

priestly libraries stored copies of funerary and religious inscriptions, composed centuries before.[72] As a result, the staff of the House of Life and the libraries associated with it likely had a direct impact on what was handed down and copied.[73] Similarly, the variations in phrasing of mortuary liturgies, originating as far back as the MK, may be viewed as intentional adaptations on the part of the scribes, rather than errors.[74] An additional system of transmission was perhaps the "*Musterbücher,*" whose periodic renewal on fresh papyrus may account for most differences between pre-Saite and Saite versions of the same texts (including glorifications).[75]

An overview of the use of *s3ḫw* spells in different periods of Egyptian history supports Assmann's suggestion. The PT that were adopted for private use as CT in the MK continue their mortuary function into the Roman era.[76] For instance, LP papyri that record *s3ḫw* II place the 25 spells of this group in the same order as MK coffins.[77] The fact that some PT and CT utterances are titled "*s3ḫw*" in later texts further supports the notion of continual use and adjustment to contemporary needs.[78] NK tomb walls often contain glorification spells, some of which already occur in early Dynasty 12.[79] Notably, the decoration of the NK Theban necropolis greatly influenced Saite tombs of the Assasif.[80] The widespread use of glorification spells in the Saite period is reflected in papyrus W551, where spells 7 and 8 of

were composed, edited, copied and recited in the *pr-ʿnḫ*. For example, spell 19 of *s3ḫw* II states that it was "found upon a leather roll in the library of the temple of Osiris from the time of Amenhotep III;" see Assmann, in S. Groll, ed., *Studies in Egyptology*, p. 9, nn. 13–14; Herbin, *SAK* 32 (2004): 175. Faulkner, *Bremner-Rhind*, pp. iii–iv, suggests that P.Bremner-Rhind, which contains the Lamentations, was "written originally as a collection of religious works for some temple library," stating, however, that there is no definite provenance for the manuscript. Notably, the occurrence of parallels for the Lamentations and the *Stundenwachen* on temple walls sustains a temple context for such liturgical texts; see Coulon, in J. Assmann, ed., *Der Abschied von den Toten*, pp. 333–34. See section 2.5, below, for a brief discussion of temple libraries.

72 Parkinson and Quirke, *Papyrus*, p. 61; Quirke, in A. Loprieno, ed., *Ancient Egyptian Literature*, p. 396; Nordh, *Aspects of Ancient Egyptian Curses and Blessings*, pp. 107–15.

73 Kahl, *Siut-Theben*, p. 354; Nordh, *Aspects of Ancient Egyptian Curses and Blessings*, p. 110; Jasnow and Zauzich, *The Ancient Egyptian Book of Thoth*, pp. 34–35.

74 Although Willems, in H. Willems, ed., *Social Aspects of Funerary Culture*, p. 257, regards the mortuary liturgies of the CT specifically, the notion could be applied to the entire genre of mortuary liturgies. See also the discussion of word play in section 1.5.1, above.

75 der Manuelian, *Living in the Past*, pp. 53–54 and 58. Der Manuelian, *ibid.*, p. 55, defines the term as "a corpus of elements gathered for any amount of later excerpting."

76 Allen, in S. D'Auria, P. Lacovara and C. Roehrig, eds., *Mummies and Magic*, p. 39, proposes that certain PT were used in non-royal burials even before their first attestations in Dynasty 6.

77 Assmann, in S. Groll, ed., *Studies in Egyptology*, p. 9.

78 See for example PT 677 (§§2018–28c) and its parallel in P.W551, lines 7, 34–45.

79 Assmann, in S. Groll, ed., *Studies in Egyptology*, p. 22. Chamber A in the tomb of Senenmut (TT 353) contains *s3ḫw* liturgies 3 and 7; see *ibid.*, p. 43, fig. 13; Dorman, *Tombs of Senenmut*, p. 99. For a list of glorification liturgies in Theban tombs of the 18th Dynasty and their MK parallels, see Kahl, *Siut-Theben*, pp. 53–168.

80 der Manuelian, *Living in the Past*, p. 55.

81 These also correspond to a number of PT, see section 1.7.3, table 4. The tomb of Mutirdis is published by Assmann, *Mutirdis*.

s3ḫw III parallel the 26th Dynasty tomb of Mutirdis.[81] In comparing the inscriptions from the tomb of Mutirdis to those in P.W551, it becomes apparent that the Saite version of these *s3ḫw* resembles more the original PT in orthography, grammar, and vocabulary.[82] Jansen-Winkeln lists numerous attestations of glorification spells from the Third Intermediate Period (TIP).[83] As mentioned previously, the Ptolemaic period yields the most examples of compilations of *s3ḫw*.

2.4. CONTENT AND PURPOSE

Glorification spells deal with several mythological themes, alluding to the story of Osiris, Horus, and Seth. More specifically, the spells are concerned with the rejuvenation of Osiris, leading to his manifestation in solar and lunar forms, his vengeance against Seth, as well as Horus' accession to the throne.[84] The effective spirit of the deceased was equated with Osiris[85] in order to be reborn from Nut and nurtured by Nephthys. Spell 9 of P.W551 addresses Osiris as "an *akh*, whom Nut bore, whom Nephthys suckled."[86]

A significant aspect of the Osirian myth lies in the reassembling of his body. Deities, such as Geb, Nut, Horus, Isis, and Nephthys, among others, reanimate the limbs of the deceased, making his body whole.[87] Naturally, the immediate family of Osiris plays the most important roles in his transformation. This is reflected in P.W551. Geb is depicted as the father by the frequently occurring epithets of Osiris, "One who Came Forth from Geb," "Oldest Child of Geb," and "Heir of Geb." Papyrus W551 portrays Geb as protecting and reassembling Osiris: "Geb, Foremost of the Great Ennead, has caused that you be healthy. He raised for you your head on your bones."[88] As the father, Geb performs the paternal function of establishing Osiris in his royal office: "… oldest child of Geb. It is his inheritance that he has given. You

82 For a further comparison, see section 1.7.3, above, and the text notes for col. 7.

83 For a list of TIP *s3ḫw*, see Jansen-Winkeln, *Text und Sprache*, pp. 137–40.

84 Smith, *Mortuary Texts of Papyrus BM 10507*, p. 21.

85 For the identification of the deceased with Osiris, see Barta, *Bedeutung der Pyramidentexte*, pp. 64–65 and 104; Allen, in S. D'Auria, P. Lacovara and C. Roehrig, eds., *Mummies and Magic*, pp. 38 and 47.

86 Line 8, 3. The parallel PT 365 (§623a) addresses the deceased king with the same words; see Allen, *The Ancient Egyptian Pyramid Texts*, p. 81.

87 See P.W551 line 7, 19: "Isis a(nd) Nephthys have reassembled you."

88 Spell 3 in lines 6, 21–22. Geb's part in providing security for his deceased son occurs from the OK to GR times in numerous PT and BD spells, NK sarcophagi, and later temples, such as Dendera, Edfu and Philae; see Bedier, *Die Rolle des Gottes Geb*, pp. 188–91. The earth-god Geb has power over snakes and thus protects the sun god against the serpents, such as Apophis, in PT 385 (§§674b–75a): *ḫfnw ḫfnwt sḏm n=f sḏm n t3 sḏm n it=k gb*, "…Male snake, female snake, listen to him, listen to the ground, listen to your father Geb!…;" see Allen, *The Ancient Egyptian Pyramid Texts*, p. 89, and Bedier, *ibid.*, pp. 186–87. Similarly, Geb's role is exemplified by the presence of his name on certain protective amulets; see for instance P.Brooklyn 47.218.50, col. XVI, 12: *rdit ẖr tp n nsw sḏr=f iwʿ k3 ḳrs m ʿt šps im3 ḫtm rn n gb ḥr=s rdit m is n it n s nty ʿnḫ ʿš ḫtm rn n gb ḥr=s*, "Placing below the head of the king as he sleeps, the heir of the bull who is buried in a noble chamber; the seal of wood (with) the name of Geb upon it. Placing in the tomb of the father of a man who is alive a seal of cedar (with) the name of Geb upon it;" Goyon, *Confirmation du pouvoir royal au nouvel an* II, pl. XI–XII and p. 115 (283), and Bedier, *ibid.*, p. 188.

have appeared as king of Upper Egypt, you have appeared as king of Lower Egypt. You prevail over all gods and their *kas*."[89] Lastly, Geb is responsible for introducing various gods, such as Isis, Nephthys, and Horus: "Geb has brought your two sisters to your side for you. It is Isis with Nephthys."[90] Similarly, Osiris' mother, Nut, functions mainly as the protector in his time of vulnerability and rejuvenation, as for example in spell 5 of P.W551: "Your mother, Nut, has spread herself over you in her name of *št-pt*. She caused you to be a god to Seth in your name of God. She protected you from all evil things."[91] Her motherly role is repeatedly stressed throughout the composition, as Osiris is referred to as the "One who Came Forth from Nut," "Son of Nut," "One whom Nut Bore," and so forth.[92]

Horus plays two roles in papyrus W551, mythological and secular. Following the mythological convention, Horus protects Osiris and avenges his murder: "It is Horus, who will make good that which Seth did against you (=Osiris)."[93] According to the secular tradition, the son and rightful heir was responsible for his father's burial and cult. Hence, Horus offers to Osiris: "He (=Horus) has bound for you (=Osiris) the wild bulls. He lassoed the goat. He tied for you the geese."[94] Horus reassembles Osiris: "May Horus be gracious to you, as he gives to you your head, and he raises for you your limbs (so that) you may exist."[95] Horus insures the deceased's acceptance into the Netherworld by placing him among the gods: "Horus caused the gods to assemble for you that they may be brotherly to you."[96] As a result, Horus is established by the text as the true heir to Osiris' throne: "Your son, Horus, is standing in your places."[97]

Isis and Nephthys perform the widest range of tasks for the deceased Osiris, including purification, protection, and reassembling. At the same time, the two sisters act as they do

89 Spell 6 in line 6, 48. Osiris and the deceased king are described as the "heir of Geb" and receive the royal office from their father; see Bedier, *Die Rolle des Gottes Geb*, pp. 176–77. Geb is clearly entitled to bestow such offices upon his heirs, as he himself is frequently referred to as king (*nswt*), ruler (*ḥk3*), etc.; see Bedier, *ibid.*, pp. 196–203. Similarly, the scenes in Dendera depicting the king in the role of Egypt's protector identify him with Geb or describe him as Geb's heir; Bedier, *ibid.*, p. 202.

90 Spell 7 in lines 7, 14–15.

91 Line 6, 42–43. While protecting her son Osiris, Nut represents a spatial principal, the sky, in which the deceased (Osiris) is reborn. In his analysis, Billing argues that in the OK corpus the PT spells, which contain a full writing of the name of Nut, appear specifically in the sarcophagus chamber and the antechamber. As such, they occur in the space literally representing the sky that extends over and incorporates the corpse and within which the transformed *3ḫ*-state is attained; see Billing, *Nut*, pp. 65–67 and 83–87. This concept develops over time, with Nut spells occupying a wider variety of surfaces in NK tombs, while typical preference is given to the lid and floor of TIP coffins; Billing, *ibid.*, pp. 133–38 and 143–47. For a summary of the evolution of the protective, motherly principal of Nut spells and a discussion of the significance of their placement, see Billing, *ibid.*, pp. 148–85.

92 The mother-son identification of Nut and Osiris parallels the relationship of Isis and Horus; see Billing, *Nut*, pp. 37–38, who points to the archetype of the motherly "uroboric Great Round," represented by the cyclical night sky, primordial ocean, earth, and the notion of femininity; see pp. 163–65.

93 Spell 7 in line 7, 19.

94 Spell 13 in line 9, 6.

95 Spell 3 in lines 6, 23–24.

96 Spell 7 in line 7, 15.

97 Spell 13 in line 9, 5.

in the lamentations, mourning and "glorifying" Osiris: "You are purified by Isis, you are made pure by Nephthys, your Two Great and Mighty Sisters, who have glorified you."[98]

Further themes of glorifications include "acceptance into the company of the gods, freedom of movement throughout the cosmos, whether in the sky, on earth, or in the underworld, reception of offerings, and participation in divine festivals and temple cults."[99] The Spirits of Pe (*b3w P*) participate in welcoming the *akh* to the sphere of the divine,[100] as the deceased joins them after his or her "transformation."[101] In light of this, the town of Pe is connected with the idea of ascension, being the place where the king went after becoming an *akh*.[102] The Spirits of Pe assist the transformation by songs and dances during the funeral, which symbolize triumph over the enemies of Osiris.[103] This performance is described in spell 2 of P.W551: "The Spirits of Pe give way to you. They strike for you their flesh. They raise for you their arms of the body, they pull for you their side-locks, they beat for you their skins, and they say, they say to you: 'Osiris, Foremost of the Westerners! You have gone and you will return, you have slept and you will awaken, you have died but you will live.'"[104]

Although *s3ḫw* primarily associate the deceased with Osiris, the latter's nightly union with Re results in a solid connection of the deceased with the sun god.[105] The transformation of the deceased into the new state of existence as an *akh* can be equated with the cyclical process of the sun, as it is newly born and rises each morning.[106] Since this morning rebirth of the sun was believed to take place in the horizon (*3ḫt*), the transformation of the deceased into the new form of existence must have occurred there as well.[107] Similarly, the PT indicate the Eastern horizon as the place of glorification through the gods Re, Geb, Nut,

98 Spell 2 in lines 6, 13–14.

99 Smith, *Liturgy of Opening the Mouth for Breathing*, p. 7, n. 33; Altenmüller, *Texte zum Begräbnisritual*, p. 62.

100 See for example PT 530 (§1253a): *i(n)ḏ ḥr m3ḳt wṯst b3w p b3w nḫn*, "Greetings, (to you, O,) ladder, which the *ba*s of Pe and the *ba*s of Nekhen raised up;" cf. Allen, *The Ancient Egyptian Pyramid Texts*, p. 164. For an overview of the Spirits of Pe, see Žabkar, *A Study of the Ba Concept*, pp. 15–22.

101 Cf. PT 468 (§904): *hy NN pw b3=k b3w iwnw is b3=k b3w nḫn is b3=k b3w p is b3=k dw3 ꜥnḫ is ḫnty snw=f*, "Ho, NN! You shall become *ba* as the *ba*s of Heliopolis, you shall become *ba* as the *ba*s of Nekhen, you shall become *ba* as the *ba*s of Pe, you shall become *ba* as the living star at the fore of his brothers;" see Allen, *The Ancient Egyptian Pyramid Texts*, p. 124.

102 Englund, *Akh*, p. 39; Žabkar, *A Study of the Ba Concept*, p. 32.

103 Piccione, in E. Teeter and J. Larson, eds., *Gold of Praise*, p. 340, proposes that the dance of the Spirits of Pe described in the PT should be understood as "ritualized fencing."

104 Lines 6, 4–6.

105 Cruz-Uribe, in E. Teeter and J. Larson, eds., *Gold of Praise*, p. 70, points out that all the rooms in Theban mortuary temples containing mortuary spells also involve themes of rebirth of the sun god, Re-Horakhty. The gods Re and Osiris unite into a giant, omnipresent deity, referred to as *dmḏy*, "The Unified One," who spans the sky and the Netherworld; see Darnell, *Enigmatic Netherworld Books of the Solar-Osirian Unity*, pp. 384–93. For another brief discussion of the close relationship between Osiris and Re in mortuary literature from the NK onwards, see Onstine, *JSSEA* 25 (1995): 66–69.

106 Allen, in S. D'Auria, P. Lacovara and C. Roehrig, eds., *Mummies and Magic*, p. 47.

107 Allen, in S. D'Auria, P. Lacovara and C. Roehrig, eds., *Mummies and Magic*, p. 47, suggests that the word *3ḫt*, "horizon," should be literally rendered as "the place of becoming *akh*." See section 2.2, above.

Horus, and Anubis.[108] Spell 8 of P.W551 addresses Osiris: "May Re find you standing with your mother Nut, that she may lead you on the two paths of the horizon."[109]

As discussed previously, *s3ḫw* are intended to assist the transition of the deceased into the *3ḫ*-form of existence suitable for the hereafter.[110] In this form, the spirit becomes incorporated into the hierarchy of the gods and blessed spirits,[111] thus escaping the worst fate of all—dying again.[112] The corpus of glorification spells implies that only "the justified" *akh* may enter into and, thus, continue existence in the hereafter. In other words, transformation into a god was a necessary part of assimilation into the Netherworld. Nevertheless, the existence of other "books" of funerary literature indicates that *s3ḫw* were not the only means of successful transition into life in the hereafter.

Unlike various other mortuary spells concerned with existence in the hereafter, *s3ḫw* were specifically designed to transform and restore the social functions[113] as well as the physical body[114] of the deceased through the connection with the sphere of the divine. Although these themes also occur in numerous other mortuary texts, such as the Liturgy of Opening the Mouth for Breathing and the Lamentations of Isis and Nephthys, among others,[115] glorifications are more precisely concerned with such transformations. It has been suggested that it is explicitly the *ba* that was transformed by these spells in mortuary cult, while glorification of the physical body took place through mummification.[116] As previously discussed, the union of the *ba* and its earthly counterpart resulted in the ascension of the *ba* to the new state of existence.[117] While the body remained on earth, the *akh*, the glorified

108 PT 419 (§§743–44) addresses the deceased king: *ind̠ ḥr=k NN m hrw=k pn ꜥḥꜥ.ti ḫft rꜥ pr=f m i3bt d̠b3.ti m sꜥḥ=k pn im 3ḫw,* "Greetings, NN, on this your day when you stand opposite the Sun as he comes forth in the east, arrayed in this insignia of yours as one of the *akhs*;" see Allen, *The Ancient Egyptian Pyramid Texts*, p. 86.

109 Line 7, 45.

110 Assmann, in S. Groll, ed., *Studies in Egyptology*, p. 16.

111 Smith, *Mortuary Texts of Papyrus BM 10507*, p. 20.

112 For the term *mwt m wḥm,* see BD 44. See, Allen, in S. D'Auria, P. Lacovara and C. Roehrig, eds., *Mummies and Magic*, p. 45.

113 For the former, see Smith, *Mortuary Texts of Papyrus BM 10507*, p. 20, and Assmann, *Liturgische Lieder*, pp. 349–50. The term, "social" refers to the deceased's renewed mental capacity and consciousness, as well as his ability to partake in offerings. For the interpretation of the participation in the offering meal as a social act, see Smith, *Papyrus Harkness*, p. 32. In other words, the transformed deceased was able to communicate with the gods, answer them, and exhibit certain knowledge; see Englund, *Akh*, p. 20; section 2.2, above. Furthermore, the notion of social functions incorporates the deceased's re-integration into a social group, divine or human, and the restoration of physical abilities, which have the ultimate purpose of social interaction.

114 Assmann, *JEA* 65 (1979): 57; Assmann, *MDAIK* 28 (1972): 122ff.

115 For this Liturgy, see Smith, *Liturgy of Opening the Mouth for Breathing*, p. 7. For the Lamentations, see Lichtheim, *Ancient Egyptian Literature* III, p. 116. See also section 2.3, above.

116 Barta, *Bedeutung der Pyramidentexte*, p. 63. For an alternate interpretation of the *ba* as one of the conditions in which a person lives after death, see Žabkar, *A Study of the Ba Concept*, pp. 113 and 149.

117 The el Kab stela of Paheri, 6 illustrates this notion: *nt̠ry b3=k ḥnꜥ 3ḫw,* "Your *ba* becomes divine with the *akhs*," see Tylor and Griffith, *Paheri*, pl. IX.

spirit, ascended to the sky.[118] Subsequently, the *ba* was believed to be the fundamental link between the two worlds, maintaining contact between the "mummy in the tomb and the world outside." [119] Nevertheless, the mummy is directly connected with the hereafter by spell 1 of P.W551: "Hail to you by the gods of the Netherworld! They praise (you) that they may venerate your mummy." [120]

Many collections of *s3ḫw* spells include precise statements indicating when, where, and under which circumstances they are to be recited. The second section of papyrus W551 is opened with one such instruction: "Glorification spell, which is made in the temple of Osiris, Foremost of the Westerners, said by the lector (priest) and chief of this temple, spoken in jubilation at every festival of the West." [121] Similar statements introduce other rituals, such as the Lamentations of Isis and Nephthys, Chapters of the Feast of the Two Kites, and the Ritual of Glorifying Osiris in the God's Domain.[122]

In his analysis of the liturgies of *s3ḫw* I, Assmann argues that their thematic development coincides with different stages of the same ritual, akin to the *Stundenwachen* texts found in GR temples.[123] According to his hypothesis, the ritual is divided into two groups, namely, the night and day liturgies. For example, *s3ḫw* I begin at night and finish on the following night. The night spells are identified by their association with embalming rites, which involve acts of protection and rejuvenation performed over the "passively outstretched deceased." [124] Accordingly, the union of the *ba* and the body takes place at night, at the time when the deceased Osiris merges with the sun god.[125] This union results in the transformation of the deceased into an *akh*, which begins life anew every morning, as does the morning sun. In other words, the arising of the sun each morning is associated with rising of the "one lying on his side." [126] The daytime spells are characterized by the importance of Re and allusion to offerings.[127] Hence, this group deals with the reactivated deceased. In this newly acquired state of existence, the spirit is assimilated into the company of the gods, in particular Re, and

118 Barta, *Bedeutung der Pyramidentexte*, p. 104. The notion that the transformed *ba* ascended to the sky is further illustrated in the 18th Dynasty statue of Huseneb, 9–10: *b3=i m pr ḫ3t=i m mḥꜥt*, "My *ba* is in the sky, my corpse is in the tomb;" see Urk. IV, 484, 14.

119 Englund, in E. Teeter and J. Larson, eds., *Gold of Praise*, p. 101.

120 Line 5, 51.

121 Line 5, 37.

122 For the Lamentations, see Faulkner, in *Mélanges Maspero* I, pl. 1. For the Chapters of the Feast of the Two Kites, see Faulkner, *Bremner-Rhind*, pp. 1–32. For the Ritual of Glorifying Osiris, see Goyon, *BIFAO* 65 (1967): 89–156. See also Smith, *Liturgy of Opening the Mouth for Breathing*, pp. 12–13.

123 Assmann, in S. Groll, ed., *Studies in Egyptology*, pp. 7–8.

124 Assmann, in S. Groll, ed., *Studies in Egyptology*, p. 8.

125 Assmann, *Re und Amun*, p. 89.

126 Assmann, *Re und Amun*, p. 70.

127 Re represents the (solar) disk of the head, while Osiris is the body of the unified solar-Osirian deity, which is in the Netherworld. As such, Re occupies the upper region of Duat (*ḥryt*), the daytime sky; see Darnell, *Enigmatic Netherworld Books of the Solar-Osirian Unity*, pp. 377–39. This corresponds to the depictions of Netherworld dwellers, such as the blessed dead or the "hour"-goddesses, who wear disks on their heads or have disks as their faces; see Darnell, *ibid.*, p. 430 and n. 21, who points to a passage from P.BM 10209 col. 1, 41–42: *iry n=k itn imy-wrtt m-ꜥḳ3 n št3.t=k psḏ=f n=k snkty m imḥ.t wbn=f m šww ḥr tp=k*, "A sun-disk has been fashioned for you (in) the necropolis opposite your tomb, that it may

requires sustenance.[128] However, the sequence of spells in P.W551 does not correspond to Assmann's description exactly, as the protective spells directed towards the passive deceased are intermixed with remarks about Re and descriptions of offerings.[129] Furthermore, certain spells refer to both the active tasks that the deceased performs and the passive ones performed for him. For example, line 10 of spell 10 of P.W551 describes Osiris as an active being: "Osiris raised himself from his side… The god stands, being powerful of his body," while the following line 11 of the same spell focuses on protection: "Horus has lifted him (=Osiris) up, he raised him in Nedit. His son protects him from Seth. Horus protects him, he repels his enemies."[130] In light of such discrepancies, Smith is correct in describing Assmann's approach as "idealized" and in making the important point that the attempt "to describe in a few sentences a complex ritual attested over a long period of time by a number of different textual witnesses is bound to yield a somewhat schematic and oversimplified picture."[131]

A brief examination of the grammar of glorification spells further elucidates their significance. The concern of glorification spells with the deceased individual's transformation, as well as the direct connection of this transformation with the gods, become apparent. Prior to the MK, *s3ḫw* spells generally show the use of the 1st and 3rd persons.[132] From the MK onwards, glorification spells utilize the 2nd person and address Osiris or the deceased associated with him, as is the case in most glorification spells of P.W551.[133] The occasional use of the 1st person in later *s3ḫw* likely originates in the PT, where the king was the intended speaker.[134] While the 2nd person is generally used in the speech of deities, as for example Horus addressing his father, Osiris, the 3rd person is preferred for texts intended to be recited by the lector priests.[135] In this respect, the use of the 2nd person in the speech of the gods tends to be made for the purpose of resurrection of the passive dead, while texts utilizing the 3rd person already identify the active deceased with a god, such as Osiris. Although most of the spells in P.W551 address Osiris in the 2nd person, the deceased is referred to from the 3rd person perspective on a number of occasions, as for example the end of spell 5 in P.W551: "Osiris of Padikakem went to his ka."[136]

illuminate the darkness in the underworld for you and shine as the sun upon your head;" see Smith, *Mortuary Texts of Papyrus BM 10507*, pp. 121–23.

128 Assmann, in S. Groll, ed., *Studies in Egyptology*, p. 8.

129 Thus, spells 2, 3, and 5 describe the deceased in a passive role, while spell 4 alludes to his travels with Re, as well as offerings.

130 Lines 8, 10–11. Similarly, the spells in P.Harkness conflict with Assmann's categorization; see Smith, *Papyrus Harkness*, pp. 28–29.

131 Smith, *Papyrus Harkness*, p. 29.

132 Assmann, *JEA* 65 (1979): 57; Servajean, *Les formules des transformations du Livre des Morts*, pp. 9–12.

133 Assmann, *Liturgische Lieder*, pp. 359–63; Assmann, *JEA* 65 (1979): 57, n. 15; Assmann *Totenliturgien* I, pp. 29–33; Smith, *Mortuary Texts of Papyrus BM 10507*, p. 20, n. 32.

134 Schott, *Mythe und Mythenbildung*, p. 46.

135 Barta, *Bedeutung der Pyramidentexte*, p. 61; Servajean, *Les formules des transformations du Livre des Morts*. Altenmüller, *Texte zum Begräbnisritual*, pp. 2–3, classifies PT spells in the 2nd person as dramatic texts.

136 Line 6, 46.

2.5. FUNCTION

Becoming an *akh* was not a simple matter of dying for an ancient Egyptian. Religious rituals and physical actions to the dead body were required in order for the deceased to attain the new form of existence. *s3ḫw* spells appear in various periods, predominantly in connection with funerary offerings and mummification in cult chambers[137] and private tombs.[138] As such, their primary function was likely during the funeral itself.[139] The precise function of glorification spells within the funerary context is a point of disagreement among a number of scholars. Smith suggests that the *Stundenwachen* ritual, which is frequently incorporated into compilations of *s3ḫw* for private individuals, must have taken place during the actual burial rites.[140] According to Frandsen, mortuary liturgies such as the *s3ḫw* assisted the deceased during the transitional phase of "separation from his previous existence."[141] Goyon proposes that glorification spells were recited specifically at the entrance of the tomb during the funeral.[142]

The association of glorification spells with embalming rituals is most clearly evident on tomb walls. A number of OK tombs depict recitation of *s3ḫw* by the embalmer (*wt*)[143] or coincide with the Opening of the Mouth (OM) ceremony performed by him.[144] In the early OK, the embalmer was responsible for preparing the body, as well as for assuring the deceased's spiritual well-being in the afterlife. The latter role would be performed by the lector priest (*ḫry-ḥbt*) from Dynasty 5 onwards.[145] At this time, the recitation of *s3ḫw* by the lector priest is known to coincide with "services being made by the embalmer."[146] Spell

137 Such as the *wꜥbt* or *writ*; see Barta, *Bedeutung der Pyramidentexte*, p. 64; Assmann, *Mutirdis*, p. 102. Similarly, the *Stundenwachen* ritual was performed for Osiris in temples of the GR period in the *wꜥbt*, "place of embalming;" see Smith, *Papyrus Harkness*, p. 34, n. 138.

138 Cf. the 6th Dynasty tomb of Kagemni and the 26th Dynasty tomb of Mutirdis; see Badawy, *ZÄS* 108 (1981): 85, fig. 1, Assmann, *Mutirdis*, pp. 101–2, and Assmann, *JEA* 65 (1979): 57, n. 17, respectively. Assmann, *Images et rites*, p. 81, suggests that a number of the spells are presumed to be found in PT, although there is no certain proof that the formula appears as part of the presentation of offerings.

139 For instance, the recitation of glorifications (*r3 s3ḫw*) is listed as part of the 'ideal burial' on line 58 of the South Stela from the 18th Dynasty tomb of Djehuty (TT110); see Davies, in S. Glanville, ed., *Studies presented to F.Ll. Griffith*, pp. 288–89, and pl. 37 and 40. For an overview of the contrasting notion that funerary spells were put to use during life on earth, see Wente, *JNES* 41 (1982): 162 and 175–76.

140 Smith, *Papyrus Harkness*, p. 34.

141 Frandsen, in E. Teeter and J. Larson, eds., *Gold of Praise*, p.141.

142 Goyon, *Rituels funéraires*, p. 169, n. 4.

143 For a representation of the embalmer reciting *s3ḫw* on the roof of the 4th Dynasty tomb of Debehni at Giza, see Lepsius, *Denkmaeler* II, p. 35.

144 See the 4th Dynasty tomb of Metjen at Saqqara; Lepsius, *Denkmaeler* II, pp. 4–6.

145 Wilson, *JNES* 3 (1944): 213 and 215. At this time, tomb walls generally depict *s3ḫw* in conjunction with the offering ritual with three or four lector priests, each with one fist on the chest and the other arm raised; see Roth, in S. D'Auria, P. Lacovara, and C. Roehrig, eds., *Mummies and Magic*, p. 58.

146 See for example the 5th Dynasty tomb of Tepemankh from Saqqara, in Urk. I, 190, 13: *i s3ḫw in ḫry-ḥbt ir n=f ḫt in wt.*

15 of P.W551 supports the association with embalming rites by evoking protection for the mummy bandages: "Mut, prevent the bandages from acting against me!"[147]

The OM ritual is also closely associated with the recitation of glorification spells. For example, the children of Horus are depicted performing this rite in spell 2 of P.W551: "They open your mouth with their fingers of copper."[148] The characteristic themes of the OM liturgy correspond to those of *s3ḫw*.[149] Much like glorification spells, the OM ritual was believed to reassemble and reanimate the deceased in order to continue life in the hereafter.[150] The OM ritual consists of several different sources, the components of which are largely similar to compilations of glorification spells. These include embalming and burial rites, offerings and slaughter, as well as temple rituals.[151] This connection is strengthened by the fact that the texts of the OM ritual are included in the compilations of *s3ḫw* III.[152] For example, the Demotic OM texts studied by Smith can be viewed as mortuary liturgies that benefited the deceased as part of the cult.[153] Evidently, the OM ritual was recited as a performance in both mortuary and temple contexts, coinciding with the use of glorification spells.[154] Notably, the OM ritual of the Late and GR periods does not appear to be a development of its NK funerary use, but rather an adaptation of earlier temple liturgies.[155] Comparable to the primary function of *s3ḫw* spells, the OM liturgies were originally meant to be recited by the mortuary priest at the tomb.[156] At the same time, such texts were also intended to be used by the deceased in the afterlife.[157]

---

147 Line 9, 40. The notion that the deceased is able to move only when his/her mummified body is rid of the bandages occurs throughout Egyptian history; see Hornung, *WdO* 14 (1983): 169–71. Cf. CT 501, VI 85m–n: *šsm=i m3ʿt n rʿ wiʿ=f ṯswt=i*, "I present right (*m3ʿt*) to Re that he may loosen my knots (*ṯswt*);" see Faulkner, *Ancient Egyptian Coffin Texts* II, p. 139. The theme of liberation from the mummy bandages is extended from the PT and CT to NK sarcophagi. For instance, the 18th Dynasty coffin of Ahmose from Dira abu an-Naga, MMA 14.10.2, records the speech of Anubis: … *h3 mwt=i 3st my dr=t ṯ3mw ḥr=i*, "…O my mother, Isis, come that you may remove the bandages (which are) upon me," Hayes, *Royal Sarcophagi*, p. 203, 52E; Hayes, *The Scepter of Egypt* II, pp. 70–71; and Badawy, *ASAE* 44 (1944): 198.

148 Line 6, 17.

149 Smith, *Liturgy of Opening the Mouth for Breathing*, pp. 6–8.

150 On the function of the OM ritual, see Roth, *JEA* 78 (1992): 113–47.

151 Smith, *Liturgy of Opening the Mouth for Breathing*, pp. 7 and 13; Otto, *Mundöffnungsritual*, pp. 2 and 8.

152 OM scene 55A=Text 171 appears as the third spell of *s3ḫw* III in P.W551 and P.BM. 10081; see cols. 6, 20–30 of the present manuscript and Assmann, in S. Groll, ed., *Studies in Egyptology*, p. 38, fig. 8.

153 OM texts frequently occur in ritual scenes of NK tombs; see Smith, *Liturgy of Opening the Mouth for Breathing*, p. 6.

154 Cruz-Uribe, in E. Teeter and J. Larson, eds., *Gold of Praise*, p. 73; Manassa, *Late Egyptian Underworld*, pp. 469, n. 187 and 190. The use of *s3ḫw* as temple liturgies is discussed in more detail below. Similarly, Quack, in K. Ryholt, ed., *Carlsberg Papyri 7*, pp. 136–50, discusses the practice of the OM ritual in temple cults, demonstrating that it was directed not only towards the deceased in funerary contexts, but frequently addressed deities, such as Sokar-Osiris and images thereof.

155 Quack, in K. Ryholt, ed., *Carlsberg Papyri 7*, pp. 140–43, n. 181.

156 Smith, *Liturgy of Opening the Mouth for Breathing*, p. 6.

157 Smith, *Liturgy of Opening the Mouth for Breathing*, pp. 17–18.

The functionality of an *akh* after death depended not only on proper spells, but also on material sustenance from offerings.[158] Spell 11 of P.W551 stresses the importance of offerings: "Behold, the court. Hail to you on this your good day on which you shine therein it (= the court) upon the districts with offerings and provisions which heaven gives and earth creates, in your name of Chief of the District."[159] The direct connection with the offering ritual is further exemplified by the preference for placing glorification spells, rather than other types of utterances from the PT corpus, in the sarcophagus chamber.[160]

The furnishing of sustenance through offerings is essential not only for survival, but also for the cyclical revival of the deceased.[161] The relation between glorification spells and offering rituals is evident in private tombs from the later OK, which depict the presentation of offerings accompanied by the recitation of *s3ḫw*.[162] Correspondingly, early representations of the deceased in front of an offering table may be interpreted as a depiction of the rite of "feeding the *akh*."[163] The tradition of placing glorification spells in conjunction with food offering rituals was continued in the 18th Dynasty.[164] Notably, a conscious distinction between mortuary liturgies and funerary literature is first evident at this time.[165] Here, mortuary liturgies begin to be recorded on the accessible cult chambers, where offerings would be presented, thus corresponding to their actual use more closely.[166] Similarly, *s3ḫw* appear on the jambs and thicknesses of Theban tombs from the Saite period.[167]

---

158 Friedman, *Serapis* 8 (1985): 40. The presentation of offerings frequently corresponds with ritual acts, such as the OM ceremony, in both funerary and temple contexts; see Cruz-Uribe, in E. Teeter and J.Larson, eds., *Gold of Praise*, p. 70.

159 Lines 8, 23–24.

160 Barta, *Bedeutung der Pyramidentexte*, p. 67.

161 Englund, in E. Teeter and J. Larson, eds., *Gold of Praise*, p. 106. Roth, in S. D'Auria, P. Lacovara, and C. Roehrig, eds., *Mummies and Magic*, pp. 58–59, proposes that the offering ritual was frequently repeated after the funeral during festivals, such as those of Sokar, Thoth, the secular New Year's feast, and so forth.

162 See for example the 5th Dynasty tomb of Hetepenptah, in Urk I, 187, 17. See also Assmann, *Images et rites*, p. 81.

163 *snmt 3ḫ* is attested throughout Egyptian history, from 1st Dynasty cylinder seals to Deir el Medina stelae; see Friedman, *Serapis* 8 (1985): 86 and 89.

164 Wilson, *JNES* 3 (1944): 217, n. 94, points to a scene on the north wall of the southern hall of offerings in Deir el Bahri, which depicts registers of offering bearers carrying food stuffs, along with a register that reads *šd s3ḫw ꜥš3 in ḫry-ḥbt*, "reciting many *s3ḫw* by the lector priest." This scene is accompanied by two texts originating in PT and CT; see Naville, *Deir el Bahari*, pl. 112.

165 The term 'funerary' is used here with regard to objects and actions pertaining to the funeral, while the term mortuary concerns the cult of the deceased and refers to the texts that were meant to be used by a living priest performing rites for the benefit of the deceased during and after the funeral. As such, mortuary liturgies "did not serve the dead as a text to be read in the hereafter;" see Assmann, in S. Groll, ed., *Studies in Egyptology*, pp. 1–2 and n. 2. There is reason to believe, however, that these liturgies acquired a secondary use in purely textual form, as is discussed below.

166 Assmann, in S. Groll, ed., *Studies in Egyptology*, p. 23.

167 Assmann, in S. Groll, ed., *Studies in Egyptology*, p. 10, describes ca. thirty-five spells, fourteen of which parallel the PT. He points out that the 26th Dynasty tomb of Padihorresnet (TT 196) records an almost complete version of *s3ḫw* II. These spells are referred to as texts 41–42 of the staircase T2; see Graefe, *Padihorresnet* I, p. 92, and II, pp. 85–97.

In addition to the connection of glorifications spells with offering and embalming rites, another important factor in understanding these spells is their specific use in rituals. The fact that each glorification spell begins with the formula *ḏd mdw,* "words to be spoken," indicates that these spells were meant to be recited.[168] However, it is also important to consider the possibility of a non-oral function of the spells. Glorification spells were recited by the lector priest during or in connection with a ritual.[169] Such recitations, particularly those accompanying the rites of the funeral and the mortuary cult, appear to be an essential part of the process of transformation into an *akh*.[170] Smith suggests that such texts as the *Stundenwachen* and related rituals were likely recited not only in conjunction with the funeral, but also at "regular intervals, perhaps on the anniversary of the original burial or on certain Osirian festivals."[171] Due to this, he describes such spells as "manifestations of a belief in the 'performative' power of speech."[172] As a consequence, the deceased was believed to become whatever the assigned speaker said he was.[173] *sꜣḫw* spells were considered to be sacred texts in their original cultic functions and could only be recited by the lector priest as the empowered speaker in cult.[174] However, the lector priests and embalmers who conducted the funeral were likely also responsible for reciting the spells on certain occasions throughout the year.[175] In sum, recitation itself was believed to transform the deceased into his or her new state of existence.

Nevertheless, the perception of *sꜣḫw* as a purely oral rite can be disputed. While not denying that *sꜣḫw* were meant to be recited, it is important to remember that they were deemed significant in written form as well. Egberts argues against a literal interpretation of the instruction *ḏd mdw,* saying that "liturgical prescriptions offer no evidence whatsoever that each and every recitation associated with the divine cult bore a dramatic stamp."[176] The

---

168 Egberts, in C. Eyre, ed., *Seventh international Congress of Egyptologists*, p. 358; Smith, *Mortuary Texts of Papyrus BM 10507*, pp. 21–22.

169 Assmann, *JEA* 65 (1979): 57.

170 Assmann, in J. Assmann and B. Gladigow, eds., *Text und Kommentar*, p. 93.

171 Smith, *Papyrus Harkness*, p. 38, n. 152. Similarly, the façade of the 6th Dynasty tomb of Idu (Giza 7102), lines 3–5, points to the frequent mortuary recitations and glorifications: *sꜣḫ.t=f in ẖry*(*w-ḥbt*) *wtw ꜥšꜣ wrt m wpt rnpt m ḏḥwtyt m rnpt m wꜣg m ḥb skr m ḥb wr m rkḥ m sꜣḏ m prt mnw m …nt ꜣbd m tpyw rnpwt m tpyw mḏw nbw m ḥb nb ꜥꜣ m ẖrt-hrw rꜥ nb,* "May he(=Idu) be glorified very greatly by lector priests and embalmers, at the New Year's festival, at the Thoth festival, at the first of the year, at the Wag feast, at the feast of Sokar, at the great festival, at the fire-lighting festival, at the Sadj festival, at the coming forth of Min, at the half month (and) month festivals, at the seasonal feasts, at the beginning of all decades, at all great festivals and throughout the course of every day;" see Simpson, *Qar and Idu*, pp. 20–21.

172 Smith, *Mortuary Texts of Papyrus BM 10507*, p. 20. For an elaborate discussion of the performative aspect of mortuary texts, see Servajean, *Les formules des transformations du Livre des Morts*.

173 Smith, *Mortuary Texts of Papyrus BM 10507*, p. 22; Roth, in S. D'Auria, P. Lacovara, and C. Roehrig, eds., *Mummies and Magic*, p. 54. See also Gillam, *Performance and Dance*, p. 38.

174 Assmann, *JEA* 65 (1979): 65; Assmann, *Liturgische Lieder*, pp. 362ff., n. 36.

175 Gillam, *Performance and Drama*, p. 43; Servajean, *Les formules des transformations du Livre des Morts*, pp. 23–48 and *passim*.

176 Egberts, in C. Eyre, ed., *Seventh international Congress of Egyptologists*, p. 359. For the periodic use of the formula *ḏd mdw* introducing a dramatic performance, see Ogdon, in *L'Égyptologie en 1979*, p. 38.

fact that glorification spells appeared on coffins, stelae, statues, and tomb walls suggests that their mere existence as texts in written form was believed to be effective.[177] In light of this, *s3ḫw* of the PT could be regarded as a written companion to the recited rituals. In written form they assured the reincarnation of the deceased with the sun god every morning.[178] The cyclical repetition of Osiris' rebirth is illustrated in spell 3 of P.W551: "Your mother bears you on this day, yearly."[179] *s3ḫw* were clearly employed in the mortuary context,[180] and, after the first transformation of the dead into an *akh* was performed, the recorded spells likely functioned on a daily basis to ensure his continuous existence.[181] The tomb scenes of lector priests reciting numerous glorifications (*s3ḫw ˁš3*), along with the papyri and inscriptions of *s3ḫw* spells, would perform this duty through the magical power of image and text.[182]

s3ḫw should not, however, be classified strictly as mortuary texts. The title of *s3ḫw* III, which instructs the ritual to be performed in the temple of Osiris and at every festival of the West, signifies the connection of glorification spells with Osirian temple liturgies. The Lamentations of Isis and Nephthys imply that a ritual similar in content to glorifications was performed in the temple of Osiris in Abydos and, perhaps, in all cult centers of Osiris during the month of *Khoiak* (4 *3ḫt*).[183] Liturgies recorded on LP mortuary papyri were frequently employed as temple rituals, suggesting that these should not be studied as separate phenomena.[184] Considering the numerous examples of temple liturgies used as mortuary texts in the tombs of Ptolemaic clergy, the distinct separation of mortuary and temple contexts should perhaps be rejected."[185] Indications that glorification spells were being composed and written in the House of Life, which was managed by the temple, further confirm the notion.[186] Moreover, these mortuary spells were known to have been recited

---

177 Barta, *Bedeutung der Pyramidentexte*, pp. 63 and 67; Smith, *Papyrus Harkness*, p. 40. Demarée, *The 3ḫ iḳr n rˁ- Stelae*, p. 222, points out that the purpose of the spells was not only for the deceased to first become an *akh*, but also to remain *akh* in the realm of the dead.

178 Barta, *Bedeutung der Pyramidentexte*, p. 67.

179 Line 6, 21.

180 Barta, *Bedeutung der Pyramidentexte*, p. 62, attributes *s3ḫw* exclusively to the mortuary genre.

181 Barta, *Bedeutung der Pyramidentexte*, p. 104.

182 Ogdon, in *L'Égyptologie en 1979*, p. 38, proposes that depictions of funerary rites caused them to be "performed *via* sympathetic magic, 'every day and at all times.'"

183 Faulkner, in *Mélanges Maspero* I, p. 346. For further discussion of the implementation of mortuary rituals in Osirian cult centers, such as Karnak, during *Khoiak*, see Coulon, in J. Assmann, ed., *Der Abschied von den Toten*, pp. 326 and 334–39; Manassa, *Late Egyptian Underworld*, p. 417, n. 41. See also section 1.7.2, above.

184 Cruz-Uribe, in E. Teeter and J. Larson, eds., *Gold of Praise*, p. 69. For an overview of such funerary literature as the BD in GR temples, see Kákosy, in *L'Égyptologie en 1979*, pp. 118 and 122. For a discussion of the correspondence between LP mortuary papyri and texts of the temple ritual, see Manassa, *Late Egyptian Underworld*, pp. 412ff., n. 6, and p. 469.

185 Cruz-Uribe, in E. Teeter and J. Larson, eds., *Gold of Praise*, p. 73.

186 This point is discussed in section 2.3, above. For the temple's administration of the House of Life (*pr-ˁnḫ*), see Gardiner, *JEA* 24 (1938): 175–77. For an overview and theories regarding the function, administration and other aspects of the House of Life, see Nordh, *Aspects of Ancient Egyptian Curses and Blessings*, pp. 106–56 and 208–16.

by the staff of the House of Life.[187] The rubric titles of many glorifications, which address the god, Osiris, Foremost of the Westerners, rather than a private Osiris NN, support the idea that *s3ḫw* spells were used as temple liturgies.[188] However, this argument is challenged by the fact that the deceased in the LP is associated with Osiris and is frequently named "Osiris, Foremost of the Westerners, Osiris of NN," as is the case in P.W551.[189] Conversely, Assmann notes the paradoxical nature of *s3ḫw* as temple liturgies and private mortuary texts, referring to them as "mortuary liturgies which were performed in the cult of Osiris at Abydos and which have survived in tombs of Ptolemaic priests as temple liturgies."[190] Szczudlowska agrees that although the titles of such compositions suggest that they are liturgical texts, they must have been adopted for funeral purposes on papyrus. She supports her claims by suggesting that the LP and GR scribes who copied these texts must have been familiar with temple liturgies.[191] The above arguments imply that glorification spells were incorporated into a dramatic temple performance, at least at some point in time.[192] The mythological themes, which establish a firm connection of *s3ḫw* spells with the tradition of Osiris, Horus, and Seth, further indicate their ritual nature. *s3ḫw* connect the cultic ritual with myth through transformations and manifestations of the glorified deceased in various forms.[193] The association of glorifications with temple performances may also be viewed from a different angle. Collections of *s3ḫw* spells written for private individuals connected the owner of the papyrus with Osirian temple celebrations, such as the mysteries (*št3w*) of Osiris at Abydos.[194] This allowed the deceased to benefit in the other world from participation in the ceremonies, even if he could not take part in these celebrations during life.[195]

187 The Book of Traversing Eternity II, 2–3 illustrates this concept: … *nw ʿt šʿt s3ḫ(w)=k m-ḫt pr-ʿnḫ dm.tw rn=k in ṯt pr-ʿnḫ ḫft šd s3ḫ(w)=f,* "… of the library, your glorifications are in the House of Life, and your name shall be pronounced by the staff of the House of Life in reading its glorifications," see Gardiner, *JEA* 24 (1938): 169 (35); Herbin, *Le livre de parcourir l'éternité*, pp. 50 and 119–20.

188 Assmann, in S. Groll, ed., *Studies in Egyptology*, p. 4.

189 See section 1.6, above.

190 Assmann, in S. Groll, ed., *Studies in Egyptology*, pp. 4–5, n. 6.

191 Szczudlowska, *ZÄS* 98 (1970): 80.

192 Schott, *Mythe und Mythenbildung*, p. 53; Goyon, *BIFAO* 78 (1978): 415–418. The scribes from the House of Life at Abydos are shown to assume the roles of various deities reciting glorifications in P.Salt 825, lines 7, 1–4: *n3w rmṯw nty ʿḳ r=f mḏ3ti pw nt rʿ sšw pr-ʿnḫ pw n3w rmṯw nty m-ẖnw=f fkty šw pw ḥnty ḥr pw nty sm3 sbiw n it=f wsir sš mḏ3t nṯr ḏḥwty pw ntf s3ḫ=f m-ẖrt nt rʿ nb nn m33 n(n) sḏm,* "The people who enter into it (=House of Life), they are the staff of Re and the scribes of the House of Life. The people who are in it, the *fkty*-priest is Shu, the slaughterer is Horus, who will slaughter those who rebel, for his father, Osiris. The scribe of the sacred book is Thoth, who will glorify him in the course of every day, unseen, unheard;" see Derchain, *Papyrus Salt 825* I, p. 139; II, pp. *8–9. See also Gardiner, *JEA* 24 (1938): 168.

193 Schott, *Mythe und Mythenbildung*, pp. 48–49. See, for example, lines 8, 5–6 of the present manuscript: "Arise Osiris, Foremost of the Westerners, Osiris of Padikakem, adorned as a wild-bull."

194 For an overview of the Osirian ceremonies that have been described as 'mysteries,' see DuQuesne, in J. Assmann and M. Bommas, eds., *Ägyptische Mysterien* p. 42. For Osirian ceremonies at Abydos during the month of *Tekh*, mentioned in P.Salt 825, see Derchain *Papyrus Salt 825* I, pp. 62–64.

195 Assmann, *Totenliturgien* II, pp. 36–37 and 454, points out that during festivals the god was believed to appear to the people, as well as the deceased tomb owners, thereby allowing the deceased to participate in the festivals of 'this world.'

2.6. CONCLUSION

s3ḫw or glorification spells belong to a complex genre of Egyptian mortuary literature that evolved through the ages into the LP. The continuous use and development of *s3ḫw* from the OK onwards is marked by the constant addition of new spells and terminology.[196] The context and etymology of the term *s3ḫ* reveal its divine connotations of mysticism, as well as the secular notions of ability and effectiveness, clarifying the Egyptian impression of the *akh*. The use of *s3ḫw* in conjunction with embalming and offering rituals suggests that they were intended to be recited during the funeral and likely accompanied the rites of the mortuary cult. *s3ḫw* were also meant to be recited cyclically at regular intervals during the year[197] and assured the daily reincarnation of the deceased (akin to the experience of the sun god every morning) by their very existence in written form. The grammar, titles, and thematic structure of glorification spells also point to their use as liturgies and dramatic performances in cult centers of Osiris.

To sum up, the term *s3ḫw* refers to various mortuary spells, which were used in very different environments. The exact definition of this term probably changed at different periods of Egyptian history. They were recited as liturgies at funerals and temples and, on a daily basis, functioned for the benefit of royal and private individuals in written form. Nevertheless, the genre of glorification spells may be defined in every era by its concern for the transformation of the deceased into a divine-like and effective form of existence in the hereafter.

196 For an overview of the spells of *s3ḫw* III in P.W551, see section 1.7.3, above. For a list of GR words and epithets in P.W551, see section 1.4 and Index.

197 See section 2.5, above; Smith, *Papyrus Harkness*, p. 38.

3
Transliteration, Translation, Commentary

The transliteration reflects only what is visible in the manuscript, while possible reconstructions are suggested in the commentary at the end of each section (stanza or spell). Completely destroyed parts of text are indicated by … . Square brackets [...] are placed around mostly destroyed hieroglyphs. Half brackets ⌜...⌝ demarcate partially destroyed text. Parentheses (...) are used around omitted and/or supplied hieroglyphs. Text on gray background specifies signs written in red ink in the manuscript. The comments for the texts of P.W551 are indicated with small capital letters in the translation sections.

3.1. RITUAL FOR INTRODUCING THE MULTITUDE ON THE LAST DAY OF *TEKH*

This little known text with an enigmatic title is a ritual that had a dual function, as a mortuary liturgy and as a temple liturgy.[1] The title of this ritual is ambiguous because of the terms *tḫ* and *ꜥšꜣ*. Based on the undoubtedly Osirian content of the text, 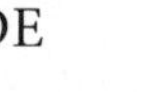 is interpreted as the name of the first month of inundation, rather than *ḥb tḫ*, "Festival of Drunkenness," held during this month. A number of references to Osirian ceremonies held in the month of *Tekh* support this assertion. In this context, the term *ꜥšꜣ*, "multitude," likely signifies the crowd of men and women (*rḫyt pꜥt*) that represents the subjects of Osiris, and whose speech is recorded in the fourth stanza.

The text, which is spoken primarily by Isis, and featuring Nephthys and Nut, addresses Osiris in seven stanzas. Its lyrical tone, speakers, and the use of the first person are reminiscent of love poetry and the Lamentations of Isis and Nephthys. As such, the ritual functioned by directly addressing Osiris in a temple context and at the same time assisting the deceased, associated with Osiris, in his transition to the hereafter in a mortuary context. In both situations, the divine speeches were probably recited by priestesses representing each goddess.

1 For a more detailed discussion of this ritual, see section 1.7.2, above. For the function of such liturgies in mortuary and temple contexts, see sections 2.4 and 2.5, above.

3.1.1. STANZA 1 — SPOKEN BY ISIS AND NEPHTHYS *Lines 1, 1-47*

Although the first address to Osiris does not explicitly name the intended speaker, the content implies that the text is recited by Isis and Nephthys. The use of 1st person singular pronouns in the beginning of the stanza points to only one speaker, while 1st person plural pronouns suggest that both sisters recite the latter part. The poetic tone and phrasing reminiscent of love poetry imply that the primary speaker is Isis, the lover and wife of Osiris. She appeals to Osiris to be rejuvenated and return hastily. Isis expresses her loyalty to Osiris by emphasizing the strong emotional bond that exists between them. She pleads with Osiris to return, asserting her devotion to him and reminding him of the joy that his return will bring. The allusion to the throne of Osiris as his "house" assures him that his position cannot be usurped.

TRANSLITERATION

(1, 1) … ⸢*ꜥšꜣ*⸣ *m ꜥrḳ tḫ*
2. … *ꜥšꜣ.kwỉ*(!) *r=ỉ mr=ỉ mꜣꜣ=k*
3. *ꜣb*(*=ỉ*) *ꜥb ỉw ḫm=k r=ỉ m ꜥnty*
4. ⸢*ḫr*(*ḫ*)⸣ *tỉ ỉw pr=k nn snḏ=k*
(1, 5) ⸢*n sḫm* … *k*⸣
6. *m wdn ꜣt=k r=ỉ*
7. *mḥ=k ḫntš n ỉw=k n=ỉ*
8. *nṯr pn sṯꜣ tw ỉw pr=k*
9. *ꜥnḫ nṯrw r tr n ỉw=k*
(1, 10) *kꜣp r šny=k ꜥnty ỉw ḥꜥw=k*
11. *n ỉn ỉb=ỉ ỉw nḏrỉw mr=k*
12. *st ỉb=k ỉm*
13. *ẖnm=k ỉm*
14. *nḏm=wy ḥḥ n=f kꜣp=k*
(1, 15) *mry-rꜥ*
ỉw=k r pr=k nn ỉṯt sw ky r=k
16. ⸢*m wrḏ*⸣ *r=k ḥwn-nfr*
17. … … *wꜥ nn nw n ꜣb*
18. … … *wꜣt m wꜥt m-ẖnw ỉb=ỉ*
19. … … … *bw mr=k ỉm=f*
(1, 20) *my mꜣꜣ ṯ*(*w*)
m ⸢*ḥ*⸣*ms m wꜥty*
21. *pꜣy šms ḏr ḫnnt=f*
22. *ꜥm ršwt n ỉw=k*
23. … .*k* … ⸢*ỉwnw ḥt*⸣*p=k ỉm=f*
24. … … … *rꜥ ḥr ẖꜣt=k*
(1, 25) ⸢*ỉw*⸣*=k r tꜣ* ⸢*n*⸣ *nỉwt=k ỉnb-ḥḏ sꜣ=k wr ỉw* ⸢*nḏ*⸣ *ḥr=k*
26. … … … … *ꜣb*
27. … … *m* … … …

28\. … … … *⸢m bi͗ty⸣ m š nb tꜣwy*
29\. … …*=k … snb=f mn=k*
APPROXIMATELY 5 LINES MISSING
(1, 35) … … *⸢m⸣y ḥḥ=n…*
36\. … … *=n i͗w tꜣ ⸢m h⸣ꜣw=f*
37\. … *i͗b=n mr-⸢ḥmwt⸣*
38\. … … … … …*=f*
APPROXIMATELY 4 LINES MISSING
43\. … … *⸢b⸣nw i͗w p⸢t⸣ … i͗wn*
44\. …*=k* … … … … *ḥḏ* …
(1, 45) *⸢pꜣy=i͗⸣ bnw*
bnbn=k i͗w pr=k
46\. … …*⸢pr-ꜥꜣ⸣ ḏdw ḥr nst=k*
47\. … *sw*
sḥb=f ḥwt-nṯr=k

TRANSLATION

(1, 1) … … ⸢Multitude⸣ on the Last Day of Tekh.[A]
2\. "… your multitude near me for I wish to see you.[B]
3\. (I) wish (to be) cleansed with myrrh from your disregard of me.[C]
4\. ⸢Rush⸣ yourself to your house without your fear,
(1, 5) ⸢… … not hold you⸣.[D]
6\. Do not delay your moment (of coming) to me,
7\. for you will be full with joy at your coming to me.[E]
8\. This god, rush yourself to your house,
9\. for the gods live at the time of your coming.[F]
(1, 10) The censing is for your hair, the myrrh is for your members.[G]
11\. My heart, which your love has grasped, has not been carried off,
12\. (for) the place of your heart is there.
13\. May you unite therewith.[H]
14\. How sweet is he who hastens to it, your censing! [I]
(1, 15) Beloved One of Re,
as you are in your house, another will not take it from you.[J]
16\. ⸢Do not be weary⸣, Beautiful Youth! [K]
17\. … … one without a moment to stop? [L]
18\. Solitude is within my heart, … … paths. [M]
19\. … … the place in which you desire to be. [N]
(1, 20) Come that you may be seen,
do not ⸢dwell⸣ in solitude! [O]
21\. My companion since his childhood,
22\. understand the joy of your return! [P]
23\. As you … ⸢Heliopolis⸣, that you may ⸢re⸣st therein,
24\. … Re will … upon your body. [Q]

(1, 25) As you ⸢are⸣ in the land of your city of the White Wall (=Memphis),
your eldest son is ⸢protecting⸣ you.[R]
26. … … … stopping …[S]
27. … … … do not …[T]
28. … … ⸢as king of Lower Egypt⸣, as the child of the lord of the two lands.
29. … … … you, he heals your pain.[U]
APPROXIMATELY 5 LINES MISSING
(1, 35) … co⸢me⸣ …, (let) us seek …[V]
36. … us … to the land ⸢ne⸣ar him,[X]
37. … our hearts, One whom ⸢Women⸣ Love.
38. … … … his …[Y]
APPROXIMATELY 4 LINES MISSING
43. … *Be⸢nu* bird⸣ to the s⸢ky⸣, … the Pillar.[Z]
44. You … … … illuminate … …[AA]
(1, 45) ⸢My⸣ *Benu* bird,
may you return to your house![BB]
46. … … ⸢pharaoh⸣ is established upon your throne,[CC]
47. … … him,
as he causes your temple to celebrate."[DD]

TEXT NOTES

This stanza introduces a number of notable allusions to Osiris through the epithets *mr-ḥmwt*, "One whom Women Love," *bnw*, "*Benu* bird," and *iwn*, "Pillar." The epithet *mr-ḥmwt* frequently refers to Osiris in the GR period, illuminating the image of Osiris as a lover and its obvious connection with regeneration and rebirth.[2] This theme appears in various Egyptian texts, as for example in P.Bremner-Rhind 3, 14–16: *ink snt=k ꜣst mrwt ib=k ḥr sꜣ mrwt=k ḥr.tw mḥ=i tꜣ pn m hrw pn*, "I am your sister Isis, the desire of your heart, (yearning) for your love, as you are far away; I flood this land (with tears) on this day." Osiris is further described as *ḏt nṯr nb mrwt tnw ꜥšꜣ mrwt*, "Body of a God, Lord of Love, the Exalted One Rich in Love," in P.Bremner-Rhind 4, 22.[3]

The notion of *bnw*, "*Benu*, phoenix," unites the murdered Osiris with his cyclical counterpart, Re. This epithet occurs in reference to Osiris and the deceased, similarly embodying the notions of regeneration after death and resurrection.[4] Thus, Osiris is here depicted as a solar symbol, denoting the phenomenon of the solar-Osirian unity, during which rebirth

2 Leitz et al., eds., *Lexikon* III, 341. Only and | | | of *ḥmwt* are visible.

3 Faulkner, *JEA* 22 (1936): 124; Faulkner, *Bremner-Rhind*, pp. 6 and 8.

4 For the possible correlation of the *bnw*-bird and the Classical phoenix myth, see Van den Broek, *Myth of the Phoenix*, pp. 4, 25–26, and 28. See also Darnell, *Enigmatic Netherworld Books of the Solar-Osirian Unity*, pp. 395–96, who demonstrates the sexual insinuations of the union of Re and Osiris. For the spelling of *bnw* with (G29), paralleled by MMA 42, 12 and BM 9, 8, see Wilson, *Ptolemaic Lexikon*, p. 316; *Wb.* I 458, 12–13.

takes place.[5] Osiris acts as the nocturnal manifestation of Re's corpse, who is cyclically reborn as the phoenix.[6] As Osiris, the deceased is said to enjoy the *Benu*'s ability to traverse the light and life of the eastern horizon and the darkness and death of the western horizon.[7] The solar association of the term *bnw* is further supported by its etymological connection with *wbn,* "to rise, shine," as well as *bnbn,* "primeval hill," both of which point to creation and rebirth."[8] Chapter 122 of the BD further illustrates the qualities of the *bnw: ꜥḳ=f m bik pr=f m bnw ỉr n=f dwꜣ-nṯr wꜣt ꜥḳ=f m ḥtp r ỉmntt ns š n wsỉr ỉr wꜣt n wsỉr NN ꜥḳ=f dwꜣ=f wsỉr nb ꜥnḫ,* "He has entered as a falcon, he has come out as a *Benu*-bird; the Morning Star made a path for him that he may enter the West in peace. He belongs to the pool of Osiris, and a path is made for Osiris NN, so that he may enter and that he may worship Osiris, the Lord of Life."[9] Here the process of cyclical transformation is explicitly explained through contrasting and complementary images: the falcon—symbolizing the deceased king—is placed in complement to the *Benu* bird—representing the resurrected Re-Osiris. Following the identification of Osiris with Re, the *bnw* is also a solar symbol associated with Heliopolis, which acts as the *ba* of both gods.[10] In support of this, Osiris is also identified as the *bnw* in CT 335, IV 199a–c: *ỉnk bnw pw ꜥꜣ nty m ỉwnw … wsỉr pw,* "I am the great Phoenix which is in Heliopolis… He is Osiris."[11] Notably, Heliopolis is here said to be the tomb of the *bnw*-phoenix.[12]

The group , interpreted here as *ỉwn,* may alternatively be read as *ỉꜥḥ,*[13] or act as an abbreviation of *ỉwn-ḥꜥꜥ,* "moon, rejoicing pillar," a GR term used to describe Osiris, and the *bas* of Osiris, among other deities.[14] The moon, which in a sense replaces the sun dur-

5 For the "solarization of Osiris," see Manassa, *Late Egyptian Underworld,* pp. 430–35. For the evolution of the concept of the solar-Osirian unity from the NK through the TIP, see Niwiński, *JEOL* 30 (1987–88): 89–91.

6 Manassa, *Late Egyptian Underworld,* pp. 425–26 and 430–32. For the designation of Osiris as the *ba* of Re, see Goyon, *RdE* 20 (1968): 90, n. 11. Similarly, Assmann, *Totenliturgien* II, p. 597, proposes that based on the connection of the *bnw*-bird with the sun god, it may also represent Osiris in the Harper's Songs.

7 Belluccio, in T. di Netro, G. Zaccone, eds., *Sesto Congresso Internazionale di Egittologia,* pp. 24 and 28.

8 Baines, *Orientalia* 39 (1970): 390–94.

9 For BD 122, see Lepsius, *Todtenbuch,* pl. xlv. Cf. Goelet, *Egyptian Book of the Dead,* p. 115.

10 Van den Broek, *Myth of the Phoenix,* pp. 17–18; Belluccio, in T. di Netro, G. Zaccone, eds., *Sesto Congresso Internazionale di Egittologia,* p. 29; Manassa, *Late Egyptian Underworld,* pp. 425–30; Leitz et al., eds., *Lexikon* II, pp. 795–97. For an overview of the Osiris-Re connection and the Heliopolitan veneration of Osiris, see El-Banna, *BIFAO* 89 (1989): 101–26.

11 Faulkner, *Ancient Egyptian Coffin Texts* I, p. 263.

12 Belluccio, in T. di Netro, G. Zaccone, eds., *Sesto Congresso Internazionale di Egittologia,* pp. 26–27; Herbin, *RdE* 54 (2003): 94; Meeks, *Mythes et légendes,* p. 173.

13 Herbin, *BIFAO* 82 (1982): 245, n. 2. For a brief discussion of *ỉꜥḥ* as the old or dying moon, in opposition to Khonsu as the young moon, see Griffiths, *JEA* 62 (1976): 158. For the symbolism of the *ỉwn*-pillar, see Van Dijk, *OMRO* 66 (1986): 8 and 12–14.

14 *ỉwn* alone is a common epithet of Osiris, as well as other deities, see Leitz et al., eds., *Lexikon* I, pp. 193–94. Wilson, *Ptolemaic Lexikon,* p. 52; *Wb.* I 53, 17; and Leitz et al., eds., *Lexikon* I, pp. 198–99. Cauville, *Le temple de Dendara* III, p. 28, similarly reads the entire group, frequently occurring in Dendera, as *ỉwn-ḥꜥꜥ*. For the iconography uniting Osiris and the moon, such as in the bronze mummiform figurines equipped with the lunar disk and crescent headdress and holding a crook and flail, see Griffiths, *JEA*

ing the night, is referred to as "(He of the) Pillar." Its association with Re-Osiris must thus indicate that the Pillar supports the night sky, in which the solar-Osirian unity and rebirth take place.[15] A passage from the Lamentations of Isis and Nephthys, col. IV 1–8, further illustrates the solar aspect of Osiris and the lunar aspect of his *ba*: *h3y iwn(y) wbn=k n=n m pt rꜥ nb nn 3b=n n m33 styw=k ḏḥwty m s3w=k sꜥḥꜥ=f b3=k m-ẖnw mꜥnḏt m rn=k(!) pwy n iꜥḥ ... iw=k wbn n=n mi rꜥ rꜥ nb psḏ=k n=n mi itm ... wbn=k n=n sḥḏ=k n=n (m) 3ḫt=k ꜥpr.ti m sšt3w=k*, "Hail Heliopolitan, may you shine for us in heaven every day, without us ceasing to behold your rays. Thoth is your protection, as he establishes your *ba* inside the day bark, in your name of Moon .... You rise for us like Re every day, and you shine for us like Atum.... You rise and shine for us (in) your horizon, equipped with your mysteries."[16] The *Benu* bird can function as the *ba* of Khonsu or the *ba* of Osiris, reinforcing the lunar theme of the couplet.[17] Similarly, the notion of Osirian rebirth in lunar form may be understood in the context of Osiris acting as the nocturnal counterpart of the sun god, Re.[18] The moon plays an important role in the festivities of the beginning of the month, as an inscription from the Khnum temple at Esna states: *ḥꜥꜥ=tw m iwn-ḥꜥꜥ tpy 3bdw sšm=f ḥbw nbw r tpy gnwt*, "One rejoices in the moon at the beginning of the months, he guides all feasts at the beginning of the seasons."[19] In this context, the Ritual of Introducing the Multitude, performed on the last day of *Tekh*, must also initiate the new month of the inundation season.[20]

1, 1

A The first composition of P.W551 is paralleled by papyrus MMA 35.9.21 (MMA), cols. 40–56,[21] as well as the unpublished P.Berlin 3057 (B), cols. 23–28, and P.BM 10081 (BM), cols. 8–15.

The beginning of this line is destroyed, but the traces of red ink support a reconstruction on the basis of MMA 40, 1: *sꜥr ꜥš3w...*, "Introducing the Multitude...." The ☉ determinative (N5) of *ꜥrḳy* is partly damaged and omitted from the MMA 40, 1 parallel. Nevertheless, this term is well attested as "the last day of the month."[22]

The term 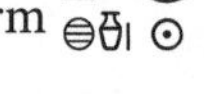 may be interpreted as *ḥb tḫ*, a "Festival of Drunkenness," which was

62 (1976): 153–59; Griffiths, *JEA* 65 (1979): 174–75; Graefe, *JEA* 65 (1979): 171–73; Darnell, *Enigmatic Netherworld Books of the Solar-Osirian Unity*, pp. 355 and 428–29.

15 Van Dijk, *OMRO* 66 (1986): 8 and 13–14, suggests that the Pillar's act of separating heaven and earth brings about sunlight and thus, represents rebirth.

16 Manassa, *Late Egyptian Underworld*, pp. 431–32; Faulkner, in *Mélanges Maspero* I, p. 339–40 and pl. II.

17 Leitz et al., eds., *Lexikon* II, p. 795. See also the bark chapel of the Khonsu temple at Karnak in Mendel, *Die kosmogonischen Inschriften*, pl. 16 (O31).

18 Herbin, *BIFAO* 82 (1982): 244; DuQuesne, in B. Backes, I. Munro, S, Stöhr, eds., *Totenbuch-Forschungen*, pp. 25, n. 25, and 26, n. 27. The moon, frequently represented as Thoth, acts as the nocturnal form of the sun, and as such unites the gods Re and Osiris at night, see Fóti, *StudAeg* 12 (1989): 18–19; Darnell, *Enigmatic Netherworld Books of the Solar-Osirian Unity*, pp. 362–63.

19 Parker, *Calendars*, p. 33; Brugsch, *Thesaurus inscriptionum Aegyptiaerum*, p. 390. For further discussion and examples of the lunar aspect of Osiris, see Derchain, *RdE* 15 (1963): 11–12 and 21–25.

20 Cf. line 1 of the present column.

held on a number of occasions in honor of Egyptian goddesses associated with the myth of the solar eye.[23] However, due to the Osirian nature of the text, the above group is translated as the name of the month *Tekh,* during which the Ritual of Introducing the Multitude was conducted.[24] Notably, the parallels of MMA 40, 1 and BM 8, 1 write *ṯḫ* with the 𓄣 determinative (F34) whose similarity with 𓏊 (W22) in hieratic likely accounts for the uncertainty. Despite the unquestionable identification of the last word in this ritual's title as a month name, in view of the dichotomy and pronounced themes of love and sexuality, the connection with Hathor and other goddesses is clearly present.

1, 2

B The imperative my may be reconstructed from the parallel MMA 40, 2 at the beginning of this line.
Since a stative form of *ꜥšꜣ* does not make sense here, the group 𓏲𓀀 (Z7 and A1) must be understood as a mistake, although it is paralleled by MMA 40, 2.
The 2nd person suffix pronoun *k* following *mꜣꜣ* is paralleled by MMA 40, 2. The use of *k* in place of the expected dependent pronoun *ṯw* is a feature of religious texts from the OK.[25] The fact that both pronouns may occur in different spells of the same version of a PT suggests that the variation does not depend on syntax.

1, 3

C In this line Isis reproaches Osiris for forgetting her with the construction *ḫm r,* "to forget something/someone."[26] Although the preposition *r* is omitted from MMA 40, 3, Goyon's rendering of the parallel line is analogous: *ꜣb ꜥbw ḫmw=k r=ỉ m ꜥnty,* "Mon souhait est d'effacer ton oubli envers moi grâce à l'oliban."
The reading of 𓐍𓅓𓂻𓈖, *ḫm,* as a *sḏm=f* with 𓈖 written in place of the 𓂜 determinative (D35) is supported by the parallels of MMA 40, 3 and BM 8, 3, both of which have the expected 𓂜 determinative (D35). The confusion in P.W551 likely stems from the frequently interchangeable use of 𓈖 (N35) and 𓂜 (D35) for phonetic *n*.[27]
The use of two homophonic *ꜣb* words is a feature of the LP and specifically Ptolemaic texts. Punning and alliteration in Egyptian religious texts must have been considered to be divinely inspired and, as such, more acceptable when addressing a god.[28] In this

21 Papyrus MMA 35.9.21 is published by Goyon, *Imouthès*, pp. 83–94. For a more detailed discussion of *ꜥšꜣt*, "multitude," see section 1.7.2, above.

22 *Wb.* I 212, 8; Černý, *ASAE* 51 (1951): 445.

23 For a more detailed discussion on this subject, see section 1.7.2, above.

24 For *ṯḫ*, "the month of *Tekh*," see *Wb.* V 325, 18–20. For the spelling of month names with the 𓎰 determinative (W3), see van Walsem, in R. Demarée and J. Janssen, eds., *Gleanings from Deir el Medina*, pp. 215–27.

25 Vernus, in H. Willems, ed., *The World of the Coffin Texts*, Annex D, pp. 188–95.

26 *Wb.* III 279, 12.

context, word play did not merely demonstrate the scribe's mastery of the language but also illuminated the divinely implied interconnections among certain terms and concepts.[29]

The use of *ỉw* in place of the preposition *r* in the construction *ʿb r,* "to be purified from," is another typical feature of Late Egyptian orthography.[30]

Myrrh figures as an essential part in the list of ideal wishes for a good afterlife in the MK stela of Seqedi Sehemre, 10–11: *t n ẖt=k mw n ẖẖ=k ṯꜣw mḥ n šrt=k ssn=k snṯr wrḥw=k ʿnty*, "Bread for your stomach, water for your throat, and the north wind for your nostril. May you inhale incense and be anointed with myrrh."[31] Furthermore, myrrh was used in the preparation of Osiris figures because it was believed to have grown from the tears of Horus.[32] Note Faulkner's translation of a similar phrase in P.Bremner-Rhind 8,12: *ẖmw m ʿntyw* as "your dust is myrrh," perhaps "your smoke is myrrh."[33]

1, 4–5

D Since 𓐍, *ẖ*, is frequently written for 𓈙, *š*, in late texts, the first verb of this line may be read as *šrš*, "to rush."[34] The parallels of MMA 40, 4 and BM 8, 4 use the more commonly attested *ẖẖ*, "to hurry." This verb is an imperative, with *ṯỉ* standing in place of the 2nd person singular dependent pronoun *ṯw*.

The more classical form of the preposition *r* stands for *ỉw* in BM 8, 4.

(G54) of *snḏ* has an unusually extended neck. The convoluted writing is amplified by the placement of the 2nd person singular suffix pronoun *k* before the determinative (Z6). However, the reading of *snḏ* is supported by its phonetic spelling with the phonetic complement (Aa27) in the parallel of BM 8, 4.

The remaining traces of line 1, 5 support a reconstruction based on MMA 40, 5: *nn sḫm šʿd ỉm=k*, "The severing will not have power over you." The spelling of the negative 𓈖 in P.W551 corresponds with BM 8, 5.

---

27 Gardiner, *Egyptian Grammar*, p. 490.

28 For a more detailed discussion of word play, see section 1.5.1, above. Wilson, *Ptolemaic Lexikon*, pp. xxiv–ix.

29 For the use of word play and homophony in religious literature in particular, see Guglielmi, in F. Junge, ed., *Studien zu Sprache und Religion Ägyptens*, pp. 491–506. See also Manassa, *Late Egyptian Underworld*, p. 9, n. 55, who suggests viewing word play, homophony, and alliteration as clues to the scribes' interpretations of the ancient texts they were copying.

30 For this specific construction, see *Wb.* I 175, 10; Meeks, *Année lexicographique* I, p. 60. For a more general discussion of the orthography of the preposition *r*, see Lustman, *Étude Grammaticale du Papyrus Bremner-Rhind*, p. 23. For *ꜣb*, "to wish," see Wilson, *Ptolemaic Lexikon*, p. 145; *Wb.* I 177, 2–3.

31 For the stela of Seqedi Sehemre (Rio de Janiero 643), see Kitchen, *Catalogue of the Egyptian Collection in the National Museum* I, p. 55; *ibid.*, II, pp. 37–38.

32 Ritner, *The Mechanics of Ancient Egyptian Magical Practice*, p. 39. For *ʿntyw*, "resin, myrrh," see *Wb.* I 206.

33 Faulkner, *JEA* 22 (1936): 123. For *ẖmw* "dust, smoke," with the determinative (P5), see Wilson, *Ptolemaic Lexikon*, p. 728.

34 *Wb.* IV 529, 1–6; Wilson, *Ptolemaic Lexikon*, p. 1026.

1, 6–7

E The negated imperative *wdn* is intended in the sense of "to delay."[35] The more widely attested translation of this term, "to be heavy," also has connotations of hindering and, hence, postponing of motion.[36] The context of this frequently occurring phrase presupposes that *3t=k*, "your moment," should be understood as the "moment of your (=Osiris) coming."

The abbreviated spelling of 𓄦, *mḥ*, "to fill," with this variant of the backbone and ribs (F37) is typical for the GR period.[37]

The last group in this line looks like the genitive *nt*, due to the shape of 𓀀 (A1). However, its position at the end of the line indicates that the group must be read as *n=i*. This is supported by the parallels of MMA 40, 7 and BM 8, 7.

1, 8–9

F The horizontal line below *sṯ3* is most likely a scribal error, which does not occur in MMA 40, 8 and BM 8, 8. Otherwise, the horizontal and the walking legs determinative (D54) may be interpreted as a corrupted suffix pronoun *n=k*, offering a number of alternative readings. For instance: *nṯr pn sṯ3.n=k tw iw pr=k*, "This God, you have rushed yourself to your house." However, it seems more logical to take *sṯ3* as an imperative strengthened by the dependent pronoun *tw*.[38] Notably, this dependent pronoun is not present in MMA 40, 8, and the preposition *r* is spelled more typically as 𓂋 (D21).

The *ꜥnḫ*, written 𓋹𓐍, is used circumstantially here. The preposition *r*, preceding *tr*, is replaced by *m* in both parallels of MMA 40, 9 and BM 8, 9.

1, 10

G Similar phrases are addressed to Osiris by Isis and Nephthys in the Lamentations of P.Bremner-Rhind 15, 14: *bt r šnw=k m ꜥnty pr ḏs=f*, "The incense cone is for your hair, (made) of myrrh which comes forth of itself (i.e., natural);" and 15, 28: *sty k3p r šnw=k m ꜥnty pr ḏs=f*, "The smell of incense on your hair is of the myrrh which comes forth of itself."[39]

The 𓈘 determinative (N24) of 𓊬𓈘𓏏, *k3p*, must be understood as a mistake for the phonetic *p*, 𓊪, while the *t* is superfluous.[40]

This line shows a number of orthographic discrepancies with the parallel texts:

1. *k3p* is written 𓊬𓈗𓊪 in both MMA 40, 10 and BM 8, 10.

---

35 Goyon, *Imouthès*, p. 85, n. 5; *Wb.* I 390, 3. The parallels of MMA 40, 6 and BM 8, 6 do not use the 𓏌-jar phonetic complement in *wdn*.

36 *Wb.* I 390.

37 *Wb.* II 116; Goyon, *Imouthès*, p. 85, n. 6.

38 For *sṯ3 r*, "to go back," see Wilson, *Ptolemaic Lexikon*, p. 968.

39 Faulkner, *JEA* 22 (1936): 123; Faulkner, *Bremner-Rhind*, pp. 28–29.

40 For *k3p*, "censing, burning of incense," see *Wb.* V 103, 8–13.

2. All three papyri spell the first preposition *r* as 𓂋, while the second one is in the form in P.W551 and MMA 40, 10.
3. BM 8, 10 uses one 𓄹 (F51) for *ḥʿw*, while the abbreviated spelling in P.W551 is paralleled by MMA 40, 10.

1, 11–13

H In the context of Isis' emotional bond and devotion for Osiris, the lack of a determinative after *mr*, "love," may suggest that a pun on *mr*, "to bind, binding," was intended here.[41]

The *iw+sḏm=f* construction of *nḏr*, "to grasp, touch," forms the Late Egyptian relative past.[42] Although the notion of being grasped by one's love is frequently encountered in Egyptian love poetry, the term *nḏr* does not occur in the corpus.[43] Rather, this concept is generally indicated by *iṯt*, "to seize," as in the 6th stanza of P.Chester Beatty I: *mrwt=f ḥr iṯ ib*, "Love of him captures the heart."[44] Cf. BM 8, 1: *n in ib=i ḏrw mr=k*, "My heart has not realized the limits of your love."

The negates a past passive *sḏmw=f*.[45] However, an alternative reading of the clause could be a future form of *in* negated by the late variant of the negation *nn*, "My love which your love has grasped will not be carried off."[46]

The 𓅆 determinative (G7), which regularly occurs with *ib*, , in MMA 40 points to the divine nature of the speaker, Isis.

Two orthographic discrepancies with the parallel texts should be noted:

1. MMA 40, 12 and BM 8, 11 omit the 𓄹 determinative (F51) after *ib*, as well as the after *im*.
2. 𓊛 (P1) stands for *im* in BM 8, 13.[47]

1, 14

I P.W551 contains a longer version of the exclamation than MMA 40, 14: *iw n=f k3p=k*; corresponding more closely to the B and BM versions: *nḏm.wy ḥḥ n=f*.[48]

---

41 *Wb.* II 105, 1–8. Similarly, both parallels of MMA 40, 11 and BM 8, 11 omit the determinative. Note the phonetic complement 𓂋 for *mr* in BM. For a more detailed discussion of word play, see section 1.5.1, above.

42 Černý and Groll, *Late Egyptian Grammar*, p. 510, 54.4.1; Johnson, *The Demotic Verbal System*, p. 182. For *nḏr*, see *Wb.* II 382, 18–383, 26. Note the frequent use of the dot below the determinative (A24), not present in the MMA parallel.

43 Mathieu, *La poésie amoureuse de l'Égypte ancienne.*

44 Lichtheim, *Ancient Egyptian Literature* II, p. 184.

45 Gardiner, *Egyptian Grammar*, §424; Hoch, *Middle Egyptian Grammar*, §§107, 2 and 115.

46 For the negative future construction, see Gardiner, *Egyptian Grammar*, §457.

47 For this use of *im*, see *Wb.* I 72, 8.

48 Goyon, *Imouthès*, p. 85, n. 7.

1, 15

J Unlike the abbreviated writing in the present manuscript, Re, , is spelled with the  determinative (G7) in MMA 40, 15. Otherwise, the first group of this line in P.W551 may have been read as *s3 mry*, "beloved son."

Goyon does not depict the circumstantial relationship of the clauses in his translation of the parallel MMA 40, 15: *mrti rꜥ iw=k r pr=k nn iṯt s(w) ky r=k*, "(O,) Bien-Aimé de Rê; tu es à ta demeure et nul autre ne pourra te la prendre."[49] The dependent pronoun *sw* refers back to "your house."

1, 16

K The beginning of this line is only partially preserved, but the traces[50] suggest that MMA 40, 16 is analogous, although there are a number of discrepancies with it and other parallels:

1. MMA 40, 16 shows a more concise writing of *ḥwn*, .
2. The  determinative (G7) modifies the entire group, *ḥwn nfr*, , in MMA 40, 16.
3. BM 8, 16 omits all  determinatives (G7) in this line.

1, 17

L The remaining traces are comparable to the intact parallels of MMA 41, 1 and BM 8, 17: *iḫ šm wꜥ nn nw n 3b n=f*, "Is this the one who walks alone, without a moment for him to stop?" *nn*, , was added later above the line in P.W551. Note also the lack of a suffix pronoun reinforcing *3b* in P.W551.

1, 18

M Cf. MMA 41, 2 and BM 8, 18: *šm=i w3wt wꜥ m-ẖnw ib=i*, "Solitude is within my heart, as I walk the paths."[51]

1, 19

N The nuances of this phrase are slightly altered in the parallels. Cf. MMA 41, 3: *nn gm=i bw šm.n=k im*, "(and) I will not find the place where you have gone!" Cf. BM 8, 19: *n gm=i bw wn.n=k im*, "(and) I have not found the place in which you are."

The spelling of the preposition im as  (P1) is typical to the GR period. This orthography is paralleled by MMA 41, 3, while BM 8, 19 shows a phonetic spelling .[52]

---

49 Goyon, *Imouthès*, p. 85.

50 For the spelling of *wrḏ* with a  determinative (G37), see *Wb.* I 337, 1–14.

51 For this GR spelling of *ẖnw*, , see *Wb.* III 368, 17.

52 *Wb.* I 72, 4–12; Fairman, *BIFAO* 43 (1945): 110. See section 1.4, above.

1, 20

O This line contains some notable orthography:

1. The imperative *my*, "come," shows an abbreviated spelling in P.W551, while the scribe of MMA 41, 4 adds the determinative (D54): .
2. *mꜣꜣ*, "to see," is spelled as here, as well as in MMA 41, 4 and BM 8, 20.[53]
3. *ḥms*, "to dwell" is rendered with (A7).[54] Cf. the longer, more unusual spelling of *ḥms*, , in MMA 41, 4.

1, 21–22

P Lines 1, 21 and 1, 22 of P.W551 are reversed in MMA, while BM combines them into one line. Note the extended spelling of *pꜣy šms* in MMA 41, 6: ; and in BM 8, 21: . The presence of determinatives (G7) for this group in the parallel texts suggests that this is an epithet.
It is difficult to say which phonetic word was intended, since only (A17 and G7) is written. *ẖnnt* fits the sense. Notably, the determinative (G7) of this word is not present in MMA 41, 6.
ꜥm, is used as an imperative. The unusual determinative (D3) for this term is paralleled by MMA 41, 5 and BM 8, 21.[55]

1, 23–24

Q The reading of this damaged line may be reconstructed from the parallels of MMA 41, 7–8 and BM 8, 22–23: *i͗w=k r i͗wnw ḥtp=k im=f ḥꜣy bꜣ n rꜥ ḥr ẖꜣt=k*, "as you are (headed) toward Heliopolis, that you may rest there, (where) the *ba* of Re will illuminate your body." Traces of (O49 and G7) following the lacuna further support the reading of *i͗wnw*, "Heliopolis," the center of the solar-Osirian unity, and thus, the resurrection of Osiris.

1, 25

R The grammatical structure of this line parallels that of line 1, 23, and is analogous to lines 9–10 of MMA 41.
Since *wr*, , lacks a determinative (G7), the phrase *sꜣ=k wr* should be understood here as "your eldest son." Cf. the similarly written *sꜣ=k ḥr*, "your son, Horus," in MMA 41, 10.
BM 8, 24 shows two orthographic divergences from P.W551:

1. A more classic form of the preposition is used in place of *i͗w*.
2. *nḏ* shows a more extended spelling: .

53 For this typically GR spelling, see Daumas, *Valeurs phonétiques* I, p. 154.

54 For this spelling, see *Wb.* III 96, 13–98, 22.

55 For *ꜥm*, "to know, understand," see *Wb.* I 184, 16–21.

1, 26

S The traces in the lacuna seem to correspond with MMA 41, 11: *nṯr wꜥt n nw n ꜣb n=f*, "Is the solitary god without a moment for him to stop?" BM 8, 25 parallels MMA, except for the negation *nn*, . *ꜣb n*, "to stop, finish," is characteristic of the Late and GR periods.

1, 27

T Cf. MMA 41, 12: *ẖwn m wdn iw iy*, "Child, do not be weary of returning." BM 8, 26 corresponds with MMA, but has in place of .

1, 28–29

U Cf. the more complete MMA 41, 13-14: *iwꜥ=k dy m bity m ẖy nb tꜣwy ḥꜣ.tw=k snb=f mnt=k*, "Your heir is a king here, a child, lord of the two lands, you are protected, as he cures your pain." Cf. the latter clause in BM 8, 28: *ḥꜣ=f ḥr=k snb=f mn=k*, "his protection is upon you, as he cures your pain."
Two orthographic features and discrepancies with the parallel texts should be noted:
1. is understood as a simplified writing of *ẖy*, "youth," written in MMA 41, 13 and BM 8, 27.[56]
2. , *snb*, has the determinative (F51) in BM 8, 28.

A large lacuna in the manuscript corresponding to 5 lines in MMA 41 follows:

MMA 41, 15	*di=f n=k ḫpš nw nbd*
	iw mꜣꜥ-ḫrw=k r iry r=k
MMA 42, 1	*i iry ḏw binw=k r=k*
	nb=n m pr=f n snḏꜣ=f
	ẖꜣr wr r=k ꜥnḫ=f ꜥnḫ it=f
MMA 41, 15	He offers to you the foreleg of the Evil One,
	as you are justified against the one who acted against you.
MMA 42, 1	O, One who Did Evil, your malevolence is (now) against you,
	Our lord is in his house, he will not suffocate.
	The child is greater than you, as he lives and his father lives.[57]

56 For this GR spelling of *ẖy*, see *Wb.* III 217, 3–8.

57 Cf. Goyon, *Imouthès*, p. 86 and pl. xxxv:

MMA 41, 15	il t'offre le cuissot du Perfide,
	et tu es triomphant sur celui qui a agi contre toi!
MMA 42, 1	Ô celui qui accomplit le mal, tes mauvaises actions se tournent contre toi,
	notre seigneur est dans sa demeure, il n'est pas dévoilé,
	l'orphelin plus puissant que toi, il vit, son père vit!

1, 35

v The traces support a reconstruction based on MMA 42, 4: *snt=ỉ my ḥḥ=n*, "My sister, come that we may search!"
Note the double *n* in the 1st person plural suffix pronoun *n*, 𓈖𓏥.

1, 36

x Cf. the variation of the preposition *n* in MMA 42, 5 and BM 9, 2: *šm=n r tꜣ n hꜣw=f*, "let us walk the land of his neighborhoods."

1, 37–38

y The beginning of this line is completely destroyed. The remaining traces are similar to MMA 42, 6–7 and BM 9, 3–4: *ꜣms ỉb n nb=n mr-ḥmwt n mḥ=f ỉb n rrw=f*, "that our lord, whom Women Love, may rejoice, as he is not concerned with his mourners."[58] The residual 𓄹 determinative (F51) in line 1, 38 was likely a part of ib, 𓄣𓏤𓄹. The significant difference in the subjects between the two texts may mean that the destroyed verb of the present manuscript did not correspond to the version of MMA.

A large lacuna in the papyrus corresponding to 4 lines in MMA 42 and 3 lines in BM 9 follows:

	n sp(!) n ỉb=ỉ m ỉb=ỉ
	ỉnk mwt mkt sꜣ=s
MMA 41, 15	*ḥmt ꜣḫ (t) hꜣy=s*
	nḏ=ỉ nb=ỉ nḏ(=ỉ) ꜥwy(!)=k sḫr=ỉ ḫftw=k ẖr=k
	My wish does not abandon my heart!
	I am the mother who protects her son,
MMA 42, 10	the beneficent wife of her husband:
	I protect my lord, and (I) protect your heir, as I cause your enemies to fall under you.[59]

1, 43

z Cf. Goyon's rendering of the complete MMA 42, 12: *bnn=k m bnw ỉw pt ntk ỉwn-ḥꜥꜥ*, "tu peux bondir comme un phénix vers le ciel car tu es *(Lunus)-Ioun-hââ.*"

58 For *ꜣms-ỉb*, "to rejoice," see Wilson, *Ptolemaic Lexikon*, p. 11.

59 Cf. Goyon, *Imouthès*, p.86, n. 14–15 and pl. xxxv:

	et mon désir ne peut demeurer dans mon cœur(?)!
	Je suis une mère qui protège son fils,
MMA 42, 10	une épouse efficient pour son époux:
	je (te) protégé, mon seigneur, je protégé ton héritier et j'abats tes ennemis sous toi.

1, 44

AA This line is completely lost. For a possible reconstruction, see MMA 42, 13: *ḫpr=k m ỉꜣbt nt ỉtm ỉw sḥḏ tꜣ n ḫʿ=k*, "You come into being in/as the left eye of Atum in order to illuminate the land with your appearance." Cf. BM 9, 9: *ḫpr=k m ỉꜣbt nt ḫpri ỉ… … tꜣ n …*, "You come into being in/as the left eye of Khepri … … the land with … ."

1, 45

BB The epithet *bnw* creates a pun on *bnw*, "to go away, leave," here.[60] Notably, the scribe omits the  determinative (G7) for *bnw*, found in the parallel MMA 42, 14 and line 43 of P.W551. The verb *bnbn*, "to return, turn back," is frequently used of the overflowing of the Nile, thus suggesting a connection between Osiris and the inundation as a source of rejuvenation.[61]

1, 46

CC The damaged line closely corresponds to MMA 42, 15 except for the phonetic spelling of 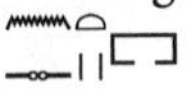, *nst*, in the parallel: *ỉw sꜣ rʿ pr-ʿꜣ ḏd.tw ḥr nst=k*, "The son of Re, pharaoh, is established upon your throne." BM 9, 10 slightly diverges: … *pr-ʿꜣ ʿnḫ wḏꜣ s(nb) ḏd ḥr nst=k*, "… the pharaoh, life, stability, he(alth), is established upon your throne."

1, 47

DD Cf. MMA 42, 16 and BM 9, 12: *ḫꜣw=k sḥb=f ḥwt-nṯr=k*. Goyon does not comment on his translation, disregarding the 2nd person singular suffix pronoun: "il (te) protège, il met en fête ton temple!"[62] Note the discrepancy between the 2nd person singular pronoun *k* in MMA and BM and the 3rd person dependent pronoun *sw* in the present manuscript.

60 *Wb.* I 456, 13.

61 See the discussion of Stanza 2, below. For *bnbn* written with the  determinative (D54), see Hannig, *Sprache der Pharaonen*, p. 254.

62 Goyon, *Imouthès*, p. 86.

3.1.2. STANZA 2 — SPOKEN BY NUT *Lines 1, 48–2, 10*

The introductory line of the second stanza indicates that the following discourse is meant to be recited by the mother of Osiris, Nut, or a priestess playing her role. The speaker explicitly identifies herself by stating, "I am your mother, Nut." In this context, the deceased is represented as a child who has been rejuvenated and became a god in the form of Osiris. As such, his golden skin and hair of lapis-lazuli, symbols of a divine and protected status, cannot be lost. Nut describes the mourning for Osiris by the gods and pleads for his quick return, much like Isis in the previous stanza. Only the appearance of the youthful Osiris will bring an end to the grief of the gods.

TRANSLITERATION

48. [*ḥwt mḥ-2*]
49. … … *i͗ i͗n nwt*
    (1, 50) … *=i͗*
        i͗rṯt=k bnr.tw nn ꜥwꜣ
    51. … …
        nn ꜣb r=k i͗m=f
    (2, 1) *i͗nk mwt⸢=k nwt⸣*
    2. *šn-m-nbw-tp=f-m-ḫsbd*
        nn wiꜣ i͗wn=f
    3. *my hꜣw ḥr=i͗*
        nḏ ti sꜣ=k n=k i͗my
    4. *nṯrw ḥr tp m mꜣst ns=k n=i͗*
        (2, 5) ⸢*bꜥḥ*⸣ *m ḥr=f*
        bgꜣ=f sꜣṯ.w
            6. *ḥr ꜣw i͗w(t)=k n=sn*
    7. *my m wn sp 2*
    8. *sꜣ šn*
    m šm n kkw m ḥrw=n
    9. *ḫy my n niwt=k*
    my nswt m ḥkꜣ nst=k
    (2, 10) *ꜣw.n wnwt sp 2*
    i͗ty wn sp 3

TRANSLATION

48. [2nd stanza]
49. … … said by Nut. [A]
    (1, 50) "… me,
        your milk is sweet, without going sour, [B]
    51. … …
        your mouth cannot evade it. [C]

(2, 1) I am ⌜your⌝ mother, ⌜Nut⌝. D
2. Golden Child, whose Head is of Lapis-lazuli,
whose colors will not fade! E
3. Come near me,
as your own son protects you. F
4. The gods are with head upon knee as you go to me, G
(2, 5) ⌜inundation⌝ is on his face,
it impregnates the ground H
6. for the length (of time when) you are coming to them. I
7. Come quickly!" Twice. J
8. "(My) young son!
Do not let darkness come to our faces! K
9. Child, come to your city.
Come, King, as ruler of your throne. L
(2, 10) The hours are very long.
Sovereign, hurry!" Three times. M

TEXT NOTES

This stanza develops the theme of rebirth by alluding to the deceased as a divine child, and by introducing a method that assists glorification and rebirth. The mention of milk (*irṯt*) in the beginning of the stanza alludes to its frequent occurrence in offering lists for the deceased and evokes the image of a suckling child. Since divine birth legends generally point to a divine father and earthly mother, the representations of a young king being suckled by a goddess cannot denote her motherly role. Rather, they suggest that milk was viewed as a source of life and power for the king as a reborn god. The Chronicle of Prince Osorkon describes him suckling from the Lady (*rpyt*), i.e., Hathor or Mut, upon his arrival at Thebes: *snḳ=f m irṯt=s ꜥḳ=sn n=f m ꜥnḫ wꜣs*: "He suckled her milk, it entered into him with life and dominion."[63] In support of this, the common GR term *ꜥnḫ-wꜣs*, "milk," explicitly demonstrates the belief in the life and power giving qualities of milk.[64]

Furthermore, the speaker addresses Osiris as a "Golden Child, whose Head is of Lapis-lazuli." The dark blue color of lapis-lazuli, commonly used in depictions of deities, such as Osiris, and the deceased, allude to their divine character.[65] P.Bremner-Rhind 15, 22–26 stresses the connection between regeneration (of Osiris, in particular) and hair of lapis-lazuli, as Isis attempts to revivify the god: *šny=k m ḫsbd n(y)=s(w) ḫsbd isk ḫsbd iw ḥr šny=k inm=k ḥꜥw=k n=k m biꜣ šmꜥw ḳsw=k nbi m ḥḏ mi ink*(!) *m ḫy*, "Your hair is lapis-lazuli and lapis-lazuli possesses it. O, lapis-lazuli is over your hair. The color of your own body is that

63 Caminos, *Chronicle of Prince Osorkon*, pp. 31–33.

64 *Wb.* I, 204, 1; Wilson, *Ptolemaic Lexikon*, p. 160.

65 For instance, the Hymn to Osiris at Philae describes Osiris as (*nbw*) *ḫsbd* (*tp*), "(Golden One), with lapis-lazuli (head)," Žabkar, *ZÄS* 108 (1981): 143 and 145. Similarly, the Great Hymn to Amun in the Hibis temple describes this god as the one *ḳsw=f m ḥḏ inm=f m nbw ḥr-tp=f m ḫsbd mꜣꜥ*, "whose bones are silver, whose skin is gold, whose hair is true lapis-lazuli…," in cols. 1–2, see Klotz, *Adoration of the Ram*, p. 71.

of Upper Egyptian metal; your bones are cast in silver; as I(!) am a child."[66] The deep blue color of divinities' hair further invokes the primordial waters of Nun, as well as associations with nighttime, in which creation and, thus, birth and rebirth occur.[67] Similarly, the Hymn to Osiris at Philae calls Osiris *nḫn-ṯḥn(w) ỉmy mnw ms.tw=f tpy rnp*, "Gleaming Child who is in the waters being born in the beginning of the year."[68]

Nut implies that numerous other gods join the immediate family of Osiris in mourning him with the idiom "head upon knee." This also touches upon the wish for rebirth expressed through mourning. Crying, as an expression of mourning, does not only represent sadness, but also assists the transformation of the deceased.[69] For instance, the glorification of Re occurs in conjunction with acts of mourning, such as screaming and crying, in lines 223–24 of the Great Litany: *ỉ3kbyw nwn=sn ḥr=k ḥwỉ=sn n=k m ˁwy=sn sbḥ=sn n=k hwt=sn n=k rmm=sn n=k ḥˁˁ b3=k hwt=sn 3ḫ ẖ3t=k*, "The mourning ones pull their sidelocks because of you, they strike for you with their arms, they shriek for you, they scream for you, and they cry for you. It is when they scream that your *ba* rejoices and when your corpse (becomes) effective."[70]

The notion of rebirth in this stanza is further alluded to through the inundation, which "impregnates the ground." In mythology, the beginning of the regenerative process of the inundation coincides with the return of Hathor, as the goddess of the eye of the sun, and her sexual union with Osiris.[71] This point elucidates the life-giving significance of the efflux of Osiris' corpse as the source of the inundation. This concept is further connected with the beneficial effects of mourning in PT 690 (§2111–12a): *h3 wsỉr ỉỉ 3ḫt sb bˁḥ 3ỉ gb ḥ3.n(=ỉ) ṯw ḥr ḥˁt(=k)*, "O, Osiris! Come, you of the Flood with Provisioning Arm, who is around Geb. I have mourned you on the site (of your) tomb…."[72]

66 Faulkner, *Bremner-Rhind*, p. 29. Cf. the translation in Faulkner, *JEA* 22 (1936): 131. Notably, the use of the second person suffix pronoun in P.Bremner-Rhind is paralleled by MMA 43, 6.

67 BD 42 explicitly identifies the hair of the deified deceased: "My hair is Nun; my face is Re…;" Goelet, *Egyptian Book of the Dead*, pl. 32. Lapis-lazuli and other minerals are likewise described as components of various deities in the context of resurrection and rebirth, see Klotz, *Adoration of the Ram*, pp. 71–73, who also points to the preference for the blue stone, lapis-lazuli, in the manufacture of scarab amulets, also symbols of regeneration. For further association of lapis-lazuli with notions of divine birth and regeneration see Daumas, in S. Aufrère, ed., *L'Univers Minéral*, pp. 465–79 and 481.

68 Žabkar, *ZÄS* 108 (1981): 143–44, notes 21 and 27, points to a similar inscription in Karnak, Opet 118–19, 254: *ỉw=k m ḥˁpy m m3ˁwy sp snnw m ḫy nfr tpy rnpt*, "You come as the inundation, as one who is being renewed continually as a perfect child, on the first of the year." See de Wit, *Les inscriptions du temple d'Opet*, p. 62, n. 2, and p. 127, n. 71, for further references.

69 For a discussion of the creative and, thus, rejuvenating aspect of crying, see Guglielmi, *CdE* 55 (1980): 73–86.

70 Hornung, *Das Buch der Anbetung des Re im Westen* I, pp. 223–24; II, pp. 90 and 145–46. For further discussion of the act of mourning assisting the deceased's transformation, see section 2.3, above; Darnell, *Enigmatic Netherworld Books of the Solar-Osirian Unity*, pp. 183–85 and 366–68, who points out that both the sound and the content of mournful screaming were deemed beneficial.

71 Manassa, in B. Rothöhler and A. Manisali, eds., *Mythos & Ritual*, pp. 122 and 129–31, nn. 102–3.

72 Allen, *The Ancient Egyptian Pyramid Texts*, p. 295 and n. 104.

1, 48–49

A The traces of red paint suggest a rubric in line 1, 48, similar to MMA 43, 1 and BM 9, 13: *ḥwt mḥ 2*, “Second stanza.”
The missing text of line 1, 49 can be reconstructed on the basis of MMA 43, 2: *nẖḥ nẖi ỉn nwt*, “Lamenting. Lamentation by Nut.” Cf. BM 9, 14: *nẖḥ ỉ.in nwt*.
Note the dot at the end of this line.

1, 50

B The translation of *bnr*, “to be sweet,” as a stative is supported by the more common ending *tỉ* in place of *tw* in BM 9, 15.
The last word of this line is translated as *ꜥwꜣ*, “to rot, go sour.”[73] However, compare Goyon’s rendering of the corresponding MMA 43, 3: *my n=ỉ ỉrtt=k bnr.tw ẖwd=s*, “Viens à moi, le lait que t’est destiné est doux, il est riche.” Goyon points out that the scribe of MMA is incorrect in having omitted *ẖꜣ* before *ꜥꜣt*, claiming that the two other versions show the full writing of *ẖwd*, “to be rich”: B: ; and BM 9, 15: .[74] Nevertheless, the close similarity of  (M12) and  (U33) in hieratic allows the possibility of transcribing the hieratic sign following *bnr* in BM 9, 15 as  (U33) and, thus, reading *bnr.tw ꜥwꜣ* in all of the versions.

1, 51

C The meaning of this line is unclear due to the break. Cf. MMA 43, 4 and BM 9, 16: *mrt=k bꜥḥ n ꜣb r=k ỉm=f*, “That which you love is abundant and your mouth will not evade it.”[75] The reading of  as “mouth” is supported by the  determinative (F51) in MMA 43, 4: 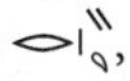, and the stroke in BM 9, 16: .

2, 1

D Unlike P.W551, the scribe of MMA 43, 5 spells the name of Nut phonetically without determinatives: .

2, 2

E This line affirms Osiris’ successful rebirth by referring to him as a (rejuvenated) child. His lapis-lazuli hair and golden skin, in turn, reiterate his divine status.
 stands for *ẖnw*, “child,” displaying a phonetic equivalency of *š* and *ẖ*, frequently occurring in LP texts.[76] The break following , *nbw*, most likely contained the de-

73 *Wb.* I 172, 3–5.
74 Goyon, *Imouthès*, p. 87, n. 17. For *ẖwd*, “to be rich,” see *Wb.* III 249, 9–15.
75 For *ꜣb*, “to separate from,” see Wilson, *Ptolemaic Lexikon*, p. 4; *Wb.* I 6, 2–8.
76 Fairman, *BIFAO* 43 (1945): 77.

terminative (N33).[77] The 3rd person singular masculine suffix pronoun of *tp* in P.W551 indicates that the group *tp=f m ḫsbd* is used here as an epithet, in a hitherto unattested form. Notably, the typically GR spelling of *tp*, 𓏽, is paralleled in BM 9, 18, which omits the suffix pronoun,[78] while MMA 43, 6 has the more usual 𓁶𓏤 (D1).

Cf. MMA 43, 6–7: *šn nbw tp=k m ḫsbd n wiꜣ.n iwn=f*, "Golden Child, your head is of lapis-lazuli and its colors cannot fade." The *nn sḏm=f* construction of P.W551 has future sense, significantly altering the present negative *n sḏm.n=f* of MMA. The transcription of the sign below *n* as 𓂡 (D41) is questionable, due to its large size, and may in fact be 𓄿 (G1). Nevertheless, the reading of the word *wiꜣ/win* remains certain here, as it is written 𓏲𓇋𓄿𓂡, with 𓂡 (D41) in MMA 43, 7; and phonetically 𓏲𓇋𓄿 in BM 9, 18. The term *wiꜣ*, "to reject, turn back," is interchangeable with *win*, "to reject."[79]

The somewhat enigmatic *iwn*, "color," can also be understood as "skin, body," as is suggested by the frequent use of this term in the stela of Herwerre in Serabit el-Khadim. With this context, the endurance of one's *iwn* points to the preservation of the physical body and at the same time authenticates the golden skin color of the deceased.[80] The GR spelling of *iwn*, 𓇋𓄿𓄿𓏥, is paralleled by MMA 43, 7 and BM 9, 18.[81]

2, 3

F In the GR period, the standard preposition *m-hꜣw* (sometimes *r-hꜣw*) was frequently written without the first component (*m/r*), but with the preposition *ḥr* at the end.[82] Cf. MMA 43, 8: *my n=i hꜣw ḥr=i*, "Come to me, near me." Notably, 𓅆 (G7) is used as the 1st person singular suffix pronoun in MMA 43, 8. Cf. BM 9, 19 : *my n=k hꜣw* … .

nḏ is understood as an active circumstantial *sḏm=f* form, with *sꜣ=k* as its subject and *ti* standing for the 2nd person singular dependent pronoun *ṯw*. *n=k+imy* acts as an emphatic possessive construction.[83] Cf. MMA 43, 9: *nḏ(=i) sꜣ n=k imy*, "(I) protect your own son." Cf. BM 9, 19: *nḏ t(w) sꜣ n=k* ⸢*imy*⸣. If it is assumed that the sign following *nḏ* is not 𓍘, but 𓁐 (B1), referring back to Nut, the speaker, this line would be read: *nḏ=i sꜣ=k n=k imy*: "as I protect your own son." This closely corresponds to Goyon's rendering. An alternate reading of this line supposes that *ti*, 𓍘, indicates a passive *tw*: *nḏ.tw sꜣ=k n=k imy*, "as your own son will be protected." However, the role of Horus as the protector of his father, rather than the one being protected, is well-attested in religious literature, such as the PT. See for example PT 357 (§591a): *nḏ.n ṯw ḥr ni ḏd.n (i).nḏ=f ṯw*, "Horus has protected you, for he could not delay protecting you," and PT 468 (§897b): *i.nḏ ṯw ḥrw*, "Horus shall protect you…."[84]

---

77 *Wb.* III 286, 18.

78 *Wb.* V 263.

79 For *wiꜣ*, see *Wb.* I 272, 3–4. For the identical *win*, see *Wb.* I 272, 12.

80 Iversen, in F. Junge, ed., *Studien zu Sprache und Religion*, pp. 507–14.

81 *Wb.* I 52, 10–17.

82 *Wb.* II 477, 12–14.

83 Gardiner, *Egyptian Grammar*, §113, 3.

84 Cf. Allen, *The Ancient Egyptian Pyramid Texts*, pp. 74, 168, and 124, respectively.

2, 4

G P.W551 uses the LP and GR term , *ns*, "to go, travel."[85] Cf. the verb in MMA 43, 10: *nṯrw ḥr tp m3st n ỉw=k*, "The gods are with head (upon) knee (because) of your departure." Cf. BM 9, 20: *nṯrw ḥr tp* ⸢*m3st*⸣ *n ỉw=k* ⸢*n=ỉ*⸣.

2, 5

H Only the determinative (G7) of *bʿḥ* remains. Cf. MMA 43, 11: *ḥʿpy m ḥr=sn bg3=f s3ṯ.w*, "Inundation is on their faces, it impregnates the ground." Note the more correct use of suffix pronouns in MMA. The 3rd person masculine singular suffix pronoun of *ḥ̣r*, "face," in P.W551 refers back to each god who is awaiting Osiris. The plural suffix pronoun *sn* in MMA more clearly refers to the gods from the previous line.
, *bg3*, "shipwrecked" must be confused with the similar sounding *bk3*, , which is used transitively here in the sense of "to impregnate (said of the Nile making fruitful the field)."[86]
Some peculiarities of this line should be noted:
1. The dot below *ḥ̣r* stands for the phonetic complement *r*.
2. The spelling of *s3ṯw*, "ground," , paralleled by MMA 43, 11 and BM 9, 21, is typical to the GR period.[87]

2, 6

I *3w*, , here again refers to the length of time until Osiris comes to Nut and the gods.[88] The determinative (V30) for this word is erroneous. The determinative (G37) in MMA 43, 12, , likely stems from the similarly spelled *ỉwi*, "bad person."[89] Note the determinative of *3w* in BM 9, 22: .

2, 7

J The presence of the determinative (D54) suggests understanding as *wn*, "to hurry."[90] At the same time, this word creates a scribal pun on , *wn*, "fault,"[91] which follows from the determinative (G37) of *wn*, , in MMA 43, 13. Here, the term bears a negative meaning of "carelessness, neglect."[92] Thus, while "come quick-

85 *Wb.* II 321, 1–3; Wilson *Ptolemaic Lexikon*, p. 544.
86 For *bg3*, "to impregnate," see *Wb.* I 482, 12–14. For the transitive use of *bk3*, "to impregnate," see *Wb.* I 481, 10–11; Wilson, *Ptolemaic Lexikon*, pp. 334–35.
87 *Wb.* III 423, 8–12.
88 For the reading of as *3w(t)*, "long (of time)," see Goyon, *Imouthès*, p. 87, n. 18; *Wb.* I 4, 15–16.
89 *Wb.* I 48, 5–10.
90 *Wb.* I 313, 10–314, 6.
91 *Wb.* I 314, 7–13. For a more detailed discussion of punning, see section 1.5.1, above.
92 Wilson, *Ptolemaic Lexikon*, p. 229.

ly" is the primary reading of the phrase, the insinuation "don't be careless (by not coming quickly)" is present, as well.

Yet another interpretation of this phrase presents a pun on *my m wn(nt)*, "come as the one who exists." The GR epithet *wn* is frequently used in the Karnak temple in reference to Osiris, supporting such punning in a mortuary text.[93] De Wit proposes that *wn* or *wnn* is, in fact, an abbreviation of *wn-nfr*, pointing to the Opet 183 inscription that refers to "Osiris-Wen(nefer)."[94]

2, 8

K The transitive use of *kkw*, "to make dark (of face; i.e., make blind)," is typical to the GR period.[95] Cf. P.Bremner-Rhind 7, 1–3: "May you come to me quickly, as I wish to see your face after I have not seen your face. Obscurity is here for us on my face, (even) while Re is in the sky."[96]

The lack of a determinative for *s3*, , suggests that the following 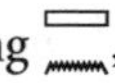, a variant of *ẖn*, , "child," may be an adjective qualifying *s3*. However, MMA 43, 14 and BM 9, 23 have the  determinative (G7) for each of the words: .[97] Cf. col. 1, 28 of the present manuscript.

Goyon translates the parallel MMA 43, 14 in a prospective sense: *s3 šn m šm kkw ḥr=n*, "mon fils, mon petit enfant! Que les ténèbres ne s'étendent pas sur nous." However, the abbreviated negation *m* clearly points to the imperative use of *šm*.[98] Note the alliterative play on sounds between *šn* and *šm* in this line.[99]

The stroke (Z5) written above the plural strokes, , following *ḥrw* in P.W551 represents the 1st person plural suffix pronoun, *n*. This reading is supported by MMA 43, 14 and BM 9, 23, which spell this suffix pronoun phonetically.

2, 9

L This line is extremely interesting due to the numerous layers of meaning it presents. The initial clause of the line, *ẖy my niwt=k*, calls to the child (Osiris), asking him to come to his city by means of an imperative verb *my*. The grammar parallels the previous lines in the typical Egyptian tendency of repeating grammatical structures. At the same time, this initial group of signs may also be transliterated *ẖy m-ʿ niwt=k*, "Child, in possession (lit. the hand) of your city," thus pointing to Osiris literally belonging in his place and position. Cf. MMA 43, 15: *š my n š=k…*, "child, come to your child …," which likely refers to Horus in his role of Osiris' offspring. Notably, *ẖy* is spelled in a

93 Leitz et al., eds., *Lexikon* II, p. 374.

94 de Wit, *Les inscriptions du temple d'Opet*, p. 127, n. 70.

95 *Wb.* V 144, 12.

96 Faulkner, *Bremner-Rhind*, pp. 12–13; Faulkner, *JEA* 22 (1936): 126.

97 *Wb.* III 286, 18.

98 For the shortened writing of the negation *im*, see Gardiner, *Egyptian Grammar*, §340.

99 For a more detailed discussion of alliteration, see section 1.5.1, above.

more classical manner here in contrast to the previous line; cf. MMA 43, 15, where only is written. Cf. for *ḫy* in BM 9, 25.

Furthermore, there are no determinatives for *nsw* or *ḥḳ3* making the sense of this phrase uncertain. The , *ḳ*, of *ḥḳ3* is followed immediately by the unusual . Considering the close resemblance in hieratic between and , as well as and , the group could have easily been confused with , *ḥwt-nṯr*, "temple." The MMA parallel permits this clause to be interpreted as *my nswt m ḥḳ3 nst=k*. Nevertheless, the above mentioned confusion between *ḥḳ3* () and *ḥwt-nṯr* () allows the possibility of reading *my sw/nswt m ḥwt-nṯr nst=k*, "Place him/the king in the temple, (which is) your throne." However, while the request to place the king in the temple is conceivable for Osiris, the context does not support this reading.

Lastly, the construction *m-ʿ*, , is at times written for a simple *m*, especially in LP texts. In this case, a third interpretation connects the two above clauses through the *m* of predication: *hy my n niwt=k m nswt m ḥḳ3 nst=k*, "Youth, come to your city as king, as ruler of your throne." Nonetheless, this option is dubious, due to the consistent differentiation between a simple *m* and *m-ʿ/my* by the scribe of P.W551.

nst is written with the determinative (G7) in MMA 43, 15.[100] Note the play on sounds between *nswt* and *nst=k*.

2, 10

M *3w* again shows an unusual spelling, , while the parallels of MMA 43, 16 and BM 9, 26 again include the determinative (G37) in . Cf. line 6 of the present column.

The -jar and determinative (N5) point to interpreting the word as *wnwt*, "hours," written in MMA 43, 16. The phrase "length of hours" refers to the time during which Nut and the gods wait for Osiris to be reborn.

Since the second *wn* lacks a determinative, it may be understood as the verb "to be," offering another interpretation for this ambiguous phrase: "The hours are long, twice, sovereign, protection exists!"

 represents *sp 3* (*ḫmt*), "3 times."[101] Alternatively, the end of this line may be understood as *ḫw*, "alone," "young," or "protection."

100 For the somewhat unusual shape of *nst*, see Möller, *Hieratische Paläographie* III, p. 396. For word play, see section 1.5.1, above.

101 Goyon, *Imouthès*, p. 87, n. 19.

3.1.3. STANZA 3 — SPOKEN BY ISIS *Lines 2, 11–48*

According to the first line, the primary speaker of the third stanza is Isis, but the 1st person plural suffix pronoun in line 2, 15 identifies both Isis and Nephthys. Isis' appeal describes the pain that the two sisters feel while mourning Osiris. Isis reminds Osiris of his heir, Horus, alluding to the revenge for Osiris' death. The theme of assurance is continued, as Osiris' throne is said to be under the control of Re, who is viewed as the rejuvenated form of Osiris.[102] The solar symbolism is emphasized as the addressee, Osiris, merges with the sun god in his daily and nightly journeys. Following further reassurance of Horus' support and protection for his father, Isis stresses her active role in reuniting with him. Thus, not only is Osiris urged to return to Isis, but she is also faithfully searching for him.

TRANSLITERATION

11. *ḥwt mḥ 3.t*

ỉ ỉr=f ỉn ꜣst mwt nty ḥr

12. *sn(=ỉ) my mꜣꜣ.tw=k*

13. *ỉw=k rf n=n m ỉrw=k mꜣꜥt*

14. *⸢p⸣ꜣy wꜥ mnḫ-sẖry-dỉ.n-nṯrw*

(2, 15) *m wdn ꜣt=k r=n*

16. *ḳsn.wy ⸢wẖd⸣=n gꜣ=k*

17. *mr.wy n=n ⸢t⸣m mꜣꜣ=n ḥr=k*

18. *bꜣ-nk*

mr=k ḥmwt

19. *ỉb n rꜥ ḥtp m ỉrw=k*

(2, 20) *⸢ỉn⸣ n=k nmtwt⸢=k⸣ nw pt tꜣ*

21. … … … …. *⸢t⸣ꜣ ꜥnẖt m ḥtp*

22. *⸢ꜥḥ⸣ꜥ n=k ḥr m ⸢nb⸣-ỉwꜥ*

23. … *rꜥ ḥr wšb ḥr nst=k*

24. … *psḏ m wsẖt*

(2, 25) *nḏ ṯ(w) sꜣ=f ẖꜥ ḥr nst=f*

26. *dgꜣ s… mꜣꜣ=k pr⸢=k⸣*

APPROXIMATELY 4 LINES MISSING

31. …*⸢m⸣y* … *mn=n*

32. … *=k* … … .*n*

33. *psḏ=k m ⸢dwꜣ⸣*

ḥtp=k m mšrw 34. *rꜥ nb*

ỉw m⸢ꜣꜣ⸣ ⸢ḥr⸣=k

(2, 35) *wb⸢ꜣ⸣* … … *⸢ꜥꜣwy⸣ nw ỉnt*

APPROXIMATELY 3 LINES MISSING

39. *ỉr=k* … … *ỉw sꜥnẖ* … *kꜣ*

… (2, 40) *⸢wꜣt r⸣=k ꜣb* …*=k*

---

102 See the text notes for col. 1, 43, above.

41. *šm=ꞽ pt tꜣ*
nn ḥm w⸢ꜣt⸣=k
42. … *ꜣw=s ḥpt n bwṯ=k ẖr*
43. *ꞽwꜥ⸢=k⸣ m št ꞽw ḫsf sp=k*
44. *šm=ꞽ m wꜥ n mr=k*
(2, 45) … *ḥḥy bw wnn=k ꞽm*
46. … … … … *nḏ* …
47. … ⸢*ꞽꜥḥ*⸣
wbn=k n=n
48. … *w=n nbd*
m r wꜣt=k

TRANSLATION

11. 3rd stanza.
Utterance for him by Isis, mother of Horus:
12. "(My) brother, may you be seen,
13. for you, indeed, belong to us in your true form.[A]
14. ⸢Th⸣e Unique One, Beneficent of the Counsels which the Gods Give.
(2, 15) Do not delay your moment (of coming) to us![B]
16. How painful it is for us ⸢to suffer⸣ the lack of you!
17. How hurtful it is for us ⸢no⸣t to see your face![C]
18. Copulating *Ba*,
as you love the wives,
19. the heart of Re is pleased with your form.[D]
(2, 20) ⸢Get⸣ for yourself ⸢your⸣ travels through the sky and the earth,
21. … … … the Land of Life … in peace,[E]
22. Horus ⸢stands⸣ up for you as the ⸢Possessor⸣ of Inheritance,[F]
23. … Re answers upon your throne.
24. … shines in the *wsḫt*-bark,[G]
(2, 25) May his son, who appears in glory upon his throne, protect you.
26. … move … that you may see your house.[H]
APPROXIMATELY 4 LINES MISSING
31. … ⸢ca⸣use … our suffering
32. your … … our …[I]
33. May you shine in ⸢the morning⸣,
may you rest in the evening, 34. every day,
so that (I) may ⸢se⸣e your ⸢face⸣![J]
(2, 35) The ⸢gates⸣ of the valley are op⸢en⸣ …[K]
APPROXIMATELY 3 LINES MISSING
39. You have made … … that … live,
… (2, 40) ⸢far from⸣ you, … stop you,[L]
41. for I have walked heaven and earth,
without reversing your pa⸢th⸣,[M]

42. … for it is long, the journey to the place where you are.[N]

43. Your heir is a youth who protects your action(s),

44. and I walk alone in love of you,[O]

(2, 45) … to search (for) the place in which you may be.

46. … … … … hail …[P]

47. … … ⸢the moon⸣,
raise yourself for us![Q]

48. We … the Evil One,
away from your path."[R]

TEXT NOTES

This stanza depicts Osiris as a brother and husband to Isis, but also refers to his union with Re.[103] Osiris is here addressed as *bꜣ-nk*, "Copulating *Ba*," explicitly describing this union in sexual terms. This LP and GR epithet of Osiris[104] implies the glorified status of its holder through the common phrase *nk m bꜣ*, "to copulate by means of (one's) *ba*."[105] As the two gods embrace and merge into one giant deity during the cycle of resurrection, their fusion may be understood as the act of copulation between (the *ba* of) Re and (the *ba* of) Osiris.[106] This notion is also exemplified in BD 17: *ptr r=f sw wsir pw ky ḏd ḥknw-rꜥ rn=f bꜣ pw n rꜥ nk=f im=f ḏs=f*, "Who is he? He is Osiris. Alternatively: acclaimer of Re is his name; he is the *ba* of Re, with whom he copulates, himself."[107] The belief that the deceased becomes one with this Great God (*nṯr ꜥꜣ*) began developing in the NK and formed completely by the 21st Dynasty.[108] As such, he or she traversed the upper sky during the day as an incarnation of the sun god and traveled the lower Duat at night as Osiris.[109] Re, in turn, acted as Osiris,

103 Cf. line 1, 43, above.

104 Leitz, et al., eds., *Lexikon* II, p. 686.

105 The sexual and creative forces of the *ba* of Osiris are illustrated in a number of CT spells. For instance, CT 94, II 67c reads: *ink bꜣ pw ꜥꜣ n wsir wḏ.n nṯrw nk=f im=f*, "I am this great *ba* of Osiris, by means of which the gods have commanded him to copulate…," see Žabkar, *A study of the Ba concept*, pp. 94–95 and 103; Barguet, *Les textes des sarcophages*, p. 233, n. 14; Faulkner, *Ancient Egyptian Coffin Texts* I, p. 93. Gee, in Z. Hawass, ed., *Egyptology at the Dawn* II, p. 233, nn. 62–64. See also CT 96, II 78 and 80; CT 874 VII 79–80.

106 The unified Re-Osiris is consequently refered to as *bꜣ-dmḏ*, "United *Ba*," as an annotation on the sarcophagus of Tjaihorpata (CG 29306) describes Isis and/or Nephthys as: "(the one) who makes protection for Osiris in the West, may she make Re into the United *Ba*;" see Manassa, *Late Egyptian Underworld*, pp. 387–88, n. 468, and pp. 430–35. The notion of a sexual union of Re and Osiris is illustrated in the stela of Amenmes (Louvre C 286); see Moret, *BIFAO* 30 (1931): 731–32, text note 11, and *passim*.

107 See Rössler-Köhler, *Kapitel 17*, pp. 214 and 241; Žabkar, *A study of the Ba concept*, p. 103. See also Darnell, *Enigmatic Netherworld Books of the Solar-Osirian Unity*, pp. 395–96, n. 113, who suggests that Osiris may act as a female counterpart to the sun, as he embodies the horizon; *ibid.*, pp. 405–6, n. 153.

108 This notion may originate as early as the MK CT; see Manassa, *Late Egyptian Underworld*, p. 432, n. 140.

109 Niwínski, *JEOL* 30 (1987–88): 93–96. This idea was particularly popular in the LP. For instance, the foot end of the lid of the sarcophagus of Tjaihorpata depicts the transformation of the sun god between the night and day barks. The text on the head end offers further clarification, "It is Re who rests in Osiris

"answering upon his throne." Lines 2, 32–34 further demonstrate the result of the cyclical joining of Re and Osiris, as Isis calls on Osiris to "shine in the morning (in the solar aspect)" and "rest in the evening (in the Osirian aspect), every day."

2, 11–13

A Cf. the introduction of this spell in MMA 44, 2: *hꜣy ir=f in ꜣst mwt nt ḥr.* The  determinative (G7) of *mwt,* , refers to the divinity of Isis, the mother of Horus.
Cf. the first statement in MMA 44, 3–4 and BM 9, 29–30: *sn=i my mꜣꜣ tw iw=k irf n=n m irw=k mꜣꜥt.*
Some orthographic features and discrepancies with the parallel texts should be noted:

1. *mwt* is written 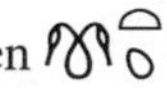 in MMA 44, 2.
2. BM 9, 28 has *ih* in place of *i*, "utterance."
3. The genitive adjective *nty* in P.W551 is replaced by the more appropriate *nt* in MMA 44, 1 and BM 9, 28.
4.  stands for the passive suffix *tw* or the reflexive dependent pronoun *ṯw.*
5. The 1st person singular suffix pronoun is written  (B1) in MMA 44, 3 and BM 9, 29.
6. *mꜣꜣ* is written  in MMA 44, 3 and BM 9, 29.
7. The enclitic particle *rf* was added above the line in P.W551.
8. *irw* is indicated only by  in MMA 44, 4 and  in BM 9, 30.

2, 14–15

B  and one  of *pꜣy* are still visible. Cf. MMA 44, 5: *pꜣ wꜥ mnḫ sḫry n nṯrw,* "Unique One, Beneficient of the Councils of the Gods." MMA 44, 6 and BM 9, 32 correspond to line 2, 15, but add the imperative *my,* "come," before the phrase.
The following orthographic features and discrepancies with the parallel texts should be noted:

1. The spelling of *sḫr,* , with  (H6) is paralleled by MMA 44, 5 and BM 9, 31.[110]
2. MMA 44, 5 spells *nṯrw* , while BM 9, 31 has .

2, 16–17

C The construction of line 2, 17 parallels the previous line. Cf. MMA 44, 8: *mr.wy n=n tm=n mꜣꜣ ḥr=k,* "How painful it is for us not to see your face!"

---

in the West, as the protection of the Osiris … NN… It is Osiris who rests in Re in the Underworld, as the protection of the Osiris … NN…," see Manassa, *Late Egyptian Underworld*, pp. 279, 386–88, and 432–35, who points to the 30th Dynasty date of this sarcophagus, as "the zenith of the revival of New Kingdom Underworld Books."

110 *Wb.* IV 258.

The determinative (Aa2) of , *wḫd,* is omitted in MMA 44, 7.

2, 18–19

D and the determinative (D53) likely point to a pun on the well-attested combination *bꜣ sty,* “ejaculating ram.”[111]
MMA 44, 9 and BM 10, 1 omit the 2nd person singular suffix pronoun: *bꜣ-nk mr-ḥmwt.* Cf. the epithet in col. 1, 37.

2, 21

E The remaining traces support a reconstruction on MMA 44, 11 and BM 10, 4: *šsp tw ỉmyw tꜣ ꜥnḫt m ḥtp,* “those who are in the Land of Life will receive you in peace.” Note the abbreviated , *ḥtp* in BM 10, 4.

2, 22

F There are two orthographic discrepancies from the parallel line of MMA:

1. Horus is spelled in MMA 44, 12.
2. , *ỉwꜥ,* has the determinative (G7) in MMA 44, 12.

2, 23–24

G The destroyed beginning of line 2, 23 may be reconstructed on the basis of MMA 44, 13 and BM 10, 6: *ỉt=k rꜥ wšb ḥr nst=k,* “Your father Re answers upon your throne!” Note the lack of *ḥr* before *wšb* in the parallels.
Cf. the slightly different MMA 44, 14: *wsir psd m ꜥnḫ mi rꜥ,* “as Osiris is shining in life like Re.” Cf. BM 10, 7 : *wsir psd m ḥnw.* The ⊙ (N5) and unusual (G7) determinatives for *psḏ,* , are paralleled by MMA 44, 14, pointing to a word play on *psḏt,* “Ennead.” Cf. the spelling of this word in BM 10, 7: .

2, 25–26

H The 3rd person singular suffix pronouns refer to Osiris.
Cf. Goyon’s translation of the corresponding MMA 44, 15: *nḏ n=f sꜣ=f ḫꜥ ḥr nst=f,* “protégé est pour lui son fils qui est apparu en gloire sur son trône!” MMA 44, 15 shows a more extended spelling of *nḏ*: ; and adds the determinative (G7) in *nst*: .
Cf. the second clause of this phrase in MMA 45, 1 and BM 10, 9: *dgs n(=ỉ) ḥr=k mꜣꜣ=k pr=k,* “May your face approach me, that you may see your house.”

---

111 Wilson, *Ptolemaic Lexikon,* p. 300. For the spelling of *bꜣ* with , see Wilson, *Ptolemaic Lexikon,* p. 293. Cf. the more typical spelling of *bꜣ* in BM 10, 1. For puns, see section 1.5.1, above.

A large lacuna in the papyrus corresponding to 4 lines in MMA 45 and BM 10 follows:

ḥr ḥr wšbt sp=k
i sṯ ibr ꜥntyw iw iwf=k
n in ib nḏriw mrt=k
MMA 45, 5 *mi mrt=i m33=k*

Horus is championing your occasion!
O, the scent of the ibr-ointment and myrrh are for your flesh,
May my heart, which your love has captured, not be carried (off),
MMA 45, 5 since I wish to see you![112]

2, 31–32

I The clearly visible arm of , *my,* and the remaining , *mn=n,* support a reconstruction of line 2, 31 based on MMA 45, 6: *i my n=n nfr mn=n,* "O, come to us that our suffering may improve." The traces of plural strokes at the end of line 2, 32 point to a possible reconstruction on the basis of B and BM 10, 15: *mr=k snby ẖ3it=n,* "for your love is what cures our illness."[113] MMA 45 omits this latter clause.

2, 33–34

J These somewhat damaged lines show a number of orthographic discrepancies with the parallel texts:

1. *psḏ* has a more typical spelling in MMA 45, 7 and BM 10, 16: 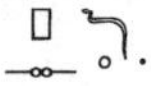.
2. The reading of *dw3* is based on the discernible  determinative (N5).
3. One of the  (D12) of *m33* is still visible in the papyrus. Cf.  (D4) for *m33* in BM 10, 17.
4. MMA 45, 8 and BM 10, 17 have a  determinative (G7) after *ḥr*, . The traces in the present manuscript suggest a simple stroke (Z1) as the determinative.

2, 35

K A part of  (O31) for *ꜥ3wy* and other remaining traces support a reconstruction based on MMA 45, 9: *wb3 n=k ꜥ3wy nw intt,* "The gates of the valley are opened for you."

---

112 Cf. Goyon, *Imouthès*, p. 88, n. 21, pl. 36:
Horus répond de ton (propre) petit enfant!
Ah, le parfum du ladanum et de l'oliban sont dirigés vers tes chairs,
Ne délaisse pas mon coeur captif de ton amour,
MMA 45, 5 puisque ce que j'aime c'est te voir!

113 Cf. Goyon's translation in Goyon, *Imouthès*, p. 88, and n. 22. He does not comment on the grammar, translating *snb* as a prospective, with *mr=k* as its subject. The word order, however, suggests reading *mr=k* as a noun and *snb* as a participle.

A large lacuna in the papyrus corresponding to 3 lines in MMA 45 and BM 10 follows:

MMA 45, 10 *ii=k n=n m33=n n tw n sš mr ib=k*
my m wdn 3t=k
wn-nfr m3ʿ-ḫrw ʿš3t šs

MMA 45, 10 May you come to us that we may look at you, and those whom your heart loves are not passed (by).
Do not delay your moment (of return)!
Wennefer, justified, One Rich of Crowds.[114]

2, 39–40

L The remaining traces appear to follow BM 10, 22-23: *ir.n=k … mw r sʿnḫ kwy w3t r=k 3b (ir=k) ds=k*. Cf. MMA 45, 13–14: *di(.tw) n=k t mw r sʿnḫ kwy w3t r=k 3b (ir=k) ds=k*, "Bread and water are giv[en] to you causing you to live. The others (=enemies) are far from you, stop yourself."[115] The determinative (F51) following *3b*, , is likely a mistake stemming from the LP term *3bw*, "fingernail."[116]

2, 41

M Goyon does not comment on his translation of the similar MMA 45, 15: *šm=i pt t3 nn gm=i w3t=k*, "car je parcours ciel et terre et je ne troupe pas tes chemins."[117] Cf. a very similar but differently expressed idea in P.Bremner-Rhind 13, 5: *ḫn=i t3 nn wrd=i m ḥḥ=k*, "I alight (upon) the earth, (but) I will not tire of searching for you."[118]

2, 42

N The location of *3w* suggests that it is not the initial group in this line, which may have been introduced by *iw*. Cf. MMA 45, 16 and BM 10, 25: *iw 3w ḥpt n bw ḫry=k*, "and going to the place where you are (takes) long."

(Aa2) is an uncommon but attested writing of the preposition *ḫr*.[119] *ḫry* is written phonetically in MMA 45, 16: and BM 10, 25: .

---

114 Goyon, *Imouthès*, p. 88, n. 23, pl. 36:
MMA 45, 10 viens à nous te voyions, ne laisse pas de côté ce que ton cœur aime,
Ne retarde pas ton instant (de venue)!
(Ô) Onnophris-le-Triomphant, riche en multitude.
For , a late writing of *mšʿ*, "crowd," see, *Wb.* II 155 and IV 54. Cf. Goyon reads this group as *šs*, "valuables," *Wb.* IV 542, 2–16.

115 Goyon, *Imouthès*, p. 88, n. 25.

116 *Wb.* I 7, 21.

117 Goyon, *Imouthès*, p. 88. For *ḥm*, "to reverse (one's path)," see Wilson, *Ptolemaic Lexikon*, p. 643; *Wb.* III 79, 21.

118 Faulkner, *Bremner-Rhind*, p. 24; Faulkner, *JEA* 22 (1936): 129.

119 *Wb.* III 386, 1–24.

2, 43–44

O Cf. Goyon's more forceful translation of MMA 46, 1: *ỉwꜥ=k m ẖ r ẖsf sp=k,* "Ton héritier est (encore) un trop petit enfant pour protéger ton action."[120]

This line has a number of discrepancies with the parallel texts:

1. *ỉwꜥ* is written  in MMA 46, 1.
2. *ẖy* is used in place of *št* in MMA 46, 1 and BM 10, 26.
3. MMA 46, 1 and BM 10, 26 do not have phonetic complements for ⊚, *sp*.
4. *wꜥ* is written very concisely in line 2, 44: . Cf. 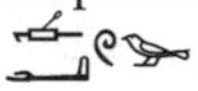 in MMA 46, 2 and  in BM 10, 27.

2, 45–46

P These partially damaged lines may be reconstructed from the parallels of MMA 46, 3–4 and BM 10, 28–29: *r ḥḥy bw wnn=k ỉm=f n mꜣꜣ(=ỉ) n sḏm(=ỉ) kꜣ tw nḏ.ty tw.*

2, 47

Q The remaining traces support a reconstruction on the basis of the B and BM 10, 30 versions: *m(y) m ỉꜥḥ wbn=k n=n,* "Come as the moon, so that you may shine for us!"[121] This line is omitted from MMA 46.

2, 48

R Cf. MMA 46, 5: *ẖr swꜣḥ=n nbd m r wꜣt=k,* "We cause the Evil One to stay far from your path." *nbd,* written very concisely in MMA 46, 5: 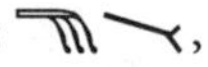, clearly refers to Seth.[122]

---

120 For *ẖsf* with the sense of "to protect," see Goyon, *Imouthès*, p. 88, n. 26; *Wb.* III 336, 19.

121 Goyon, *Imouthès*, p. 88 and n. 27. For a discussion of the lunar theme in this Osirian ritual, see the notes for col. 1, 43–44, above.

122 *Wb.* II 247, 7; Leitz et al., eds., *Lexikon* IV, pp. 199–201.

3.1.4. STANZA 4 — SPOKEN BY ISIS (POSSIBLY WITH NEPHTHYS)

Lines 2, 49–3, 25

The use of 1st person singular suffix pronouns by the speaker demonstrates that the fourth stanza is spoken by one of the sisters. Based on this sister's description of her search for Osiris, the speaker is probably Isis. She quotes the recitation of "the men and women" who may represent the "multitude" from this ritual's title. Immediately following their speech, Isis addresses these men and women, inviting them to hear about her ordeal. Interestingly, in this address to the mortals, she refers to Osiris exclusively as "lord," an epithet that is otherwise used rarely in this text. Isis then proceeds to call on her sister, Nephthys, to join the lamentation in line 3, 15. It is unclear if Isis alone or both sisters are the speakers of the following passage. The text points to the fresh and continuous supply of the necessary offerings and protection for the deceased Osiris. The last couplet of this stanza reinforces the significance of the rejuvenated Osiris for the living and his role as the founder of the existing world order.

TRANSLITERATION

49. *[ḥwt] mḥ 4.t*
ỉw ṯꜣy ḥmwt ḥr nḥt n ỉw=k
(3, 1) *mỉ ỉr=k n=sn ḥtpw*
2. *ỉ.ẖpr ḏfꜣw n ỉw=f*
3. *ỉn wnwt-nbt-m-r-ꜥwy=f*
4. *šps-prw-m-ḏfꜣw*
(3, 5) *ỉw mỉn kꜣ=k rꜥ nb*
6. *mỉ ntk ỉry ꜥnẖ=sn*
7. *ḥtp.tw m pr=k*
mn.tw m st=k
8. *ỉ ṯꜣyw ḥmwt ḥr ḥḥy nb=sn*
9. *ỉ.hꜣy my n=n mꜣn=tn*
(3, 10) *ỉ.hꜣy my sḏm=tn*
11. *šm=ỉ pt tꜣ m wꜥ ḥr ḥḥy nb*
12. *n gm=ỉ bw wnn nb ỉm*
13. *smꜣyw nbd ꜥšꜣw m pẖr=ỉ*
14. *n(n) mr ỉm=ỉ ỉmt=sn*
sšm=f n=ỉ wꜣt
(3, 15) *⸢m⸣y sn(t)=ỉ*
rm=n sw
16. *ỉ ỉwny mr-ỉnb-ḥḏ*
mk wꜣt r nỉwt sn.t
17. *nn ꜥš nn ḏw r=k*
18. *⸢gnn⸣ ꜥnty ⸢nn d⸣š r=k rf*
19. *nhm ỉw rn ḥwt-nṯr=k*
(3, 20) *ỉw=k m pr=k nn s(n)ḏ=k*

21. *wnn rḫyt p*⸢*ʿt*⸣ *ḥr dw3=k*
22. *ḥḥy ʿnḫ=sn …=k*
23. ⸢*mk*⸣ *ʿnḫw=sn m tr n iw=k m rn=k* 24. ⸢*pfy*⸣ *n ḥ*⸢*ʿpy*⸣
(3, 25) ⸢*iw*⸣*… pr-ʿ3 m ḥk3 ḥr nst=k*
t3wy m-ḫt=f

TRANSLATION

49. 4th [stanza].
"Men and women are praying for your coming,
(3, 1) as you made the offerings for them: A
2. It is because of his coming that the provisions occur.B
3. One who Brings Everything that Exists by the Action of his Hands,
4. One with whose Provisions the Temples are Made Splendid.C
(3, 5) Now, but your *ka* (exists) every day,
6. for you are the one who makes their life.D
7. You are resting in your house,
you are established in your place." E
8. "O, men and women seeking their lord! F
9. O, come to us that you may see,
(3, 10) O, come that you may hear! G
11. I have walked the sky and the earth alone seeking the lord,
12. (but) I have not found the place in which the lord is.
13. The accomplices of the Evil One are numerous around me, H
14. (and) there is none among those who follow me,
that can show me the path. I
(3, 15) ⸢Co⸣me, my sister,
let us mourn him! J
16. O, Heliopolitan, the One who Loves Memphis,
look, the path to the two cities.
17. There is no groaning, there is no evil against you.K
18. The myrrh is ⸢soft, without being re⸣moved from you, indeed.L
19. One shouts the name of your temple,
(3, 20) as you are in your house without your fear.M
21. The commoners and man⸢kind⸣ will praise you,
22. seeking their life … you.N
23. ⸢Now⸢, they live at the time of your coming, in ⸢that⸣ name of yours 24. of ⸢In⸣un⸢dation⸣.O
(3, 25) … pharaoh is the ruler upon your throne,
and the two lands are in his following." P

TEXT NOTES

The prayer of the men and women at the beginning of this stanza portrays Osiris in a much more religious fashion than the often familial attitude of Isis, Nephthys, and Nut in the previous stanzas. From the point of view of the men and women, Osiris is a creator who makes life and provides the temples with the offerings that he fashioned. The men and women refer to him as the "One who Brings Everything that Exists by the Action of his Hands," "One with whose Provisions the Temples are Made Splendid," and the one who "makes their life."[123] The all-encompasing image of this god similarly occurs in the Hymn to Osiris at Philae. Osiris' qualities of a ruler are expressed in this hymn with the epithets "Lord of Eternity… King of the Two Lands … who Came Forth from the Womb with Uraei on his Head… King of Heaven, Ruler of the Lands, Great Sovereign in the Underworld," etc. This hymn alludes to the creative force of Osiris by referring to him as *ir iššp m ẖt mwt=f … ms m3ʿt sḥtm is(ft)*, "the one who created light in the womb of his mother… the one who fashioned truth and abolished falsehood." He is similarly called *nṯr špss wp ẖt*, "August (God) who Inaugurated Offerings," demonstrating his role in establishing cultic practices.[124]

As the speech of the men and women concludes, Isis addresses Osiris in a more familiar manner, alluding to his role in the cycle of rebirth and, accordingly, his association with Re. The epithets "Heliopolitan" (*iwny*) and "One who Loves Memphis" (*mr-inb-ḥḏ*)[125] again underline the close bond of Osiris with Re, the solar deity of Heliopolis.

At the end of the stanza, Isis reminds Osiris of his significance for the life of the commoners and mankind, literally naming him , "Inundation."[126] The use of this epithet equates Osiris with the Nile's flood and its regenerative qualities, alluded to in stanzas 2 and 5. Thus, just as the successful burial of his assembled body provides for his regeneration, the rebirth of nature is brought about by the inundation. The correlation between the inundated Nile and Osiris is seen from the OK onwards.[127] More specifically, the efflux of Osiris' corpse (*pr m wsir*) that was cast into the 'source' of the Nile emerges as the life-giving inundation. As such, the flood waters not only lead to the rebirth of the dismembered god but also bring renewed life to the Nile valley.[128] This notion is illustrated in PT 423 (§766a),

123 This notion is supported by the epithet of the deceased, identified with Re and Thoth, *ir-ʿnḫ-n-ḥnmmt*, Leitz et al., eds., *Lexikon* I, p. 446. For a similar epithet of various deities, *ir-ʿnḫ*, "The One who Makes Life," see Leitz et al., eds., *Lexikon* I, 445.

124 Žabkar, *ZÄS* 108 (1981): 142–44 and 165, points to the existence of such descriptions of the "universality of Osiris' character" from the MK onwards. For instance, lines 4–13 of the NK stela of Amenmes (Louvre C 286) describe Osiris' role in his rule and creation, see Moret, *BIFAO* 30 (1931): 733–38 and 749.

125 Leitz et al., eds., *Lexikon* I, p. 189, and *ibid.*, III, p. 335, respectively.

126 This typically late spelling involves the spewing mouth,  (D26), which derives from the analogous spewing pustule,  (Aa3), used in *rḏw*, "efflux (of Osiris)," thus alluding to the origin of the Nile and its inundation, see Darnell, *Enigmatic Netherworld Books of the Solar-Osirian Unity*, p. 99, n. 297. Cf. P.Brooklyn 47.218.50 1, 3 in Goyon, *Confirmation du pouvoir royal au nouvel an* II, pl. 1; and see also P.BM 10209 1, 34, in Haikal, *Nesmin* II, p. 29.

127 See Koemoth, *Osiris et les arbres*, pp. 5–10, and n. 22 for further references on this topic.

128 Assmann, in N. Grimal, A. Kamel, C. May-Sheikholeslami, eds., *Hommages Fayza Haikal*, pp. 8–16, refers to the depictions of libation offerings where water is represented as a chain of *ʿnḫ*-signs, stressing

which refers to the deceased king as *pr m ḳbḥw,* "the one who comes in/as the cool water," continuing, *m n=k rdw pr im=k… ip kw ḥr rnpty rnpwt m rn=k pw n mw-rnpi,* "Accept the outflow that comes from you… Horus shall take account of you year by year, rejuvenated in your name of the Rejuvenated Waters (of the inundation)." [129] The annual flooding of the Nile, paralleled by the cyclical rebirth of Osiris, was central to the Egyptian concept of time. This association is clearly visible in the etymologic connection of *rnpt,* "year," and *rnpi,* "to be young, new." [130]

2, 49–3, 1

A MMA 46, 8 uses the rather rare *mi sḏm.n=f* construction in the parallel of line 3, 1: *mi iry.n=k n=sn ḥtpw.*[131] Note the determinative (A1) for *ḥmt,* here, paralleled in MMA 46, 7 and BM 10, 33. Cf. col. 1, 37 of the present manuscript.

3, 2

B The prayer to be spoken by the men and women begins with this line. It is introduced by an initial 2nd tense of *ḫpr,* written with the *i*-prefix.[132] The 3rd person singular suffix pronoun *f* refers to Osiris, who is designated by a number of epithets in lines 3, 3–4. The determinative (G7) for *ḏf3w,* , in P.W551 most likely stems from a scribal confusion with (T14). Note the consistent use of and (G38) for *ḏf3w,* , in the MMA parallel.

3, 3–4

C The GR epithet *in-wnnt-nbt-m-r-ʿwy=f,* "He who Brings Everything that Exists by the Action of his Hands," names Osiris, the addressee of this stanza.[133] Note the discrepancy between the verb *in* of the present manuscript and *ir* of MMA 46, 10: *iry-wntw-m-r-ʿwy=f,* "He who Makes that which Exists by the Action of his Hands." The construction *m r-ʿwy,* "in the hands" may mean "work, action" in the GR period.[134]
The similarity between (A52) for *šps* and (U39) for *wṯs* in hieratic suggests the possibility of a graphic pun on the expression *ṯs-prt,* "to plant seeds," which is associated with offerings, and connects this phrase with the concept of rebirth and creation.[135] The association of Osiris with regeneration and growing vegetation supports this notion.

the connection between libation, inundation, and life. Similarly, the chaotic waters of Nun play an analogous life-giving role in Egyptian creation myths.

129 Allen, *The Ancient Egyptian Pyramid Texts,* p. 101.

130 *Wb.* II 429 and 432, 11ff., respectively.

131 For the *mi sḏm=f* and *mi sḏm.n=f* constructions, see Gardiner, *Egyptian Grammar,* §§156 and 170, 5.

132 Cassonnet, *Les temps seconds,* pp. 21–22 and *passim.*; Černý and Groll, *Late Egyptian Grammar,* p. 382, 26.18.6.

133 This epithet is also used for a number of other deities, see Leitz et al., eds., *Lexikon* I, p. 451.

134 *Wb.* II 395, 13–18 and *Wb.* II 396, 1–3, respectively.

135 See section 1.5.1, above. Wilson, *Ptolemaic Lexikon,* p. 1173.

3, 5–6

D The meaning of this line is elusive, but likely points to the cyclical and eternal existence of Osiris' *ka*. Cf. the more intelligible MMA 46, 12 and BM 11, 5: *iw min kꜣ=k m r nbt,* "Today (the subject of) your *ka* is in every mouth."[136]
The 3rd person plural suffix pronoun of line 3, 6 must refer to the men and women reciting this text.

3, 7

E The prayer spoken by the men and women ends here.
The verbs *ḥtp* and *mn*[137] are used as statives. Cf. the second verb and lack of the 2nd person singular stative ending in MMA 46, 14: *ḥtp tw m pr=k šn m st=k,* "resting in your house, enveloped in your place." The corresponding lines of B and BM 11, 7 read *spd,* , in place of MMA's *sꜥḥ,* , and P.W551's *mn,* .[138]

3, 8

F Cf. P.Bremner-Rhind 12, 13–14: *ihꜣy my (n)=n ḥnꜥ=i pꜣ ṯꜣyw ḥmwt m niwt ḥḥ nb=n,* "O, come (to) us with me! The men and women in the city are seeking our lord."[139]
MMA 46, 15, BM 11, 8, and the corresponding line of B have a clause omitted from P.W551: *i ḫr stḫ pfy my m-ḥtp,* "O, that Seth has fallen! Come in peace."[140]
This line shows a number of peculiarities and discrepancies with the parallel texts:

1. The vocative *i* is written  (A26) in BM 11, 9.
2. The verb *ḥḥ* is omitted from MMA 46, 16: *i ṯꜣyw ḥmtw n nb=n.*
3. *ṯꜣy* is spelled more concisely  in MMA 46, 16 and BM 11, 9.
4. *nb* is spelled with the phonetic complement *n*, above, in P.W551.

3, 9–10

G *mꜣ(n)* is the non-initial prospective form of the verb *mꜣ*.[141] Compare the very similar MMA 47, 1 and BM 11, 10: *hꜣy my (n)=n mꜣꜣ=ṯn,* "Hey, come to us that you may see!"[142]
Cf. the use of pronouns in the parallels of MMA 47, 2 and BM 11, 11: *hꜣy my=n sḏm tn.*

136 For *iw min*, "now, but (as a beginning of a sentence)," see *Wb.* I 43, 4.

137 For the spelling of *mn* with  (O25), see *Wb.* II 60, 6–11.

138 Goyon, *Imouthès*, p. 88, n. 28.

139 Faulkner, *Bremner-Rhind*, p. 22; Faulkner, *JEA* 22 (1936): 129.

140 Goyon, *Imouthès*, p. 89, n. 29.

141 For this form, see Gardiner, *Egyptian Grammar*, §448; Smith, in H. Thissen and K. Zauzich, eds., *Grammata Demotika*, p. 204.

142 Goyon, *Imouthès*, p. 89. Notably, the scribe of MMA regularly spells *hꜣy* without the initial *i*. Cf. the consistent spelling of this vocative with  (A26) or 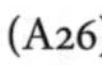 in BM 11, 10.

3, 11–13

H Here Isis describes the troubles of searching for her husband's body. The 1st person singular suffix pronoun, written (B1) in MMA 47, 3 and BM 11, 12, refers to Isis, the speaker. Based on this, the 2nd person plural suffix pronoun of line 3, 9 must refer to Isis and Nephthys. Cf. col. 2, 41 of the present manuscript: *šm=i pt tꜣ nn ḥm w⸢ꜣt⸣=k,* "for I have walked heaven and earth, without reversing your pa⸢th⸣."

The LP and GR epithet *smꜣyw nbd,* "Accomplices of the Evil One," which is written in red ink in MMA 47, 5 and BM 11, 14, refers to the followers of Seth.[143]

There are a number of orthographic features and discrepancies from the parallel texts:

1. The determinative (G7) follows *pt tꜣ* in MMA 47, 3.
2. *wꜥ* is written in MMA 47, 3 and in BM 11, 12.
3. (D54) stands for *ḥḥy* in BM 11, 12.
4. MMA 47, 3 uses the negation *nn,* rather than *n*.
5. is used for *gm* in BM 11, 13.
6. The 1st person singular suffix pronoun is erroneously written with (A1) and (B1) in P.W551. Cf. (A1) in MMA 47, 4, while the pronoun is omitted from BM 11, 13.
7. The scribe of BM 11, 13 includes the resumptive 3rd person singular suffix pronoun after *im*: *nn gm(=i) bw wnn nb im=f.*
8. The spelling of *pẖr* as , paralleled by MMA 47, 5 and BM 11, 14, is typical to the Ptolemaic period.[144]
9. MMA 47, 5 and BM 11, 14 omit the 1st person singular suffix pronoun of *pẖr*.

3, 14

I The appeal to the men and women ends with this line.

Goyon transliterates the group in MMA 47, 6 as *iw wꜥ*, pointing to the phonetic (M17) in the B and BM parallels: .[145] Although this reading is possible, *mr,* "follower, member," referring, in this case, to the accomplices of Seth is more probable.[146]

3, 15

J This line has two orthographic discrepancies from the parallel texts:

1. The determinative (B1) is written after *my* in the parallels of MMA 47, 7 and BM 11, 16.
2. Cf. the full phonetic spelling of *rm* in MMA 47, 7: .

143 Leitz et al., eds., *Lexikon* VI, p. 318; Wilson, *Ptolemaic Lexikon*, pp. 508–9 and 842; Caminos, *JEA* 58 (1972): 209, n. 7 and 220. Cf. the determinative (D3) in *nbd* of MMA 47, 5.

144 Fairman, *BIFAO* 43 (1945): 115.

145 Goyon, *Imouthès*, p. 89, n. 30.

146 Daumas, *Valeurs phonétiques* III, p. 467. For *mr*, "follower, member," see *Wb.* II 98, 2–6.

3, 16–17

K The somewhat rare medical term *ʿš*, "groaning," occurs in all parallels.[147]
The following discrepancies with the parallel texts should be noted:

1. The determinatives, , are omitted from *iwny*, , in MMA 47, 8, while only (G7) determines *iwny*, , in BM 11, 17.
2. *inb-ḥḏ* is abbreviated to in BM 11, 17.
3. The second negation in MMA 47, 9 and BM 11, 18 is a simple *n*, .
4. The preposition *ḫr* stands in place of *r* in BM 11, 18: … *ʿš n ḏw ḫr=k*.

3, 18

L Cf. the suffix pronouns in MMA 47, 10: *gnn ʿnty n dš=f r=k*, "The myrrh is soft, it has not been removed from you." Cf. BM 11, 19 : *gnn ʿnty n dš=k rf*.[148] *ʿnty* is written in MMA 47, 10 and BM 11, 19.
dš is written in P.W551.[149] Cf. the more correct in MMA 47, 10.

3, 19–20

M This line carries on the theme of the sustained cult of Osiris. Cf. MMA 47, 11 and BM 11, 20: *hn r r hwt-nṯr=k*, "Jubilation is at the entrance to your temple." This phrase is paralleled by P.Bremner-Rhind 13, 11: *ihꜣy hn r r ḥwt=k*.[150]
Cf. the negation in MMA 47, 12: *iw=k m pr=k n snḏ=k*. Cf. BM 11, 21: *ḥr… pr=k n snḏ=k*.[151]

3, 21–22

N *wnn=f ḥr sḏm* is understood as a 2nd tense construction, although Goyon translates the corresponding line of MMA 47, 13 in the present tense: "et les *Rekhyt* et les *Pât* t'adorent."[152] There are no phonetic complements for *rḫyt*, , in MMA 47, 13. The somewhat unusual -ending of *pʿt*, , is paralleled by MMA 47, 13 and BM 11, 22.
The damaged portion of line 3, 22 may be reconstructed on the basis of MMA 47, 14 and BM 11, 23: *ḥr ḥḥy ʿnḫ=sn m-ʿ=k*, "seeking their life in your hand." Note the lack of the preposition *ḥr* at the beginning of this line in P.W551.

---

147 *Wb.* I 227, 18.
148 For *gnn*, "to be soft," see *Wb.* V 175, 16–17.
149 For the reading of this sign as a phonetic *d*, see Daumas, *Valeurs phonétiques* IV, p. 722.
150 Faulkner, *Bremner-Rhind*, p. 24; Goyon, *Imouthès*, p. 89, n. 33.
151 For the phonetic spelling of *snḏ*, paralleled by MMA 47, 12 and BM 11, 21, see *Wb.* IV 182, 2–14.
152 Goyon, *Imouthès*, p. 89.

3, 23–24

O The corresponding line 15 of MMA 47 ends after *iw=k,* the rest is paralleled by MMA 47, 16.
Cf. the demonstrative in MMA 47, 16 and BM 11, 24: *m rn=k pwy n ḥʿpy,* "in this your name of the Inundation." The spelling of *rn* as  (V10) is different from MMA 47, 16, where it is written .[153]

3, 25

P This line shows a number of discrepancies with the parallel texts:

1. MMA 48, 1 has the  determinative (G7) for *ḥḳꜣ,* .
2. The preposition *ḥr* is not used in MMA 48, 1: *iw pr-ʿꜣ m ḥḳꜣ nst=k tꜣwy m ḫt=f,* "the pharaoh is the ruler of your throne, and the two lands are behind him!"
3. *tꜣwy* is written  in MMA 48, 1 and BM 11, 25.
4. BM 11, 25 shows a more elaborate spelling of *ḫt*: .

153 *Wb.* II 425.

3.1.5. STANZA 5 — SPOKEN BY ISIS *Lines 3, 26–4, 26*

Isis, established in line 3, 27 as the wife and sister of Osiris, recites the fifth stanza. She commands Osiris to arise and, thus, become rejuvenated. The security of Osiris involves his immediate family, as well as a broad population of gods. Mehenyt is named first among the powerful deities concerned with protecting Osiris. After asserting the protection of Osiris and the victory over Seth, Isis calls on her deceased husband to be rejuvenated. The text points to the stability of Horus' position on the throne of Osiris, implying that his office and cult are being maintained. Having been assured of safety, Osiris is to resume his place as king in the Netherworld by adorning himself appropriately. While lines 3, 21–25 of the fourth stanza emphasize the significance of Osiris for *rḫyt pꜥt,* "commoners and mankind," i.e., the living, line 4, 18 of this stanza points to the devotion to Osiris by the *wrḏw* (written ), "the weary," i.e., the dead. As the Memphite and Heliopolitan veneration of Osiris is placed in contrast to the evil of Seth, the throne of Egypt remains with Osiris and his family. Isis draws attention to the affection and grief of the family and people, and also alludes to the rights and duties of Osiris as the possessor of the throne. Thus, this stanza combines emotional, political, and religious aspects of the Osirian cycle.

TRANSLITERATION

26. *⸢ḥwt⸣ mḥ 5*
⸢ỉn⸣k ỉmw n sšr=k
27. *ḥmwt sn(=ỉ) n mwt=k*
28. *nn r=k sp 2*
ḥp-ꜥnḫ m wdn ꜣt=k r=ỉ
APPROXIMATELY 4 LINES MISSING
33. *…=k wpt b… …s*
34. *my mꜣn … … … ⸢ḫnt⸣*
(3, 35) *my m ḥtp*
sꜣ=k m bỉty m nḏ⸢=k⸣
36. *ꜥwyw=ỉ ⸢ḥ⸣ꜣ r ḫw ḏt=k mr=k*
37. *ỉ ḥwn nfr*
my r pr=k
nḏ⸢=k nb⸣ …
APPROXIMATELY 2 LINES MISSING
(3, 40) *mk … … … … …*
41. *ṯs tw rk m ỉꜥḥ m-hꜣ ⸢ḥḳꜣ⸣-ꜣnḏ*
42. *snḏ n=n pfy m ꜣt=f*
43. *… …=k … mꜣꜥ ḫrw*
44. *nṯrw m sꜣw n ḥꜣ=k*
(3, 45) *mḥnt ḥr tp=k m nbt-nsr*
46. *nr=s pẖr m šn=k*
47. *m n=k ẖkrw=k m-ꜥ nbw*
48. *sḫw=s ḏt=k mi ꜣwt ḥr it=s*

49. … …

… *iw ẖft=k*

(3, 50) [*ib*] *n rꜥ r=k*

51. … *sḥḏ-tꜣ-nṯrw-n-iw*(*t*)*=f*

52. … … *rk*

sḥri nbd

53. [*d*]*wn ḥꜥw*⸢*=k*⸣ *pd ꜥwt=k*

(4, 1) *sꜣ=k ḥr m-ḥry nst=k*

2. *rdwy wsir m sšm ḥrw*

3. *ti-sw iwꜥ wdn s*

4. *hꜣy ṯꜣi-nfr nn iꜣby n ḏt=k*

(4, 5) *ḳnw my*

mꜣr

6. *ity my n ẖrw=n*

i ity mꜣꜣ=n ti

7. *nn wn ḫsf ẖy=k*

8. *my ḥꜣ.n=i m bw wnn=k im=f*

9. *nn wḫd n=i ꜣt=k*

(4, 10) *mꜣꜣ* … *min nn ḥꜣw ḥꜣt*

11. *nḫn ẖy iw nḏ ḥr=k*

12. *sn=i m wꜥ=f*

sn(*t*)*=f m iw=s*

13. *nḫn mkt ky m ẖrwyw*

14. *ny-m iw=f r ẖrw=n*

(4, 15) *ihꜣi ṯꜣi nn šm=i m kf ḏw*

16. *tꜣ bꜥḥy ẖr iꜥby=k*

17. *my rk nn ꜥn sp=k*

18. *rmṯw wrḏw ḥr nḥbt n mrwt=k*

19. *imw* ⸢*r*⸣*=k* (*i*)*n rpwty=k*

(4, 20) ⸢*mrtyw*⸣ *mrt-ḥmwt*

21. *iry-tꜣ ḳnw*

m tštš ꜥwt=k

22. *sš*⸢*d*⸣*=k r iwnw*

ḥpt ti inb-ḥḏ

23. ⸢*iw ḏw*⸣ *ꜣbḫt m ir s*

24. *iw* ⸢*n*⸣*=k st rꜥ m* ⸢*ẖnw*⸣ *sw*⸢*ḥt*⸣

(4, 25) *my rk*

m ⸢*wiꜣ nst=f*⸣

26. *pꜣ* ⸢*ꜥšꜣ*⸣*-m-mrwt-*⸢*wꜥt*⸣

TRANSLATION

26. Fifth ⸢stanza⸣.

"⸢I⸣ am the one who grieves over your condition,

27. the wife of (my) brother, of your mother.[A]

28. There is no one against you." Twice.

"Living Apis, do not be heavy in your moment to me! [B]

APPROXIMATELY 4 LINES MISSING

33. … … brow … its … [C]

34. Come that … may see … … ⸢before⸣

(3, 35) Come in peace,

for your son is the king and ⸢your⸣ protector.[D]

36. My arms are ⸢rai⸣sed in order to protect your body (with) love of you! [E]

37. O, Beautiful ⸢You⸣th,

come to your house,

that you may pro⸢tect the lord⸣… [F]

APPROXIMATELY 2 LINES MISSING

(3, 40) Look, … … … … … [G]

41. Raise yourself, indeed, as the moon around the ⸢Helio⸣politan nome,

42. for That One fears us in his moment, [H]

43. … your … … justified.[I]

44. The gods are protecting you:

(3, 45) Mehenyt is upon your head as the Mistress of Flame,

46. as the terror of her encircles that which you surround.[J]

47. Take for yourself your adornments of gold, [K]

48. for she has caused your body to be protected, as the one who extends on behalf of her father, [L]

49. … …

… against your enemy,

(3, 50) [as the heart] of Re is (turned) towards you! [M]

51. … One who Illuminates the Land (for) the Gods by his Coming.

52. … indeed,

the Evil One is driven away! [N]

53. [Str]etch ⸢your⸣ body, loosen your limbs! [O]

(4, 1) Your son, Horus, is the one upon your throne.[P]

2. The two legs of Osiris are what Horus guides,

3. for he is, indeed, the heir who offers it.[Q]

4. O, good husband, there is no smell to your body! [R]

(4, 5) Brave One, come!

Miserable One! [S]

6. Sovereign, come toward our voice!

O, Sovereign, let us see you! [T]

7. There is no one who opposes your child.

8. Come, I will mourn in the place where you are.[U]

9. The moment (of your arrival) will not be painful for me,
(4, 10) (but) seeing … today, this extends (joy in) the heart.[V]
11. Young child, hail to you!
12. My brother is in his solitude;
his sister, she is separated.[W]
13. The youth who protects another in turmoil,
14. will he come towards our voice?[X]
(4, 15) O, husband, I shall not come as the one who reveals evil,[Y]
16. for the land is overwhelmed by your evil![Z]
17. Come, indeed, your occasion will not repeat.[AA]
18. The weary people are praying for your love.
19. The lamentation is for you b(y) your two goddesses.[BB]
(4, 20) ⸢Beloved One⸣, who Loves Women,
21. Brave Protector of the Land,
do not separate (from) your flock.[CC]
22. The White Wall (Memphis) will embrace you,
as soon as you ⸢arri⸣ve in Heliopolis,[DD]
23. ⸢while evil⸣ mixes with the one who did it,
24. because the seat of Re was ⸢yo⸣urs from (the time when you were) ⸢in the eg⸣g.[EE]
(4, 25) Come indeed,
do not let ⸢his throne be rejected⸣,[FF]
26. One ⸢Rich⸣ of Love for ⸢the Sole One⸣."[GG]

TEXT NOTES

Isis requests that Osiris return to his role as a rejuvenated sovereign, husband, and brother, while assuring him of the gods' protection. Mehenyt, as the uraeus, is mentioned first among the gods protecting Osiris. This choice is interesting due to her close connection with the coiled serpent, Mehen, who similarly plays a protective role, encompassing and shielding Osiris and Re.[154] While Mehen's place is in the night bark of Re, as it sails on the fiery roads of the Netherworld,[155] the Mehen-serpent also represents these roads. This

154 For instance, Mehen encircles Osiris in the Seventh Hour of the Amduat, upper register, see Hornung, *Das Amduat* I, pp. 119–20, pl. Siebente Stunde. Mehen similarly encircles and protects the sun god in the Seventh Hour of the Amduat, middle register, and in the Second Hour of the Book of Gates, see Hornung, *ibid.* I, pp. 122–24; II, pp. 130–31; Piccione, *JARCE* 27 (1990): 43–48 and Piankoff, *Le livre des portes*, pp. 70–71, fig. 9, respectively. Mehen also protects the sun god by surrounding his enemies and keeping them contained: Ritner, *JNES* 43 (1984): 219; Darnell, *Enigmatic Netherworld Books of the Solar-Osirian Unity*, pp. 380–85. Piccione, *ibid.*: 47–52, suggests a connection between the deity and the *mḥn*-gameboard, successful passage through which represented rebirth from the body of the Mehen-serpent. The name and protective qualities of Mehen are annexed to the uraeus of Re (*tꜣ mḥnt*) from the NK, onwards, see Ritner, *JNES* 43 (1984): 220.

155 Thus, the close association of Mehen with fire permits the interchangeability of Nesret and Mehenyt, which is reflected in the hieroglyphs, see text notes for lines 3, 44–46.

concept is illustrated already in the MK, as for instance in CT spells 758-60: *ir wnnt mḥn pwy pw n rʿ...*, "As for this Coiled One, he is the Coiled One of Re...;" *ir n=i w3wt wn n=i sbḫwt imyw mḥnw iw rḫ.kwi šnw n rʿ ḥnʿ imywt=f...*, "Prepare paths for me, open for me the gates which are among the Coiled Ones, for I know the circuit of Re and of those who are with him...;" *ir mḥn pw inn ist n s3=s ḥr imy-ḥ3t wsḫt...*, "As for this Coiled One whom Isis brought to her son Horus, who is in the bow of the bark...."[156]

The underlying theme of the solar-Osirian unity is further reflected in the LP epithet "One who Illuminates the Land for the Gods by his Coming" (*sḥḏ-t3-n-nṯrw-m-iwt=f*), which frequently refers to both Osiris and Re, emphasizing their close association.[157] The notion that this union is destined to cyclically occur is illustrated with Isis' statement, "the seat of Re was yours from (the time when you were) in the egg (i.e., before birth)." The arrival of Osiris in Heliopolis is yet another reference to the joining of the two gods. Isis' request that Osiris arise as "the moon around the Heliopolitan nome" similarly points to the instance of unity of Re and Osiris, when the United *Ba* acts as the lunar disk, filling the lack of the *wadjet*-eye.[158] In support, Osiris plays an important role in the GR Hymn to the Crescent Moon: *ḫnty-mk=s ḫnm.n=f i3bt wsir ḏd wbn(w) m nṯr im=s ḫprr šps ḥr mḥ ḫb=s*, "*Khentymekes* has united with the left eye (=moon), and Osiris is established and shining as a god therein it, the noble scarab filling its lack."[159] The fusion of the sun and the moon, or Re and Osiris, denotes the triumph of these gods over their enemies and thus assists their cycle of rebirth: *ḏḥwty wr pr m m3ʿ ḫrw i3b(t) šsp(w) wnm(t) iʿḥ iyw r ss=f*, "The great Thoth has come forth as justification, the left eye (=moon) has seized the right eye (=sun), and the moon has come at its (proper) time."[160]

The stanza again alludes to the theme of the regenerative properties of the inundation and its connection with Osiris in line 4, 16 by the phrase *t3 bʿḥy*, literally meaning "the inundated land."[161] This, along with the pun on *iʿby*, "unity (of Osiris' limbs),"[162] invokes the fertile aspects of Osiris.

3, 26–27

A The initial phrase of this stanza, *imw n sšr=k*, "one who grieves over your condition," may present a possible word play on an epithet of Isis, *imn-sḫrw*, "The One Hidden of Forms."[163] The word *imw*, "to mourn, grieve," is used here as a participle.[164] The common phonetic change from *ḫ* to *š* allows for the reading of *sḫr(w)*, "state, condition,"[165]

156 CT 759, VI 387n–o; CT 759, VI 389a–b; CT 760, VI 390a–b, respectively. See Faulkner, *Ancient Egyptian Coffin Texts* II, pp. 290–92.

157 Leitz et al., eds., *Lexikon* VI, p. 483.

158 Manassa, *Late Egyptian Underworld*, pp. 117–18 and 388.

159 Herbin, *BIFAO* 82 (1982): 249; Manassa, *Late Egyptian Underworld*, p. 117.

160 Herbin, *BIFAO* 82 (1982): 251; Manassa, *Late Egyptian Underworld*, pp. 117–18.

161 *Wb.* I 448, 11. Cf. the role of the inundation in lines 2, 5 and 3, 23, above.

162 Wilson, *Ptolemaic Lexikon*, p. 43. For a discussion of puns, see section 1.5.1, above.

163 See section 1.5.1, above. Wilson, *Ptolemaic Lexikon*, p. 909; Leitz et al., eds., *Lexikon* I, p. 349.

164 *Wb.* I 77, 12 and 14–15.

165 Fairman, *BIFAO* 43 (1945): 64.

which is supported by the gloss *sḫr=k,* , written next to *sšt=k,* , in BM 11, 27, and *sš=i*(!), , in the B variant.[166] MMA 48, 3 slightly elaborates the situation of Isis: *ink wꜥt im n sš=k,* "I am alone, grieving your condition."

The parallels of B and BM 11, 26 include an invocation written in red ink preceding this line: *i my irk stẖ ḫr*(*w*), "O, come then, Seth is fallen!" The invocation is omitted from MMA and P.W551.[167]

Some orthographic peculiarities and discrepancies with the parallel texts should be noted:

1. P.W551 has superficial plural strokes for *ḥmt,* , omitted from MMA 48, 4 and BM 11, 28.
2. The 1st person singular suffix pronoun after *sn* is written  (B1) in MMA 48, 4.
3. *mwt* is written  in MMA 48, 4 and  in BM 11, 28.

3, 28

B *ꜣt=k r=i* should be understood as "the moment of your coming."[168] Cf. the 1st person plural suffix pronoun, referring to both sisters, in MMA 48, 6 and BM 11, 30: *m wdn ꜣt=k r=n,* "Do not delay your moment (of coming) to us."

This line has some orthographic discrepancies with the parallel texts:

1. *ḥp,* , has the  determinative (E1) in MMA 48, 5.
2. The phonetic complement *n* of *ꜥnḫ,* 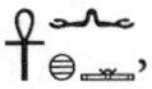, is written with  (D35) in P.W551, while BM 11, 29 omits all phonetic complements for this word.
3. *wdn* has an abbreviated writing with  (U32) in MMA 48, 6 and BM 11, 30.

A large lacuna in the papyrus corresponding to 4 lines in MMA 48 and BM 11–12 follows:

	rnp=k rnp=ti wḥm=k rnp(*t*) *n rnp*
	siw nṯr pn iw r sw=f
	nṯrw nṯrwt m ršit sp 2
MMA 48, 10	*nṯr nfr wṯs r ḥrt*
	May you renew being rejuvenated, as you repeat the rejuvenation annually!
	May this god, who comes on his day, be announced.
	The gods and goddesses are rejoicing, twice,
MMA 48, 10	(when) the good god rises up to the sky.[169]

166 Goyon, *Imouthès*, p. 89, n. 35, points to the word play on *sḫr* and *sštꜣ*, "hidden form."

167 Goyon, *Imouthès*, p. 89, n. 34.

168 Cf. lines 1, 6 and 2, 15 of P.W551.

169 Cf. Goyon, *Imouthès*, pp. 89–90, n. 36, pl. 38:

	Rajeunis étant rajeuni, puisqu tu renouvelles le rajeunissement du cycle annuel!
	Si ce dieu vient au jour convenu que est sien,
	Les dieux et les déesses son heureux, *bis*,
MMA 48, 10	si le dieu parfait s'élève vers le ciel.

3, 33

C The remaining traces support a reconstruction based on MMA 48, 11 and BM 12, 2: *im wpt=f bḳ.tw m tkꜣw=s,* "One who is on his brow is bright as its flame."

3, 34–35

D P.W551 omits the line: *sẖr=s n=k nbd m hh=s,* "it defeats the Evil One for you with its flame!" in MMA 48, 12 and BM 12, 3. Cf. MMA 48, 14: *my mꜣꜣ=i ḥr=k mi ḫnty,* "Come that I may see your face as before." Lines 3, 34 and 3, 35 are reversed in MMA 48 and BM 12. There are two notable orthographic discrepancies with the parallels:

1. *bity,* 𓆤𓏏𓅆, shows a 𓅆 determinative (G7), but lacks the cartouche in MMA 48, 13 and BM 12, 4.
2. B and BM 12, 4 spell *nḏ* phonetically: 𓈖𓆓.[170]

3, 36

E Cf. the second part of this clause in the parallels of B: *ḏt=k mr=i,* "your body which I love" and BM 12, 6: *ḏt=k mr(w)t=k r=i,* "your body and your love to me."[171] The lacuna at the end of this line suggests that *r=i,* present in the BM variant, should be considered as a possible reconstruction.
Cf. P.Bremner-Rhind 8, 9: *ꜥwy=i ḳꜣ r ḫw.tw=k mrwt.n=i,* "My arms are raised in order to protect you, the one whom I have loved."[172]
There are some orthographic discrepancies with the parallels texts:

1. *ḥꜣ,* 𓁐, lacks the phonetic complements in MMA 48, 15 and BM 12, 6.
2. *ḫw* is spelled 𓐍𓐍𓐍 in MMA 48, 15 and BM 12, 6.
3. *ḏt* shows a fuller phonetic spelling in MMA 48, 15: 𓆓𓏏𓏭 and in the margin of BM 12, 6. Notably, it is spelled as a simple 𓆓 in the original line of BM.

3, 37

F Cf. MMA 48, 16: *i ḥwn nfr my r pr=k nḏ=k nb tꜣwy,* "O, Beautiful Youth, come to your house, that you may protect the lord of the two lands!" The lack of the 𓀐 determinative (A17) for *ḥwn,* 𓎛𓅱𓈖, in MMA 48, 16 implies an association with Wennefer.
A lacuna in the papyrus corresponding to 2 lines in MMA 49 and BM 12 follows:

MMA 49, 1 *sbi=k ḫr nn wnn=f*
šm=i m kfꜣ n wꜥ=k

170 Goyon, *Imouthès*, p. 90, n. 37.

171 Goyon, *Imouthès*, p. 90, n. 38.

172 Faulkner, *JEA* 22 (1936): 127; Faulkner, *Bremner-Rhind*, p. 15.

MMA 49, 1 Your rebel has fallen, he will be no more,
(but) I walk endlessly (because) of your solitude.[173]

The parallel texts suggest that this portion of the stanza is again addressed to Osiris.

3, 40

G The remaining traces support a reconstruction on the basis of MMA 49, 3 and BM 12, 10: *mk m dpt m ꜣb r=i͗*, "Look, One who is in the Bark, do not separate from me!"

3, 41–42

H *ḥkꜣ-ꜥnḏ* is the name of the twelfth Lower Egyptian Heliopolitan nome, whose capital was *i͗wnw* (Heliopolis), pointing to the solar connection invoked by this line.[174]
The abbreviated  determinative (Z6) of *pfy* in MMA 49, 5 relates this demonstrative to Seth, the enemy of Osiris and his immediate family.
ṯs is written 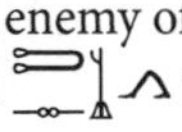 in MMA 49, 4 and just  (U39) in BM 12, 11.

3, 43

I This damaged line may be reconstructed on the basis of MMA 49, 6 and BM 12, 13: *sḥꜣ=k r pr=k n mꜣꜥ ḫrw*, "May you hurry to your house, in justification!"

3, 44–46

J Cf. the lack of the preposition *n* in the initial statement of MMA 49, 7: *nṯrw m sꜣw ḥꜣ=k*.
Cf. BM 12, 14: *nṯrw m sꜣw=k ḥꜣ=k*.[175]
The epithet *nbt-nsrt*, "Mistress of Flame," is frequently attested for Mehenyt and Isis, stressing their close association.[176] The gloss in the margin of BM 12, 15 reads , *nbt tꜣw*.[177]
The similarity of  (D26) and  (Q7) in hieratic may have caused confusion for the copyist. The  determinative frequently employed for Nesret or Mehenyt was likely replaced in this case by  (D26). Nevertheless,  (D26) logically occurs as a determinative in the name of this goddess, who may spit fire against enemies. The 3rd person

173 Cf. Goyon, *Imouthès*, p. 90, pl. 38:
MMA 49, 1 Celui que t'est rebelle est tombé. Il ne sera plus,
mais je chemine sans fin à cause de ta solitude!

174 Wilson, *Ptolemaic Lexikon*, p. 681.

175 For the GR construction *sꜣw ḥꜣ*, "to protect (someone/something)," see *Wb.* III 416, 12; Wilson, *Ptolemaic Lexikon*, p. 782.

176 Leitz, et al., eds., *Lexikon* IV, pp. 82-83.

177 Goyon, *Imouthès*, p. 90, n. 39.

singular feminine suffix pronoun of line 3, 46 refers to Mehenyt, elaborating on her role in repelling the enemies of Osiris.

There are two orthographic discrepancies in the parallels texts:

1. *nṯrw* is spelled phonetically in MMA 49, 7: .
2. *nsrt* has a more typical spelling in MMA 49, 9, and BM 12, 15.

3, 47

K The reading of *ḫkr* is questionable, because the determinative most resembles (S2). However, the phonetic in MMA 49, 10 supports this interpretation.

Cf. MMA 49, 10: *m n=k ḫkrw=k m ꜥwy nbi.* Goyon suggests that *ꜥwy,* , is a mistake for *kꜣt,* , translating this line "Prends pour toi ta parure ouvragée d'or!"[178] However, the existing , *m-ꜥ,* should be taken more seriously, considering the parallel of P.W551.

Note the phonetic *nbi,* , in MMA 49, 10 and the B variant, while BM, 12, 17 corresponds with P.W551.[179]

3, 48

L Cf. MMA 49, 11: *sḫw=s ḏt=k mi ꜣwy ḥr it=s,* and the variants in B: *sḫw=s ḏt=k mi ꜣw it=s,* and BM 12, 18: *sḫw=s ḏt=k mi ꜣw id=s.*[180] Goyon translates this phrase "car elle protégé ton corps comme une chapelle(?) au-dessus de son père." He proposes that the presence of the determinative (O1) for *ꜣw* in B and BM suggests the reading of *ꜣwt* as "chapel," without, however, accounting for the preposition *ḥr* in the MMA version.[181]

There are two orthographic discrepancies with the parallel texts:

1. *sḫw* shows a phonetic spelling, , in MMA 49, 11 and BM 12, 18.
2. *it,* spelled here, is written phonetically in MMA 49, 11: , and in BM 12, 18.

3, 49–50

M The damaged portion of line 3, 49 may be reconstructed on the basis of MMA 49, 12: *ii=tw wḏꜣ.tw n ḫftw=k,* "You have come being sound, as there are no enemies of yours." Note the (D35) of the MMA version, in place of *iw* in P.W551.

The reading of the somewhat damaged line 3, 50 is supported by MMA 49, 13 and BM 12, 20: *ib n rꜥ r=k.* The surviving stroke immediately following the break suggests that the lost word should be read as , *ib,* "heart."

178 Goyon, *Imouthès*, p. 90, n. 40. For the construction *m n=k*, see Gardiner, *Egyptian Grammar*, §336.

179 Goyon, *Imouthès*, p. 90, n. 40.

180 Goyon, *Imouthès*, p. 90, n. 40.

181 Goyon, *Imouthès*, p. 90, n. 41; Meeks, *Année lexicographique* III, p. 2.

3, 51–52

N Cf. the more complete examples in MMA 49, 14–15 and BM 12, 21–22: *i sḥḏ-tꜣ-n-nṯrw-n-iwt=f psd rk sḥr nbd.*[182] If the epithet, One who Illuminates the Land for the Gods by his Coming, is assumed to refer to Re, *sḥr* may be understood as an imperative: "O, One who Illuminates the Land for the Gods at his Coming, [Brilliant One], indeed, expel the Evil One." However, the context indicates that this entire speech is addressed to Osiris specifically. Thus, reading *sḥr* as a passive *sḏmw=f* is more reasonable. The determinative for *sḥr*, , in P.W551 represents this word in MMA 49, 15: .[183]

3, 53

O This reading is supported by the intact MMA 49, 16 and BM 12, 23: *dwn ḥꜥw=k pd ꜥwt=k.*[184]

4, 1

P Cf. Goyon's translation of the parallel MMA 50, 1, "ton fils Horus est l'héritier de ton trône!" *ḥry* is written  in MMA 50, 1 and phonetically in BM 12, 24: .[185]

4, 2–3

Q The grammar of line 4, 2 is understood as the *m*+infinitive construction.[186] Cf. Goyon's rendering of MMA 50, 2 and BM 12, 25: *šm wsir msw ḥr*, "Osiris chemine grâce aux Enfants d'Horus!"[187] Goyon reads  in the beginning of MMA 50, 2 as *šm*.[188] The  following the  determinative (G7) of Horus are unusual and must determine the entire phrase. Cf. *ḥr* written 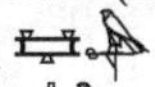 in MMA 50, 2.[189]
The name of Osiris is spelled  in line 4, 2. This form of the god's name, with the  (N5) replacing the earlier  (D4), first appears in the 21st Dynasty, and becomes popular in late hieratic texts.[190]  stands for *wsir* in MMA 50, 2 and BM 12, 25.
Cf. Goyon's rendering of MMA 50, 3: *ti-sw iw.n wdn s*, "et il est tenu à l'écart de celui qui commet cela," and BM 12, 26: *ti-sw iw.n wdn im*. The 3rd person singular dependent pronoun *sw* refers to Horus, emphasizing the importance of maintaining Osiris' cult by

182 Note the phonetic writing of *nṯrw* in MMA 49, 14.

183 Möller, *Hieratische Paläographie* III, p. 17.

184  (E34) of *dwn* is clearly visible in P.W551. The top intact sign of this line looks like , but should be understood as a mistake for the somewhat similar (T9) of *pd*.

185 For the spelling of *ḥry* as  in P.W551, see *Wb.* III 193.

186 Gardiner, *Egyptian Grammar*, § 331.

187 The corresponding B version also has *msw ḥr*; see Goyon, *Imouthès*, p. 91, n. 42.

188 Goyon, *Imouthès*, p. 91, n. 42.

189 This spelling is common in the CT, see *Wb.* III 123, 1.

190 DuQuesne, in B. Backes, I. Munro, S, Stöhr, eds., *Totenbuch-Forschungen*, pp. 31–32, and n. 74.

his son and rightful heir.[191] *s* stands for the dependent pronoun *st,* referring back to the throne. The reading of *ỉwꜥ* is uncertain due to the lack of a phonetic complement expected with *ỉwꜥ*, "heir." Cf. for this word in MMA 50, 3. However, of P.W551 is paralleled by the B version with the determinative and BM 12, 16 with the determinative (G37).[192]

4, 4

R Cf. MMA 50, 4: *nṯr nfr nn ꜣb=k r=ỉ,* "Good god, may you not separate from me!" Cf. also BM 12, 27 and the B version: *ỉh nfr n(n) ꜣb.n nḏ=k pn,* "O, good one, this protector of yours does not separate."[193]

4, 5

S The meaning of *mꜣr,* as referring to a person who has been wronged, fits well here and is frequently encountered in GR texts.[194] An alternate reading of the group is *m ꜣr=ỉ,* "don't drive me out."[195] However, (G7 and A1), which follow the phonetic signs, suggest understanding this group as the epithet "Miserable One."[196]
MMA 50 and BM 12 omit this line.

4, 6

T Cf. the more abbreviated MMA 50, 5 and BM 12, 28: *ỉty my mꜣꜣ(=ỉ) t(w) m twt=k,* "Sovereign, come that (I) may see you in your (true) form."
There are two orthographic peculiarities in this appeal to Osiris:

1. The plural strokes are omitted from the 1st person plural suffix pronoun.[197]
2. , *ti,* stands for the 2nd person singular dependent pronoun *ṯw.*

4, 7–8

U Cf. MMA 50, 6: *n ẖsf ẖy=k*[198] *my ẖrd n=n,* "Your child is not opposed. Come to us, child!" Notably, the second part of this phrase in BM 12, 29 and B differs slightly: *ẖ(y)=k m-m ẖrd.w,* "your child is among the children."[199]

---

191 For the enclitic particle *ti-sw,* frequently used with circumstantial clauses, see Gardiner, *Egyptian Grammar,* §§119.4 and 243.

192 Goyon, *Imouthès,* p. 91, n. 43.

193 Goyon, *Imouthès,* p. 91, n. 44.

194 Wilson, *Ptolemaic Lexikon,* p. 403.

195 *Wb.* I 11, 9–16.

196 Leitz et al., eds., *Lexikon* III, p. 237.

197 *Wb.* II 194.

198 Cf. for *ẖy* in MMA 50, 6.

199 Goyon, *Imouthès,* p. 91, n. 45.

Note the lack of the dot under the  determinative (A24) of *ẖsf,* which is generally characteristic to this scribe.
The  following  is attested as part of the verb *ḥ3,* "to mourn" in GR times.[200] Cf. the use of *ḥ3,* , "would that," in MMA 50, 7: *ḥ3 wnn=i bw wnn=k im,* "Would that I existed (in) the place where you exist!"[201]

4, 9–10

v In this line Isis stresses that she will be happy to see Osiris resurrected and strengthens this statement by describing the pain that the current unfortunate state of Osiris causes her in the following line.
Line 4, 9 of P.W551 agrees with BM 13, 1 and the B version.[202] Cf. the divergent MMA 50, 8: *n wšr mw m ḥrw=n,* "Water (from tears) has not dried on our faces."
A 2nd person pronoun is expected in the lacuna of line 4, 10, but the traces are ambiguous. Cf. , *ṯ* in MMA 50, 9 and BM 13, 2 support this reading: *m33 ṯ(n) min m=sn ḥ3w ḥ3t,* "(and) seeing you today among them would extend the heart." *ḥ3w* is written with the  determinative (V32) in MMA 50, 9 and the  determinative (G37) in BM 13, 2, which point to a pun on *ḥ3i,* "to mourn."[203]
The following orthographic peculiarities and discrepancies from the parallel texts should be noted:

1. The  determinative (P1) for 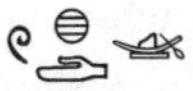, *wḫd,* likely originates from the similar *ḫd,* "to travel north." Cf. the determinatives for *wḫd* in BM 13, 1: .
2. *m3* is spelled as  in MMA 50, 9.

4, 11–12

w Cf. Goyon's rendering of MMA 50, 10–11: *n sp ḫy r nḏt=i šn(=i) m wꜥ=f šnt=f m iw s(w),* "Jamais il ne (suffira) d'un petit enfant pour me protéger. Mon frère est dans la solitude, sa sœur est dans la séparation d'avec lui." MMA 50, 10 and BM 13, 3 have 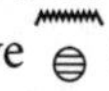 in the beginning of this line, which Goyon understands as *n sp.*[204] However, the extended spelling in the present manuscript, , supports the reading of *nḫn.*
The following orthographic peculiarities and discrepancies from the parallel texts should be noted:

1. *šn,* "brother," is written phonetically, , in MMA 50, 11.

200 *Wb.* III 7, 1–4.
201 Cf. the phonetic spelling of *im* in MMA 50, 7.
202 Goyon, *Imouthés*, p. 91, n. 46.
203 Thus, Wilson, *Ptolemaic Lexikon*, p. 614, proposes reading the expression *ḥ3w-ib*, as "sorrow, sickness of heart," suggesting the origin of this term in the verb *ḥ3i*, "to mourn." For punning, see section 1.5.1, above.
204 Goyon, *Imouthès*, p. 91, n. 47.

2. The word , *snt,* "sister," mistakenly has the seated man, , instead of the expected seated woman determinative, , in P.W551. This differentiates it from , "brother," in the beginning of this line.[205]
3. The  determinative of *iw,* "to detach, separate," in P.W551 must be a mistake. The  (V32) in MMA 50, 11 and  (G37) determinatives for *iw* in BM 13, 4 clarify the reading of this word.[206]

4, 13–14

X These lines continue the appeal, as the tradition of Horus' protection of Osiris is alluded to with a Late Egyptian interrogative .[207]
nḫn, "youth," clearly refers to Horus, the protector of Osiris.  stands in place of *nḫn mkt* [208] in the otherwise similar versions of MMA 50, 12 and BM 13, 5: *nḫ kt ky m ḫrwyw,* "One protects another in turmoil." In the context of this line the word *nḫn* presents a pun on *nḫ,* "to protect, protector" of MMA.[209] Cf.  in BM 13, 5.
Note the play on sounds between *ḫrw,* "voice," of line 4, 14 and *ḫrwyw,* "turmoil," of line 4, 13.[210]

4, 15

Y This line has notable differences with every parallel. Goyon proposes the following translation of the elusive MMA 50, 14: *ihy šr*(!)=*i m kf twt*=*k,* "Malheur! Je chemine sans fin et ta momie." The parallel of B 49, 2 supports his reading of the verb *šm* by spelling out the phonetic . [211] However, the variation in the last word of this line in BM 13, 7 considerably changes its meaning: *ih3* [212] *šm*=*i m kf mn*. The use of , *mn,* in the parallel of BM 13, 7 suggests a connection with the GR epithet of Imhotep, *kf-mnt,* "He who Expels Suffering." [213]

4, 16

Z *ʿb*=*k,* "your evil," should be understood as the evil that was done against Osiris.[214]

---

205 For variant spellings of *snt* in B, 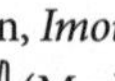 (with a phonetic *t*) and BM 13, 4, , see Goyon, *Imouthès,* p. 91, n. 48.
206 For *iw,* "to detach, separate," see *Wb.* I 48, 1–2.
207 For the interrogative *ny-m,* see Gardiner, *Egyptian Grammar,* §496.
208 For *mki,* "to protect," see *Wb.* II 160, 1–21. See section 1.5.1, above.
209 *Wb.* II 304, 9–14.
210 Cf. the phonetic complements for *ḫrw,* , in MMA 50, 13 and BM 13, 6. See section 1.5.1, above.
211 MMA 50, 14 has , see Goyon, *Imouthès,* p. 91, n. 49.
212 Note the lack of the expected (M17) in the vocative of BM 13, 7.
213 Leitz et al., eds., *Lexikon* VII, p. 283.
214 For (*i*)*ʿb,* "impurity, evil," see *Wb.* I 174, 15–18; Wilson, *Ptolemaic Lexikon,* p. 144. Cf. the determinative (G37) for *iʿby* in MMA 50, 15 and BM 13, 8.

Despite the attested spelling of *t3* as , cf. Goyon's translation of MMA 50, 15: *t3/ḫpr* () *bꜥḥy ẖr iꜥby,* "se met à être submergée sous les impuretés!" [215]
The preposition *ẖr* is spelled as  in P.W551.[216] This reading is supported by the phonetic  in BM 13, 8 and  in MMA 50, 15.

4, 17

AA Cf. the vocative in MMA 50, 16: *i my rk n ꜥn sp=k,* and the more elaborate BM 13, 9: *i my n=i n ꜥn sp=k.*[217] *sp=k,* "your occasion," refers to the occasion of Osiris' murder.

4, 18

BB Cf. MMA 51, 1: *rmṯw ḥr nḥbt n iw=k,* "People are praying for your coming." P.W551 corresponds more closely to B and BM 13, 10 which read: *rmṯw ḥr nḥbt n mrwt=k.*[218] The spelling of *rmṯ,* 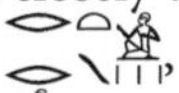, is paralleled by MMA 51, 1. Cf. the phonetic spelling of *rmṯw* in BM 13, 10: 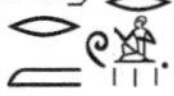.
Osiris is mourned by the inhabitants of the Netherworld as well as the "two ladies, goddesses" (*rpwty*), clearly referring to Isis and Nephthys.[219] The oo determinative (N33) of  represents the duality of this word. Cf. the  determinative for *rpwty* in MMA 51, 2 and  in BM 13, 11.

4, 20

CC Lines 4, 20–21 address Osiris with a series of epithets.[220] Cf. the epithet of line 4, 20 with cols. 1, 37, and 2, 18. The GR term *tštš,* "to crush, cut up," [221] is reminiscent of an Osirian epithet, *tštš,* which frequently occurs in rituals where Horus and the deceased address the "Hacked up One." [222] P.W551 col. 4 and MMA col. 51 omit line 13, 12 of BM: *i my nb r=i(!) pr=k.*
There are some notable discrepancies with the parallel texts:

1. *ḳnw* appears as  in MMA 51, 5, but lacks  in BM 13, 14.
2. The phonetic 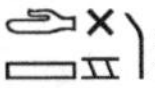 is written in place of *tštš* in MMA 51, 5 and BM 13, 14.
3.  (F28) represents *ꜥwt* in BM 13, 14.

215 For the reading of  as *t3*, see Daumas, *Valeurs phonétiques* II, p. 389; and *Wb.* V 212.
216 *Wb.* III 386.
217  (D55) is used as an ideogram for *ꜥn* in MMA 50, 16 and BM 13, 9.
218 Goyon, *Imouthès*, p. 91, n. 50.
219 *Wb.* II 415, 5–6.
220 For the GR epithet *iry-t3*, "Protector of the Land," see Leitz et al., eds., *Lexikon* I, p. 413.
221 *Wb.* V 330, 5–10.
222 Leitz et al., eds., *Lexikon* VII, p. 441.

4, 22

DD Both verbs in this sentence are 2nd tenses forming a *Wechselsatz.* Cf. the variant in MMA 51, 6: *sšd=k r pr=k ḥn*(!) *ḥpt tw ỉnb-ḥḏ,* "The White-Wall will embrace you when you arrive at your house!" BM 13, 15, in turn, corresponds with P.W551, except for the lack of *ḥḏ*. Cf. the phonetic in BM 13, 15. The following *ḥpt* in the present text stands for the 2nd person singular masculine dependent pronoun *ṯw*.
Goyon follows the proposition of Wilson regarding the origin of the GR verb of motion, *sšd,* "to go fast, to harpoon," in *sšd* "flash (of stars).[223] This is supported by the presence of the ★ determinative (N14) in the corresponding lines of B and BM 13, 15. The choice of this stellar term perhaps points to the association of Osiris and Orion, the ruler of the stars.[224]
The reading of as *ỉwnw* in P.W551 is supported by its more typical spelling with (O28) in BM 13, 15 and in MMA 51, 6, which Goyon overlooked in his translation.[225] Otherwise, the circular sign may also be understood as ⊙ (N5), allowing the entire group to be read as *ḥb,* "festival."

4, 23–24

EE P.W551 corresponds to the parallels of B and BM 13, 16.[226] Cf. MMA 51, 7: *r tꜣ ꜣbḫ t*(*w*) *m ỉr=s,* "to the land, join yourself to the one who made it."

4, 25

FF Cf. the spelling of *wiꜣ* in col. 2, 2 of P.W551: . Cf. also BM 13, 18: and the phonetic complements and determinative of *wiꜣ,* , in MMA 51, 9.

4, 26

GG The remaining traces correspond to the versions of B and BM 13, 19. Cf. MMA 51, 10: *pꜣ nb ꜥšꜣ-m-mrwt-wꜥt,* "The lord, Rich of Love for the Sole One."[227] The GR epithet *ꜥšꜣt-m-mrwt-wꜥt,* "One Rich of Love for the Sole One," refers to Osiris,[228] while the "Sole One" must be understood as Isis. The determinative (G37) of , *wꜥ* in MMA 51, 10, points to the negative connotations of Isis' condition.
The present manuscript omits MMA 51, 11 and BM 13, 20: *ỉ my rk stš ḫr,* "O, come indeed. Seth has fallen!"

---

223 Goyon, *Imouthès*, p. 91, n. 51; Wilson, *Ptolemaic Lexikon*, p. 936; *Wb.* IV 300, 8–9 and 301, 1–2; Meeks, *Année lexicographique* II, p. 355.

224 Darnell, *Enigmatic Netherworld Books of the Solar-Osirian Unity*, p. 280. For the connection of Osiris and Orion, illustrated in P.Vienne 3865, line 28: *bꜣ=k m pt ꜥnḫ.tw m sꜣḥ*, "Your *ba* is in the sky (and) you are living as Orion," see Herbin, *RdE* 35 (1984): 109, 121–22 and 126.

225 For this LP spelling of *ỉwnw*, see *Wb.* I 54.

226 Goyon, *Imouthès*, p. 91, n. 52.

227 Goyon, *Imouthès*, p. 91, n. 53.

228 Leitz et al., eds., *Lexikon* II, p. 216.

3.1.6. STANZA 6 — SPOKEN PROBABLY BY ISIS *Lines 4, 27–43*

Although no speaker is provided by the text, Isis is most likely intended to continue her recitation from the previous stanza. Isis describes her grief over the sudden death of Osiris, calling him with such poetic epithets as "One whose Form is at Rest" (*ḥtp-ỉrw=f*).[229] Despite her pleas for his return, Isis acknowledges that Osiris will never be the same. Nevertheless, the epithet "One who Changes his Forms" (*sn-ỉrw=f*), representing Sokar-Osiris, points to Isis' anticipation of the rejuvenation of her husband.[230] The second portion of the stanza calls for Osiris' rebirth, stressing the role of his son, Horus, and the importance of the proper order of inheritance.

TRANSLITERATION

27. *ḥwt mḥ 6*

ḥnty=k tkn r ḥry

28. *ḳsn wḏ.tw ỉỉ=k r=ỉ*

29. *ꜣb(=ỉ) mꜣꜣ ⸢k⸣ sp 2*

ḥtp-m-ỉrw=f ꜣb.n(=ỉ) mꜣꜣ=k

(4, 30) *s⸢ḏr⸣-ḥr-psd=f-mỉ-ḫt-ḥḏỉ*

31. … … … *ḳy-m-ẖnw⸢=f⸣*

32. … … … … *m ḏrwt=f*

33. … … … … *⸢nn⸣ ḳr⸢=f sw⸣*

34. … *r*… *ḫ ⸢ḳs⸣w=f*

(4, 35) *[nḫ]ỉ pw nn ỉw=f r nḥḥ*

36. *mnt ỉm=f ⸢sn⸣-ỉrw=f*

37. *ỉ⸢w⸣=f m pr kkt rꜥ nb*

38. *m-ḏr ꜣb* … *⸢mꜣ⸣n(=ỉ) ḥr=k nfr*

39. … … … … *nt ꜥnḫt*

(4, 40) … *m⸢y r p⸣r=k*

ḥr … *ẖr ẖkrw=k ḏt*

41. *⸢nḏ⸣ ỉt=k ⸢šw⸣ sꜣ rꜥ ỉwꜥ=k*

my n sꜣ=k

42. *nn ỉt=k ⸢ḥr⸣ ỉwꜥ=k m ỉry nst=k*

43. … … *⸢my r pr=k⸣* … … … … …

TRANSLATION

27. Sixth stanza.

"Your extent is what reaches up to the sky.[A]

28. Painful is the (fact that) you are charged to leave me.[B]

---

229 Leitz et al., eds., *Lexikon* V, p. 570.

230 For this predominantly GR epithet, see Leitz et al., eds., *Lexikon* VI, p. 361; Wilson, *Ptolemaic Lexikon*, p. 853.

29. (I) wish to see ⸢you⸣." Twice.
"One whose Form is at Rest, (I) wish to see you.
(4, 30) One who Re⸢sts⸣ upon his Back like a Damaged Tree, C
31. … Insect(?) … … on ⸢his⸣ Interior, D
32. … … … … at his sides E
33. … … … … ⸢without him⸣ bending ⸢it⸣ F
34. … … his bo⸢nes⸣! G
(4, 35) It is [disheart]ening, he will never return! H
36. Misery is in him, the One who ⸢Changes⸣ his Forms,
37. for he is in the house of darkness every day,
38. when (I) ⸢w⸣ish to ⸢se⸣e your beautiful face! I
39. … … … … of life. J
(4, 40) … co⸢me⸣ to your hou⸢se⸣,
Horus … your adornments of the body. K
41. Your father, ⸢Shu⸣, the son of Re, ⸢protects your⸣ heir.
Come to your son,
42. and your father will not be ⸢with⸣ your inheritance as the guardian of your throne! L
43. … … ⸢come to your house⸣ … … … … …" M

TEXT NOTES

This stanza addresses Osiris as a giant solar-Osirian deity in the process of transformation. The statement "your extent is what reaches up to the sky" depicts the unified Re-Osiris who fills heaven and earth.[231] More specifically, the head of the giant deity is located in the daytime sky (*ḥryt*), while his feet extend over the Netherworld (*ḫtmyt*). Despite this transformation, the speaker chooses epithets denoting the immobility of the deceased Osiris, such as "One who Rests upon his Back like a Damaged Tree" (*sḏr-ḥr-psd=f-m-ḫt-šʿd*).[232]

This dichotomy is further reflected in the allusion to the transformations that Osiris goes through after death, i.e., in the darkness. The rather rare expression *pr kkw*, "house of darkness,"[233] appears also in the MK stela of Seqedi Sehemre, 11–12: *wbꜣ ḥr=k m pr kkw*, "May you have clear sight in the house of darkness."[234] Furthermore, this phrase may present an intentional pun on the epithet of Hapy and the Great Lion (*rw-ʿꜣ*), "He who Comes Forth from Darkness (*pr-m-kkw*)," pointing to the cyclical regeneration of Osiris and his asso-

231 For a discussion of the giant solar-Osirian deity, see Darnell, *Enigmatic Netherworld Books of the Solar-Osirian Unity*, pp. 374–424 and *passim*, especially pp. 375–79.

232 Leitz et al., eds., *Lexikon* VI, p. 743. Cf. the more familiar *sḏr-ḥr-psḏ=f*, "One who Rests upon his Back." For a detailed discussion of the connections between Osiris and various trees, as well as other plants, see Koemoth, *Osiris et les arbres*.

233 Assmann, *Totenliturgien* I, p. 158, n. 195. Cf. *ʿt kky*, "place of darkness," which likely designates a portion of the underworld or an inner chamber of the temple associated with the "edge of the universe;" see Jasnow and Zauzich, *The Ancient Egyptian Book of Thoth*, pp. 36–38.

234 Kitchen, *Catalogue of the Egyptian Collection in the National Museum* I, p. 55, n. 22; *ibid.*, II, pp. 37–38.

ciation with the inundation.[235] Nevertheless, the position of Osiris in darkness commonly appears in Netherworld books, as for instance in the Book of Caverns: *nṯr ꜥꜣ tp=f m kkw pḥwy=f m kkw,* "O, Osiris, Great God, the one whose head is in darkness, the one whose two hind parts are in darkness." [236]

4, 27

A Goyon translates the closely corresponding MMA 51, 13: "L'espace que tu laisses vide atteint jusqu'à la hauteur du ciel." He supplies *wšr* based on BM 13, 22, which reads: *ḫnty wš(r)=k tkn iw ḥry.*[237]

There are a number of notable peculiarities in this line:

1. The 2nd person singular suffix pronoun of *ḫnty* is placed below the line due to the size of 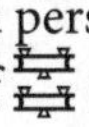 (N31). Cf. one  (N31) in 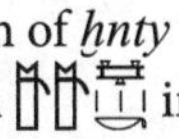 in MMA 51, 13.[238]
2.  and  are reversed in *tkn,* 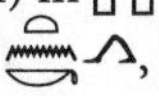, "to reach." [239] Cf. the more correct spelling in MMA 51, 13:  and BM 13, 22: .

4, 28

B Cf. MMA 51, 14: *ḳsn.wy wḏ.tw ii=r(!) r=i,* "How painful it is that you were sent to go from me." MMA 51, 14 has an erroneous  in place of the 2nd person singular suffix pronoun. Cf. BM 13, 23: *ḳsn.wy wḏ ii=k r=i.*

4, 29–30

C The presence of the suffix pronoun rather than the dependent pronoun, *ṯw,* following both *mꜣꜣ* verbs suggests a passive reading. However, the use of *k* in place of the 2nd person singular dependent pronoun is commonly attested.[240] Cf. the use of *n* in MMA 51, 15: *ꜣb.n=(i) mꜣꜣ k(w) sp 2 ḥtp-ir=f ꜣb.n(=i) mꜣꜣ=k,* "(I) wish to see you, twice, One whose Form is at Rest, (I) wish to see you."

The group , replaced by  (T30) in MMA 51, 16 and BM 13, 25, is understood as an abbreviated writing of *šꜥd.*[241] The same term is applied to the tree that contained the life force of Bata in the Tale of the Two Brothers, col. 12, 6–7: *iw=sn ḥr šꜥd tꜣ bḥḥ*(?) *nty ḥꜣty n bꜣ-tꜣ ḥr r=st iw=f hꜣyt mt m tꜣ wnwt wrt,* "They cut down the blossom(?) on which the heart of Bata was and he fell dead at that moment." [242]

235 Leitz et al., eds., *Lexikon* III, p. 86.

236 See the introductory text of the 6th division of the Book of Caverns, lines 2–3, in Piankoff, *BIFAO* 43 (1945): 16 and pl. CII.

237 Goyon, *Imouthès*, p. 91, n. 54.

238 For *ḫnty*, "space, area," rarely in the BD "the end of the sky," see *Wb.* III 105, 10–106, 16.

239 *Wb.* V 335, 1.

240 See text notes for line 1, 2 of the present manuscript.

241 *Wb.* IV 423, 6.

242 Gardiner, *Late Egyptian Stories*, p. 22; Lichtheim, *Ancient Egyptian Literature* II, p. 208.

There are some orthographic discrepancies with the parallels:

1.  has no determinatives in BM 13, 24.
2. *irw,* , has no plural strokes in MMA 51, 15 and BM 13, 24.
3. *m33* is written  in MMA 51, 15.
4. Both *3b* words are spelled  in the MMA parallel. Note the presence of a determinative and *n* in the second *3b.n,* .

4, 31

D The damaged portion of this line may be reconstructed on the basis of MMA 52, 1 and BM 13, 26: *ḥw-ḳy-m-ẖnw=f,* "One who Strikes the Insect(?) inside Him(self)." Goyon suggests reading , *ḳy,* which is plural in B and BM 13, 26: 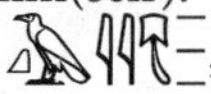, as *ḳ33,* "necrophagus" of the CT.[243]

4, 32

E The remaining traces support a reconstruction from MMA 52, 2 and BM 13, 27: *ʿwyw=f sẖ3 m ḏrwt=f,* "while his arms extend on his sides."

4, 33

F The remaining end of the line supports a reconstruction following MMA 52, 3: *rdwy=f dwn n(n) ḳr=f s(t),* "and his legs stretch with(out) him bending th(em)."

4, 34

G This line is largely damaged. The reading of *r* and *ẖ* is reasonable, but does not appear to correspond to the MMA or BM parallels. Cf. MMA 52, 4 and BM 13, 29: *imy-wt ḥr ẖw ḳsw=f,* "as the embalmer is protecting his bones."

4, 35

H The reading of this line is supported by MMA 52, 5 and BM 13, 30: *nẖi pw nn iw=f r nḥḥ.*[244] Note the consistent use of the negation *n* in BM 13, 30. Only the  determinative (G37) of *nẖi* remains.[245]

---

243 Goyon, *Imouthès,* p. 92, n. 55. For *ḳ33,* "necrophagus," see Meeks, *Année lexicographique* II, p. 385. The epithet of Osiris, *ḥw-ḳy-m-ẖnw=f,* "One who Strikes the Insect(?) inside Him(self)," is not attested outside of this ritual, see Leitz et al., eds., *Lexikon* V, p. 64.

244 For *iw* in the sense of "to return," see *Wb.* I 44, 7.

245 For *nẖi,* "to lament, mourning," see *Wb.* II 305, 11–17.

4, 36–38

I Cf. Goyon's rendering of MMA 52, 6–7: *mnt im=f sni irw=f iw=i m pr kkw rʿ nb,* "La misère est en lui, sa forme est changée, et moi je suis au royaume des ténèbres, chaque jour…" Goyon reads 𓉐𓏤 as the verb "to come forth" despite the lack of the 𓂻 determinative (D54). Cf. BM 13, 31: *mnt im=f nn sn iry ir=f iw=i m pr=i kkt rʿ nb.*
Although the text returns to the use of the 2nd person in line 4, 38, the Late Egyptian subordinate temporal construction *m-ḏr sḏm=f* indicates that this clause continues the sentence from the previous line.[246] Cf. MMA 52, 8: *m-ḏr ꜣb=i n mꜣꜣ ḥr=k nfr,* "since I want to see your beautiful face." Note the variant form *mꜣn* here. Cf. line 3, 9 of P.W551.
Two peculiarities in the present manuscript should be noted:

1. 𓊃 and 𓈖 of *sni* are reversed.
2. [hieroglyphs] is written with the 𓅆 determinative (G7).

4, 39

J This largely broken line may be reconstructed on the basis of MMA 52, 9: *wn-nfr mꜣʿ ḫrw wsir nb tꜣ ʿnḫt,* "Wennefer, the justified, Osiris, Lord of the Land of Life," or BM 14, 2: *wn-nfr wsir nb tꜣ ʿnḫt.*

4, 40

K The remaining 𓅆 (G7) in the beginning, as well as the traces of the rest of this line suggest a reconstruction in accordance with MMA 52, 10–11 and BM 14, 3: *ity my r pr=k ḥr im=f ḥr ḫkrw=k,* "Sovereign, come to your house, Horus is in it in your adornments." 𓅃 (G5) stands for Horus in MMA 52, 11.

4, 41–42

L In these lines, Isis stresses the significance of the correct order of inheritance.
Cf. MMA 52, 12–14: *nḏ k(w) it=k šw sꜣ rʿ iwʿ=k m-ʿ sꜣ=k nn ky ḥr iwʿ=k m iry nst=k,* "Your father, Shu, protects you. Your inheritance is in the possession of your son, no other is your heir, the guardian of your throne!" Cf. BM 14, 4–5: *nḏ=k it=k šw sꜣ rʿ iwʿ m-ʿ sꜣ=k nn ky ḥr iwʿ=k m iry nst=k.* The latter clause in MMA 52, 14 corresponds with BM 14, 5.
Two discrepancies with the parallel texts should be noted:

1. BM 14, 4 includes the 𓇳 determinative (N5) for Shu.
2. [hieroglyphs] and [hieroglyphs] have the 𓅆 determinative (G7) in MMA 52, 14.

246 Černý and Groll, *Late Egyptian Grammar*, pp. 410 ff.

4, 43

M The remaining traces correspond with MMA 52, 15–16: *i ity my r pr=k m wšr mw m ḥr=n,* "Sovereign, come to your house, drying the water (of tears) from our face(s)!" Cf. BM 14, 6: *i ity nfr my r pr=k wšr mw m ḥr=n.*

3.1.7. STANZA 7 — SPOKEN BY ISIS *Lines 4, 44–5, 36*

The appellation "my beloved" suggests that the seventh stanza is again spoken by Isis. The statement "you have fertilized and I became pregnant," which clearly refers to Isis' conception of Horus, supports this. As the theme of Isis' conception of Horus parallels the relationship of Nut and Osiris, the reassembling of Osiris by his mother, Nut, is explored in the beginning of this stanza. Having become complete again, and being promised not to experience pain or discomfort, Osiris is now able to return. After alluding to the conception of Horus, Isis speaks of her grief. However, the text shifts focus to Seth and his punishment for the crimes against Osiris. At this point the poetic discourse of the previous stanzas is replaced with legalistic terminology, such as *wšbyt,* "statement," and *wḏb,* "to turn back," often said of a dispute.[247] Going along with the legalistic theme, Isis indicates that her testimony will be supported by witnesses.

The more emotional tone of the previous stanzas, describing Isis' suffering, is then revisited. She speaks of the memory of *šr,* "the child," clearly referring to the rejuvenated Osiris. Remembering is a significant aspect of mourning, with which Isis supports the existence of the deceased Osiris in the Netherworld.[248] An already familiar theme of the importance of the correct order of succession is stressed by Isis at the end of this stanza. The throne of Osiris is inherited by his son and rightful heir, Horus, who protects Osiris and avenges his death. The last lines of the ritual allude to the place of the pharaoh in this divine order of inheritance, and his role in supporting the Osirian cult.

TRANSLITERATION

44. *ḥwt mḥ 7*
(4, 45) *i my n=i mrt=i*
sip.n k(w) mwt=k nwt
46. *nn g⌜ꜣ⌝*
⌜n⌝n ꜥšw im=k
47. *nḏry … m-ꜥ=k*
di=s šfi=k n ḫftw=k

247 *Wb.* I 408, 3–15; Meeks, *Année lexicographique* II, p. 108; and Wilson, *Ptolemaic Lexikon*, pp. 289–90; Hannig, *Sprache der Pharaonen*, p. 234.

248 For *sḫꜣ*, "to remember, think about," see *Wb.* IV 233, 7.

48. šd… tw m hrw psḏntyw
49. wꜣ …
… mꜣꜣ tw
(4, 50) ꜥšꜣt … … ⸢m⸣ ỉbb
51. rm … … sp 2
sn=ỉ ⸢rm⸣=ỉ n=k
52. ḥr ḳnw … … ỉm=k
53. nt⸢k⸣ ỉs … … ⸢mwt⸣=ỉ
54. … … … …
(5, 1) pꜣ.n=k šsp m (ỉ)wr=ỉ
2. šm=ỉ n=k
nn mꜣꜣ=k s(w)
3. ỉw=ỉ dy m-ḫnt nꜣy(t) pfy smꜣr-nb-pt
4. mk ỉb=ỉ ꜣw
ꜣhd m mḥ
(5, 5) wḏꜣty=ỉ ḥm n rm
6. ḥwy.tw sḏm=ỉ ḫrw=ỉ
7. rm=ỉ m ikk
8. nḫb.tw bꜣkiw tp hrw 30 9. ỉn pfy wd ḳnw
(5, 10) ḏd=ỉ n=k
ḫbn i.ir r=ỉ m sn ỉw ḫpr ḫr=k
11. šm=ỉ m wꜥ nn ỉw ḥnꜥ=ỉ
12. nwḥ ḥꜣ n=ỉ
ꜣs.tw ỉw ḥpt=ỉ sꜣ=k
13. (n-)ỉb-n ỉry wšbyt
14. wḏb.tw=ỉ n ḥḏ pfy
sꜣw wḏb=f ḳnw r=f
(5, 15) ḥtp ỉb=ỉ ḥr mt r ꜥnḫ
16. ꜣw.n ỉry wšbyt
17. rm=ỉ ḥr ꜣw n mḥw=k
18. mn=ỉ smtr.n wy nty m sꜣ=ỉ
19. ỉb=ỉ mḥw
nn gꜣ=k
(5, 20) … wḫd m ꜣt=k
21. ngꜣ ḥꜥw=ỉ m ⸢mn⸣
22. ḥr ḳnw wr ⸢r=k n=ỉ
ky ḏd⸣ sḫꜣ.n=s šr m ḫy
23. nḫ sw ⸢šn⸣tꜣyt
⸢ỉw⸣ sḫꜣ.n=s sp 2 ḫr=s
24. rm⸢=ỉ n=k⸣
ỉb=ỉ ḥr mn=f n ꜣw ⸢mr⸣=k r=ỉ
(5, 25) sn=ỉ m ꜥ[mḏ]
mk ⸢sꜣ⸣=k m ⸢ḥr⸣ nḏ=k

26. *ḥr wn.n=f m ḥḳ(ꜣ) nst=k*
wd.n=f ḳnw ỉ.ỉr s(w)
27. *ỉw=f ḥtm r ẖbt=f n ḏt*
28. *nḏ=k ẖpr*
nn mn=k
29. *nṯrw nṯrwt ỉb=sn nḏm*
(5, 30) *mwt-nṯr m ꜣw-ỉbw*
31. *nbt-ẖwt m ꜥfn(t)=s*
mꜣꜣ stš ẖr ḥr ḥr=f
32. *ỉw ḥr ḥr ỉꜣwt=f nty ḥḳ(ꜣ) nst=f*
33. … ⸢*ỉỉ*⸣ *m rnpy*
34. ⸢*t*⸣*nw sw r nṯr nb*
(5, 35) *ỉw pr-ꜥꜣ ꜥ(nẖ)* ⸢*wḏꜣ*⸣ *s(nb) ḏd ḥr nst=f ḏt*
36. *ḥr sḏfꜣw ḥr* ⸢*prw*⸣ *nb(w) kꜣ=k*
ỉw=f pw nfr

TRANSLATION

44. Seventh stanza.[A]
(4, 45) "O, come to me, my beloved,
your mother, Nut, has reconstituted you.[B]
46. There is no ⸢la⸣ck,
there is no groaning in you,[C]
47. … grasps your hand,
she causes terror of you in your enemies,[D]
48. … nourishes you on the day of the New Moon festival![E]
49. Far away …
… see you,[F]
(4, 50) … numerous … do not be silent.[G]
51. … weep … my brother," Twice.
"I weep for you,
52. because of the misfortune … … in you,[H]
53. yo⸢u are⸣ indeed, … … my ⸢mother⸣,
54. … … … …[I]
(5, 1) You have fertilized and I became pregnant;
2. when I came to you
you did not see him.[J]
3. I am here before that den of Him who Makes Wretched the Lord of Heaven.[K]
4. Now, my heart is stretching,
being weakened through worry,
(5, 5) as my eyes resist weeping.[L]
6. Please, let me hear my (*sic*) voice,
7. as I weep, lamenting.[M]

8. A service of the beginning of 30 days is instructed 9. by That One who committed the offence.[N]
(5, 10) I say to you:
the crime which was done against me resembles that which occurred against you.[O]
11. I come alone, without (anyone) with me.[P]
12. Lamentation is bound to me,
as I rush so that I may embrace your son
13. (for) the sake of making a statement.[Q]
14. I am turned back by the harm of That One,
for fear that he turn back to the crime against him![R]
(5, 15) My heart wishes for death more than life,
16. for making a statement (takes) long.[S]
17. I weep as long as (I am) grieving you.[T]
18. I suffer, and those who care for me bear witness to me.[U]
19. My heart is grieving,
there being no more lack (of) you,
(5, 20) … suffering in your moment.[V]
21. My limbs are torn up in ⸢suffering⸣
22. because of the great crime ⸢against you and towards me."
Another reading:⸣ (because) she remembers the child as a youth.[W]
23. "Shentayt mourns him,
she has remembered keenly regarding it:[X]
24. '⸢I⸣ weep ⸢for you⸣.
My heart, it is suffering at the extent of your ⸢love⸣ for me![Y]
(5, 25) My brother, do not [be weak]!
Look, your ⸢son⸣ is ⸢Horus⸣, your protector.[Z]
26. Horus, he is the ruler of your throne.
He reversed the crime of the one who committed i(t),
27. (and) he is destroyed at the place of punishment, forever.[AA]
28. Your protector has come into being,
and there will be no (more) pain for you.'[BB]
29. The gods and goddesses, their hearts are cheerful,
(5, 30) as the god's mother rejoices.[CC]
31. Nephthys is in her *ꜥfnt*-veil,
seeing Seth fallen on his face,
32. while Horus is in his office of the Possessor of his Throne.[DD]
33. … ⸢has come⸣ as the Rejuvenated One.[EE]
34. He is more distinguished than any god,
(5, 35) as the Pharaoh, l(ife), ⸢prosperity,⸣ he(alth), is enduring upon his throne, forever.[FF]
36. supplying all ⸢the temples⸣ for your *ka*."
It has come (to an end) well.[GG]

TEXT NOTES

The initial portion of this stanza focuses on the transformation of Osiris. As Isis points to her conception and birth of Horus, her speech suggests a parallel between this line's theme of Isis and Horus and the Osirian rebirth through Nut.[249] Thus, the epithet *nb-pt,* "Lord of Heaven," refers to Osiris as the offspring of the sky goddess and as the transformed solar-Osirian deity. The transformation occurs as Osiris' mother, Nut, reconstitutes (*sip*) him. The term *sip,* in the sense "to organize, revise, inspect (of limbs; i.e., to make well)," likely stems from the notion of accounting for each limb of the deceased.[250] *sip* is used in the same sense in CT 44, I 185: *sip=k b3=k m pt iwf=k ẖ3t=k m iwnw,* "May you inspect (*sip*) your *ba* in the sky, as your flesh and your corpse are in Heliopolis."[251] Notably, *sip* also implies the notion of judgment in the common expression *sip m/ḥr/r mḫ3t,* "to examine on the scale," alluding to the assessment not only of the deceased him/herself, but also of the heart in the judgement hall of Osiris.[252]

The legalistic theme in the middle of the stanza points to the mythological context of the trials of Seth. The term *wšbyt,* understood as "statement, justification,"[253] has the legal sense of answering for "crimes (allegedly) committed ... 'that which has to be answered.'"[254] However, this term may also have the sense of "to answer for (someone)," or even "to protect, avenge, champion," which better illustrates the actions of Isis. Furthermore, the latter translation is significant in its implication of protection, as is clearly illustrated by the Great Karnak inscription of Merneptah, line 9: *bityw m-ʿḳ3 dmi=sn inḥ(w) m sšmw-t3wy n g3w mšʿw bn n=w pḏwt r wšb ḥr=w,* "Lower Egyptian kings were opposite their town, surrounded by He who Guides the Two Lands through lack of military forces. They had no bowmen to champion them."[255]

The successful outcome of the trials and the triumph of Osiris are clear, as the transformed god is literally addressed by the well-attested epithet *rnpy,* "Rejuvenated One."[256] Horus, his rightful heir, is accordingly called the "Possessor of his (=Osiris') Throne."

---

249 Notably, the act of conception (*iwr*), as opposed to birth (*msi*), is rarely associated with Nut, who primarily focuses on the latter; see Billing, *Nut*, pp. 33–36. Cf. CT 684, VI 313a–f: *i nrty iptwty nty rʿ iwr. ty rʿ (m w)ḫ sp 2 ms.ty sw (m) dw3t sp 2 iwr=tn NN pn (m w)ḫ sp 2 ms=tn sw (m) dw3t sp 2 mi rʿ rʿ nb,* "O, you two vultures of Re, you two who conceived Re (in) the night, you two who bore him (in) the morning, may you conceive this NN (in) the night, may you bare him(!) (in) the morning, like Re every day," see Faulkner, *Ancient Egyptian Coffin Texts* II, p. 250.

250 *Wb.* IV 35, 2–3. Wilson, *Ptolemaic Lexikon*, p. 798, proposes that the term alludes to "ensuring that the mummy has all its limbs and none are lost."

251 Cf. Faulkner, *Ancient Egyptian Coffin Texts* I, p. 36.

252 Seeber, *Untersuchungen zur Darstellung des Totengerichts*, p. 78, nn. 283–85.

253 Hannig, *Sprache der Pharaonen*, p. 220. This spelling of *wšbyt* likely originates from *šbn*, "to mix," *Wb.* IV 442, 1.

254 Green, *GM* 41 (1980): 43. Cf. the translation of *iry wšb*, "to give an answer," in Goyon, *Imouthès*, p. 93, n. 67; *Wb.* I 372, 4–6; Meeks, *Année lexicographique* II, p. 108.

255 See Manassa, *The Great Karnak Inscription*, pp. 16 and 19, n. g, who offers further examples of this rendering of the term. See also *Wb.* I 371, 17–18; Wilson, *Ptolemaic Lexikon*, p. 267.

256 Leitz et al., eds., *Lexikon* IV, pp. 682–83.

4, 44

A Note the horizontal spelling of the number seven , with the phonetic complement *t* in MMA 53, 1 and BM 14, 7.

4, 45

B Cf. slightly extended MMA 53, 2–3: *i my n=i mrt=i sip ti n mwt=k nṯrt nwt,* "O, come to me, my beloved, your divine mother, Nut, has reconstituted you!" The  that follows *sip.n* in P.W551 may be explained by the passive use of *sip* in BM 14, 8–9: *i my n=i mrt(=i) sip.n.tw=k mwt=k nwt.*
Some orthography and discrepancies with the parallels of this line should be noted:

1.  does not have the  determinative (D54) in MMA 53, 2 and BM 14, 8.
2. This is the first instance of the use of  (S3) for a phonetic *n* in this text, paralleling MMA 53, 2 and BM 14, 8.
3.  stands for the 1st person singular suffix pronoun in MMA 53, 2, but it is omitted in BM 14, 8. Cf.  in P.W551.
4.  (F45) stands for *mwt* in MMA 53, 3.
5. Cf. the simple phonetic  for Nut in MMA 53, 3 and the  (B1) determinative of Nut in BM 14, 9.

4, 46

C Cf. line 3, 17 of the present manuscript: *nn ꜥš nn ḏw r=k,* "There is no groaning, there is no evil against you." Note the  (Aa2) determinative for 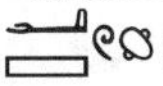 in MMA 53, 4 and BM 14, 10.

4, 47

D The lacuna in this line likely contained a 3rd person singular feminine suffix pronoun as the subject of *nḏry,* paralleling the second clause of this line. This pronoun refers to Nut, who is mentioned in line 4, 45 above. Cf. the shorter version of this line in MMA 53, 5 and BM 14, 11: *nḏry=s ꜥ=k di=s šfiw=k,* "She grasps your hand and she causes terror (of) you." Since Egyptian notions of terror and respect are closely related, the nuance of the enemies respecting Osiris should also be considered in this context. The spelling of *di* as  in MMA 53, 5 and 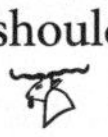 (F7) for *šfy* in BM 14, 11 should be mentioned.[257]
Note the dot at the end of this line.

257 For a discussion of *šfy*, "awe inspired terror," see Wilson, *Ptolemaic Lexikon*, p. 1004.

4, 48

E This manuscript parallels versions B and BM 14, 12: *šd=s tw m iw=k m hrw psḏntyw.*[258] Cf. MMA 53, 6: *ḥnty=s tw m iw=k hrw psḏn,* "She provides (for) you on your return, on the day of the New Moon fesitval!" The group appears as *psḏntyw* from the MK onwards.[259] Cf. the (G4) in *psḏntyw* in BM 14, 12: .
Cf. PT 437 (§794): *sd3 n=k psḏt irw n=k tpyw wꜥb=k n psḏntyw ḫꜥ=k n tp 3bd,* "You at whom the nine shake and for whom the first ones act, [you] will become clean at the New Moon day and appear at the first of the month."[260]

4, 49

F Cf. MMA 53, 7: *w3 r=k ḫ3yt rm(=i) tw,* "Your malady is far from you, (but) I grieve you." Note the marginal glosses in B and BM 14, 13: *w3w r=k ḫ3yt.*[261]

4, 50

G The remaining is understood as *3bb,* "to be silent, mute,"[262] following Goyon. The damaged portion of this line may be reconstructed on the basis of MMA 53, 8 and BM 14, 14: *ꜥš3 hrw m ibb,* "(My) cries are numerous, do not be silent!"

4, 51–52

H The remains of this line support a reconstruction from MMA 53, 9 and BM 14, 15: *rm=i n=k sp 2 šn(=i) rm=i n=k,* "I weep for you, twice, (my) brother, I weep for you."
Cf. the clause of line 4, 52 in MMA 53, 10: *ḥr ḳnw (w)r ḫpr im=k,* "because of the (gr) eat misfortune which happened to you." The scribe of BM 14, 16 writes out *wr* fully in: *ḥr ḳnw wr ḫpr im=k.*
There are two orthographic discrepancies with the parallel texts:

1. The first *rm* has the determinative (D9) in MMA 53, 9 and BM 14, 15.
2. *šn* is written without a determinative in MMA 53, 9 and with (T22) in BM 14, 15.

---

258 Goyon, *Imouthès*, p. 92, n. 60.

259 Wilson, *Ptolemaic Lexikon*, p. 374. For a discussion of the term *psḏntyw*, "new moon," and its hieroglyphic representation, see Depuydt, in L. Lesko, ed., *Ancient Egyptian and Mediterranean Studies*, pp. 71–89. Depuydt, *Civil Calendar and Lunar Calendar in Ancient Egypt*, p. 154, argues that *psḏntyw* not only describes the first day of the lunar month, but likely also refers to the first day of the civil month. See also Spalinger, *Private Feast Lists of Ancient Egypt*, p. 6.

260 Allen, *The Ancient Egyptian Pyramid Texts*, p. 105.

261 Goyon, *Imouthès*, p. 92, n. 61; *Wb.* III 360; Meeks, *Année lexicographique* I, p. 268.

262 Goyon, *Imouthès*, p. 92, n. 62. See also Meeks, *Année lexicographique* I, p. 4, who equates the term with *inb*; Meeks, *Année lexicographique* I, p. 33.

4, 53–54

I Cf. MMA 53, 11: *ntk is sn mwt=i,* "You are, indeed, the brother (also born to) my mother." (F45) again stands for *mwt* in MMA 53, 11 and BM 14, 17.
Indiscernible traces of at least one more line are visible following this line.

5, 1–2

J Cf. the presence of a suffix pronoun after *šsp* and the lack of one after *iwr* in MMA 53, 13: *pꜣ.n=k šsp=i m iwr* and in BM 14, 18: *pꜣ.n=k šsp=i n iwr.*
The omission of the 1st person suffix pronoun considerably alters the sense of MMA 53, 14: *šm.n=k nn mꜣꜣ=k sw,* "you have gone, not having seen him (=the child)." The 3rd person singular dependent pronoun *sw* refers to Horus, with whom Isis was pregnant. As the negative construction of this phrase in line 5, 2 is unclear, is understood as a late writing of *n*, making the phrase a *n sḏm=f* circumstantial past.[263] The abbreviated negation in BM 14, 18 supports this interpretation.
This line has some notable orthographic features and discrepancies with the parallel texts:

1. The expected determinative (D52) is omitted from *pꜣ* in all texts.[264]
2. Cf. the more complete spelling of *iwr* in MMA 53, 13 and BM 14, 18: .[265]
3. stands for the 1st person singular suffix pronoun in P.W551.
4. The dependent pronoun *sw* has a full writing in MMA 53, 14: .

5, 3

K The context suggests understanding the phrase *nꜣyt pfy smꜣr-nb-pt* as referring to the den of Seth. Accordingly, the epithet *nb-pt,* "Lord of Heaven," refers to Osiris.[266]
This line shows some orthographic discrepancies with the parallel texts:

1. is used consistently for the 1st person suffix pronoun in MMA 53.
2. *ḫnt,* , lacks determinatives in BM 14, 19.
3. is omitted from in MMA 53, 15.
4. The demonstrative *pfy* has the determinative (Z6) in BM 14, 19.
5. *smꜣr,* , has the determinative (G37) in BM 14, 19.[267]
6. has one determinative (G7) in MMA 53, 15 and none in BM 14, 19.

263 Gardiner, *Egyptian Grammar*, p. 376, § 455.5.

264 For *pꜣy*, "to copulate, fertilize," see *Wb.* I 497, 13–14. According to Wilson, *Ptolemaic Lexikon*, p. 345, this term may originate in *pwi* or *pꜣi*, "to pour out."

265 For *šsp*, "to conceive (with *iwr*)," see *Wb.* IV 533, 6–7.

266 Leitz et al., eds., *Lexikon* III, pp. 624–25.

267 For *smꜣr*, "to make wretched, to dispossess," see *Wb.* IV 127, 1–4; Wilson, *Ptolemaic Lexikon*, p. 844.

5, 4–5

L The clearly negative connotation of the word *3w*, "to be long," is unusual, as the phrase *3w-ib*, "to rejoice," is generally a positive notion.[268] Isis' description of her grief is followed by the verb *3hd*, "to be weak,"[269] the weight of which is strengthened by its probable origin in *nhd*, "painful."[270] Cf. the less descriptive but eloquent MMA 53, 16: *mk ib=i iwh n mḥ*, "Look, my heart is overloaded with worry."

 is understood as *ḥm*, "to give way, repel."[271] However, considering the spelling of *ḥm*  in MMA 54, 1, Goyon suggests that it is used in place of *ḥ3m*, *ḥm3*, "to fade."[272] BM 14, 21, in turn, uses the  determinative (D9) for *ḥm*, adding a gloss for the expression in the left margin: , *irt(=i) gw3 n rm(t)*, "(my) eye is bonded with crying."[273]

These orthographic features and discrepancies from the parallel texts should be noted:

1.  stands for the 1st person suffix pronoun in BM 14, 20.
2.  has phonetic complements in MMA 53, 16.
3. The 1st person singular suffix pronoun is written with  here.
4. *wḏ3ty* is spelled phonetically in MMA 54, 1: 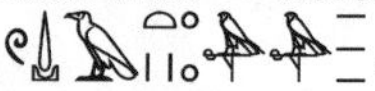.[274]

5, 6–7

M Isis expresses her hope that Osiris will heed her pleas through the term , *ḥwy*, "please," used frequently before imperative and prospective verb forms.

The 1st person singular suffix pronoun of *sḏm* must be understood as a mistake for the 2nd person pronoun. Otherwise, *sḏm* may be a participle, resulting in: "please, one who hears my voice."

The scarcely attested GR noun for the sun, *ikk*, does not fit the sense of line 5, 7.[275] The context as well as the  determinative lead to a similar sounding *ik*, "to lament."[276] This term occurs in the PT, as for instance spell 337 (§550b) calls on the nursing cows to mourn Osiris: *pḫr ḥ3=f rmi sw ik sw*, "Go around him, bewail him, lament him." The preceeding verb *rm*, "to weep," supports this reading. On the other hand, Goyon sug-

---

268 For *3w*, "to be long (of illness)," see *Wb.* I 4, 2. Notably, an example of a very negative meaning for the group appears in the similar sounding term , *3w*, "death," used from the MK onwards, see *Wb.* I 5, 16.

269 *Wb.* I 12, 9.

270 *Wb.* II 288, 2–4.

271 For *ḥm* with the  determinative (D55), "to give way, repel," see *Wb.* III 79, 1–21.

272 Goyon, *Imouthès*, p. 93, n. 63. For *ḥ3m*, *ḥm3*, "to fade," see Meeks, *Année lexicographique* I, p. 244.

273 Goyon, *Imouthès*, p. 93, n. 63.

274 For *wḏ3ty*, "the two eyes of god," see Wilson, *Ptolemaic Lexikon*, p. 287.

275 *Wb.* I 140, 10.

276 *Wb.* I 138, 21. This term also occurs in the Book of Traversing Eternity, P.Leiden T32, III 27, see Herbin, *Le livre de parcourir l'éternité*, pp. 56, 167–68, and 443.

gests that *ikk* is used for *ggw,* "to be astonished," and renders the slightly different MMA 54, 3: *rm=i n=k m ikk,* as "je pleure pour toi, ne sois pas étonné(?)!"[277] Goyon places a question mark next to *ikk,* but does not address the problematic translation, although the concept of Osiris being surprised by Isis' mourning is unusual.

There are two orthographic features and discrepancies with the parallels:

1. *ḥwy* is spelled 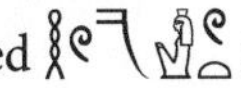 in the B and BM 14, 22 versions.[278]
2. The 1st person singular suffix pronoun  is inserted above line 5, 7.

5, 8–9

N The expression *tp 30,* written  in MMA 54, 4 and BM 14, 23,[279] is unclear. It likely refers to the festival of offering to the dead.[280] Another notable consideration is the typical 30-day length of priestly service (*wrš*).[281]

The demonstrative *pfy* refers to Seth, which is supported by the  determinative (Z6) for *pfy* in MMA 54, 5 and BM 14, 24. Accordingly, *ḳnw,* "offence," must be understood as the murder of Osiris. Note the dot above the determinative of 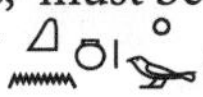 in P.W551.

5, 10

O 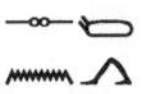 is understood here as *sn,* "to resemble." However, the  determinative (D54) of *sn* suggests that it may also be interpreted as "to pass, exceed," allowing for a much stronger sense. Thus, Isis' pain would be greater than that of Osiris. The exact sense of this statement is difficult to ascertain, since the choice of these terms was most likely intended as a pun, adding poetic subtlety to this religious text.[282]

Cf. *ẖbi,* "to lessen," in place of the phonetically similar *ẖbn,* "to punish, criminal,"[283] in MMA 54, 6–7: *ḏd=i n=k ẖbi iry r=i m sni r ḫpr ḥr=k,* "I say to you: the devastation which was done against me resembles that which occurred against you." This manuscript follows the B version and BM 14, 26: *ḏd(=i) n=k ẖbn iry r=i m sni r ḫpr ḥr=k.*

This line shows some notable orthographic peculiarities:

1. The participial prefix *i* is spelled as  here.[284]

277 Goyon, *Imouthès*, p. 93, n. 65; *Wb.* V 157, 4–6.

278 Goyon, *Imouthès*, p. 93, n. 64. For the grammatical use of *ḥwy*, "please," see *Wb.* III 45, 8–9.

279 Möller, *Hieratische Paläographie* III, p. 625.

280 *Wb.* V 269, 12.

281 The temple service performed by priests generally lasted 29 or 30 days throughout Egyptian history; see Depuydt, *Civil Calendar and Lunar Calendar in Ancient Egypt*, pp. 147–48.

282 Ockinga, *JEA* 69 (1983): 88–95, demonstrates that *sni* construed with the preposition *r* should be translated "to imitate." For the latter interpretation, see *Wb.* III 455, 7. For a discussion of puns, see section 1.5.1, above.

283 For *ẖbi*, used similarly to *ẖbꜣ*, "to destroy," from the NK, see *Wb.* III, 251 and 253; for *ẖbn*, see *Wb.* III 254; Goyon, *Imouthès*, p. 93, n. 66.

284 Junge, *Einführung in die Grammatik des Neuägyptischen*, p. 68, 2.1.

2. *ỉr* is written (D12).[285]
3. There is an extra stroke at the bottom of the reed leaf (M17) of *ỉw*, which stands for *r* in the *m*+infinitive+*r* construction of *m snỉ r*, "to resemble."[286]
4. *ẖr* is spelled in the GR manner with phonetic .[287]

5, 11

P Cf. MMA 54, 8 and BM 14, 27: *šm=ỉ m wꜥ nn r ḥnꜥ=ỉ*. MMA 54, 8 has a phonetic spelling of *wꜥ*: .

5, 12–13

Q The presence of the 2nd person singular suffix pronoun after *sꜣ* in P.W551 and BM 14, 28 reinforces the notion that Isis is speaking to Osiris concerning their son, Horus. This reading is questionable, however. Goyon does not comment on his translation of MMA 54, 9: *nwḥ=ỉ ꜣs.tw r ḥpt sꜣ(=ỉ)*, "Je suis courbée, me hâtant pour aller recueillir (mon) fils."
The following orthographic features and discrepancies should be noted:

1. The unexpected (D55) determinative of *nwḥ* in P.W551 is paralleled by MMA 54, 9, while this term lacks a determinative in BM 14, 28.
2. *ỉb* is spelled in MMA 54, 10.

5, 14

R The similarity between (G54) and (M11) in hieratic points to a visual pun on the words *snḏ*, "fear," and *wḏb*, "to turn back."[288] Note the phonetic complement *d* for *wḏb* in P.W551. MMA 54, 11–12 and BM 14, 30 use *snḏ* in place of the first *wḏb*: *snḏt=ỉ n ḥḏ n pfy sꜣw wḏb=f ḳnw r=f*, "I am terrified of the harm of That One, for fear that he turn back to the crime against him (=Osiris)!" Note the more usual determinative for *ḳnw*, , in MMA 54, 12 and the lack of a determinative in BM 14, 30.

5, 16

S Cf. MMA 54, 14: *n ꜣw n ỉry wšbt*, "for long is the making of a statement." *ꜣw* should be understood in the temporal sense of "to take a long (time)."[289] Cf. only (D4) for *ỉry* in BM 14, 31.

---

285 For this spelling of *ir*, see Daumas, *Valeurs phonétiques* I, p. 153.
286 *Wb.* III 456, 15–457, 2; Wilson, *Ptolemaic Lexikon*, p. 853.
287 *Wb.* III 315.
288 Derchain-Urtel, in M. Minas and J. Zeidler, eds., *Aspekte spätägyptischer Kultur*, p. 79. For puns, see section 1.5.1, above.
289 *Wb.* I 4, 1.

5, 17

T The verb *mḥ,* "to worry, grieve," is frequently used in reference to Osiris.[290] The determinative points to a possible pun on *mḥ,* "flood," or idiomatically, "to be loyal (to someone)."[291] Note the superfluous *n* of *mḥ,* in P.W551. Cf. the determinatives of *mḥ,* , in MMA 54, 15.
Cf. the passive *mḥ* of MMA 54, 15: *rm=i n=k ḥr ꜣw n mḥ.tw=k,* "I weep for you as long as you are mourned."

5, 18

U Cf. the slightly different MMA 54, 15: *mdw=i ḥr smt.n wy nty m sꜣ=i,* "My words bear witness to me (as they are) behind me!"

5, 19–20

V MMA 55, 1 is likely correct in its use of the 3rd person suffix pronoun referring to *ib,* "heart:" *ib=i mḥw nn gꜣ=f,* "My heart is grieving, there being no lack." Note the pun on *mḥ,* "to grieve," and *mḥ,* "to overflow" in both texts.[292] The scribe of MMA chose clearly different suffix pronouns in 55, 2: *nn ḫd m ꜣt=f,* "There is no suffering in his moment." The B version uses *wḫd=i* in place of *ḫd.*[293]

5, 21–22

W is understood as *mn* here.[294] The determinative (A2) of *mn* most likely originates from *mr,* "to love," similarly written in LP texts.
Cf. MMA 55, 3: *(n)gꜣ=i ḥꜥw=i m šntt,* "I am torn up (and) my limbs are prisoner(s)." BM 15, 5 has *m ntt* in place of *šntt.*[295]
Lines 5, 21 and 5, 22 are combined into one in the MMA and BM parallels. Cf. the second part of MMA 55, 3 and BM 15, 5: *ḥr ḳnw wr mꜣꜣ=i,* "because of the great crime which I saw." The second part of line 5, 22, which presents another interpretation by the scribe of P.W551, is omitted from all the parallels. This is marked by , a GR spelling of *ky ḏd,* "another reading."[296]
Cf. the determinatives of *ḳnw,* in MMA 55, 3. Note the possible word play of *ḫy,* "youth," and *ḫw,* "uniqueness."

---

290 *Wb.* II 120, 14.

291 See section 1.5.1, above. *Wb.* II 122, 19.

292 See section 1.5.1, above.

293 Goyon, *Imouthès*, p. 93, n. 68.

294 Daumas, *Valeurs phonétiques* I, p. 154.

295 Goyon, *Imouthès*, p. 93, n. 69.

296 For the GR group , transcribed as *ky ḏd*, "another reading," see *Wb.* V 111, 11.

5, 23

X Shentayt, spelled  in MMA 55, 4, is an epithet of Isis in mourning.[297]
 (M3) at the end of this line has a number of readings: *imy, m, nḫt, ḫ, ḫt, ḫr, sms,* but none of these is convincing in this case.[298] The reading *ḫr,* "regarding," seems most plausible. Cf. Goyon's translation of MMA 55, 4: *nḫ sw šnt3yt sḫ3.n=s ḫmt=s,* "et Shentayt le déplore quand elle se souvient qu'elle le prévoyait." Goyon understands the group  in MMA 55, 4 as *ḫmt,* "to think, foresee," pointing to  in the B version.[299] However, cf. the remaining phrase in the partially damaged parallel of BM 15, 7: 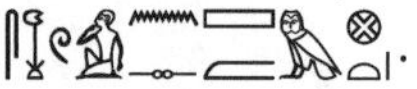.

5, 24

Y The reading of this partially destroyed line is supported by MMA 55, 5–6: *rm=i n=k ib=i ḥr mnt=f n 3w n mr=i r=k,* "I weep for you. My heart, it is suffering at the extent of my love for you!" Note the more typical emphasis on Isis' love for Osiris here, rather than Osiris' love for Isis in P.W551 and BM 15, 7.
 is consistently used for the 1st person singular suffix pronoun in BM 15, 8.

5, 25

Z Cf. MMA 55, 7–8: *šn(=i) m wrd r iw(=k) mk s3=k ḥr m nḏ=k,* "(My) brother, do not be weak in (your) return! Look, your son, Horus, is your protector." The remaining traces suggest that the present manuscript corresponds to B and BM 15, 8 in using *ʿmd,* "to be weak." [300] However, BM 15, 8 omits the particle *mk*: *sn=i m ʿmd s3=k ḥr m nḏ=k.*
There are two orthographic discrepancies with the parallel texts:

1.  following the phonetic  stands for the 1st person singular suffix pronoun in MMA 55, 7.
2. *nḏ,*  has a determinative in MMA 55, 8 and BM 15, 9.

5, 26–27

AA Cf. the form of the participle in MMA 55, 9–10 and BM 15, 10: *ḥr wn.n=f m ḥḳ3 nst=k wd.n=f ḳnw r ir s.*[301] Cf. the slight differences of the second statement in MMA 55, 11: *ḥtm=f m ḫbt=f ḏt,* "He is destroyed in his place of punishment, forever."

---

297 Leitz et al., eds., *Lexikon* VII, p. 105; Coulon, in Z. Hawass, ed., *Egyptology at the Dawn*, p. 138. For *nḫ*, "to mourn," see *Wb.* II 305, 11–14.

298 Daumas, *Valeurs phonétiques* II, p. 396.

299 Goyon, *Imouthès*, p. 93, n. 70; *Wb.* III 285, 5–11; Meeks, *Année lexicographique* I, p. 278.

300 *Wb.* I 187, 6–7; Goyon, *Imouthès*, p. 93, n. 71.

301 For *i.ir* as a Late Egyptian participle, see Černý and Groll, *Late Egyptian Grammar*, p. 463.

The 3rd person suffix pronoun of line 5, 27 refers to Seth, who is described in the previous line as the "one who committed the crime." His destruction is said to happen at the place of punishment/execution (*ḫbt*).[302]
Some orthographic features and discrepancies with the parallel texts should be noted:

1. *ḥkꜣ,* , shows an abbreviated spelling in BM 15, 10.
2. Note the determinative in *nst,*  in MMA 55, 9.
3. *wdn,* 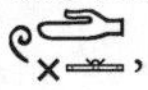, lacks determinatives in BM 15, 10.
4. The superfluous *n* below the determinative of  does not appear in the parallels.
5. The  (A8) determinative in this LP writing of *ḫbt,* , likely originates from *ḫbb,* "to dance." Cf. the phonetic spelling of 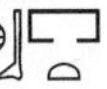 in MMA 55, 11.

5, 28

BB This passage clearly refers to Horus as the protector of Osiris. Cf. the very different interpretation of the text in MMA 55, 12: *nḏt.n=f ḫpr n mnt=k,* "He has protected that which came into being of your suffering."

5, 29–30

CC Note the poetic play on *nḏ,* "to protect," in line 5, 28, with *nṯrw,* "gods," and the stative form of *nḏm,* "to be sweet," in line 5, 29.[303] Cf. the synonymous MMA 55, 13: *nṯrw nṯrwt ibw=sn ꜣw,* "The gods and goddesses, their hearts are rejoicing."
Line 5, 30 is omitted from MMA 55 but is paralleled in BM 15, 14. The epithet *mwt-nṯr,* "god's mother," relates to Isis as the mother of Horus.[304]
There are two orthographic discrepancies with the parallel texts:

1. *nṯrw* is spelled  in BM 15, 13. The orthography of MMA 55, 13 corresponds to P.W551 more closely: 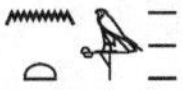 and 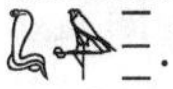.
2. Note the  determinative (F51) for 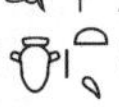 in MMA 55, 13.

5, 31–32

DD Cf. the use of the verb *mꜣꜣ* in MMA 55, 14–16 and BM 15, 15–16: *nbt-ḥwt m ꜥfn(t)=s mꜣꜣ=s stš ḫr ḥr ḥr=f iw ḥr ḥr iꜣwt=f nt ḥkꜣ nst,* "Nephthys is in her ꜥ*fnt*-veil, as she sees Seth fallen on his face, while Horus is in his office of the Possessor of the Throne." The ꜥ*fnt*-headdress is frequently depicted being worn by pharaohs. Cf. P.Westcar 10, 10–11: *ẖrd n mḥ 1 rwd ḳsw=f nḫbt ꜥwt=f m nbw ꜥfnt=f m ḫsbd mꜣꜥ,* "A child (Userkaf) of one

302 *Wb.* III 252, 9–14. For a brief discussion of *ḫbt* as the place where Seth is punished, see Zandee, *Death as an Enemy*, p. 16.

303 See section 1.5.1, above.

304 Leitz et al., eds., *Lexikon* III, pp. 261–62.

cubit, strong boned, his limbs overlaid with gold, his *ꜥfnt*-headdress of true lapis-lazuli."[305] The term *ꜥfn* involves enveloping a person or object in cloth for protection from outside danger.[306]

There are some peculiarities and orthographic discrepancies with the parallel texts:

1. The spelling of Nephthys, with (F32) is unusual for the scribe of P.W551, but it is paralleled by MMA 55, 14 and BM 15, 15.[307]
2. The *ꜥfnt*, "head-cloth," is written with the determinative (A24) in MMA 55, 14.
3. *ẖr* is written as in MMA 55, 15 and BM 15, 15. Goyon transcribes its determinative as (V12) over (D54), probably due to the similarity of this hieratic group with (A15).
4. *nty* also appears as a genitive in line 2, 11 of the present manuscript.[308]
5. *ỉꜣwt* is written as in MMA 55, 16.
6. *ḥḳꜣ* shows an abbreviated spelling in BM 15, 16.
7. *nst* is spelled phonetically in MMA 55, 16: .

5, 33

EE The damaged text appears to correspond to MMA 56, 1 and BM 15, 17: *wsir iy.tw m rnpi*, "Osiris has come as the Rejuvenated One." Note the extra determinative (M4) for in both parallels.

5, 35

FF While line 5, 35 of P.W551 states the fact of pharaoh's rule, the text of MMA 56, 3 addresses Osiris with the 2nd person suffix pronoun: *ỉw pr-ꜥꜣ ꜥnḫ wḏꜣ snb ḏdwt ḥr nst=k*, "The Pharaoh, life, prosperity, health, is established upon your throne." BM 15, 18 corresponds to P.W551 more closely: *ỉw pr-ꜥꜣ ꜥ(nḫ) wḏꜣ s(nb) ḏd ḥr nst=f*.

Two discrepancies with the parallel texts should be noted:

1. *pr-ꜥꜣ* is written as in MMA 56, 3.
2. *nst* has the determinative (G7) in MMA 56, 3: .

---

305 Erman, *Die Märchen des Papyrus Westcar*, pl. X; Lichtheim, *Ancient Egyptian Literature* I, p. 220.

306 Vernus, *RdE* 33 (1982): 93–94. For *ꜥfnt*, "head-cloth," see *Wb.* I 183, 4; for *ꜥfn*, "to wrap," see *Wb.* I 183, 1–3.

307 This spelling points to a pun on *nbt-ẖt*, "Mistress of the Womb," with the allusions to tomb. For the play between *ẖt* and *ḥt*, see Smith, *Mortuary Texts of Papyrus BM 10507*, pp. 97–98. For puns, see section 1.5.1, above.

308 For the epithet of Horus, *ḥḳꜣ-nst*, "Possessor of the Throne," see Leitz et al., eds., *Lexikon*, V, p. 514; *Wb.* III 172, 11.

5, 36

GG This last couplet is similar to a portion of the Glorification of Osiris in the papyrus MMA 25, 9: *wsir ḫnty-imntyw iw m rnpy tnw iw nṯr nb s3=f ḥr sḏf3w rw prw n k3=f...*, "Osiris, Foremost of the Westerners has come as the Rejuvenated One, more distinguished than any god. His son, Horus, is supplying the entrances of the temples of his *ka...*"[309]

The 2nd person singular suffix pronoun refers to the *ka* of Osiris. Cf. the slightly abbreviated MMA 56, 4–5: *ḥr sḏf3w m prw n k3=k iw=f pw*, "supplying the temples for your *ka*! It has come (to an end.)" Note the shift of focus to Re in BM 15, 19: *ḥr sḏf3w pr rʿ n k3=f*, "supplying the temple(s) of Re of his *ka*.

A space the size of one line follows.

3.2. GLORIFICATIONS

This section comprises sixteen glorification spells, which belong to the category of *s3ḫw* III. Each of the spells begins with the rubricized title *s3ḫw*, "Glorification spell."[310] The initial six spells of *s3ḫw* III concern acts of mourning and protection, subsequently leading to successful rebirth and rejuvenation. The speech of the Spirits of Pe, addressing the deceased, demonstrates the intent of this group of spells: "You (=Osiris/the deceased) have gone and you will return, you have slept and you will awaken, you have died but you will live."[311] The following spells 7–9 involve various deities, namely Geb, Horus, Thoth, Nut, Isis, and Nephthys, revivifying the corpse. Here the body of the deceased Osiris is symbolically assembled; his mouth and eyes being opened so that he may be "more effective than the glorified gods."[312] Spells 10–15 are of the *Stundenwachen* type,[313] describing the release and slaughter of four geese.[314] Here Atum and the Ennead are depicted slaughtering geese and cattle, as well as bulls. Subsequently, the sacrifice of animals represents triumph over the enemies of Osiris, in particular, Seth. This concept is illustrated in the statement "Your son, Horus, is standing in your places. He has caught for you the confederates of Seth. He has smitten for you the bulls. He has bound for you the wild bulls. He lassoed the goat. He tied for you the geese."[315] The final spell 16 provides instructions for recitation and action. Column 10 closes the papyrus with a familiar *iw=f pw nfr*, "It has come (to an end) well."

309 Goyon, *Imouthès*, pp. 61, and 94, n. 73.

310 See section 1.7.3 and chapter 2 for further discussion of glorification spells.

311 Line 6, 6.

312 Line 8, 4.

313 Of these, the initial three parallel spell 2 of *s3ḫw* I. Assmann, in S. Groll, ed., *Studies in Egyptology*, p. 38, fig. 8.

314 Assmann, in S. Groll, ed., *Studies in Egyptology*, p. 7, connects this rite to the dramatic performance in the *wryt*.

315 Lines 9, 5–6.

3.2.1. *sꜣḫw* III, SPELL 1 — SPOKEN BY THE LECTOR PRIEST

Lines 5, 37–6, 1[316]

The title in the beginning identifies this spell as a recitation performed in the temple of Osiris during "every festival of the West." The end of the spell clarifies its function as a standard ritual to be recited from the "festival service book" (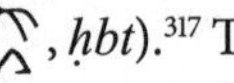, *ḥbt*).[317] This initial spell of *sꜣḫw* III establishes Osiris as the son of Geb and Nut. Emphasis is put on his status as the former king of Upper and Lower Egypt and on Osiris' power over the gods, both on earth and in the Netherworld. As the gods hail and praise Osiris, he is protected.

TRANSLITERATION

37. *sꜣḫ*
ir m ḥwt-nṯr nty wsir ḫnty-imnt(tyw)
i in ḫry(-ḥbt) 38. *⸢ḥr⸣ tp n pr tn*
ḏdw m hꜣ-snḏ m ḥb nb n imntt
39. *⸢nṯr⸣ m hꜣ-snḏ sp 4*
irt ḥb=f
ḫtm=f n inp ḏt r nḥḥ
(5, 40) … … … …*k* … *tw wsir*
ḏd mdw in ḫry-ḥbt
41. *hy ⸢wsir⸣ ḫnty-imnt(tyw)*
⸢nḏ=k⸣ … *gmw fꜣw* 42. *=k*
m iḫtmw nṯrw wr snḏ=k m nṯrw imyw ẖrt-nṯr
43. *inp is ḫnty-imntt*
hy wsir ḫnty-imntyw ḥry-tp
44. *n=k wnp-ḥr*
bit
n=k wnp stš
ḫ⸢ʿ⸣=kw⸣ (5, 45) *m nsw bit*
sḫm=kw m psḏt
kꜣw=sn is
46. *dfꜣw=sn is*
hy wsir ḫnty-imntyw
n=k 47. *imy pt tꜣ*
n=k imy ʿnḫ mt
n=k imy ḥry-tp 48. *spꜣt igrt*

---

316 For a detailed discussion of Assmann's and Goyon's classification of *sꜣḫw* spells, see section 1.1 and Assmann, in S. Groll, ed., *Studies in Egyptology*, pp. 1–45. For the description of the spells of *sꜣḫw* III, see section 1.7.3 and chapter 2, above.

317 For *ḥbt*, "festival service book (recited by lector priests)," see *Wb.* III 61, 1–4; Wilson, *Ptolemaic Lexikon*, p. 637.

hy wsir ḫnty-imntyw
ꜣḫ=k
ꜣḫt 49. *imnt m ḥꜥꜥ*
ḥkn=sn n kꜣ=k šps=k
rs (5, 50)*=k r sꜣw mꜣꜥt mꜣstyw m ksm*
51. *nḏ ḥr=k in nṯrw ḳrtyw*
dwꜣ=sn r snsn sꜥḥ 52. *=k*
⌜*nḏ*⌝ *ḥr=k*
ii nṯrw sp 2
ḥꜣ=sn rm 53. … … [*n=k*]
… … *nb tꜣ sḫm-spd pr m nwt*
h(*ꜣ*)*-snḏ.n=k*
54. … [*pꜣ*]*wtyw sni nbwt tꜣ n bꜣw* (5, 55) ⌜*=k hꜣ-snḏ*⌝
… *wr pr m gb nṯr-šps pr m nwt*
(6, 1) *hnw n=k nṯr nb sꜣṯw sp 4*
ḏd mdw in ḫry-ḥbt tnw sp nbt
šd ḥbt

TRANSLATION

37. Glorification spell,
which is made in the temple of Osiris, Foremost of the West(erners),
said by the lector (priest) and chi⌜ef⌝ 38. of this temple,
spoken in jubilation at every festival of the West.[A]
39. ⌜The god⌝ is in jubilation," Four times.
"making his festival,
which he sealed for Anubis, forever and ever.
(5, 40) … … … … you … Osiris.[B]
Words spoken by the lector priest:
41. "O, ⌜Osiris⌝, Foremost of the West(erners),
Those who recognize your splendor ⌜protect you⌝ …,
42. while the Great Gods provide your respect among the gods who are in the necropolis.
43. Anubis is, indeed, the Foremost of the West.[C]
O, Osiris, Foremost of the Westerners, Chief!
44. To you belongs the One whom Horus Stabbed.
King of Lower Egypt!
To you belongs the Stabbed One, Seth.[D]
⌜You⌝ have appeared (5, 45) as the king of Upper and Lower Egypt,
you have power over the Ennead, indeed,
(over) their *ka*s, indeed,[E]
46. (and over) their provisions, indeed.
O, Osiris, Foremost of the Westerners!
Yours are 47. those who are in the sky and the land.

Yours are those who are alive and dead.
Yours are those who are upon the 48. district of the necropolis.[F]
O, Osiris, Foremost of the Westerners.
May you be effective,
as 49. the horizon of the West is in jubilation.[G]
They praise your noble *ka*
so that you may awaken (5, 50) at the wall of truth, (with) the *m3styw*-divinities bowing.[H]
51. Hail to you by the gods of the Netherworld!
They praise (you) that they may venerate your mummy.[I]
52. Hail to you,
the gods have come." Twice.
"They mourn, ... cry 53. ... [is yours]
... ... lord of the land! Powerful and Effective One, who Came Forth from Nut!
Veneration is yours! [J]
54. ... [primeval beings] and the ladies prostrate themselves to your
(5, 55) might (in) ⸢veneration⸣.[K]
Great ... who Came Forth from Geb, Noble God,
One who Came Forth from Nut.[L]
(6, 1) Every god of the land rejoices for you." 4 times.
Words spoken by the lector priest on every occasion,
reciting the festival service book.[M]

TEXT NOTES

The first spell of *s3ḫw* III establishes Osiris as a victorious and transformed god. Accordingly, Seth is repeatedly referred to as the "Stabbed One" and as belonging to Osiris. The epithets of Osiris, such as "Powerful and Effective One" and "Noble God," among others, emphasize the triumph over his enemies, as well as his successful transformation. In this new state of existence, Osiris becomes the ruler of this world and the hereafter. The fact that "those who are upon the district of the necropolis" (*ḥry-tp sp3t-igrt*) belong to Osiris further accentuates his newly established role as the ruler of the Netherworld.[318] The statements of lines 5, 46–47 closely parallel a portion of the Ritual of the Glorification of Osiris in MMA 21, 10–11: *n=k imy pt t3 n=k imy nty mw n=k imy imwt=sn nb,* "Yours are those who are in the sky and the land. Yours are those who are in the water. Yours are all those who are among them." [319]

The *m3styw*-divinities bow down before Osiris and the still unnamed deceased associated with him. The bowing *m3styw* are a group of protective deities that appear most frequently in the CT. More specifically, these mysterious deities are depicted in the Book of the Two Ways as squatting, dangerous, animal-headed beings called *sšt3w ḥrw ʿnḫw m ʿmʿ3wt=sn,*

318 This statement resembles the Osirian epithet "Chief of the District of the Necropolis," known from the NK onwards; see Leitz et al., eds., *Lexikon* V, p. 399. For *igr* as an old form of *gr*, "necropolis, realm of the dead," see *Wb.* I 141, 4–5.

319 Goyon, *Imouthès*, p. 56.

"the ones whose faces are hidden; who live by means of their throw-sticks."[320] They are established by CT 1079, VII 351b–f as the guardians of Osiris, acquaintance with whom extended the protection upon the deceased: *ir mꜣstyw ipw in gb smn=sn m r-stꜣw m ḏr sꜣ=f wsir n snḏ sn=f stš im=f bs.n sw ir s nb r rḫ rn mꜣstyw ipw wnn=f ḥnꜥ wsir r nḥḥ n sk.n=f ḏt,* "As for the *mꜣstyw,* it is Geb who established them in Rosetau in the territory of his son, Osiris, for fear of his brother, Seth. He will not harm him! As for any man who knows the name of the *mꜣstyw,* he is the one who will exist with Osiris for eternity, and he will not perish."[321] Knowing the name of the *mꜣstyw* allowed the deceased to safely pass them in order to enter the hereafter. Such epithets of the *mꜣstyw* as *irw ꜥrrwt,* "Guardians of the Gates," and *wpwtyw nw ẖbt,* "Messengers of the Place of Execution," support this notion, further connecting these deities with the dangers of the Netherworld.[322] The destructive and protective aspects of the *mꜣstyw* are balanced as they are said to *ꜥnḫyw m mꜣꜥt rnpwt=sn rnpwt wsir NN,* "live in *maat,* as their years are the years of Osiris NN."[323]

5, 37–38

A Cf. the more abbreviated beginning of the introduction in BM 16, 1–2: *sꜣḫ ir ḥwt-nṯr nt wsir in ẖry-ḥbt ḥry-tp n ḥwt pn*. Note the masculine *pn* in place of the expected *tn* in BM 16, 2.

The context suggests reconstructing *ḥbt* of *ẖry-ḥbt,* "lector priest," in the lacuna. Cf. the full writing of the title in BM 16, 2: 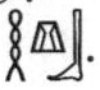.

The traces at the beginning of 5, 38 support a reconstruction of , *ḥr,* parallel to BM 16, 2. *ḥry-tp* likely acts as a substantive in the group *ẖry-ḥbt ḥry-tp* and should thus be translated as a separate title: "chief" or "magician."[324]

5, 38–40

B The phrase *hꜣ-snḏ* was used as the beginning of a praising formula in the MK and the verb "to revere" in the GR time.[325] 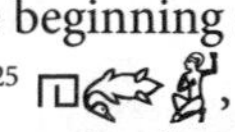, *hꜣ-snḏ,* "jubilation (with *hnw*-gesticulations),"[326] is a gesture that appears most often during the presentation of offerings and expresses a state of intense emotion from a divine presence, such as a pharaoh, a god, or the deceased.[327] Moreover, this group is also acknowledged as a GR spelling of *hy,*

---

320 CT 1073, VII 342a–b and CT 1184, VII 520a–b; see Lesko, *The Ancient Egyptian Book of Two Ways*, p. 81; Zandee, *Death as an Enemy*, p. 204.

321 Cf. Lesko, *The Ancient Egyptian Book of Two Ways*, p. 84.

322 CT 1081, VII, 354b and CT 45, I 196d, respectively.

323 BD 147; see Verhoeven, *Das Saitische Totenbuch der Iahtesnacht* II, p. 119, col. 111, 9–12. For further references, see Leitz et al., eds., *Lexikon* III, p. 238; *Wb.* II 32, 17–18.

324 Quaegebeur, in G. Dreyer, G. Fecht, and J. Osing, eds., *Form und Mass*, pp. 368–94.

325 *Wb.* II 471, 11–14.

326 Assmann, in S. Groll, ed., *Studies in Egyptology*, p. 12.

327 Assmann, *Images et rites*, p. 2; Darnell, *Enigmatic Netherworld Books of the Solar-Osirian Unity*, pp. 404–6, n. 148.

"cheers, jubilation," seemingly equivalent with *ḥꜣ-snḏ*.[328] Thus, while the exact transliteration of this group is uncertain, the expression of cheers and praises on the part of the lector priest is clear.[329]

Cf. *ỉr šsp=f* in BM 16, 5 in place of *ỉrt ḥb=f* in P.W551. Much of BM 16, 6–7 corresponding to the lacuna is also damaged, although is visible before a lacuna containing traces of presumably Osiris: .

The 3rd person singular masculine suffix pronoun of *ẖtm* refers to the god (*nṯr*).

5, 41–43

C The reading of *wsir* is supported by the remaining .

fꜣw appears in LP and GR texts as , replacing the typical determinative (Y1) with (F7), which is written on the following line.[330]

Cf. the slightly different BM 16, 9–11: *snḏ=k r ỉ.ḫtmw gmw fꜣw=k*.

Here, *ḫnty-ỉmntt,* "Foremost of the West," is used as an epithet of Anubis. This shortened form of the epithet frequently occurs in the present manuscript in reference to Osiris, although in these cases it is likely an abbreviation of *ḫnty-ỉmntyw*.[331]

5, 43–44

D While the text clearly addresses Osiris here, the title *ḥry-tp,* "chief" or "magician" is considerably more common for various other deities including Geb, Thoth and Amun.[332]

The scribe of BM 16 consistently writes without (D19).

The reading of the first , *n=k,* is questionable, due to the thickness of the upper sign. However, it is supported by the clear parallel further in this line and in BM 16, 13.

The term *wnp,* "to stab," commonly occurs in GR texts in regard to the destruction of the enemies of Horus, but may also be rendered as "victory, triumph."[333]

5, 44–45

E *sḫm* is a stative form mirroring *ḫꜥ*, which begins this thought in line 5, 44. Cf. a similar formula addressing Nut in PT 444 (§824): *mdw nwt ḫꜥ.n=ṯ(w) m bỉt n sḫm=ṯ(w) m nṯrw kꜣw=sn ỉsṯ ỉwꜥt=sn ỉsṯ dfꜣw=sn ỉsṯ ỉšwt=sn nbt ỉs nwt dd=ṯ sḏb=f/NN ꜥnḫ=f,* "Recitation. Nut, you have appeared as a bee, for you control the gods and their *ka*s as

328 Assmann, *ibid.*, p. 84; see also *Wb.* II 483, 1–13.

329 For further discussion of the term *ḥꜣ-snḏ*, see Hays, *GM* 204 (2005): 51–56.

330 *Wb.* I 575, 3–12. For a brief discussion of this term, see Wilson, *Ptolemaic Lexikon*, p. 388.

331 For the use of *ḫnty-ỉmntt* in reference to Anubis, see Leitz et al., eds., *Lexikon* V, pp. 783–86.

332 Leitz et al., eds., *Lexikon* V, p. 387; Quaegebeur, in G. Dreyer, G. Fecht, and J. Osing, eds., *Form und Mass*, pp. 368–94.

333 *Wb.* I 319, 3–5; Wilson, *Ptolemaic Lexikon*, p. 234.

well, and their inheritance as well, and their nourishment as well, and all their things as well. Nut, when you make him/NN revive, he will live."[334]

5, 47–48

F For an unexplained reason (M17), which belongs to *imy*, , of 5, 47 is written on 5, 46.

5, 48–49

G The two *ꜣḫ*-words of this couplet create a poetic play on sounds.[335] The diacritical following the second , *ꜣḫt*, indicates that the determinative of this word () is on the following line. The spelling of the term *ꜣḫt* in BM 16, 20, , supports this notion.

5, 49–50

H Cf. the first portion of this phrase in BM 16, 21: *ḥknw=sn n kꜣ=k šps ḥms=k pr=k*. The determinative (Aa2) of *šps*, , likely originates from the similar sounding GR form of , *špt*, "anger."[336]
The choice of the word *sꜣw*, "wall,"[337] must be due to the play on sounds that it creates with the preceding *rs=k r*, as well as the pun on *sꜣw*, "protection," evoking the shielding aspects of a wall.[338] Similarly, the play on the sounds of *mꜣst*, "knee," in the name of the *mꜣstyw* and the concept of bending or bowing, *m ksm*, are further examples of the poetic aspect of this text.

5, 51

I Cf. the latter part of this phrase in BM 16, 23–24: *nḏ ḥr=k in nṯrw ḳrtyw dwꜣ=sn k(w) snsn sꜥḥw=k*. The indicate plurality of *nṯrw*, , in BM 16, 23.[339]

5, 52–53

J Much of the lacuna may be reconstructed on the basis of BM 16, 26–27: *rm=sn n=k hꜣ-snḏ n=k nṯr pt tꜣ sḫm spd pr m nwt hꜣ-snḏ n=k*, "They cry for you, veneration is yours.

334 Allen, *The Ancient Egyptian Pyramid Texts*, p. 107.

335 See section 1.5.1, above.

336 *Wb.* IV 454, 1–12.

337 For *sꜣw*, "wall," often used for temple walls, see *Wb.* IV 14, 4–14; Wilson, *Ptolemaic Lexikon*, p. 789. For further discussion of punning, see section 1.5.1, above.

338 See section 1.5.1, above.

339 For *nṯrw ḳrtyw*, "gods in the Netherworld," see *Wb.* V 562, 10.

God of the sky and the land! Powerful and effective one, who Came Forth from Nut! Veneration is yours." The epithet *pr m nwt,* "He who Came Forth from Nut," is commonly used to designate Osiris.[340]

5, 54–55

K Cf. BM 16, 28–29: *nbwt pꜣwtyw sni nbwt tꜣ r bꜣw=k hꜣ-snḏ.*[341]

5, 55

L The sequence of epithets in this line clearly addresses Osiris. Cf. BM 16, 30: *sḫm wr pr m gb nṯr šps pr m nwt.*
The spelling of the name of Geb as appears as early as Dynasty 21.[342] Cf. the more typical in BM 16, 30.

6, 1

M There are two orthographic peculiarities in this clause:

1. *hn,* "to rejoice," is written as .[343]
2. The scribe repeats the determinative (G7) of *nb* twice, the first sign being a more elaborate falcon on a staff attested from Dynasty 25 onwards.[344]

---

340 Leitz et al., eds., *Lexikon* III, p. 65.

341 For the GR spelling of *pꜣwtyw*, , "primeval beings," paralleled by BM 16, 28, see *Wb.* I, 496, 10–15.

342 *Wb.* V 164, 6–11. For a discussion of this spelling, see Bedier, *Die Rolle des Gottes Geb*, pp. 163–64, who points to the phonetic similarity of *ḳ* and *g*, seen in non-literary texts as early as the NK. For the epithet of Osiris *pr-m-gb*, "He who Came Forth from Geb," see Leitz et al., eds., *Lexikon* III, p. 86.

343 Möller, *Hieratische Paläographie* III, p. 36, n. 1.

344 Möller, *Hieratische Paläographie* III, p. 188.

3.2.2. *s3ḫw* III, SPELL 2 — SPOKEN BY THE LECTOR PRIEST IN THE EVENING *Lines 6, 2–20*[345]

The end of this spell indicates that it is meant to be recited by the lector priest in the evening. This priest describes the process of Osiris' glorification. As the spell opens, various deities mourn the deceased Osiris. The Spirits of Pe welcome him into the Netherworld and express their grief over his death by "striking their flesh," "pulling their side-locks," and "beating their skins." Following the gods' mourning, prospective *sḏm=fs* balance Osiris' previous dismal condition with the hope for his resurrected and active state. His rejuvenation is emphasized with the epithet *wḥm-ʿnḫ,* "Repeater of Life,"[346] as the enemies of Osiris are overcome by Horus and the Oldest Daughter who is in Qedem. This spell provides the mythological context for the funeral, as Isis and Nephthys reassemble, guard, and glorify Osiris, while the four sons of Horus purify him and perform the Opening of the Mouth ritual.

TRANSLITERATION

2. *s3ḫ*
ḏd mdw in ḫry-ḥbt
wn ʿ3wy pt
sš ʿ3wy sb(3) n pḏt
mḫ3w nṯrw imyw 3. *p*
ii=sn n wsir ḫnty-imntyw
ḥr ḫrw rm n 3st sbḥt nbt-ḥwt
ḥr siw 3ḫty
4. *iptn nty wr pn*
pr m sb3
rwi n=k b3w p
ḥw=sn n=k iwf (6, 5)*=sn*
sk3=sn n=k ʿwyw=sn n ḫ(t)
nwn=sn n=k m sm3=sn n(!)
sḫ=sn n=k ḫr msk3wy=sn
i 6.*=sn ḏd=sn n=k*
wsir ḫnty-imntyw
šm=k ii=k
sḏr=k rs=k
mni=k ʿnḫ=k
7. *ʿḥʿ n=k m3=k ir n=k s3=k*
rs=k sḏm=k iry n=k ḥr
ḥw=f n=k ḥw=k(!) *tw m k3-k3w*
sm3.n=f 8. *n=k st m sm3w*

345 For further discussion see section 1.7.3, above.

346 Line 6, 11. This epithet identifies Osiris, among other gods, see Leitz, et al., eds., *Lexikon* II, p. 519. For the phrase *m wḥm-ʿnḫ*, "resurrection," see *Wb.* I 341, 6.

ḥw n=k s3t-wrt-imy-ḳdm
iꜥb.n=s ḳs n ẖft=k
wdn=s sw ẖr 9.*=k*
ẖft=f
w3=f m-ꜥ=k
im sfẖ=k im=f tm i3kb snty
m i3kb=sn ti m dd (6, 10) *wsir n s3=f ḥr*
dr.n=f dw r=f m fd=f hrw
šm.n=f irw r=f m ẖmnw=f hrw
11. *pr=k m wḥm-ꜥnẖ*
wꜥb=k m š ḳbḥw
ẖprw m wp-w3wt
sšm=k n s3=k ḥr
rdit=f n=k nṯrw 12. *ẖft=k*
snbw im=sn r=k
di=sn n=k ẖftyw=k ẖr=k
m rdi.n sw n=k ḏḥwty
nfr.wy m33
⌜*p*…⌝ 13. *.wy ptr m33 ḥr*
dit=f ꜥnẖ n it=f
3w=f w3s in wsir m-ẖnt nṯrw mntyw
wꜥb=k in 3st
14. *swꜥb=k in nbt-ḥwt snty=k-wr(ty)-ꜥ3(ty)=k*
3ẖ kw
s3 kw
di kw
s3ḳ iwf=k
ṯs (6, 15) *ꜥ(w)t=k*
wn st ẖꜥ irty m tp=k
m (m)sktt (m)ꜥnḏt
rdi n=k nṯr tm psḏt 16. *ẖr=k*
wṯs tw msw msw
imsty ḥpy dw3-mwt=f ḳbḥ-snw=f
iꜥi=sn n=k ḥr=k
17. *sk=sn n=k rmt=k*
wp=sn r=k m ḏbꜥw=sn ipw bi3t
pr=k iw nst tm
šm=k r sẖt 18. *i3rw*
šn m š šw pw ḥnꜥ tfnwt nṯrw(y)-ꜥ3w-m-pt
rs nṯr ꜥḥꜥ nṯr
3ẖ 19. *pwy nn pr m gb*
ẖrp-šps pr m nwt
ḏd ẖry(-ḥbt) nn m mšrw n rꜥ ḥtp=f (6, 20) *m ꜥnẖ*

TRANSLATION

2. Glorification spell.
Words spoken by the lector priest:
"The doors of heaven are opened,
the doors of the gate of heaven are opened.
Suffering are the gods who are in 3. Pe.[A]
They come to Osiris, Foremost of the Westerners,
at the sound of the cry of Isis (and) the shriek of Nephthys,[B]
at the complaints of these two *akh*s,
4. which are the(se) Great One(s),
who have come forth from the gate.[C]
The Spirits of Pe give way to you.
They strike for you their flesh.[D]
(6, 5) They raise for you their arms of the body,
they pull for you their side-locks,
they beat for you their skins,[E]
and they say, 6. they say to you:
'Osiris, Foremost of the Westerners![F]
You have gone and you will return,
you have slept and you will awaken,
you have died but you will live.[G]
7. Stand up that you may see what your son made for you.
May you awaken so that you may hear (about) what Horus did for you:[H]
He smote for you the one who smote you, as the Bull of Bulls,[I]
he slaughtered 8. them for you as wild bulls.'[J]
The Oldest Daughter who is in Qedem strikes for you.
She has gathered up the flesh of your enemy,[K]
she placed it under 9. you.
He (was) opposed,
his plan (being) against you.[L]
Do not let go of him that the two sisters may mourn no more.[M]
They mourn you as (6, 10) Osiris speaks to his son, Horus,
for he has removed evil from him on his four(th) day,
he has nullified that which was done against him on his eigh(th) day.[N]
11. You have come forth as the Repeater of Life.
You have been purified in the Lake of Cool Water,
having become as Wepwawet.[O]
You are guided by your son, Horus,
he having placed for you the gods 12. before you.[P]
Those who are against you are destroyed.
They placed for you your enemy under you,
Thoth having given him to you.[Q]

How beautiful is the si⌜ght⌝!
How … 13. to view the sight of Horus,
as he gives life to his father
and extends the *was*-scepter to Osiris before the Western gods.[R]
You are purified by Isis, [S]
14. you are made pure by Nephthys, your Two Great and Mighty Sisters,
who have glorified you,
who have guarded you,
who have placed you,
who have gathered your flesh,
who have raised up (6, 15) your members.[T]
Now indeed, the two eyes appear on your head,
namely the Night bark and the Day bark.[U]
The god, Atum, has placed for you the Ennead 16. under you.[V]
The children of (your) children raised you,
(namely), Imsety, Hapy, Duamutef, Kebehsenuef.
They wash your face for you, [W]
they 17. wipe your tears for you.
They open your mouth with their fingers of copper,
so that you may go forth toward the throne of Atum,
that you may travel to the Field 18. of Rushes.[X]
Those who row on the lake, it is Shu with Tefnut, the Two Great Gods in Heaven.
The god awakens, the god stands up.[Y]
It is this spirit 19. who Came Forth from Geb,
The Noble Leader, who Came Forth from Nut."
The lector (priest) says this in the evening, as Re is (6, 20) setting.[Z]

TEXT NOTES

The beginning of this spell describes the progression of Osiris through his transformation. As Osiris transforms inside the sky goddess, Nut, his rebirth may only take place when he has attained the new *3ḫ*-state of existence and is ready to be born. Thus, the image of the open doors of heaven literally depicts the deceased god's approach to being (re)born from his mother, Nut. [347] However, since the process of transformation is not yet complete, Osiris must be assisted by the mourning Isis and Nephthys, as well as the Spirits of Pe, among others.

The acts of self-injury by the Spirits of Pe express the suffering experience of mourning.[348] For instance, the term *nwn,* "to pull (of hair)," implies unkempt hair as a gesture that associ-

347 Billing, *Nut*, pp. 106–7.

348 Lines 6, 4–5. Meuli, *Gesammelte Schriften* I, pp. 347–48; Darnell, *Enigmatic Netherworld Books of the Solar-Osirian Unity*, pp. 183–84. Piccione, in E. Teeter and J. Larson, eds., *Gold of Praise*, pp. 340 and 346, interprets this as a funerary dance with sticks and a representation of ritualized fencing.

ates the mourner with "the chaos of death."[349] As the face is covered by hair, the inability to see places the mourner in a "state of obscurity," comparable to death.[350] Furthermore, the pulling of hair, which may be connected with vegetation, implies Nut's customary pose with her hair falling forward — all of which invoke the notion of rebirth.[351] Accordingly, the various terms for mourning and lamentation typically include the determinative (D3).[352] The lamenting Isis is described in P.Boulaq 6, recto VII, 6: *pꜣy=s ḳꜣs wꜣḥ m-bꜣḥ=st,* "Her hair lock remains before her."[353] Although this gesture is typically performed by women, the presumably masculine Spirits of Pe are supported in this act of mourning by the male deities of the Second Division of Caverns.[354]

The Spirits of Pe describe Horus' protection of Osiris, referred to with the epithet *kꜣ-kꜣw,* "Bull of Bulls."[355] Although various deities possess this epithet, its Osirian aspect is significant in this context. Accordingly, for instance, the east exterior wall at the temple of Medamud addresses Trajan as Osiris, the son of the sky goddess Nut: *ntk kꜣ-kꜣw ꜥšꜣ iwnw nḫt pḥw r nṯrw dmḏw iwꜥ rk nt pt …,* "You are the Bull of the Bulls, with numerous colors, mighty and strong more than the unified gods, the heir of the Sky(-goddess) indeed …."[356] The association of the regenerative qualities and fecundity of the bull with Osiris[357] becomes evident as the sounds of the fourth cavern of the Eighth Hour of the Amduat are characterized on certain LP sarcophagi[358] as *nim kꜣ-kꜣw,* "Bull of Bulls becoming pleased."[359] The cry of satisfaction of the Bull of Bulls appears to result from the Bull's sexual union with his consort, Hathor, the goddess of the eye of the sun, and her return in the new year, coinciding with the beginning of the inundation.[360] Furthermore, the Litany of Re associates the moment of pleasure experienced by the Bull of Bulls with the union of Re and Osiris: *ḫꜥ rꜥ*

349 Line 6, 5. See Manassa, *Late Egyptian Underworld*, p. 31, n. 123–24, who points to P.Bremner-Rhind 9, 21: *iꜣkbw=sn n=k m iꜣr(=sn) msbb tp,* "They mourn for you with (their) wigs, being disheveled of head," as well as the reference to the lamenting Isis and Nephthys as "they of the hair locks (*ḥnsktyw*)" in P.Bremner-Rhind 6, 23.

350 See also Valdesogo Martín, in Z. Hawass, ed., *Egyptology at the Dawn* II, pp. 548–50.

351 Valdesogo Martín, *ibid.*, pp. 551–53; Manassa, *Late Egyptian Underworld*, p. 31.

352 See, for instance: *gꜣs,* "to mourn," in *Wb.* V, 156, 1 and *iꜣkb,* "to lament," in *Wb.* I, 34, 9–12. For further references, see also Koenig, *Le Papyrus Boulaq 6*, pp. 78–79, and Desroches-Noblecourt, *BIFAO* 45 (1947): 219 and n. 4.

353 Koenig, *Le Papyrus Boulaq 6*, p. 76.

354 Manassa, *Late Egyptian Underworld*, p. 30, n. 122. For the depiction of the male deities in mourning in the second register, see Piankoff, *BIFAO* 42 (1944): pl. X.

355 Leitz et al., eds., *Lexikon* VII, p. 273; Manassa, in B. Rothöhler and A. Manisali, eds., *Mythos & Ritual*, p. 121.

356 Drioton, *Fouilles de Médamoud* III, 2, pp. 52–53, no. 120, 7.

357 For the *kꜣ-imntt*, "Bull of the West," see Leitz et al., eds., *Lexikon* VII, p. 251–52. For further references see Manassa, in B. Rothöhler and A. Manisali, eds., *Mythos & Ritual*, p. 121, n. 58.

358 Manassa, *Late Egyptian Underworld*, pp. 157–61, 256, and 262–63; Manassa, in B. Rothöhler and A. Manisali, eds., *Mythos & Ritual*, p. 122 and 133–34.

359 Manassa, in B. Rothöhler and A. Manisali, eds., *Mythos & Ritual*, pp. 113, 116–17, and 134, points out that the epithet Bull of Bulls designates Tatenen in the Amduat Cosmogony of the Eighth Hour of the Amduat.

360 Manassa, in B. Rothöhler and A. Manisali, eds., *Mythos & Ritual*, pp. 121–22.

m ḫnty dwꜣt nim rf kꜣ m knst ntk rꜥ ḥtp=k ẖꜣwt=k, "May Re appear as the foremost of the Underworld that the bull becomes pleased in Kenset. You are Re as you rest (upon) your corpses!"[361]

Osiris is similarly assisted by the enigmatic "Oldest Daughter who is in Qedem," who destroys his enemies.[362] Although this epithet occurs as early as the PT, the identification of the powerful goddess remains ambiguous. Nevertheless, the epithet itself, as well as the violent and protective role of the goddess in the present text, are comparable to certain aspects of the goddesses of the eye of the sun. The fact that this goddess is in Qedem, a distant eastern land, may connect her to the myth of the Wandering Eye. While various manifestations of the eye of the sun have the epithet Daughter of Re (*sꜣt rꜥ*), Sakhmet best fits the fierce and aggressive character of this goddess' actions. Sakhmet's more usual role in the security of Re grants her the responsibility of securing the solar aspect of Osiris as she fights Seth and his accomplices.[363] Similarly, Sakhmet's epithet, Daughter of Osiris (*sꜣt wsir*), unifies Re and Osiris under her protection.[364] Nevertheless, while the identification with Sakhmet is appropriate to the ferocious and protective nature of the Oldest Daughter who is in Qedem, the exact name of the owner of this epithet remains questionable. For instance, Bastet appears on *wadjet*-eye amulets as the goddess of the eye of the sun who protects the Eye of Horus.[365] Notably, Isis is another strong candidate for holding the title of the Oldest Daughter who is in Qedem, as she acts in place of the solar eye, destroying the enemies in the Seventh Hour of the Amduat.[366] Nonetheless, Hathor's role as the consort of the Bull of Bulls, in addition to her defense of Re and Osiris as the goddess of the eye of the sun in numerous texts, suggests that she is the goddess denoted by this epithet.[367]

Following the mourning of Osiris and the destruction of his enemies, the text alludes to the process of mummification. Osiris is purified and the Opening of the Mouth ritual is performed for him, while Horus executes his duties as the son and rightful heir. His act of "giving life" and "extending the *was*-scepter" to his father, Osiris, is an accurate description of the "Awakening of Osiris" scene, attested in various royal and private burial chambers

361 See Manassa, in B. Rothöhler and A. Manisali, eds., *Mythos & Ritual*, p. 122, who quotes Hornung, *Das Buch der Anbetung des Re im Westen* I, p. 157.

362 For the obscure epithet *sꜣt-wrt-imyt-ḳdm*, "Great Daughter who is in Qedem," see Leitz et al., eds., *Lexikon* VI, p. 103. For *ḳdm*, "Eastern land," see *Wb.* V 82, 1–2.

363 Germond, *Sekhmet et la protection du monde*, pp. 148–50.

364 Gauthier, *ASAE* 19 (1920): 186, n. 7, and 195. Germond, *Sekhmet et la protection du monde*, pp. 151–52 and 160–61, points to further examples of Sakhmet's protection of Osiris as well as Re.

365 See Darnell, *SAK* 24 (1997): 42–48, who points to the association of the goddesses of the solar eye with the rising of Sothis and the beginning of the new year.

366 Hornung, *Das Amduat*, p. 123, pl. Siebente Stunde; II, p. 123–34; Manassa, *Late Egyptian Underworld*, pp. 251–52, notes that several Osirian festivals were held simultaneously with the return of the goddess of the eye of the sun. See also Germond, *Sekhmet et la protection du monde*, pp. 148–61. For further discussion of the belligerent aspect of Isis and her identification with the eye of the sun and the uraeus from the NK onwards, see Münster, *Untersuchungen zur Göttin Isis*, pp. 109–10 and 198.

367 Hathor is referred to in Edfu by a similar epithet: *sꜣt-wrt-nt-nb-pt*, "Oldest Daughter of the Lord of the Sky," see Leitz et al., eds., *Lexikon* VI, p. 103.

and temples from the NK onwards. In this scene, Horus holds the *was*-scepter, while literally giving life to his dead father by presenting the *ankh*-symbol to his nostrils.[368]

Furthermore, the cyclical union of Re and Osiris plays a significant part in the transformation of the deceased god. The explicit connection of the two eyes of the god with the Night and Day barks invokes the solar-Osirian unity, as the two eyes in question are generally those of Re. These eyes are depicted in the middle register of the Second Hour of the Amduat: the Hathoric sistrum on the fourth bark represents the right, *3ḫt*-eye, associated with Hathor. The lunar crescent with a disc on the fifth bark, in turn, symbolizes the left, lunar eye.[369]

6, 2–3

A This line corresponds with the beginning of PT 670 (§§1972–86), var. 482 (§§1004b–10c).[370] Cf. PT §1004b: *wn n=k ʿ3wy pt isn n=k ʿ3wy pḏt,* and PT §1972: *wn ʿ3wy pt isn ʿ3wy pḏt.*

The presence of the 𓏛 determinative (Y1) in *sb(3)*, , points to a word play on *sb3,* "knowledge," implying that the specific knowledge required to pass into the afterlife has become available to the deceased Osiris as heaven's doors have been opened for him.[371] The opening of the celestial doors suggests that the deceased has completed the process of rejuvenation, having become an *akh.*[372]

This line contains some notable orthographic and comparative features with the parallel texts:

1. The spelling of *wn,* , corresponds with BM 17, 2 and PT §1004b in the pyramid of Pepi.
2. *ʿ3wy* is consistently spelled 𓉿 (O31) in PT §1004b.
3. The 𓅆 determinative (G7) of *pt,* , is not paralleled by the PT. Cf. the phonetic complement of *pt* in BM 17, 2: .
4. The spelling of *pḏt,* , is unusually short, as 𓇯 (N1) acts as a phonetic *p* and a determinative for the entire word.[373] Cf. in all versions of PT §1004b.

---

368 I am indebted to Colleen Manassa for calling attention to this notable parallel. See Willems, in J. Van Dijk, ed., *Essays on Ancient Egypt in Honour of Herman te Velde*, p. 359, nn. 57–58, who further points to the suggestion that this scene belongs to the hourly vigil of Osiris. For further references to the scene of "Awakening Osiris" in temples, as well as tombs, see Manassa, *Late Egyptian Underworld*, p. 149 and n. 392.

369 Hegenbarth, *SAK* 30 (2002): 182–84; Hornung, *Das Amduat* I, pl. Zweite Stunde; II, p. 51.

370 The translation of the subsequent spells is based on Allen, *The Ancient Egyptian Pyramid Texts*, pp. 266–67, and 130–31, respectively.

371 For *sb3*, "gate," more specifically "gate of heaven, necropolis, etc.," see *Wb.* IV 83, 9–17. For a discussion of the gate of heaven as an image of the bolt to an opened tomb, see Schott, *Mythe und Mythenbildung*, p. 47. For word play, see section 1.5.1, above.

372 Billing, *Nut*, pp. 106–7.

373 For *pḏt*, "expanse of heaven," see *Wb.* I 569, 2.

5. Cf. the phonetic spelling of *mẖ3w*, in PT §1004c and §1973a, with the variant in PT §1004c in the pyramid of Pepi.[374] The must originate in the word , *mẖ3w*, "corpse."[375]
6. *nṯrw* is written in BM 17, 2.
7. The presence of *ỉmyw*, , is paralleled in PT §1973a and PT §1004c from the pyramid of Neferkare.

6, 3

B The corresponding PT §1004d and §1973a do not give Osiris the typical epithet, *ḫnty-ỉmntyw*. The clause is paralleled only by PT §1973a–b: *ỉw=sn n wsỉr NN ḥr ḫrw rmm 3st ḥr sbḥt nbt-ḥwt*. Cf. PT §1004d: *ỉw=sn n wsỉr ḥr ḫrw sbḥ.n 3st ḥnꜥ nbt-ḥwt*.
Some orthographic discrepancies should be noted:

1. , *ỉỉ*, has no determinative, but the reading is supported by ( ) , *ỉw*, in PT §1004d, §1973a, and BM 17, 3.
2. *ḫrw*, , has phonetic complements in BM 17, 3.
3. *rm* is written in PT §1973b.

6, 3–4

C BM 17, 4 parallels P.W551, except for the genitive *nt* in place of *nty*. Cf. the corresponding PT §1973c–d: *ỉww 3ḫty ỉptwt n wr pn pr m dw3t*, "The wailing of those two *akhs* [for this Great One] who comes forth from the Duat."[376] PT §1973c uses the verb *ỉww*, "to wail," in place of *sỉw*, "to praise, complain."[377]
3ḫt, , begins on line 3. The and (D4 and D6) determinatives are unusual for this word and likely originate in *3ḫt*, "shining eye," commonly written with either of these determinatives.[378] Due to the Old Egyptian plural demonstrative *ỉptn* the translation follows the corresponding PT §1973c: , *3ḫty*, "two *akhs*."[379]
pr, , is written with a phonetic complement in PT §1973d. The deviation between *dw3t*, "Netherworld," and *sb3*, "gate," may stem from the use of the ☆ determinative (N14) in both words.[380] Notably, the ☆ determinative (N14) is not present in the PT parallel.

374 For the spelling of this word with (K4), see *Wb.* II 133, 4–5.
375 *Wb.* II 133, 7.
376 Allen, *The Ancient Egyptian Pyramid Texts*, p. 266.
377 *Wb.* I 18, 17–19 and *Wb.* IV 34, 3–5, respectively.
378 For *3ḫt*, "Shining Eye," said of various goddesses, see Leitz et al., eds., *Lexikon* I, p. 46.
379 Allen, *The Ancient Egyptian Pyramid Texts*, p. 266; Faulkner, *Ancient Egyptian Pyramid Texts*, p. 285. For *ỉptn*, "these," see *Wb.* I 70, 6.
380 For the epithet of various deities, including Osiris and Shu, *pr-m-dw3t*, "He who Came Forth from the Netherworld," see Leitz et al., eds., *Lexikon* III, p. 89.

6, 4

D Spirits of Pe are spelled without determinatives in both PT variants. , *rwi,* is understood in its intransitive sense "to move away, give way."[381] In contrast, Faulkner translates *rwi* as "to clash (sticks)." He points out that the same verb without an object is used for "clapping (hands)" in PT 676 (§2014a). Allen, in turn, offers the variation "to drum."[382] The determinative of *rwi,* , in both PT parallels likely originates in *rwi,* "to dance."[383]
The parallel of PT 482 omits this and the following phrases.

6, 4–5

e The 3rd person plural suffix pronoun of *i͗wf* is omitted from PT §1974b.
The principal translation of *sẖ,* , often written with the determinative (D46), is "to beat,"[384] but the term also carries the sense of "flailing (the arms in sadness)."[385] The significance of such expressions of lament for the process of glorification is supported by a passage from the Great Litany in the tomb of Ramses VI: *i͗ꜣkbyw nwn=sn ḥr=k ḥwi=sn n=k m ꜥwy=sn sbḥ=sn n=k hwt=sn n=k rmm=sn n=k ḥꜥꜥ bꜣ=k hwt=sn ꜣḫ ẖꜣt=k,* "The mourning ones toss their hair because of you and they flail for you with their arms, they cry out for you, and they scream for you, and they shed tears for you. That your *ba* rejoices, is when they scream and when your corpse becomes effective."[386]
Cf. the first clause with PT §1005b: *sẖ=sn n=k ꜥwy=sn* and PT §1974b: *sḳ=sn n=k ꜥwy=sn.*
n=k in the clause *nwn=sn n=k m smꜣ=sn* is paralleled only by PT §1005c of Neferkare and PT §1974c from the same pyramid.
Cf. the end of this line with PT §1974d of Neferkare and BM 17, 6: *sẖ=sn n=k mnwt=sn.*
The following orthographic peculiarities and discrepancies with the parallel texts should be noted:

1. *ꜥwyw* is spelled and in the variants of PT §1005b and in PT §1974b.
2. *nwn* is spelled ( ) in all PT variants.[387]

---

381 *Wb.* II 406, 2–15.

382 Allen, *The Ancient Egyptian Pyramid Texts,* p. 267. See also, Faulkner, *Ancient Egyptian Pyramid Texts,* p. 170, n. 2.

383 *Wb.* II 407, 7.

384 Line 6, 5. *Wb.* III 466, 13–467, 13.

385 Line 6, 5. *Wb.* III 48, 6.

386 Tomb of Ramses VI (KV 9), corridor G, register 1, scene 1, 223–24; see Darnell, *Enigmatic Netherworld Books of the Solar-Osirian Unity,* pp. 183–84 and nn. 89–90; Hornung, *Das Buch der Anbetung des Re im Westen* II, pp. 90 and 145–46.

387 *Wb.* II 222, 5.

3. *smꜣ* has phonetic complements in BM 17, 6: .[388]
4. The *n* of the 3rd person plural suffix pronoun of *sẖ* is written as in P.W551.
5. (Aa2) stands for the preposition *ẖr*.

6, 5–6

F Cf. the PT parallels §1975a and §1005d: *i.ḏd=sn n/irk wsir*. The *ỉ=sn* must originate from the Old Egyptian "to say."[389]
Note that the epithet *ḫnty-ỉmntyw* is again omitted from the PT. Cf. BM 17, 7: *ḏsr=k smꜣꜥ=sn n=k wsir ḫnty-ỉmntyw*.

6, 6

G While PT §1975b corresponds to this line, PT §1006 uses the *sḏm.n=f* form: *šm.n=k ỉw.n=k rs.n=k sḏr.n=k mn.ti ꜥnḫ*. This phrase is also found in CT 785, VI 414j–k: *šm.n=k ỉwt=k sḏr=k rs.n=k*; at this point the CT spell diverges from the present manuscript. This clause has some notable orthographic features:

1. The 3rd person plural suffix pronoun *sn,* following *ḏd,* is written .
2. The in , *sḏr,* must be a mistake.
3. The unusual determinative of *mnỉ,* , literally "to moor," suggests understanding this word as the verb "to die."[390]
4. The below the 2nd person singular suffix pronoun of , *ꜥnḫ=k,* is a phonetic complement for *ꜥḥꜥ*, , of the following line.

6, 7

H Cf. the slightly different PT §1007a–b: *ꜥḥꜥ mꜣ=k nn ꜥḥꜥ sḏm=k nn ỉr.n n=k sꜣ=k ỉr.n n=k ḥr*. PT §1976a–b presents a closer parallel: *ꜥḥꜥ mꜣꜣ=k ỉrt.n n=k sꜣ=k i.rs sḏm=k ỉrt.n n=k ḥr*. See also CT 761, VI 391c–d: *mꜣꜣ=k ỉrt.n n=k sꜣ=k ḥr sḏm=k ỉrt.n n=k ỉt=k gb*. The deeds of Geb, rather than Horus, are described here.
Some discrepancies with the parallel texts should be noted:

1. *ꜥḥꜥ* has the determinative (A21) here and in BM 17, 8.[391] The parallels of PT §1007a and §1976a spell the word phonetically: .
2. *ỉr* is spelled in BM 17, 8.
3. *sꜣ=k,* , lacks the determinative (G7) in both PT parallels.
4. *rs* is spelled in BM 17, 9.

388 *Wb.* IV 122, 1–6.
389 *Wb.* I 89, 8–9.
390 Allen, *The Ancient Egyptian Pyramid Texts*, p. 267, n. 44.
391 *Wb.* I 218.

5. *sḏm,* , has a superfluous , probably stemming from *nḏ,* , common to this text. See the more conventional spelling of *sḏm* in PT §1007a, §1976b, and BM 17, 9: .
6. The abbreviated (D4) stands for *iry* in BM 17, 9.
7. The PT versions omit the determinative (G7) for Horus, present in BM 17, 9.

I The plurality of the epithet in the present manuscript, , is not replicated in BM 17, 9: .
The after *ḥw* is a scribal mistake, as the following , *tw,* is the correct and expected dependent pronoun here. The version of PT §1007c from the pyramid of Neferkare corresponds to the grammar of this phrase the closest: *ḥw.n=f n=k ḥw ṯw*, but diverges in the latter part of the line: *ḳ3s.n=f n=k ḳ3s ṯw*. Cf. PT §1977a: *ḥw.n=f n=k ḥw ṯw m iḥw*. Cf. this phrase in BM 17, 9: *ḥw=k m k3*.

6, 7–8

J Cf. the longer PT §1977b–c: *sm3.n=f n=k sm3 ṯw m sm3 ḳ3s.n=f n=k ḳ3s ṯw*. This clause is also reminiscent of PT 580 (§1544a–b) from the pyramid of Pepi I: *ḥw.n=i n=k ḥw tw m iḥ sm3.n=i n=k sm3 tw m sm3,* "I have struck for you as an ox the one who struck you, I have killed for you as a wild bull the one who killed you." [392]
The determinative (T30) written between the bulls, *sm3w,* , is paralleled in BM 17, 10.

6, 8

K Cf. PT §1008a and §1977d: *d=f/.n=f sw ẖr s3t=f/k-wrt-imt-ḳdm*. Here the enemies are being placed beneath the Oldest Daughter who is in Qedem, rather than Osiris. The phonetic complement *m* is omitted from *ḳdm,* , in BM 17, 10.

6, 8–9

L The "enemy" opposed the correct order of inheritance, i.e., Horus' ascension to the throne of Osiris. The failed "plan" ( ) involved the murder of Osiris in order to rule on his throne.[393] Thus, the 3rd person singular masculine suffix pronoun of *ẖft* refers to the enemy, Seth, while the 2nd person singular masculine suffix pronoun in this line refers to Osiris.

392 Allen, *The Ancient Egyptian Pyramid Texts*, p. 185.
393 *Wb.* I 244, 12. For the reading of (V4) as the phonetic *w*, see Daumas, *Valeurs phonétiques* IV, p. 740. The determinative (F51) is unusual for this word, but paralleled in BM 17, 11.

6, 9

M The construction of this clause is interesting in its use of the suffix pronoun with the negatival complement *sfḫ*.[394]
The negative verb *tm* is in prospective form and is followed by *ỉ3kb*+dependent pronoun in the sense of "to mourn (someone)."[395] Note the poetic play on sounds of *ỉ3kb snty* and *ỉ3kb=sn ti*. Cf. PT §1009a–b of Merenre and Neferkare and PT §1978a: *tm m ỉ3kb ḥr itrty nṯrw*, "so that mourning over the Dual Shrines may end."
The following discrepancies with the parallels should be noted:

1. The spelling of *ỉ3kb* with  (D13) is paralleled by BM 17, 12.[396] Cf. *ỉ3kb*, , with the more common determinative  (D3) in both PT versions.
2. The *ti*, , following *ỉ3kb=sn* stands for the 2nd person singular dependent pronoun *ṯw*.

6, 9–10

N The 3rd person singular masculine suffix pronoun of *dr* refers to Horus.
Cf. the more poetic PT §1978b–d: *mdw wsir n ḥr fd.n=f ḏw ir NN m fdnw=f hrw ẖm.n=f i.irt ir=f m ḫmnt=f hrw*, "Osiris shall speak for Horus, because he has forcibly removed the bad (that was against the deceased king) on his fourth day and has annihilated what was done against him on his eighth day."[397] The PT version has *fd* instead of *dr*, creating a pun with the word *fdw*, "4," which was overlooked in this text.
The Spell for the Existence of a Man and what is in his House, CT 754, VI 383–84, parallels this passage.[398] Cf. CT VI 383 i–k: *mdw wsir n s3=f ḥr ẖm.n=f iryt r=f m hrw 8 fd.n=f fdt irtw iwf=f m hrw fdnw=f*, "Osiris speaks to his son Horus, for he has nullified what was done to him on his eighth day, he has removed the sweat which was on his flesh on his fourth day."
This clause of P.W551 has some notable orthographic features:

1. The name of Horus shows a late spelling in BM 17: .
2. *šm*, , should be understood as *ẖm*, "to demolish."[399]
3. A part of *hrw*, , is written on the following line.

394 Gardiner, *Egyptian Grammar*, §343, n. 5.

395 Wilson, *Ptolemaic Lexikon*, p. 35.

396 Wilson, *Ptolemaic Lexikon*, p. 35.

397 Allen, *The Ancient Egyptian Pyramid Texts*, p. 267, n. 45, suggests that the 4th and 8th days are a reference to mummification.

398 The translation of the subsequent spells is based on Faulkner, *Ancient Egyptian Coffin Texts* II, p. 288.

399 *Wb.* III 281, 1–4.

6, 11

O The rejuvenation of Osiris is stressed by the epithet *wḥm-ꜥnḫ,* "Repeater of Life."[400] The process of rejuvenation is described with a *sḏmw=f* passive form of *wꜥb* and stative *ḫprw,* "having become (Wepwawet)."
Cf. PT §1009c: *pr=k r=k ir pt ḫpr=k m wp-wꜣwt*; §1979a–b: *pr.n=k m š n ꜥnḫ wꜥb.ti m š n ḳbḥw ḫpr.ti m wp-wꜣwt*. Cf. CT VI 383l–m: *ii n=k ii.tw m š pn ꜥnḫ.ti wꜥb.ti m š ḳbḥy,* "Those who should come will come to you in the garden, for you are alive and cleansed in the pool of cold water."
This clause has three notable orthographic features and discrepancies with the parallel texts:

1. The two *t*s of *ḳbḥw,* , are likely influenced by the spelling of *imntt.*
2. *pr* lacks the determinative (D54) in BM 17, 14.
3. Wepwawet has a more elaborate spelling in PT §1009c and §1979b: . BM 17, 15 corresponds with P.W551.

6, 11–12

P Cf. PT §1010a: *sšm ṯw sꜣ=k ḥr m wꜣwt pt*; §1979b–c: *sšm ṯw sꜣ=k ḥr rdi.n=f n=k nṯrw*. Cf. CT VI 383n: *sšm ṯw sꜣ=k ḥr,* "your son Horus will guide you."
sšm should be read as a passive *sḏmw=f* paralleling the form of *wꜥb* in the above clause. However, the presence of the 2nd person singular dependent pronoun in all parallels points to a different interpretation of this text. This grammar allows Osiris to become the active guide of Horus after assuming the role of Wepwawet, thus: "You guide your son, Horus, having become Wepwawet." Another possibility is to understand *sšm* as a participle, with *k* standing for the 2nd person dependent pronoun:[401] "...Wepwawet, who guides you for your son Horus." Yet, these readings are questionable.
Cf. the last phrase in BM 17, 16: *rdi.n=f n=k nṯrw.*

6, 12

Q The Oldest Daughter who is in Qedem is indicated by the 3rd person plural suffix pronoun of *di,* as well as Thoth, whose name is written (G26) in PT §1979c.
There is a confusion in the number of enemies in this line. See the more consistent PT §1979c: *rdi.n=f n=k nṯrw ḫftyw=k in n=k sn ḏḥwty*. This phrase is omitted from PT 482 and CT 754.
The determinative (Y1) of the participle *snb,* , "to destroy," must originate from the common *snb,* "to be healthy."[402] The clause *snb im=sn r=k* is not included in PT 670. BM 17, 16 omits determinatives for *im,* .

---

400 This epithet identifies Osiris, among other gods; see Leitz et al., eds., *Lexikon* II, p. 519. For the phrase *m wḥm ꜥnḫ*, "repeating life, resurrection," see *Wb.* I 341, 6.

401 See line 1, 2 of the present manuscript.

402 *Wb.* III 458, 8–9 and *Wb.* IV 158, 2–159, 5, respectively.

6, 12–13

R The  following *nfr* and *ptr* should be understood as the exclamatory particle *wy*. For a reconstruction of the damage, see PT §1980a–c: *nfrw ꜣ mꜣꜣw ḥtpw ꜣ ptrw mꜣꜣw ḥr di=f ꜥnḫ n it=f* [*ꜣw=f*] *wꜣs n wsir m-ḫnt ntrw imntyw,* "How beautiful it is to see, how satisfying it is to see the sight of Horus giving life to his father [and extending] authority to Osiris, Foremost of the Westerners!"[403] CT VI 383o–q closely follows the PT version, adding an auditory aspect to Horus' actions: *nfrw ꜣ mꜣꜣ ḥtpw ꜣ sḏm mꜣꜣ ḥr ḥr ꜣwt wꜣs n it=f wsir,* "How beautiful is to see, how satisfying is to hear and to see Horus extending the *was*-scepter to his father, Osiris."[404] This phrase also occurs in *Stundenwachen* XIV and the Abydos ritual S 26.[405] BM 17, 17–18 alters the phrase slightly: *nfr.w(y) mꜣꜣ r pw ḫr mꜣꜣ ḥr dit=f ꜥnḫ ntr ꜣw r=f wꜣs n wsir m ḫnty-mntyw.*
Some orthographic features and discrepancies with the parallel texts should be noted:

1. The spelling of *n it=f,* , is very simplified here. Cf. the  determinative (G7) for *it,* , in PT §1980b.
2. The  determinative (D41) of *ꜣw,* , replaces the expected determinative (Y1) here.
3. *wꜣs* is spelled  in P.W551. Cf. the phonetic *wꜣs* in PT §1980b: .
4.  should be read as *imntyw,* "western," in parallel to PT §1980c, which spells .
5. Note the visual pun on  of *(i)mntyw,* , in this line and in the line above, with the spelling of Thoth: 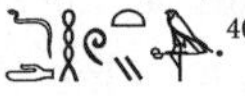.[406]

6, 13

S The causative *s* of *wꜥb* is omitted here. Cf. PT §1981a: *st st=k in ꜣst.* Cf. CT VI 384a: *stw sꜣt=k in ꜣst,* "Your libation is poured by Isis."
The unusual spelling of Isis, , with  (D4) points to the confusion between her name and that of Osiris. The reading is supported by the more typical spelling of Isis in all the parallels.

6, 14–15

T Isis and Nephthys, who are responsible for much of the actions necessary for Osiris' rebirth, are referred to by the epithet *snty-wrty-ꜥꜣty,* "Two Great and Mighty Sisters,"

403 Cf. Allen, *The Ancient Egyptian Pyramid Texts*, p. 267.

404 Cf. the translation of Faulkner, *Ancient Egyptian Coffin Texts* II, p. 288: "How happy are those who see, how content are those who hear, when Horus is seen extending the *wꜣs*-staff to his father Osiris."

405 Junker, *Stundenwachen*, p. 81.

406 For puns, see section 1.5.1, above.

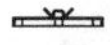

found also in CT 693, VI 325 o.[407] The group  following *wr* creates a common writing of *iw,* "to go," which makes no sense here and must be a mistake of the scribe. Cf. the more typical short spelling of *wr*(*ty*) in BM 17, 19: . The group  following *ꜥꜣ* should likely be understood as the 2nd person singular suffix pronoun, reinforcing the possessive *k* of *snty,* "sisters." This notion is supported by the abbreviated spelling of *ꜥꜣ*(*ty*) and the presence of *k* following *wr,* , and *ꜥꜣ,* , in BM 17, 19.
The verbs *ꜣḫ, sꜣ, di, sḳ,* and *ṯs* are perfect participles. *ꜣḫ kw sꜣ kw* are made obscure by their abbreviated forms.[408] The expected causative *s* of *ꜣḫ* is omitted here, as well as in the previous line.
PT §1981a–b omits the clause *ꜣḫ kw sꜣ kw di kw: wꜥb.n ṯw nbt-ḥwt snty-wrti-ꜥꜣti sꜣḳ ti iwf=k.* Cf. CT VI 384b–e: *wꜥb ṯw nbt-ḥwt snty=k wrty ḥkꜣw ṯs.ti ḳsw=k inḳ.ti n=k ꜥwt=k,* "Nephthys cleanses you, (even) your two sisters, great of magic. Your bones are knit together for you, your members are collected for you."
Cf. the end of this phrase in BM 17, 19: *sbḳ iwf=k. iwf,* , has the more typical  determinative (F51) in PT §1981b.

6, 15

u Cf. PT §§1981c–82a: *ṯs.ti ꜥwt=k i.sḫꜥ.ti irty=k m tp=k msktt ꜥnḏt,* "(sisters) who have collected your flesh, raised your limbs, and made your eye appear in your head: the Nightboat and the Dayboat." Cf. also BM 17, 20: *ṯs ꜥt=k wnn ḫꜥ irty m tp=k msktt ꜥnḏt.* Different phrasing is used to express a parallel subject in CT VI 384f–g: *rdit n=k irty=k m ḫnt=k msktt ꜥnḏt,* "Your eyes are set in your face for you (by) the Night-bark and the Day-bark." The CT spell ends here.
The  before *msktt* must be serving a dual purpose: that of the *m* of predication and as a phonetic complement for *msktt,* . The initial *m* is omitted from *mꜥnḏt,* , as well. Note the hieroglyphic-like  determinatives (P1) for both *msktt* and *mꜥnḏt,* while in BM 19, 20 the determinatives are more typically hieratic. Cf. the more extended phonetic spelling of these boats in PT §1982a:  and .

6, 15–16

v *rdi* is a participle. Cf. PT §1982b: *rd n=k tm ir.n n=k psḏty,* "Atum has given to you, the Dual Ennead has acted for you." BM 17, 21 omits *nṯr* before *tm* as well.
psḏt is spelled 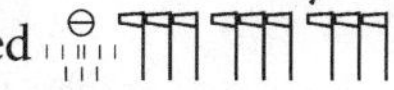 in P.W551[409] and  in BM 17, 21. However, the PT parallel has 18 *nṯr* signs representing the "Dual Ennead."

407 Leitz, et al., eds., *Lexikon* VI, p. 377. Note the variant translation of Allen, *The Ancient Egyptian Pyramid Texts,* p. 267, of *snty-wrty-ꜥꜣty* in the corresponding PT: "your [two] elder and great [sisters]."
408 For *sꜣ,* "to guard," see *Wb.* III 416, which gives only one example of its spelling with (G39).
409 Möller, *Hieratische Paläographie* III, p. 62.

6, 16

w Cf. PT §1983a–c: *ṯs.n ṯw msw msw=k twt ḥp imsti dwꜣ-mwt=f ḳbḥ-snw=f irw.n=k rnw=sn m twt*. This clause in BM 17, 21 corresponds to P.W551, except for the 2nd person singular suffix pronoun following the second *msw*.

The reading of is supported by the phonetic complements for *iꜥi* in PT §1983d: . Otherwise, this group may also be read *ḏsr*, "to purify," or *ḫwi*, "to protect." Cf. the end of this phrase in BM 17, 22: *iꜥi=sn ḥr=k*[410] and in PT §1983d: *iꜥi ḥr=k*.

There are some notable orthographic features and discrepancies with the parallel texts:

1. Imsety is spelled here.[411] Cf. the more typical spelling of Imsety in BM 17, 21: .
2. Cf. the more common phonetic spelling of the names of the four sons of Horus in PT §1983b: .
3. The at the end of this line serves as a phonetic complement for *sk*, , of the following line.

6, 17–18

x *pr* is a prospective *sḏm=f*. Cf. PT §§1983d–84a: *iꜥḥw rmt=k wpw r=k m ḏbꜥw=sn biꜣw prr=k pr=k r wsḫt tm*, "dried your tears, and opened your mouth with their copper fingers. When you go forth you shall go forth to Atum's broadhall."

The term *biꜣt*, "copper," frequently occurs in connection with the tool used in the OM ceremony.[412]

Some discrepancies with the parallel texts should be noted:

1. *rmt* is spelled phonetically in PT §1983d: and BM 17, 22: .
2. PT §1983e has a more elaborate spelling of *wp*: .
3. *ḏbꜥw* is spelled phonetically in PT §1983e: .
4. *nst*, , has no phonetic complements in BM 17, 23.
5. The of *sḫt*, , are written on the following line.

6, 18

y Cf. the longer PT §§1984b–85c: *šm=k ir sḫt iꜣrw ḫns=k swt nṯr ꜥꜣ rdi n=k pt rdi n=k tꜣ rdi n=k sḫt iꜣrw in nṯrw ꜥꜣw ḫnn ṯw šw ḥnꜥ tfnt nṯrwy ꜥꜣwy iwnw*, "Go to the Marsh of Reeds, and course the Great God's places, for you have been given the sky, you have been given the earth, you have been given the Marsh of Reeds (by) the two Great Gods who row you: Shu and Tefnut, the two Great Gods in Heliopolis."

---

410 For *iꜥi*, "to wash," see *Wb.* I 39, 5–6.

411 Leitz et al., eds., *Lexikon* I, p. 367.

412 *Wb.* I 436, 2. For a discussion of the fingers of *biꜣ* in the OM ceremony, see Roth, *JEA* 79 (1993): 57 and 66.

The epithet *nṯrwy-ꜥ3wy-nw-pt,* "Two Great Gods in Heaven," is generally attributed to Nut and Orion.[413] The better-attested *nṯrwy-ꜥ3wy-iwnw,* which refers to Shu and Tefnut, is used in the PT parallel.[414]  stands for the participle of *ẖnn,* "to row." [415]
Some orthographic discrepancies with the parallels should be noted:

1. PT §1984b uses the more common determinative (M2) for *i3rw,* , while BM 17, 24 has 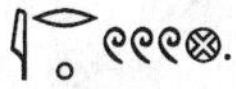.
2. Shu and Tefnut do not show  determinatives (G7) in PT §1985c and BM 17, 24.
3. PT §1985c and BM 17, 24 have the more accurate *nṯrwy,* , in place of *nṯrw,* 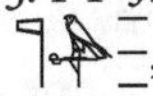, in P.W551.
4. *rs* is written with phonetic complements in PT §1986a: 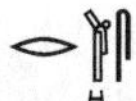 and BM 17, 25: .
5. *ꜥḥꜥ* is spelled  here.[416] Cf. the more common spelling 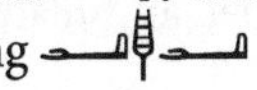 in PT §1986a.

6, 19–20

z This line refers to Osiris, the son of Geb (spelled ) and Nut. Cf. the more elaborate PT §1986b: *n 3ḫ pn pr m dw3t wsir NN pr m gb.*
The phrase *ḥtp m ꜥnḫ* is understood here as an idiom for "to set (of the sun), to descend (of one's death)." [417] Cf. BM 17, 26: *ḏdw ẖry-(ḥbt) m mšrw rꜥ ḥtp=f m ꜥnḫtt.*
There are two notable discrepancies with the parallels:

1. *ẖry-(ḥbt)* is spelled 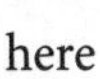 here and in BM 17, 26.
2. Cf. 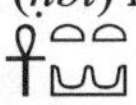 for *ꜥnḫt* in BM 17, 26.

413 Leitz et al., eds., *Lexikon* IV, p. 448.
414 Leitz et al., eds., *Lexikon* IV, p. 448.
415 *Wb.* III 383, 3–9.
416 *Wb.* I 218, 3–5.
417 *Wb.* I 200, 2–3.

3.2.3. *sꜣḫw* III, SPELL 3 — SPOKEN BY THE LECTOR PRIEST

Lines 6, 20–30 [418]

Much like the previous spells, this one is meant to be recited by the lector priest, although the text offers no further instructions regarding the time and place of the recitations. The initial line of this spell provides the first occurrence of the name of the original owner of the present manuscript, Padikakem. Cyclical rebirth is wished upon the deceased Osiris of Padikakem, so that he may be as effective as the living and the dead. Having been equated with Osiris, the deceased is reassembled by his father and son, Geb and Horus, and joined by his *ka*. Osiris is then invited to exist through his heir. The conclusion of the spell implies that after the murder of Osiris and revenge by Horus, this ordeal is over, and the deceased is again complete and ready to be accepted among the gods.

TRANSLITERATION

sꜣḫ
ḏd mdw ỉn ẖry-ḥbt
hy wsỉr ḫnty-ỉmntyw wsỉr n Pꜣ-dỉt-kꜣ-km
21. *ms tỉ mwt=k m hrw pn ẖrt rnpt*
rs ỉr=k ỉry.tw rḫ tỉ ḫm kw
swḏꜣ.n kw gb 22. *ḫnty-psḏt-ꜥꜣt*
ṯs=f n=k tp=k r ḳsw=k
… ⸢*ḏd*⸣*=f* … … *m* ꜥ⸢*nḫw*⸣
23. ⸢… *m*⸣ [*hr*]*w* ⸢*p*⸣*n*
ḥtp ⸢*n*⸣*=k gb*
rdỉt=f n=k tp=k
s(ꜣ)*ḳ*⸢*=f n*⸣*=k ỉwf=k*
ḥtp n=k ḥr
rdỉ=f n=k 24. *tp=k*
sḳ=f n=k ꜥt=k
wn=kw(!)
šsp n=k sw kꜣ n nṯr=k
nn bṯ kꜣ=k nṯr=k
ḥtp (6, 25) *n=k kꜣ=k*
ḥtp n=k ntr=k
kꜣ=k m-bꜣḥ=k
nṯr=k m-ḫt=k
šsp n=k tp=k
ḏd mdw sp 4
26. *sꜣḫ*

418 See section 1.7.3, above.

ḏd mdw ꞽn ẖry-(ḥ)b(t)

ꜥnḫ=k ḫr ḥr

wsꞽr ḫnty-ꞽmntyw wsꞽr n Pꜣ-dꞽt-kꜣ-km

27. *ms tw mwt=k m hrw pn*

ꜥḫn.n=k ꞽrty=k ẖnw-ꜥwy=k m-ẖnw-ꜥwy=k

ꞽr.n=k ꞽw ꞽry r=k

28. *ꞽry.tw rḫ.tw ḫm.tw*

swꜣḏ.n tw gb ḫnty-psḏt-ꜥꜣt

rdꞽt=f n=k tp=k 29. *r ḳsw=k*

ḥtp n=k gb

rdꞽt=f n=k tp=k

sšm=f …

[ḥt]p n=k ḥr

rdꞽt=f n=k tp=k

⸢šsp⸣ (6, 30) *n=k sw kꜣ=k nṯr=k*

m bṯ tw

ḥtp n=k kꜣ=k

ḥtp n=k nṯr=k m ⸢hrw⸣ pn

TRANSLATION

Glorification spell.

Words spoken by the lector priest:

"O, Osiris, Foremost of the Westerners, Osiris of Padikakem.

21. Your mother bears you on this day, yearly.

Awaken, that you may do that which those who know you and those who are ignorant of you did.

Geb, Foremost of the Great Ennead, has caused that you be healthy.

22. He raised for you your head on your bones (i.e., skeleton),

… he ⸢said⸣ … … among the l⸢iving⸣ [A]

23. … ⸢th⸣is [da]y.

May Geb be gracious ⸢to⸣ you,

as he gives to you your head,

and he assembles for you your limbs.

May Horus be gracious to you, [B]

as he gives to you 24. your head,

and he raises for you your limbs

(so that) you may exist. [C]

The *ka* of your god seizes it for you.

The *ka* of your god will not leave.

May (6, 25) your *ka* be gracious to you! [D]

May your god be gracious to you!

Your *ka* is before you,
your god is behind you,
your head is held for you." E

Words spoken four times.
26. Glorification spell.
Words spoken by the lector priest:
"May you live through Horus!
Osiris, Foremost of the Westerners, Osiris of Padikakem.
27. Your mother bears you on this day.
You shut your eyes, embracing with your embrace.
You act against the one who acted against you.F
28. What is known, and what is not known is done.
Geb, Foremost of the Great Ennead, has caused that you be healthy.
He placed for you your head 29. on your bones.G
May Geb be gracious to you!
He gave to you your head,
as he guided ...
May Horus [be grac]ious to you!
He gave to you your head, H
(and) (6, 30) the *ka* of your god ⸢accepted⸣ it for you
as that which left you.
May your *ka* be gracious to you!
May your god be gracious to you on this ⸢day⸣!" I

TEXT NOTES

The cyclical nature of this spell is exemplified by the statement of the annual (*ẖrt rnpt*) birth of Osiris.[419] The phrase "Your mother bears you on this day" in the middle of the spell points to the more specific event in linear time. In other words, Osiris' birth and rejuvenation are represented through the yearly ritual, as well as at each point when this spell may come into reality.

The wish for Osiris' action reflects the all-encompassing character of this transformed god, as the epithet "those who know you" is understood in reference to the inhabitants of the Netherworld, i.e., the gods and the dead, while "those who do not know" Osiris are the living. Subsequently, this expresses the notion that Osiris and the glorified deceased associated with him will be as effective as the living and the blessed dead.

Osiris benefits from the reconstructive and protective acts of deities, such as Horus and Geb. Among these, "your god" likely signifies Osiris, with whom the deceased Padikakem is identified. In this sense, Osiris performs a dual role of the first king, who has been resurrected and upon whom all mortuary rituals are modeled, and of the ultimate Netherworldly judge. Thus, the wish that "your god be gracious to you (=Padikakem)" establishes Osiris in his place as the king of the Netherworld, responsible for deciding the fate of the deceased.

---

419 *Wb.* III 391, 18–21; Wilson, *Ptolemaic Lexikon*, p. 775.

6, 20–22

A This spell is paralleled by scene 55A of the OM[420] and the Ptolemaic coffin of Ankhhophi, 2–12.[421]

ḫnty-psḏt-ꜥꜣt, "Foremost of the Great Ennead," is a common epithet of Geb, as well as Osiris and Atum.[422]

Cf. the very different interpretation of a similar OM formula, scene 55A, b–e: *hꜣ NN ms tw n mwt=k m hrw pn ir.n=k rḫ.ti ḫm.ti swḏꜣ tw gb ḫnty-ḫt-tpy-n-psḏt-ꜥꜣt ṯs=f n=k tp=k r ḳsw=k ḏd=f n=k sḏm psḏt ꜥꜣt imyw ꜥnḫw,* "O NN, your mother bore you on this day. You have done what is known and what is ignored. Geb, Foremost of the First Body of the Great Ennead, has caused that you be healthy. He raised for you your head on your bones so that what he said to you is heard. The great Ennead is among the living."[423]

The Ankhhophi, 2–4 records a parallel but slightly abbreviated text: *ms.n tw… pn pr nfr ir=k ir.tw rḫw ḫmw tw sw[ḏꜣ] … ḫnty-ḫt-n-psḏt-ꜥꜣt im ꜥnḫ,* "… bears you … this good (?) … may you do that which those who know you and those who are ignorant of you did. … the Foremost of the Body of the Great Ennead has caused that [you be hea]lthy among the living."

Despite the distinctive pronouns, a possible reconstruction may be based on BM 18, 3–9: *ms tw mwt=k m hrw pn ḫrt rnpt iry=k ir kw rḫ tw ḫm k(w) swꜣḏ.n kw gb ṯs=f n=k tp=k r ḳsw=k ḏd=f n=k sḏm psḏt ꜥꜣt im ꜥnḫw.*

The following peculiarities and discrepancies with the parallel texts should be noted:

1.  following *ms* stands for the 2nd person singular dependent pronoun *tw*.
2. *psḏt* is written 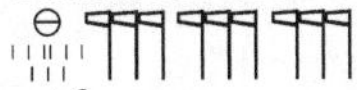 in P.W551, while BM 18, 6 again has .
3. BM 18, 7 has the  determinative (A24) for *ṯs,* 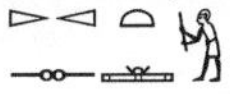.

6, 23

B Ankhhophi, 4–5 is very similar to the present manuscript, replacing *iwf* with *ꜥwt,* "members." Cf. also OM 55A, e, from which Geb is omitted: *rdi=f n=k tp=k sḳ=f n=k ḥꜥw=k ḥtp n=k ḥr,* "He gives to you your head, he assembles for you your members. May Horus be gracious to you."[424] Notably, Horus is mentioned in texts 4 and 6 of OM only.

---

420 The transliteration and translation of the subsequent spells of scene 55A of the OM is based on Otto, *Mundöffnungsritual* I, pp. 139–42; *ibid.*, II pp. 124–26.

421 The transliteration and translation of the subsequent spells on the coffin of Ankhhophi (CG 29311) is based on Maspero, *Sarcophages des époques persane et ptolémaïque*, p. 59.

422 Leitz et al., eds., *Lexikon* V, p. 814.

423 *imyw ꜥnḫw* occurs only in text 6. Cf. Otto, *Mundöffnungsritual* I, pp. 139–40; II p. 124, who reads *ḫm.ti* as a participle: "O, N! Geboren hat dich deine Mutter an diesem Tage. Du bist gemacht als ein Wissender dessen, was nicht gewusst wird. Es hat dich unversehrt gemacht Geb." Otto, *ibid.*, II, p. 125, n. 2, also offers an alternate translation of this phrase: "Das, was du tust, ist das Bekannte; das was du tust, ist das Unbekannte."

424 *ḥꜥw* is replaced with *iwf* and *ꜥwt* in texts 6 and 7, respectively.

Cf. variation of *sḏm.n=f* forms in BM 18, 9–11: *ḥtp n=k gb rdi.n=f n=k tp=k sḳ=f n=k iwf=k ḥtp n=k ḥr rdi.n=f n=k tp=k.*
The following peculiarities and discrepancies with the parallel texts should be noted:

1. *ḥtp* shows an abbreviated spelling, , in BM 18, 9.
2. *s3ḳ* is written (I3), and the name of Horus, , omits the determinative (G7) in Ankhhophi, 5.
3. , usually read *iwꜥt,* "inheritance,"[425] does not make much sense here. The reading *iwf* is supported by the phonetic complements in BM 18, 11: and OM 55A, e: .

6, 24

C The following peculiarities and discrepancies with the parallel texts should be noted:

1. The prospective form of *wn=k* has a superfluous *w*, , following the 2nd person singular suffix pronoun.
2. The 3rd person singular dependent pronoun following *šsp.n=k* refers to *tp,* "head," i.e., "the *ka* of your god seizes your head."
3. *šsp,* , does not have determinatives in BM 18, 13.
4. *ꜥt=k* is replaced by *ḥꜥw=k* in the parallel OM 55A, f, which otherwise corresponds to the present manuscript.

6, 24–25

D Only a horizontal line is visible below the first *k3,* , which may be read as the genitival *n* or the 2nd person singular suffix pronoun *k*. OM 55A, g–h, awkwardly uses first person pronouns: *šsp n=t sw k3 nṯr m bṯ=i ḥtp n=t k3=i ḥtp n=t nṯr=i,* "My *ka* of my god seizes it for you, lest I leave. May my *ka* be gracious to you! May my god be gracious to you!"
See also Ankhhophi, 5–6: *šsp… nṯr=k m bṯ=k ḥtp n=k k3=k ḥtp n=k nṯr*[*=k*], "… of your god seizes … …. You will not leave. May your *ka* be gracious to you! May [your] god be gracious to you!" Cf. BM 18, 13–14: *sšp n=k sw k3=k nṯr=k ḥtp n=k k3=k.*

6, 25

E Cf. the variation in OM 55A, i: *šsp n=k tp=k sp 4,* "Your head is held for you, four times." The remaining traces of Ankhhophi, 7 closely correspond to P.W551.
Some orthographic discrepancies with the parallels should be noted:

1. *ḫt* shows a very abbreviated spelling in BM 18, 16: .
2. *šsp,* , again lacks phonetic complements in BM 18, 16.
3. *tp,* , lacks the determinative (F51) in BM 18, 16.

425 *Wb.* I 51, 1–7.

6, 26–27

F While the first portion of this statement parallels the corresponding lines of OM 55A and the remaining signs on the coffin of Ankhhopi, the latter statements differ considerably. Text 4 of OM 55A, k–m differs from P.W551: *ʿnẖ=k ḥr ḥr ms tỉ n mwt=k m hrw pn ỉrt st ỉrty=k ẖnw-ʿwy ḏs=k ẖn-ʿwy*..., "May you live through Horus! You are borne by your mother on this day. She makes your eyes, embracing yourself." Text 7 of OM 55A, k–l, is closer to the present manuscript, although it seems to be somewhat corrupted: *ʿẖn.n=s ỉrty ẖnw-ʿwy(?) ỉwʿ n ḏs=s ỉr.n=t ỉr r=t.* Ankhhophi, 7–9 similarly ascribes the action of shutting the eyes to the mother: *ʿnẖ=k ḥr ...=k m hrw pn ʿẖn.n=s ỉrty=k ẖnw-ʿwy=k n=f ...n=k r ỉr ỉr=k*, "May you live through ...! Your ... ... this day. She shuts your eyes, embracing him... You ... against the one who acted against you." The remaining traces of BM 19, 6–8 correspond more closely to P.W551: ... *ỉrty=k m-ẖnw-ʿwy=k ỉr.n=k r ỉỉ n=k.*

The phrase *ẖnw-ʿwy=k m-ẖnw-ʿwy=k* likely refers to the common embracing position of the arms on an embalmed body, as well as the mythological notion of Osirian rebirth inside (the embrace of) his mother, Nut.

6, 28–29

G The suffix *tw,* following *ỉr, rẖ,* and *ẖm* points to the passive use of these verbs.

Cf. the dependent pronoun in the same phrase in line 21 of this column: *swꜣḏ.n kw gb ẖnty-psḏt-ʿꜣt.*

OM 55A, m–o closely corresponds but again alters Geb's title and substitutes *ṯs* in place of *rdỉ* in the last clause, as does Ankhhophi 9–10, amending *ṯs =f* in place of *rdỉt=f* and the preposition *r* with *ỉw*. BM 19 parallels this line except for the *sḏm.n=f* form of *rdỉ,* the lack of determinatives for *swꜣḏ,* , and the consistent spelling of Geb as  in BM 19, 9–10. Cf. line 22 of this column: *ṯs=f n=k tp=k r ḳsw=k,* "He (=Geb) raised for you your head on your bones."

6, 29

H OM 55A, p–q again replaces *rdỉ* with *ṯs* in both instances.

A 2nd person singular dependent pronoun and the initial sign of *ḥtp,* 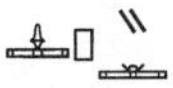, were likely in the break, see BM 19, 13–17: *ḥtp n=k gb rdỉ.n=f n=k tp=k sšm.n=f tw ḥtp n=k ḥr rdỉt.n=f n=k tp=k.*

6, 30

I The 2nd person dependent pronoun *tw* following the participle *bṯ* refers to the head of Osiris, which was severed by Seth.

Cf. the different interpretation and 3rd person perspective of text 4 of OM 55A, r–s: *šsp n=k sw kꜣ n NN m bw ỉṯt sw nṯr=f m bw ỉṯt sw ḥtp n=f nṯr=f m hrw pn,* "The *ka* of NN accepted it for you in the place (where) his god seized it, in the place of seizing it.

May his god be gracious to him on this day!" The remaining traces of OM text 7 and Ankhhophi, 11–12 correspond to P.W551.
The ⊙| in BM 19, 20 supports the reading of the damaged portion of this line as *hrw*, "day." The phrase "on this day" begins and ends this spell.

3.2.4. *sꜣḫw* III, SPELL 4 — SPOKEN BY THE LECTOR PRIEST

Lines 6, 31–39 [426]

This spell, again recited by a lector priest, addresses Osiris with the common epithet *sꜣ-nwt*, "Son of Nut,"[427] underscoring his relationship with the sky goddess. As offerings are promised to the deceased, the connection of Osiris and Re is emphasized. In this context, the unification of the rejuvenated Osiris with Re relates to the necessity of provisions at this stage of resurrection. The text corresponds with the CT spell "The Beautiful West is Joyful at Meeting the Man."[428]

TRANSLITERATION

31. *sꜣḫ*
ḏd mdw [in] ẖry-ḥ(bt)
ꜥnḫ(=ỉ) ⸢r=k⸣ sꜣ nwt
pḥ=k rꜥ ỉsk nṯrw m-ẖnw [ỉꜣkb] 32.*=sn*
⸢smꜣ⸣ šꜥd m wsḫt
pḥ=k nwt
mꜣ=k [šs]tꜣw
šd=k šw
p⸢ḏ …⸣
33. *mꜣ wrrt ḏr ꜣḫt*
ỉw n=k ḥw ḏr nwt hrw pw⸢y …⸣ spḥw ngꜣw
st ỉmnt 34. *m ḥꜥꜥ*
mꜣꜣ=sn ḥꜥwt nṯr
nḏ ḥr=k … …
dỉ=tn n wsỉr ḫnty-(6, 35) *ỉmntyw wsỉr n Pꜣ-dỉt-kꜣ-km ḥb*
p⸢sš⸣=ṯn ⸢n⸣=f ⸢sḫt⸣
ḥtpw ỉmꜣ 36.*=tn n wsỉr ⸢ḫnty⸣-ỉmntyw wsỉr n Pꜣ-dỉt-kꜣ-km m ꜥwt=f mỉ … … …*
37. … *⸢ws⸣ỉr ḫnty-ỉmntyw wsỉr n Pꜣ-dỉt-kꜣ-km*
… … … … *⸢nwn šwtw⸣*
38. *nṯr ỉm=sn šwt(y)*
nṯr ẖnn rꜥ m pt
r sḳddt rꜥ m kbḥw
ẖnm m šw 39. *sp 2*
ỉm=tn ḏd mdw ẖnm m šw

---

426 See section 1.7.3, above.
427 Leitz et al., eds., *Lexikon* VI, pp. 82–83.
428 CT 363, V 23b–24c.

TRANSLATION

31. Glorification spell.
Words spoken (by) the lector priest:
"(I) live for you, Son of Nut.
May you reach Re when the gods are in their [mourning], A
32. ⌜... see⌝ the slaughter at the hall.
May you reach Nut.
May you see the [sec]ret things.
May you protect Shu.B
... s⌜tretch out⌝,
33. for the Great One sees those pertaining to the limit of the horizon.
The flood of the end of Nut (i.e., sky) has come to you (on) th⌜is⌝ day of lassoing the cattle,
as the West 34. is rejoicing,
for they see the limbs of the god.C
Hail to you ... ...
You have given to Osiris, Foremost (6, 35) of the Westerners, Osiris of Padikakem, the catch of fish and fowl.D
You have ⌜divided up⌝ the ⌜Field⌝ of Offerings ⌜for⌝ him.
May you be gracious 36. to Osiris, ⌜Foremost⌝ of the Westerners, Osiris of Padikakem in his members like ... ...E
37. ... ⌜Osi⌝ris, Foremost of the Westerners, Osiris of Padikakem.
... ... ⌜ruffled plumage⌝.F
38. God among them, (who is) plumed,
the god who rows Re in the sky,
as Re sails in heaven,
the offspring, like Shu." 39. Twice.G
"May you (pl) not speak, Offspring of Shu!"

TEXT NOTES

This spell emphasizes the symbolism of captured animals in the Osirian myth. The West (=Netherworld) celebrates the victory of Osiris "on the day of lassoing the cattle." As the motif of capturing and binding the enemies frequently occurs in mortuary and religious texts,[429] the term *spḥ,* "to lasso," refers to capturing evil-doers and foes of Osiris and Re in order to slaughter them.[430] In this context, lassoing an enemy of the deceased or Osiris parallels the act of capturing cattle that are to be slaughtered.[431] Thus, the lassoing and sub-

429 Cf. the idea of capturing and binding the enemies with fetters (*inṯ*) by the *inṯti*-demon in the Litany to Re and the Amduat; see Hornung, *Das Buch der Anbetung des Re im Westen* I, p. 73; II, pp. 71, 118, and nn. 176–78. See also Griffiths, *The Origins of Osiris and his Cult*, pp. 110–11.

430 *Wb.* IV 105, 6–10; Wilson, *Ptolemaic Lexikon*, p. 829.

431 Zandee, *Death as an Enemy*, p. 233.

sequent slaughter becomes the fate of cattle, as well as any potential enemy of the god or the deceased. For instance, BD 17 and its parallel CT 335 wish the deceased to be protected by a demon who *dd sp*ḥ *m isftyw r* ḫ*bt=f dn.tw b*ȝ*w*, "places a lasso on the evil-doers at his slaughtering block, (on) which *ba*s are pierced." [432]

Some lines later, Osiris is offered a "catch of fish and fowl," which may be viewed as part of a mortuary process for the drowned god.[433] Similarly, fishing and fowling scenes in the funerary context present one of the "icons" of tomb painting. Various fish and birds are loaded with the mythological symbolism of conquering the enemies of Osiris, as well as with the symbolism of sexuality. At the same time, scenes of fishing and fowling in tombs act for the benefit of the deceased, suggesting rebirth and providing functionality and sustenance in the hereafter.[434] Furthermore, as fishing, fowling and bull hunting frequently take place in the marshes, these acts possess a dual significance. On the one hand, the capture and slaughter of various animals is equated with analogous acts against the enemies of Osiris. Conversely, since these hunts predominantly occur in the marshes, Osiris' rebirth is invoked through the association of this environment with acts of creation and the inundation.

6, 31

A A large *in*, , must have originally been in the lacuna following ḏ*d mdw*. ḫ*ry-*ḥ*bt*, , was omitted initially and added later slightly above the line.

The temporal nuances of this clause are expressed with the enclitic particle *isk*, indicating a circumstantial clause of time, and with the preposition *m-*ḫ*nw*, used in the temporal sense.[435]

This text is paralleled by CT 363, V 23b–24c.[436] Cf. CT V 23b–d: *ii.n=i* ḫ*r=k s*ȝ *nwt p*ḥ*=k r*ʿ *hrw* ḥ*b=f sk n*ṯ*rw m-*ḫ*nw i*ȝ*kbw*, "I have come to you, O, Son of Nut; may you reach Re (on) the day of his festival, while the gods are in mourning." Re is spelled without phonetic complements in CT V 23c:  and lacks determinatives in BM 20, 2: .

The reading of *i*ȝ*kb*, , is supported by its phonetic complements and determinative on the following line.

6, 32

B *š*ʿ*d* is understood as the verb "to slaughter, cut up," frequently used as a variant of *nrw* or *sn*ḏ in the PT.[437]

The sign after *m*, 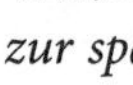, is not found in Möller, *Hieratische Paläographie* III or Verhoeven, *Untersuchungen zur späthieratischen Buchschrift*. Its interpretation as an unusual writ-

432 CT 335, IV 300b–301a.

433 Griffiths, *The Origins of Osiris and his Cult*, pp. 25 and 111.

434 For an overview of the various theories regarding the function of fishing and fowling themes in the funerary context, see Hartwig, *Tomb Painting and Identity*, pp. 103–6.

435 Gardiner, *Egyptian Grammar*, §119.3, and Wilson, *Ptolemaic Lexikon*, p. 767, respectively.

436 The translation of the subsequent spells is based on Faulkner, *Ancient Egyptian Coffin Texts* II, pp. 5–6.

437 *Wb.* IV 422, 3–17; Wilson, *Ptolemaic Lexikon*, p. 526.

ing of *wsẖt,* (O13), is supported by the parallels of CT V 23e: and the hieroglyphic-like (O15) in BM 20, 4.[438] The context suggests understanding *wsẖt* in its sense of "slaughter place (for bulls),"[439] rather than the more familiar *wsẖt,* "hall, court." However, compare Faulkner's translation of the parallel CT V 23e–g: *m3.n=sn šꜥt wsẖt pḥ=k nwt m3=k sšt3w šd=k šw,* "for they have seen the terror of the Broad Hall (var. B1C: sky). May you reach Nut, may you see the hidden things, may you rescue(?) Shu."[440]

Cf. the 2nd person singular suffix pronoun in BM 20, 3–5: ... *i3kb=sn m3=k ... wsẖt pḥ=k nwt m3=k sšt3w šd=k šw*. The in the name of Shu, , is paralleled only by BM 20, 5.

6, 32–34

C Cf. BM 20, 5–6: *pḏ m3 wr... ḏr 3ḫt iw.n=k imy mw ḏr pt*. Cf. also CT V 23h–24c: *pḏ=k irt=k m3.n=sn imyw ḏrw 3ḫt iw.n n=k imyw nwt hrw pw n spḥ.n ng3 sk imnt nfrt m ḥꜥwt m33=sn ꜥt m nṯr ink pw,* "May you extend your vision for they have seen those who are in the limits of the horizon. Those who are in the sky have come to you on the day when the long-horn is lassoed, while the beautiful West is in joy, for they have seen the limb of the god. Such am I." The CT spell ends here.

Some orthographic features and discrepancies from the parallel texts should be noted:

1. Only the of *pḏ* is visible in the end of 6, 32. This term is spelled in BM 20, 5 and CT V 23h.
2. *3ḫt* shows a more extended spelling in CT V 23i: or , and lacks phonetic complements in BM 20, 6: .
3. Note the determinatives of *ng3,* , in CT V 23g and BM 20, 7.
4. *st,* , stands for the enclitic particle *isṯ*.
5. The 3rd person plural suffix pronoun of *m33,* written in CT V 24b and in BM 20, 8, refers to the inhabitants of the West.
6. *nṯr* shows an abbreviated spelling in CT V 24b: , but is spelled phonetically in BM 20, 8: .

6, 34–35

D The parallel with CT 429, V 275a–76d begins here.[441] Cf. CT V 275a–b: *nḏ ḥr=k ṯn nbw ḥb di.n=ṯn n=i/N ḥb,* "Hail to you, you lords of fishing and fowling! You have given me/N a catch of fish and fowl." Cf. the similar BM 20, 9–10: *nḏ ḥr=k tn nbw nṯrw ḥb di=tn n wsir.*

---

438 *Wb.* I 366, 5-367, 2.

439 Wilson, *Ptolemaic Lexikon*, p. 264.

440 Faulkner, *Ancient Egyptian Coffin Texts* II, pp. 5 and 6, n. 2.

441 The translation of the subsequent spells is based on Faulkner, *Ancient Egyptian Coffin Texts* II, p. 72.

6, 35–36

E The 2nd person plural suffix pronoun of *imꜣ,* written without the phonetic *i* in BM 20, 11: , refers to the lords of fishing and fowling, greeted in the previous line. Cf. Faulkner's rendering of the parallel CT V 275c–d: *psš.n=ṯn n=i/N sḫt ḥtpw imꜣ=ṯn n=i/N ꜥwt ḏt=ṯn ḏs=ṯn,* "You have divided up the Field of Offerings for me/N. May you be well-disposed to me/N as regards your own bodily members."[442] Cf. the later part of this clause in BM 20, 13–4: *mꜣ=tn ḏt=tn ḏs=tn di=tn wsir.*
Some orthographic features and discrepancies from the parallel texts should be noted:

1. (G4) is omitted from *imn(tyw),* (R14), in BM 20, 10.
2. The name of Padikakem is spelled with a Demotic form of (I6).[443] and the following round sign, which looks like (D3)[444] are also part of the name Padikakem.

6, 37

F Traces of ☉ (N5) and the following epithet support the reconstruction of *wsir* at the beginning of this line. The remaining name of Padikakem is again spelled with the determinative (D3). The following lacuna may be reconstructed on the basis of BM 20, 15–16: *ḫnty-imntyw ḥw.n bik ṯꜣw in wn ṯꜣw šwt.* Cf. CT V 275e: *rdi.n=ṯn n=i/N sn bik nwn šwt/ṯꜣw nwn ṯꜣw šwt,* "for you have granted to me/N to outsoar the falcon with ruffled plumage."
The terms used to describe Horus' ruffled plumage, *ṯꜣw šwt,* in the parallel texts point to his connection with life-giving air and breath (*ṯꜣw*), as well as the concept of *maat* and life, symbolized by the *šwty*-plumes.[445] The term *nwn,* used in P.W551, similarly refers to "unkempt hair," invoking, however, a rather different association with mourning.[446]

6, 38–39

G Cf. the question in the similar CT V 276a–d: *nṯr sp 2 in-m šwty ẖnnw m ꜣḫt sḳddw rꜥ m ḳbḥw ẖnm šw sp 2 im=ṯn mdw ẖnm šw,* "O, you gods, you gods, who are the plumed ones who row in the horizon when Re sails in the firmament? Offspring of Shu!

---

442 Faulkner, *Ancient Egyptian Coffin Texts* II, p. 72, n. 1. For *ḥb,* "catch of fish and fowl," see *Wb.* III 62, 2–7.

443 *CDD*, k, p. 21.

444 Möller, *Hieratische Paläographie* III, p. 7, 81b.

445 Wilson, *Ptolemaic Lexikon*, p. 1158. For a detailed discussion of the (crown with) two plumes piercing heaven, and thus being an appropriate attribute of the Horus-falcon and the gods who row in the horizon (mentioned in the following lines), see Budde, *SAK* 30 (2002): 57–102.

446 *Wb.* II 222, 5 and I, 318 9. See also the text notes for lines 6, 4–5, above.

Offspring of Shu! May you not speak, O, offspring of Shu!"[447] Cf. BM 20, 16–17: *nṯr ỉm=s šwt nṯr n ẖnn rꜥ m ꜣḫt r sḳdd.tw rꜥ m ḳbḥw pt.*[448]
[hieroglyph] and [hieroglyph] (W9, T34) for *ẖnm*, [hieroglyphs], are similar in hieratic to the group [hieroglyphs] (P5, M29 and G17), evoking visual associations with the familiar phrase *ṯꜣw nḏm šw*, "sweet breath of Shu," perhaps an intentional graphic pun.[449]
Some orthographic features and discrepancies from the parallels should be noted:

1. *ḳbḥw*, [hieroglyphs], is spelled with phonetic complements and fewer determinatives in BM 20, 16.
2. CT V 276c includes the common [hieroglyph] determinative (A17) for *ẖnm*: [hieroglyphs].
3. [hieroglyph] is the phonetic complement for the name of Shu, [hieroglyphs], in line 6, 39, which is spelled with the [hieroglyph] determinative (N5).[450]

3.2.5. *sꜣḫw* III, SPELL 5 — *Lines 6, 39–46*[451]

Following the previous spells, the speaker here is presumably again the lector priest, who is not specified, however. This spell concerns Nut, the mother and protector of Osiris. Following the death of her son, she is depicted as the protector of his heir, Horus. As Padikakem, the deceased owner of this papyrus, is equated with Osiris and other deities, Nut's protection is implied for him as well.

TRANSLITERATION

39. *sꜣḫ*
ḏd mdw
sšpt n pḏt (6, 40) *ẖr ẖr nṯr ỉm=s*
ỉ.nḏ ḥr=k sꜣḫw
ms.n kw mwt=k r tr siwꜥ.n=s kw
r 41. *nw sfḫ.n kw tm*
m sk iwf nwt
ḥꜥ=k m psḏt
hy wsir ḫnty-imntyw wsir 42. *Pꜣ-dit-kꜣ-km*
pšš.n s mwt=k nwt ḥr=k m rn=s n št-pt
rdi.n=s wn 43. *n=k m nṯr m stš m rn=k n nṯr*
ẖnm.n=s ti m-ꜥ ḫt nbt ḏw m rn=s n ẖnm-wr

447 Faulkner, *Ancient Egyptian Coffin Texts* II, p. 72, nn. 4–5.
448 For *ḳbḥw*, "heaven," see *Wb.* V 30, 1–6.
449 For the epithet *ẖnm šw*, "Offspring(?) of Shu," see Faulkner, *Ancient Egyptian Coffin Texts* II, p. 72, n. 6. For a discussion of graphic puns, see section 1.5.1, above.
450 *Wb.* IV 429, 1–4.
451 See section 1.7.3.

nwt s3 44. ḫr s3 wsir
n ṯw(t) s(t) wr im msw=s
sb sp 2 ḫr k3=f
sb wsir ḫr k3 (6, 45) *=f*
sb ḥr ḫr k3=f
sb nṯr ḫr k3=f
sb sšm ḫr k3=f
sb ḫnty-ʿ3t 46. *ḫr k3=f*
sb ti ḏd.ti ḫr k3=k
sb wsir n P3-dit-k3-km ḫr k3=f

TRANSLATION

Glorification spell.
Words spoken:
"The Luminous Ones are in heaven (6, 40) in the possession of the god therein.
Hail to you, Orion!
Your mother bore you at the time that she made you heir,
at 41. the moment when Atum released you,
wiping the flesh of Nut.
May you appear as the Ennead.[A]
O, Osiris, Foremost of the Westerners, Osiris (of) 42. Padikakem.
Your mother, Nut, has spread herself over you in her name of *št-pt*.[B]
She caused you to be 43. a god to Seth in your name of God.
She protected you from all evil things in her name of Great Well.[C]
Nut is protecting 44. the son of Osiris,
for you are, indeed, the greatest among her children.[D]
Gone is the one who went to his *ka*.
Osiris went to his *ka*.[E]
(6, 45) Horus went to his *ka*,
the god went to his *ka*,
the Leader went to his *ka*,
the Foremost of the Great One went 46. to his *ka*,
the Durable Ones went to your *ka*.
Osiris of Padikakem went to his *ka*." [F]

TEXT NOTES

As this spell focuses on Nut, her son Osiris is addressed by one of his common epithets, *s3ḥw*, "Orion,"[452] which literally places him in the body of his mother, the sky-goddess Nut. Nut performs her significant role of the motherly protector of Osiris. Nut's act of "embracing" or "spreading herself" explicitly refers to this protection, as Osiris is enclosed in the

452 *Wb.* IV 22, 1–3; Leitz et al., eds., *Lexikon* VI, pp. 152–54.

space of Nut during his transformation.[453] A text known from the OK onwards illustrates this point: *ḏd mdw in nwt pd(=i) wy ḥr=k ẖw=i ḥꜥw=k ḫr=i ḏwt n ꜥr=s n=k sꜣḫ=i sꜣ=i ir=i mkt=k mi irt=i ḥr wnn-nfr,* "Recitation by Nut: (I) spread myself over you that I may protect your limbs in me. Evil has not reached up to you. I make my protection *akh* that I may protect you like I did for Wennefer." [454] In turn, Nut is referred to by the well-attested epithet *št-pt,*[455] which may originate in *štꜣ-pt,* "secrecy of the sky," relating it to the nocturnal mystery of the sky goddess who conceals life within her body.[456]

6, 39–41

A The GR causative *siw(ꜥ),* , "to inherit," [457] may present a visual pun on *iwr,* , "to conceive;" [458] thus: "the time when she conceived you."
Cf. one *ḫr* in BM 21, 1–3: *sšpt pḏt ḫrtyw nṯr im=s.*
The group may also be read as *sf,* , "yesterday," but *sfḫ,* "to release, set apart," makes more sense here.[459]
The reading of *sk,* , "to wipe," is questionable due to the lack of a determinative. Other potential translations, such as "to destroy," are possible interpretations as well. Nonetheless, considering the context, "wiping the flesh" is the more appropriate reading.[460]
Some orthography and discrepancies with the parallel texts should be noted:

1. *mwt* shows an unusual spelling, , paralleled by BM 21, 4.[461]
2. Nut, , is consistently written without determinatives in BM 21, 6 and further.
3. *ḥꜥ,* , has an abbreviated spelling in BM 21, 7.
4. A superfluous follows *ḥꜥ=k* in P.W551.

6, 42

B This line corresponds with the beginning of PT 588 (§§1607–08), known largely from the pyramid of Merenre, and a part of PT 368 (§638), attested in numerous pyramids. The parallel with PT 588 and 368 ends following line 6, 44.

---

453 Billing, *Nut,* pp. 90–93 and 133.

454 NK shrine of Hepu, TT 66, see Billing, *Nut,* p. 133.

455 Leitz et al., eds., *Lexikon* VII, p. 128.

456 Billing, *Nut,* pp. 92–93 and 126–27, suggests that texts belonging to this category were likely meant to be recited first, in order to introduce the goddess Nut, and thus indicate the beginning of the process of transformation by Osiris and the deceased associated with him.

457 For the spelling of *iwꜥ* with the determinative (Y1), see *Wb.* I 50, 8–10.

458 *Wb.* I 56, 1–7. For puns see section 1.5.1, above.

459 *Wb.* IV 116, 2–117, 5.

460 For a brief overview of the uses of *sk,* "to wipe, touch" in various mortuary texts, see Wilson, *Ptolemaic Lexikon,* pp. 941–42.

461 *Wb.* II 54, 1–10.

The  that follows *psš.n* stands for the 3rd person singular feminine dependent pronoun *st*. Cf. a similar statement in the *Stundenwachen* V, 53–54: *psš.n(=i) ḥr=k m wꜥwt m rn pwy n št-pt,* "I have spread myself over you as *wꜥw(i)t* in this my name of *št-pt*."[462]
Some discrepancies with the parallel texts should be noted:

1. *mwt* is written  in PT §1607a, §638a, and BM 21, 8.
2. *štpt*, 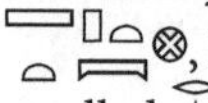, has the  determinative (O49) in PT §1607a and §638a.
3. *rdi* is spelled  in PT §1607b and §638b.
4. *wn* is written  in PT §1607b, while  of P.W551 is paralleled by PT §638b from the pyramids of Teti and Pepi.

6, 42–43

C Cf. PT §1607a and §638b: *rdi.n=s wn=k m nṯr n ḫft=k*. The epithet *ḫnmt-wrt*, "Great Well," refers to Nut, among other goddesses.[463]
Some discrepancies with the parallel texts should be noted:

1. *ḫnm* has phonetic complements in PT §1608a:  and §638c: .
2.  stands for the 2nd person singular dependent pronoun, acting as direct object of *ḫnm*. Cf. *tw*, , in BM 21, 11 and *kw*, , in PT §1608a.
3. *ḫt*, , does not have determinatives or  in the PT parallels.
4. The spelling of *ḫnm-wrt* varies in PT §1608a: 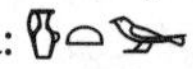 and §638c in the pyramid of Merenre: . Cf. the other variants of PT §638c: .
5. The superfluous  following *s3*, , is paralleled by BM 21, 13.

6, 43–44

D The phrase *nwt s3 ḥr s3 wsir* is omitted from PT §1608 and §638.
Some discrepancies with the parallel texts should be noted:

1. *ṯwt* is written  in PT §1608b and §638d.
2. *ist* is written  in BM 21, 14.
3. *wr*, , has the  determinative (G7) in BM 21, 14.

6, 44

E The phrase *sb sp 2*, , occurs in several Pyramid spells and should be understood as *sb sb*.[464] See, for instance PT 447 (§826a): *sb sb* () *ḥr k3=f*, "(someone) has gone to be with his *ka*,"[465] and PT 568 (§1431a): *sb sb* (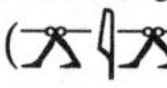) *ḥr k3=f*, "(someone)

462 Junker, *Stundenwachen*, p. 55.
463 Billing, *Nut*, pp. 179–80; Leitz et al., eds., *Lexikon* VI, p. 21.
464 For *sb*, "to go," see *Wb.* III 429, 13–15.
465 Allen, *The Ancient Egyptian Pyramid Texts*, p. 108.

has gone where his *ka* is."[466] The expression *sb n/ẖr k3*, "to go to one's *ka*," generally refers to death, particularly of gods.[467] Cf. *ii=sn sp 2*, 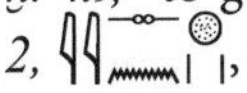, in BM 21, 15.
The 3rd person singular suffix pronoun of the last *k3* in 6, 44 is written on the following line.

6, 45–46

F Cf. the third clause in this series in BM 21, 18: *sb ḏḥwty ẖr k3=f.*
sšm, "The Leader," spelled  in BM 21, 19, is an epithet that refers to various deities, including Thoth.[468]
The feminine ending of *ḫnty-ꜥ3t* suggests that this may be an abbreviated version of the common Osirian epithet *ḫnty-psḏt-ꜥ3t*, "Foremost of the Great Ennead."[469]
ḏdt, "The Durable Ones," spelled  in BM 21, 21, is a LP and GR epithet referring to various goddesses, including Isis.[470] Note the unusual, hieroglyphic-like 2nd person singular suffix pronoun following *ḏd.ti ẖr k3.*
Note the dot at the end of 6, 45.

3.2.6. *s3ḫw* III, SPELL 6 — *Lines 6, 47–7, 2*[471]

The speaker of this spell is again not specified by the text, but is presumed to be the lector priest. While the previous spell concerns Nut, this spell focuses on Geb as the father of Osiris, pointing to his role as the source of Osiris' status as king of Upper and Lower Egypt. Geb brings Horus and other gods to protect Osiris, who is said to be accepted by the gods without opposition. The latter part of the spell reverts to Nut, who loves and protects Osiris. With the support of his parents, Osiris is called to arise and command his rightful position.

TRANSLITERATION

47. *s3ḫ*
ḏd mdw
  hy wsir ḫnty-imntyw wsir n P3-dit-k3-km
    twt s3 wr=s ms 48. *smsw gb*
      wdd=f iwꜥ=f
    ḫꜥ.n=k m nsw
    ḫꜥ.n=k m bity

466 Allen, *The Ancient Egyptian Pyramid Texts*, p. 176.
467 Wilson, *Ptolemaic Lexikon*, p. 1073.
468 Leitz et al., eds., *Lexikon* VI, p. 121.
469 Leitz et al., eds., *Lexikon* V, p. 814.
470 Leitz et al., eds., *Lexikon* VII, pp. 680–81.
471 See section 1.7.3, above.

sḫm.ti m nṯrw nbw k3=sn
sw3 49. *df3w=sn*
hy wsir ḫnty-imntyw wsir n P3-dit-k3-km
in.n n=k gb ḥr
(6, 50) *nḏ=f k*[*w*]
in.n=f n=k ibw nṯrw
nn bin im=sn m-ʿ=f
hy wsir ḫnty-(*imn*)*tyw wsir* 51. *n P3*[*-dit-k3-*]*km*
ms=n-pt
iwr.n-nwt
iwʿ gb
mrt=f
⸢*ps*⸣*š mwt=k*
(7, 1) *nwt ḥr=k m rn=s n št-pt*
n ḥr.n mwt=k nwt r=k m rn=s n ḥrt
hy wsir ḫnty-imntyw
ṯs tw
šsp n=k sʿḥ=k
2. *ir n=k psḏt ʿ3t*
sḫnt.n=s st=k
st ḥr nṯrw ḫnty-pt
hy wsir ḫnty-imntyw
ʿḥʿ r=k
di ʿ=k in ḥr d=f ʿḥʿ=k
grḥ

TRANSLATION

47. Glorification spell.
Words spoken:
"O, Osiris, Foremost of the Westerners, Osiris of Padikakem.
You are her eldest son, 48. the oldest child of Geb.
It is his inheritance that he has given.[A]
You have appeared as king of Upper Egypt,
you have appeared as king of Lower Egypt,
you prevail over all gods and their *ka*s,
as their provisions have 49. diminished.[B]
O, Osiris, Foremost of the Westerners, Osiris of Padikakem.
Geb brought Horus to you
(6, 50) that he may protect y[o]u.[C]
He brought to you the hearts of the gods,
and there is no evil among them from him.[D]
O, Osiris, Foremost (of the Wester)ners, Osiris 51. of Pa[dika]kem.
One whom the Sky Bore,

One whom Nut Conceived,
Heir of Geb,
whom he loves,
whom your mother ⌜pro⌝tects.
(7, 1) Nut is upon you in her name of *št-pt*.
Your mother, Nut, is not far from you in her name of Heaven.[E]
O, Osiris, Foremost of the Westerners.
Raise yourself! [F]
Seize for yourself your dignity,
2. which the Great Ennead made for you.
It extolled your place,
it being near the gods, the Foremost of Heaven.[F]
O, Osiris, Foremost of the Westerners.
Stand yourself up,
give your hand to Horus that he may help you stand." [G]

Pause.

TEXT NOTES

6, 47–48

A  stands for the 2nd person independent pronoun *ṯwt,* which commonly occurs in Old Egyptian.[472]
Judging by the context, the 3rd person feminine suffix pronoun following *wr* refers to Nut. *wr* is written  in BM 22, 3. The 3rd person masculine suffix pronoun of *wdi,* "to place," [473] refers to Geb.

6, 48–49

B The first *ḫꜥ* is understood as a prospective 2nd tense and the second *ḫꜥ* as a circumstantial form with an erroneous *n* following it, although the second *ḫꜥ* may also be read as a *sḏm.n=f* form. This reading corresponds to Allen's translation of the parallel PT 426 (§776a–b) in the pyramid of Pepi: *wsir NN ḫꜥ.n=k m* ⌜*n*⌝*swt bit n sḫm=k m nṯrw* (*nbw*) *k3w=sn isṯ,* "Osiris NN (=Pepi), you have appeared as the Dual King, for you control the gods and their *ka*s as well." [474] Notably, Faulkner reads *ḫꜥ* as an imperative with a reinforcing dative, "appear as King of Upper and Lower Egypt…." [475] The scribe of BM 22, 4–5 uses both *ḫꜥ* verbs as *sḏm=f* forms.

---

472 Gardiner, *Egyptian Grammar*, §64.
473 *Wb.* I 384, 15–387, 21.
474 Allen, *The Ancient Egyptian Pyramid Texts*, p. 103.
475 Faulkner, *Ancient Egyptian Pyramid Texts*, p. 141, n. 1

sḫm acts as a stative in the construction *sḫm m,* "to prevail over,"[476] while *swꜣ,* "to pass, diminish," is used as a passive *sḏmw=f,*[477] implying the negative effects of the lack of Osirian leadership.
This line has two notable orthographic features:

1. and in the clause *ḫꜥ.n=k m bity* are reversed.
2. and in the clause *sḫm.ti m nṯrw nbw kꜣ=sn* are reversed.

6, 49–50

C This line is similar to PT 357 (§590b–c) var. PT 367 (§634a–b).[478] Cf. PT §590b: *in n=k gb ḥr*. Cf. also the dependent pronoun in PT §634a: *hꜣ wsir NN in.n n=k gb ḥrw i.nḏ=f ṯw*. Note the lack of determinatives (G7) for both deities in PT §590b and §634a. and of *ḏfꜣw=sn* are reversed again.

6, 50

D Cf. PT §590b–c: *ip=f n=k ibw=sn in.n=f n=k nṯrw nb(w) m sp ni biꜣ im=sn m ꜥ=f,* "(Geb has gotten Horus for you,) that he may allot their hearts to you. He has gotten you all the gods together, and there is none of them who are away from you."[479] Rather than indicating the lack of negativity in the hearts of the gods, PT §634b–c emphasizes the positive influence of Geb's actions on Osiris: *in.n=f n=k ibw nṯrw im=k gꜣw im=k ꜥšw,* "(Geb has fetched Horus for you, that he might tend you.) He has fetched you the gods' hearts, that you might not groan, that you might not moan."
This line has some notable orthographic features:

1. The reading of the unusual group as *nn* is supported by BM 22, 10.
2. stands for the phonetic *i* in *bin,* .[480] Cf. *bin,* , in BM 22, 10.
3. *imnt* is omitted in the epithet *ḫnty-(imn)tyw,* .

6, 51–7, 1

E *ms.n-pt,* "One whom the Sky Bore," is a predominantly Saite epithet of Osiris.[481] The ceiling vault of Bakenrenef is similar to this line: *wsir imy-r niwt ṯꜣty bꜣk-n-rn=f ms.n-pt iwr.n-nwt iwꜥ gb mr=f psš mwt=k nwt ḥr=k m rn=s n št-pt rdi.n=s wn=k m nṯr n ḫft=k*

476 *Wb.* IV 248, 15.

477 *Wb.* IV 60, 8–61, 20.

478 Allen, *The Ancient Egyptian Pyramid Texts,* pp. 73 and 82, respectively.

479 Allen, *The Ancient Egyptian Pyramid Texts,* p. 73, does not comment on the 2nd person singular pronoun in his translation, despite the apparent 3rd person singular masculine suffix pronoun in the original.

480 Daumas, *Valeurs phonétiques* II, p. 156.

481 Leitz et al., eds., *Lexikon* III, p. 402.

wsir NN mꜣꜥ-ḫrw.[482] The parallel from the tomb of Bakenrenef ends following this line. Two discrepancies with the parallel texts should be noted:

1. *pt*, , lacks phonetic complements and determinatives in BM 22, 11.
2. The determinative (G7) is consistently omitted from the names of gods on the ceiling inscription of Bakenrenef.

7, 1–2

F The phrase *ṯs tw* begins the parallel with a section of PT 677 (§2020a–b). *dmḏ ti*, , stands in place of Ts tw in BM 22, 17.
Cf. the form of *ir* in PT §2020b: *šsp n=k sꜥḥ=k ir.n n=k psḏti*. The 3rd person singular feminine suffix pronoun of *sḫnt*, "to exalt,"[483] refers to the Ennead. The epithet *ḫnty-pt*, "Foremost of Heaven," is employed for various deities in the entourage of the Great Ennead.[484]
The following peculiarities and discrepancies from the parallel texts should be noted:

1. *rn*, , has no determinative (G7) in BM 22, 13.
2. *sꜥḥ* is written in BM 22, 17 and in PT §2020b.
3. *psḏty* is spelled in PT §2020b.
4. *pt* is spelled phonetically in BM 22, 20: .

G The following corresponds with the beginning of PT 593 (§§1627–37)[485] from the pyramids of Merenre and Neferkare, which are in turn similar to PT 366 (§§626–33).[486] A variant of this spell also occurs as texts 91 and 92 in the tomb of Mutirdis.[487] The parallel continues on to the subsequent spell.
di, , is interpreted as an imperative, although it is not spelled *my*, while *in*, , is understood as the preposition *n*. Otherwise, the verb *di* may be taken in the passive sense: *di ꜥ=k in ḥr*, "your hand is placed by Horus …." Cf. the grammar of PT §1627a: *ꜥḥꜥ di n=k ꜥ=k n ḥr di=f ꜥḥꜥ=k*, "Stand up, give your arm to Horus, that he may make you stand up." Cf. the prospective verbs in Mutirdis 91, 3: *ꜥḥꜥ=k di=k ꜥwy=k n ḥr di=f nmi=k*, "May you stand and give your hands to Horus, that he may give your bier."
Some orthographic features of this line and discrepancies with the parallel texts should be noted:

1. *ꜥḥꜥ* is consistently spelled in PT §626a and §1627a from the pyramid of Merenre and lacks phonetic complements in PT §1627a of the pyramid of Neferkare.

482 For the tomb of Bakenrenef (L24), see El-Naggar, *EVO* 9 (1986): 28.
483 *Wb*. IV 255, 6–256, 11.
484 Leitz et al., eds., *Lexikon* V, p. 805.
485 The translation of the subsequent texts is based on Allen, *The Ancient Egyptian Pyramid Texts*, p. 217.
486 The translation of the subsequent texts is based on Allen, *The Ancient Egyptian Pyramid Texts*, p. 81.
487 Assmann, *Mutirdis*, pp. 84–85.

2. The PT regularly omit 𓅆 determinatives (G7) for the names of gods.
3. *di* is consistently spelled 𓏙 (X8) in PT §1627a.
4. *grḥ*, , is used here as a verse separator.[488]

3.2.7. *sꜣḫw* III, SPELL 7 *Lines 7, 2–34*[489]

No speaker is mentioned in the text of spell 7. The beginning of this spell continues the theme of establishing Osiris' paternity from the previous spell. Osiris is again assured of his victory, as well as of the protection by the gods of the Great Ennead and their acceptance. It is their decision that places Osiris above his enemies. Nut protects and reassembles Osiris, as he is said to be the greatest among her children. Following this introduction, the focus of the spell shifts to the other family members of Osiris: Isis, Nephthys, and Horus, who assist in reassembling and reanimating him. The role of Thoth in the resurrection is protecting and driving away the enemies of Osiris. Geb, responsible for introducing various gods to his son, establishes the correct succession for Osiris and Horus. In turn, Horus designates the deceased Osiris as the chief among the gods, complementing his own status in this world. Consequently, the end of the spell commands Osiris to arise as an effective and glorified spirit.

TRANSLITERATION

hy wsir ḫnty-(imn)tyw
3. sk n=k gb r=k
wp=f n=k irty=k
hy wsir ḫnty-(imn)tyw wsir n Pꜣ-dit-kꜣ-km
nḏ.n kw psḏt ꜥꜣt
di=s ḫftw=k ẖr=k
ḫw.n=s ꜥꜥwt 4. isd=f r=k
hy wsir ḫnty-(imn)tyw wsir n Pꜣ-dit-kꜣ-km
ḫw.n k(w) mwt=k nwt
dr.n(=s) iꜣkb=k
ẖnm=s kw inḳ=s kw (7, 5) *wṯs=s kw*
ṯwt wr im msw=s
iw n=k snty=k r gs=k
ꜣst pw ḥnꜥ nbt-ḥwt
wn=sn m bw ẖr=k im n=i(!)
nḏr.n snt 6.=k ꜣst im=k
gm.n=s tw km.ti wr.ti m rn=k n km-wr
šn.n=k ḥwt nbt m-ẖnw ꜥwy=k m rn=k n šn-wr-7.-dbn-ḥꜣw-nbw
ꜥꜣ.tw

488 Möller, *Hieratische Paläographie* III, p. 9, n. 1.
489 See section 1.7.3, above.

mk ṯw wr šn ṯw m rn=k n šn-wr-sk

ỉn n=k ḥr stš

dỉ=f sw ẖr=k

sẖr 8. *ẖr=k*

wr pḥty=k r=f

rdỉt.n ḥr šn.n=k nṯr nb m-ẖnw ʿwy=k

mr ḥr ỉt=f ỉm=k

n rdỉt ḥr bỉꜣ n ỉt=f ỉm 9.*=k*

ʿnḫ.ti m ʿnḫ ḫpr

nḏ=k m ḏdwt

sꜣ n=k ꜣst ḥnʿ nbt-ḥwt

m sꜣwt sỉꜣ=sn nb=sn ỉm=k m rn=k n nb-s(!)-(7, 10)*-sꜣwt*

nṯr=sn ỉm=k m rn=k n mr-nṯr

dwꜣ=sn kw

ỉm=k ḥr=sn

ỉỉ n=k sn(t)=k ꜣst

ḥʿʿ.tw n mr=k

pr mtwt=k ỉm=s

spd m spdt

11. *ḥr-spd pr ỉm=k*

ꜣḫ.n=f ỉm=k m rn=k n ꜣḫ-ỉmy-ḏndrw

nḏ.n kw ḥr m rn=f n ḥr sꜣ-nḏ-ỉt(=f)

12. *hy wsỉr ḫnty-ỉmntyw*

nḏ n=k ḥr

nḏ.n nḏ=f tw

hy wsỉr ḫnty-ỉmntyw wsỉr n Pꜣ-dỉt-kꜣ-km

ỉw n=k ḥr

nḥm.n=f tw ỉry=f

s-13.*-ẖt n=k ḏḥwty ỉmyw-ẖt stš*

ỉn=f n=k nṯrw

(s)ḥm.n=f n=k ỉb n stš

twt wr r=f

pr.n=k m-bꜣḥ=f

ḳd=k m-14.*-bꜣḥ=f*

mꜣꜣ=f gb ḳd=k d.n=f k(w) m st=f

hy wsỉr ḫnty-ỉmntyw wsỉr n Pꜣ-dỉt-kꜣ-km

ỉn n=k gb snty=k r gs=k

(7, 15) *ꜣst pw ḥnʿ nbt-ḥwt*

rdỉ.n ḥr dmḏ tw nṯrw

snsn=s(n) r=k m rn=sn snwty

hy wsỉr ḫnty-ỉmntyw wsỉr n Pꜣ-(dỉt)-16.*-kꜣ-km*

ỉm gꜣ ỉm ʿšw

wp n=k ḥr r=k

wn=f n=k ỉrty=k

hy wsir ḫnty-imntyw wsir n P3-dit-k3-km
in.n n=k 17. *gb ḥr ḥni*
ip=f n=k ibw=sn
in=f n=k nṯrw nb(w) m sp wꜥ
nn bi3 im=sn m-ꜥ=f
nḏ.n kw ḥr n 18. *ḏdt*
nḏ=f tw
nḥm.n=f irt=f m-ꜥ ḫft=k
sḫm.n=f ib stš
di.n=f n=k irt=f
tw nn bnr
snḫḫ n=k
sip n=k 19. *s*
h(y) nḫḫ s ḫr=k
ꜥb.n kw 3st ḥ(nꜥ) nbt-ḥwt
ḫnt-ib.n ḥr ḫr=k m rn=k n ḫnty-imnt
in ḥr nḏ iry.n stš r=k
hy (7, 20) *wsir ḫnty-imntyw wsir n P3-dit-k3-km*
ꜥḥꜥ r=k
ii ḥr ip ṯ(w) mm-ꜥ nṯrw
mr.n kw ḥr
ḥtm.n=f 21. *tw m nṯr*
dmi n=k ḥr irt=f r=k
wp=f n=k irty=k
m33=k im=sn
hy wsir ḫnty-imntyw wsir n P3-dit-k3-km
22. *ṯs n=k nṯrw ḥr=k*
mr=sn tw
sw3ḏ.n tw 3st ḥnꜥ nbt-ḥwt
n ḥr ḥr r=k
twt n k3=f
ḥtp=k ḥr=f
wnn=k šsp 23. *mdt=f*
ḥtp=k ḥr=s
sḏm n ḥr nis.n=k
rdit.n ḥr šms tw nṯrw
hy wsir ḫnty-imntyw wsir n P3-dit-k3-km
24. *rs r=k*
in n=k gb ḥr
ip=f tw
gm.n kw ḥr
3ḫ.n=f im=k
sꜥr n=k ḥr nṯrw

rdit.n=f n=k sn
(7, 25) sḥḏ=sn ḥr=k
d(i).n kw ḥr m-ḥ3t nṯrw
rdit.n=f n=k iṯt=k nbt
mrt.n sw ḥr r=k
n wp.n ḥr m rn=k n ꜥnḏti
26. *di.n n=k ḥr irt=f rwḏt*
d n=k imim⸢=k⸣
⸢nr⸣ …=k nb ⸢tw
m⸣ḥ kw ḥr tm.ti m irt=f m rn=s pfy 27. *m …*
… ḥr nṯrw
n bi3=sn r=k
ḏr bw nb ⸢mḥ⸣.n=k im
inḳ ⸢n=k⸣ nbt-ḥwt ⸢ꜥt⸣w=k nbt m 28. *rn=s ⸢pw n sš3t nbt-ḳdw*
sw3ḏ n=k⸣ …
di.n=k mwt=k nwt ꜥ… m rn=s pw n ḏrwt
inḳ 29.*=s ⸢kw m … ḳrs⸣ … … … … …*
(7, 30) … … … … … nwtwy
hy ⸢wsir⸣ [ḫnty-imntyw] wsir [n P3-dit-]k3-km
ṯs 31. *…=k r=f*
… … …
…[n] ḏd nḏ=f ṯ(w)
hy wsir ḫnty-imn(tyw) wsir ⸢n P3-dit-k3-km
twt⸣ nṯr wꜥ.ti
nn 32. *⸢mr⸣=k*
[r]di … … ⸢ms⸣wt …
wṯs=sn kw
rdit.n=f n=k nṯrw nb(w)
m šms=sn kw
sḫm=k im=sn
f3i.n k(w) ḥr 33. *m rn=k n nṯr-im-ḥnw*
wṯs.n=f tw m rn=k n skr
ꜥnḫ.ṯ
šn=k rꜥ nb
3ḫ.tw m rn=k n 3ḫt-34.*-pr-rꜥ-im=s*
w3š.ti spd.ti b3.ti 3ḫ.tw sḫm.tw ḏt ḏt
grḥ

TRANSLATION

"O, Osiris, Foremost of the (West)erners.
3. Geb wiped for you your mouth,
as he opened your eyes for you.[A]
O, Osiris, Foremost of the (West)erners, Osiris of Padikakem.
The Great Ennead has protected you,
as it has placed your enemies under you.[B]
It has warded off the saliva 4. which he spat out against you.[C]
O, Osiris, Foremost of the (West)erners, Osiris of Padikakem.
Your mother, Nut, protects you,
(she) has driven away your mourning.
She enfolds you, she embraces you, (7, 5) she lifts you up,
for you are the greatest among her children.[D]
Your two sisters at your side come to you,
it is Isis with Nephthys.
They are in the place where you are.
Your sister, 6. Isis, has taken hold of you.[E]
She found you very black in your name of *km-wr*.
May you surround all things inside your arms in your name of *šn-wr,* 7. who Encircles the Islands,
you being great. F
Look, you are great and round in your name of *šn-wr-sk*.
Horus brought Seth to you,
he placed him under you,
(he) having fallen 8. under you,
for your strength is greater than his.[G]
Horus caused you to encircle every god inside your arms.
Horus loves his father in you.
Horus will not let his father in you be far, [H]
9. you being alive as the Living Scarab,
as you are protected in Mendes.
Isis with Nephthys waited for you in Asyut;
they recognize their lord in you, in your name of Lord of (7, 10) Asyut, [I]
as their god is in you, in your name of Canal of the God.
They worship you.
Do not let them be far!
Your sister, Isis, comes to you
rejoicing in your love,
as your seed goes forth into her,
(she) being ready as Sothis.[J]
11. Horus-Soped came forth from you.
He has power through you in your name of Spirit who is in the *ḏndrw*-Bark.
Horus protected you in his name of Horus, the Son who Protects (his) Father.[K]

12. O, Osiris, Foremost of the Westerners.
Horus protects for you,
his protection protects you.
O, Osiris, Foremost of the Westerners, Osiris of Padikakem.
Horus comes to you,
he has rescued you.[L]
13. Thoth has caused the followers of Seth to retreat for you.
He brought to you the gods.
He has driven back the heart of Seth for you,
for you are greater than he.[M]
You have gone forth in front of him,
your form being 14. before him.
Geb, he has seen your form and he set you in his place.
O, Osiris, Foremost of the Westerners, Osiris of Padikakem.
Geb has brought your two sisters to your side for you.[N]
(7, 15) It is Isis with Nephthys.
Horus caused the gods to assemble for you
that they may be brotherly to you, in their name of *Senwt*-Shrines.[O]
O, Osiris, Foremost of the Westerners, Osiris of Pa(di)-16.-kakem.
Do not languish, do not shout!
Horus has opened for you your mouth.
He has opened for you your two eyes.
O, Osiris, Foremost of the Westerners, Osiris of Padikakem. P
Geb brought for you 17. Horus (in) the *Henw*-Bark,
so that he may claim for you their hearts.
He brought for you all the gods at once.
There are none among them who will escape from him.[Q]
Horus of Mendes has protected 18. you,
he has protected you.
He rescued his eye from your enemy.
He has destroyed the heart of Seth.
He has given (it) to you.[R]
This is his sweet eye,
cause it to come back to you,
assign it for yourself.
19. O, may it be (as) new for you![S]
Isis a(nd) Nephthys have reassembled you.
Horus is glad on account of you in your name of Foremost of the Westerners.
It is Horus, who will make good that which Seth did against you.[T]
O, (7, 20) Osiris, Foremost of the Westerners, Osiris of Padikakem,
Raise yourself!
Horus, who claimed you from the gods, has come.
Horus has loved you,
he has provided for 21. you as a god.

Horus has joined for you his eye to you.[U]
He has opened for you your two eyes,
that you may see with them.[V]
O, Osiris, Foremost of the Westerners, Osiris of Padikakem.
22. The gods have bound your face for you,
as they loved you.
Isis and Nephthys made you healthy.
Horus is not far from you,
for you are his *ka*.
May you be pleased with him![W]
May you hurry and receive 23. his word.
May you be pleased with it!
Listen to Horus, whom you have summoned.
Horus caused the gods to follow you.[X]
O, Osiris, Foremost of the Westerners, Osiris of Padikakem.
24. Awaken yourself!
Geb brought to you Horus,
that he may claim you.
Horus found you,
and he has power through you.
Horus caused the gods to ascend to you.
He has given them to you,
(7, 25) that they may illuminate your face.[Y]
Horus placed you in front of the gods,
and gave to you everything which you have seized.
Horus bound it for you.
Horus will not separate (from you) in your name of Andjety.[Z]
26. Horus has given to you his strong eye,
and caused you to be strong,
so that your every … ⸢fear you⸣.[AA]
Horus fil⸢led yo⸣u completely with his eye in this its name 27. of ….
Horus has … the gods …
they will not be far from you,
from ⸢every⸣ place (where) you ⸢have drowned⸣.[BB]
Nephthys has collected ⸢for you⸣ all your ⸢lim⸣bs in 28. ⸢this⸣ name of hers,
⸢Seshat, Lady of Builders.⸣
… ⸢made them hale for you⸣.
Your mother, Nut, has placed you … in this her name of Coffin.[CC]
She has embraced 29. you in … … … Coffin … … … … …[DD]
(7, 30) … … … unsteadiness.[EE]
O, ⸢Osiris⸣, [Foremost of the Westerners,] Osiris [of Padi]kakem.
Lift up 31. your … toward him
… … …
(For) his protection of you [will not] fail.[FF]

O, Osiris, Foremost of the Westerners, Osiris [of Padikakem].
You are the sole god,
and there is none 32. ⸢li⸣ke you
... gave ... ... ⸢child⸣ren,
that they may raise you.[GG]
He gave to you all the gods
that they may follow you,
(as) you have power over them.[HH]
Horus has raised you 33. in your name of God who is in the *Henw*-Bark.
He raised you in your name of Sokar.
Live,
so that you may encircle every day![II]
Be a spirit in your name of Horizon 34. from which Re Comes Forth.
Be strong, be effective, be a *Ba*, be glorified, be powerful of body, forever!"[JJ]
Pause.

TEXT NOTES

Various deities protect Osiris by deflecting from him the negative qualities associated with Seth. For instance, the Great Ennead repels , *ꜥꜥwt*, "saliva," that Seth spits out against Osiris.[490] Notably, this term replaces *ꜥꜣꜥ*, "evil influence," which occurs in the parallel texts, and explains the origin of the unusual determinative (F44) of this term, which is written on the following line.[491] This evil is exemplified by the term *isd*, "to spit," which carries particularly negative connotations in the context of Egyptian magic.[492]

Having been safeguarded by the Great Ennead, as well as Geb and Nut, Osiris appears before Isis, having become *km.ti wr.ti*. This ambiguous phrase leads to two different but appropriate readings: "very black" or "complete and great."[493] The first reading points to the typical color for Osiris' skin, as well as the rich soil of the Nile valley, as symbols of regeneration. At the same time, Osiris is rejuvenated only after being completely reassembled and made hale, as is implied by the second reading. The following epithet of Osiris, *km-wr*, is generally translated as the name of the city of Athribis, "Bitter Lakes" or "Great Black Wall,"[494] because of the determinative (O36), omitted from P.W551 but present in PT 366 (§628b) and PT 593 (§1630d). Although the PT spelling of *km-wr*, , points to

490 As PT 222 (§205) suggests that Seth was born when Nut spewed him out, he uses spitting against Osiris and Horus; see te Velde, *Seth*, pp. 85 and 104, n. 3, and Ritner, *The Mechanics of Ancient Egyptian Magical Practice*, p. 84, who points to Seth's capacity as the Spewer (*iššy*), connecting him to the forces of rain and thunderstorms.

491 Cf. the more typical determinative (Aa2) in Mutirdis, 5. See *Wb.* I 167, 2–4. For a brief discussion of *ꜥꜣꜥ*, see Dawson, *JEA* 21 (1935): 30–40.

492 Ritner, *The Mechanics of Ancient Egyptian Magical Practice*, pp. 83–84.

493 For the ambiguity of meaning in Egyptian puns, see section 1.5.1, above.

494 *Wb.* V 126, 1. Allen, *The Ancient Egyptian Pyramid Texts*, p. 217, reads the group literally as "Great Black Wall."

a geographical interpretation of the term, the choice of this curious epithet may in fact be intended as a pun on *km.ti wr.ti,* "very black,"[495] that describes Osiris in the same clause.

Osiris is further referred to by other unusual epithets, *šn-wr,* who Encircles the Islands, and *šn-wr-sk.*[496] The term *šn,* "One who Encircles, Surrounds," in these epithets refers to Osiris' all-encompassing aspect of the giant solar-Osirian deity, which is supported by the clause in the following line 7, 8: "Horus caused you to encircle every god inside your arms."

The rejuvenation of Osiris and his existence in the next world is assured by his ability to procreate through Isis. However, the transliteration of the phrase 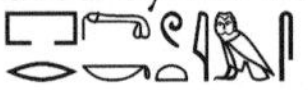 is somewhat ambiguous. The basic reading of this phrase, *pr mtwt=k im=s,* "your seed goes forth into her (=Isis)," contains a word play on *pr,* "to go forth," and *prt,* "seed."[497] Thus, 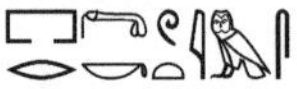 may also be read as *prt=k im=s,* "your seed is in her." Appropriately, Isis is said to be *spd m spdt,* "ready as Sothis," where the stative form of *spd* presents an alliterative pun on the name of *spd,* "Sothis," not only pointing to the astronomical signal of the coming inundation but also to the explicitly sexual connotations of the phrase.[498]

In the latter part of this spell, Horus performs numerous duties for his father, including the integration of Osiris into the sphere of the divine. The phrase *bw nb mḥ.n=k im* charges the gods with staying close to Osiris "in every place where you (=Osiris) have drowned." This statement refers to the severed parts of the god that Seth scattered throughout the Nile. As such, following Allen's suggestion, this clause refers to "Osiris as the force of life in the inundation."[499]

7, 2–3

A The parallel with PT 366 (§§626b–33a) and PT 593 (§§1627b–37a) continues in this spell.[500] Cf. the extra clause in PT §626b: *ms.n ṯw mwt=k nwt sk.n n=k gb r=k,* "Your mother Nut has given birth to you and Geb has wiped your mouth for you." Cf. the form of *sk* in PT §1627b: *sk.n n=k gb r=k.* The expression *sk r,* "wiping the mouth," is typically used in the OM ritual.[501] The phrase *wp=f n=k irty=k* is omitted from PT 593 and 366, as well as text 91 in the tomb of Mutirdis.[502] It is paralleled in BM 23, 1–2. There are two notable features in these lines:

1. *imnt* is omitted from the second *ḫnty-(imn)tyw* and in a number of following lines.
2. The dot, paralleled by BM 22, 20, is placed at the end of line 7, 2.

---

495 Or "complete and great;" see Faulkner, *Ancient Egyptian Pyramid Texts*, p. 244, n. 4.

496 This title is reminiscent of *šn-ʿ3-sk*, a "name of a sea," *Wb.* IV 310, 8–9.

497 *Wb.* I 530, 9–531, 4. For further discussion of word play, see section 1.5.1, above.

498 Englund, *Akh*, p. 56.

499 Allen, *The Ancient Egyptian Pyramid Texts*, p. 80, n. 26. See also, Koemoth, *Osiris et les arbres*, pp. 9–10, who demonstrates that the contact between Osiris' body and the Nile is generally referred to by the term *mḥ*.

500 The subsequent translations of these are based on Allen, *The Ancient Egyptian Pyramid Texts*, pp. 81 and 217, respectively.

501 Wilson, *Ptolemaic Lexikon*, pp. 941–42.

502 The transliteration and translation of the subsequent parallel spells from the tomb of Mutirdis are based on Assmann, *Mutirdis*, pp. 84–85.

7, 3

B Cf. PT §627d: *di.n=sn n=k ḫftw=k ẖr=k,* "They place for you your enemies under you." PT §1628b and Mutirdis 91, 4 replace *ḫftw=k* with "Seth:" *di.n=sn n=k stš ẖr=k ḥnk=f ẖr=k.* The scribe of P.W551 views the Ennead as a whole, referring to it by the 3rd person singular feminine suffix pronoun, as opposed to the plural suffix pronoun of the PT. Accordingly, *psḏt* is written  with nine *nṯr* signs (R8) in PT §1628a and §626c.

The following orthographic peculiarities and discrepancies with the parallels should be noted:

1. Note the dot following *hy wsir ḫnty-(imn)tyw.*
2. *nḏ* is written without phonetic complements in BM 23, 2: .
3. *ḫft* is written  in PT §626d and  in BM 23, 2.

7, 3–4

C The *d,* , of *isd,* , is written slightly above the line.
Cf. 3rd person plural suffix pronoun in PT §1628c and Mutirdis 91, 5: *ḥw.n=sn ꜥ3ꜥ isd=f ir=k.* At this point, PT 366 diverges from the present manuscript. The spelling of *ḫw* in P.W551 is similar to that of PT §1628c: .

7, 4–5

D Cf. the dependent pronouns in PT §1629a–b: *nwt ḫrt ḥr s3=s im=k ḫw=s ṯw ḫnm=s ṯw inḳ=s ṯw ṯs=s ṯw,* "Nut has fallen over her son in you. She defends you, she (re)unites you, she embraces you, she raises you." PT §1629b has *ṯs* in place of *wṯs*. Mutirdis 91, 5–6 is slightly closer to P.W551: *nwt ḫw=s s3=s im=k nw=s tw inḳ=s tw,* "Nut, she protects her son in you, she provides for you, she embraces you."

The phrase *dr.n(=s) i3kb=k,* "she has driven away your mourning,"[503] is more grammatically consistent in BM 23, 3: *dr.n=s i3kb=k ḫnm.n=s tw inḳ.n=s tw.* The initial phrase, omitted from the PT parallel and Mutirdis 91, is reminiscent of the GR epithet of a temple god in procession, *dr-i3kb,* "One who Drives Away Mourning."[504] Cf. the spelling of *i3kb* in col. 6, 9 of the present manuscript.

The following orthographic peculiarities and discrepancies with the parallel texts should be noted:

1. *inḳ,* , is written with the -jar here.[505] BM 23, 3 spells the term phonetically: 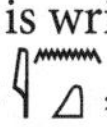, while PT §1629b in the pyramid of Merenre shows the more usual determinative for *inḳ*: .

503 Wilson, *Ptolemaic Lexikon*, p. 1203.

504 Leitz et al., eds., *Lexikon*, VII, p. 554.

505 *Wb.* I 100, 19–22.

2. *ṯwt* is spelled in PT §1629c.
3. *wr,* , has no determinative (G7) in PT §1629c.

7, 5–6

E PT 366 again parallels P.W551. PT §628a and §1630a are more concise: *ii n=k snty=k ꜣst nbt-ḥwt,* "Your two sisters, Isis and Nephthys, have returned to you." Cf. PT §1630a from the pyramid of Neferkare: *ii n=k snty=k ꜣst ḥnꜥ nbt-ḥwt,* while the version of this spell recorded in the pyramid of Merenre omits *ḥnꜥ,* "with." Mutirdis 91, 7 corresponds more closely: ... *ꜣst pw ḥnꜥ nbt-ḥwt.* Cf. the verb in PT §1630b and Mutirdis 91, 7–8: *ḥm.n=sn m bw ḫr=k im nḏr.n snt=k ꜣst im=k,* "after having gone off from where you are. Your sister Isis has taken hold of you."

Some orthographic features of this line and discrepancies with the parallel texts should be noted:

1. *iw,* , is spelled phonetically in BM 23, 4.
2. *bw* shows a more extended writing in PT §1630b: .
3. is assumed to be a mistake here, as it is omitted from all the parallel versions.
4. *nḏr* is written in PT §1630c.[506]

7, 6–7

F Cf. Allen's translation of PT §628a–b: *swꜣḏ=sn kw kmt wrt m rn=k n km-wr,* "(They) making you sound and very black in your name of Great Black (Wall)."[507] PT §1630c–d and Mutirdis 91, 9 correspond to the present manuscript, omitting *wr.ti.*

The second clause is rather different in PT §§628c–29b: *wꜣḏt wrt m rn=k n wꜣḏ-wr mk wr.ti šn.ti m šn-wr mk dbn.ti šnt m dbn pḫr-ḥꜣw-nbwt,* "very green in your name of the Great Green (=sea). Look, you are great and round, as the Great Round. Look, you are encircled and round, as the circuit that surrounds the Islands." Faulkner suggests reading *šn,* spelled in PT §629c, as an imperative with a reflexive dative.[508] The version of PT §1631a corresponds to P.W551, except for the epithet, written : *šn.n=k ḫt nbt m-ḫnw ꜥ=k m rn=k n dbn-pḫr-ḥꜣw-nbwt,* "you having encircled everything inside your arms in your name of the Circuit that Goes Around the External Isles." Faulkner reads the epithet as *dbn-pḫr-ḥꜣw-nbwt* due to the phonetic rendering of its first part in PT §629b: and . However, (F46) in PT §1631a may be a determinative for *dbn,* as it is understood here. Assmann, in turn, reads (F46), the only sign for this word in Mutirdis 91, 10, as *pḫr.*[509]

---

506 For *nḏr,* "to take hold of," see *Wb.* II 382, 21.

507 Allen, *The Ancient Egyptian Pyramid Texts,* p. 81.

508 For the spelling of *šn* with the determinative (G37), see Faulkner, *Ancient Egyptian Pyramid Texts,* p. 244, n. 5.

509 Assmann, *Mutirdis,* p. 85, n. k.

Some discrepancies with the parallel texts should be noted:

1. *ḫwt* is written as a singular  in PT §1631a and BM 23, 5.
2. Similarly, *ʿwy* appears as the singular  in BM 23, 5.
3. Note the determinative of *šn-wr* in BM 23, 5: .

7, 7–8

G Cf. Allen's translation of PT §629c: *mk šn.ti ʿ3.ti m šn-ʿ3-sk,* "Look, you have become round and great, as he who surrounds the Great Waters that Perish." See also PT §1631b and Mutirdis 92, 1, which read: *ʿ3.tw m rn=k n ʿ3-sk-mw,* "(You) having become great in your name of the Great Waters that Perish."

Cf. PT §1632b and Mutirdis 92, 1–2: *in n=k ḥr stš di.n=f n=k sw ksi ẖr=k wr pḥt=k ir=f,* "Horus has gotten Seth for you and given him to you bowed down under you: your strength is greater than his." The following three lines of PT 366 diverge from the present manuscript.

Some discrepancies with the parallel texts should be noted:

1.  regularly appears in place of *tw* in PT §629c and BM 23, 5.
2. *mk* is spelled simply  in PT §629c.
3. Horus is consistently spelled 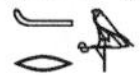 in BM 23, 5.
4. The phonetic complement is omitted in the name of Seth, , written in black ink, in BM 23, 6.
5. *sḫr,* , has phonetic complements in BM 23, 6.
6. The double  (F9) is paralleled in BM 23, 6, while PT §1632b has the phonetic .

7, 8

H Cf. the slightly longer PT §§1632c–1633b and Mutirdis 92, 2–3: *rdi.n ḥr šn=k n=k nṯrw nb m-ẖnw ʿwy=k i.mr n ḥr it=f im=k n di.n ḥr bḫn=k n bi3.n ḥr ir=k nḏ.n ḥr it=f im=k,* "Horus has made you encircle all the gods inside your arms. Horus has desired his father in you, and Horus cannot let you disappear. Horus cannot be away from you, for Horus has tended his father in you." BM 23, 7 closely corresponds to P.W551, except for the *sḏm.n=f* form of *mr*.

The presence of the  determinative (G7) after *it=f im=k* suggests that this phrase should be understood as an epithet. The 2nd person singular suffix pronoun following *im* refers to Osiris, the father of Horus.

Some discrepancies with the parallel texts should be noted:

1. The verb *rdi* shows a phonetic *t* in P.W551.
2. Note the determinative for *bi3,* , in PT §1633a and its spelling in BM 23, 7: .

3. *it* is spelled with the phonetic *d* in P.W551. BM 23, 7 has an abbreviated spelling of *it=f*: .

7, 9–10

I Every parallel presents a slightly different version of this statement. Cf. PT §1633c: *ꜥnḫ.ti m ḫpr-ꜥnḫ n ḏdd=k m ḏdt,* “You are alive as the Living Scarab, enduring in Mendes.” See also Mutirdis 92, 3–4: *ꜥnḫ.ti m ꜥnḫ n ḏdd=k m ḏdt,* “You are alive as the Living One, enduring in Mendes.” Cf. BM 23, 7: *ꜥnḫ.ti m ḫpr dd=k m ḏdt,* “You are alive as the Beetle, enduring in Mendes.”
The epithet *nb-sꜣwt,* “Lord of Asyut,” refers to Osiris, as well as various other deities.[510]
Some orthographic peculiarities and discrepancies with the parallel texts should be noted:

1. *ꜥnḫ,* , is very abbreviated in this line, but has phonetic complements in PT §1633c from the pyramid of Neferkare: .
2. *ḏdwt* is spelled or in PT §1633c, while BM 23, 7 has .
3. *sꜣ* is spelled phonetically here .[511] Cf. the spelling of *sꜣ* as in PT §630a and §1634a.
4. *nb* has a determinative (G7), paralleled only by PT §630b from the pyramid of Teti.
5. *s,* , of line 7, 9 is a phonetic complement of *sꜣwt,* , in line 7, 10. Cf. in PT §630a and §1634a.[512]

7, 10

J Cf. the more extended PT §§630c–32c: *…n nṯr=sn im=k m rn=k n nṯr dwꜣ=sn ṯw im=k ḥr ir=sn m rn=k n dwꜣ-nṯr iꜥb=sn ṯw im=k ḏnd m rn=k n ḏndrw i n=k snt=k ist (i). ḥꜥꜥ=t n mrwt=k d.n=k s tp ḥms=k pr mtwt=k im=s spd.t m spdt,* “…for their god in you, in your name of God. They worship you so that you do not become far from them in your name of *dwꜣ-nṯr*; gathering you, so that you do not become angry, in your name of the *ḏndrw*-Bark. Your sister Isis has come to you, aroused [for] love of you. You have put her on your phallus so that your seed might emerge into her, sharp as Sothis.” PT §§1634c–35a is close to the present manuscript: *n nṯr=sn im=k m rn=k n mr-nṯr dwꜣ=sn ṯw im=k ḥr r=sn*. Cf. the somewhat different Mutirdis 92, 5–7: *mꜣꜣ.n ḥr it=f im=k m rn=k n nṯr nṯrw=sn im=k m rn=k n … dwꜣ=sn ṯw nn wꜣi=k r=sn,* “Horus sees his father in you, in your name of God, their divinity is in you in your name of … They worship you and you are not far from them.”
PT §1635b and Mutirdis 92, 7 do not include *sn=k* in the latter clause of this line. The rest of the texts parallel P.W551.

510 Leitz et al., eds., *Lexikon* III, p. 725.
511 *Wb.* III 416, 12.
512 For *sꜣwt*, “Asyut,” see *Wb.* III 420, 2.

Some discrepancies with the parallel texts should be noted:

1. *mr-nṯr* is spelled in PT §1634c from the pyramid of Merenre.[513]
Cf. , *nṯr-spꜣt* in place of *mr-nṯr* in BM 23, 8.
2. PT §631a and §1635a spell *dwꜣ* in a more typical manner: , while
BM 23, 8 has .
3. The in the 3rd person plural suffix pronoun of *dwꜣ* is mistakenly written
below of the 2nd person singular dependent pronoun *kw*: .
4. *im* is written in PT §1635a.
5. *ḥr* is written in most PT parallels.

7, 11

K Cf. PT §§632d–33a: *ḥr spd pr im=k m ḥr-im-spdt ꜣḫ.n=k im=f m rn=f/k n ꜣḫ-im-ḏndrw*; Cf. PT §§1636b–37a: *ḥr-spd pr im=k m rn=f n ḥr im spdt ꜣḫ=k im=f m rn=f n ꜣḫ-im-ḏndrw*. The very slight difference in the suffix pronouns of the latter clauses creates a great difference in meaning. While the PT spell states that Hor-Soped provides power to the deceased, the present manuscript suggests that it is the deceased through whom Hor-Soped receives his power. This latter clause is reminiscent of the OK epithet *ꜣḫ-imy-ḏndrw*, "Spirit who is in the *Djenderu*-Bark."[514]
The epithet *ḥr-sꜣ-nḏ-it=f*, "Horus, the Son who Protects his Father," refers to Horus, as well as his son, Kebehsenuef.[515]
The parallels of PT 366 and 593 end here.

7, 12

L This line corresponds with the beginning of PT 356 (§§575–77).[516] Cf. PT §575a: *iw.n ḥr sḫn=f ṯw*. The present manuscript uses *nḥm*, "to take away, rescue," which is visually similar to PT's *sḫn*.[517] Cf. the *sḏm.n=f* forms in BM 23, 11: *nḥm.n=f tw ir.n=f*. The 3rd person singular masculine suffix pronoun refers to Horus.
Some peculiarities and discrepancies with the parallel texts should be noted:

1. (*imnt*) of the epithet *ḫnty-imntyw* is inserted above the line.
2. *nḏ* is written with the phonetic complement *d*.
3. The omitted determinative (D54) of *iw*, , "to come," is present in the variants of PT §575a as or , and in BM 23, 11 as .

513 For the PT epithet of the deceased, *mr-nṯr*, "Canal of the God," see Leitz et al., eds., *Lexikon* III, p. 328.

514 Leitz et al., eds., *Lexikon* I, p. 36. For *ḏndrw*, see *Wb.* V 579, 9–12.

515 Leitz et al., eds., *Lexikon* VI, p. 85.

516 The translation of the subsequent spells is based on Allen, *The Ancient Egyptian Pyramid Texts*, pp. 72–73.

517 *Wb.* II 294, 12–297, 4.

7, 13

M Cf. PT §§575b–76a: *rdi.n=f sḫt n=k ḏḥwty m-ḫt stš in.n=f n=k sn iwnw sḥm.n=f (n=k) ib stš ṯwt wr ir=f,* "He (=Horus) has made Thoth drive back Seth's followers for you, he has gotten them corralled for you, and has turned away the desire of Seth. You are greater than he." The dative *n=k* occurs only in the pyramid of Neferkare. The 3rd person singular masculine suffix pronouns of *in* and *sḫm* refer to Thoth, whose name is written (G26) in PT §575b. The causative of the verb *sḫt,* , is written in line 7, 12.[518] This verb lacks determinatives in BM 23, 11: .
Cf. the latter part of this phrase in BM 23, 11–12: *in[.n=f] n=k s(n) srwy sḥm.n=f n=k ib stš ṯwt wr ir=f.*

7, 14

N Cf. the suffix pronouns in PT §576c and BM 23, 12: *m3.n gb ḳd=k d.n=f kw m st=k.* BM 23, 13 corresponds to P.W551 except for the form of the verb *ini*: *in.n n=k gb.*
Some discrepancies with the parallel texts should be noted:

1. *m33* has an abbreviated writing in PT §576c: and BM 23, 12: .
2. *st,* , does not have the determinative (O1) in PT §576c.
3. (*imnt*) of the epithet *ḫnty-imntyw* is inserted above the line.

7, 15

O PT §577a has the correct feminine demonstrative in place of the masculine *pw* of P.W551 in the phrase *3st tw ḥnʿ nbt-ḥwt.*
The parallel with PT 356 ends with this line. PT §577b corresponds with the beginning of PT 370 (§645). Cf. the very similar PT §645a–b: *hy wsir NN rdi.n ḥr dmḏ ṯw nṯrw snsn=sn ir=k m rn=k n snwt.* Cf. also *Stundenwachen* XIV, 71–72: *sn=sn r=k ḫpr rn=sn ipw n snwti,* "They unite with you and this their name of *snwti* comes into being."[519] The term *snwt,* "chapel," is frequently used to mean cabin of a bark-shrine or cult image.[520]
Some discrepancies with the parallel texts should be noted:

1. *dmḏ,* , has a phonetic complement in PT §577b and §645a.
2. *snsn,* "to be brotherly," is spelled as a visual pun on the *snwt* shrine.[521]
Cf. PT §645b: and the phonetic rendering in PT §577c.
3. The of the 3rd person plural suffix pronoun of *snsn* is omitted.
4. (*imnt*) of the epithet *ḫnty-imntyw* is inserted above the line.

518 For *ḫt,* "to drive back, repel," see *Wb.* III 342, 15–343, 4.
519 Cf. Junker, *Stundenwachen,* p. 83: "und vereinigen sich mit dir, und so wird ihr Name: *snti.*"
520 Wilson, *Ptolemaic Lexikon,* p. 855.
521 *Wb.* IV 172, 14. For puns, see section 1.5.1, above.

7, 16

P The address in this line begins with two *im+sḏm* constructions, negating the Old Egyptian subjunctive/imperative.[522]
The following passage corresponds with PT 367 (§§634c–35)[523] and PT 357 (§§590–92).[524] Cf. the prospective forms in PT §634c: *im=k gꜣ im=k ꜥšw rdi.n n=k ḥr irt=f,* "(He [=Horus] has fetched for you the god's hearts,) that you might not groan, that you might not moan. Horus has given you his eye." The expression im *gꜣ (i)m ꜥšw* is paralleled by PT §590a.[525] The following statement of P.W551, which describes Horus performing the Opening of the Mouth, parallels PT §589b exactly: *wp n=k ḥr r=k.* Thus, this and the previous phrases are reversed in the PT parallel. *wn=f n=k irty=k* is omitted from PT 357.
Some discrepancies with the parallel texts should be noted:

1. *di* is omitted from the name of Padikakem, probably due to the lack of space at the end of the line.
2. *ꜥšw,* 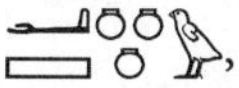, shows a more extended spelling in PT §590a and §634c, and is written  in BM 23, 14.
3. *wn,* , lacks the  determinative (D40) in BM 23, 14.
4.  (*imnt*) of the epithet *ḫnty-imntyw* is inserted above the line again.

7, 17

Q The 3rd person plural suffix pronoun of *ibw* refers to the gods in the following clause. Cf. PT §590b–c: *in.n n=k gb ḥr ip=f n=k ibw=sn,* "Geb brought Horus to you that he may allot to you their hearts." Cf. the *sḏm=f* form in BM 23, 14: *in n=k gb.*
ḥnw is a personification of the Sokar bark, on which the falcon-headed god stands.[526]
All the parallels omit *wꜥ* after *sp* in the latter part of this line. See PT §590c: *in.n=f n=k nṯrw nb m sp n biꜣ im=sn m-ꜥ=f,* "He has brought to you all the gods together, and there is not one of them who will be away from you." Cf. also BM: *in.n=f n=k nṯrw nbw m sp nn biꜣ im=sn r=k. biꜣ* is written without determinatives in BM 23, 15.[527] This line also occurs in PT §647a: *in.n=f n=k nṯrw m sp n biꜣ im=sn m-ꜥ=f.*

522 Allen, *Inflection of the Verb*, p. 13.

523 The translation of the subsequent spells is based on Allen, *The Ancient Egyptian Pyramid Texts*, p. 82.

524 The translation of the subsequent spells is based on Allen, *The Ancient Egyptian Pyramid Texts*, pp. 73–74.

525 For *gꜣ*, "languish," see Faulkner, *Ancient Egyptian Pyramid Texts*, p. 115, n. 8.

526 Leitz et al., eds., *Lexikon* V, p. 159. For the epithet *ḥr-m-ḥnw*, "Horus in the *Henw*-Bark," see Leitz et al., eds., *Lexikon* V, p. 274.

527 For *biꜣ*, "to leave, escape," see *Wb.* I 439, 10.

7, 17–18

R A variant reading of the first clause, *nḏ.n kw ḥr n ḏdw,* is "Horus of Buto protects you." Cf. the more complete PT §591a–c: *nḏ.n ṯw ḥr ni ḏd.n nḏ=f ṯw nḥm.n ḥr irt=f m-ʿ stš rdi. n=f n=k s,* "Horus has protected you, and he will not delay protecting you. Horus has wrestled his eye from Seth and given it to you." Cf. the latter part of BM 23, 16: *sḥm.n=f n=k ib n stš di.n=f n=k.*

Some discrepancies with the parallel texts should be noted:

1. *nḥm,* , does not have determinatives in BM 23, 15.
2. Note the abbreviated spelling of Seth, written in black ink in BM 23, 16: .

7, 18–19

S This phrase is grammatically unusual, since a prospective *sḏm=f* is expected in place of the *sḏm.n=f* form.[528] Cf. PT §591c: *irt=f tn bnt sḫt n=k s ip n=k s ḥ3 nḫḫ ḫr=k,* "This sweet eye of his, return it to yourself, allot it to yourself. O, may it endure with you." The latter clause is also paralleled by PT 169 (§100). Cf. BM 23, 16: *hy snḫḫ.n=s ḫr=k.*

7, 19

T Note the omission of Nephthys and the slight variantion of the participial statement in PT §592a–c: *iʿb.n ṯw 3st ḫnt ib ḥr ḫr=k m rn=k n ḫnty-imntyw in ḥr nḏ=f irt.n stš ir=k.* See also BM 23, 16–17: *iʿb.n=k tw 3st ḥnʿ nbt-ḥwt.*

Some discrepancies with the parallel texts should be noted:

1. The abbreviated *ḥnʿ,* , of P.W551 is spelled phonetically in BM 23, 16: 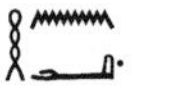.
2. *ḫnty,* 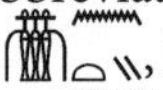, has phonetic complements in BM 23, 17.
3. *imntyw,* 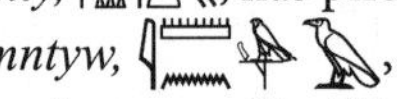, has the more extended phonetic spelling in PT §592b from the pyramid of Teti.

7, 20–21

U This line corresponds with the beginning of PT 364 (§§609–21)[529] and text 104a in the tomb of Mutirdis.[530]

ip is a participle. PT §609b closely corresponds, replacing *kw* with *ṯw*: *ii ḥr ip=f ṯw m-ʿ nṯrw mr.n ṯw ḥr*. Cf. BM 23, 17: *ip=f ṯw.*

528 For an overview of the variation of the *sḏm=f* and *sḏm.n=f* forms in late texts, see Lustman, *Étude Grammaticale du Papyrus Bremner-Rhind*, p. 116, n. 9, and p. 137.

529 The translation of the subsequent spells is based on Allen, *The Ancient Egyptian Pyramid Texts*, p. 80.

530 The transliteration and translation of the subsequent spells is based on Assmann, *Mutirdis*, pp. 94ff. This text also occurs in the tomb of Psametik; see Daressy, *RdT* 17 (1895): 17–25.

Cf. PT §609c: *ḥtm.n=f ṯw sdmy.n n=k ḥr irt=f ir=k,* "He has provided you; Horus has painted his eye on you." The clause *m irt=f* appears only in the pyramid of Merenre. Cf. Mutirdis 104a, 2: *ḥtm=f ṯw m irty=f sdmi n=k ḥr irty=f r=k,* "He provides you with his eyes; he has joined his eye to you."

Some points of comparison with the parallel texts should be noted:

1. *ʿḥʿ* is written  in PT §609a.
2. A dot is placed between *ḥr,* , and *ip,* 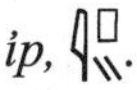.
3. *nṯrw,* , is written in PT §609b and BM 23, 18.
4. The spelling of *ḥtm,* , in P.W551 is similar to the version of PT §609c in the pyramid of Teti: .[531]

7, 21

v Cf. PT §610a: *wp.n n=k ḥr irt=k mꜣ=k im=s,* "Horus opened your eye, that you might see with it." Cf. also the nominal subject in Mutirdis 104a, 3 and BM 23, 18: *wp n=k ḥr irt=f mꜣ=k im=s*. Cf. the shorter writing of *mꜣꜣ* in PT §610a:  and BM 23, 18: .

7, 22

w Mutirdis 104a, 3 uses *nṯrt* in place of "Isis with Nephthys."
Faulkner and Allen offer a more literal rendering of PT §611a: *ḥtp ḥr=k n=f,* "May your face be well-disposed/peaceful to him."[532] Cf. Mutirdis 104a, 4: … *n wn nmtt=k.*
Some discrepancies with the parallel texts should be noted:

1. Cf. the phonetic complements of *ṯs* in PT §610b:  and BM 23, 19: .
2. The  and  in the suffix pronoun *sn* of *mr=sn* are reversed.
3. *swꜣḏ* shows a simpler spelling in PT §610c: .
4. *ḥnʿ* has an abbreviated spelling in BM 23, 19: .
5. *ḥr* shows an extended writing in PT §610d:  and BM 23, 19: .
6. *ḥtp* is more abbreviated in PT §611a:  and BM 23, 19: .

7, 22–23

x *šsp* is an imperative in P.W551. Cf. the very similar PT §611a: *wn=k šsp n=k mdt ḥr ḥtp=k ḥr=s*. Mutirdis 104a, 4 considerably shortens the first statement: *šsp=k mdwt=f ḥr=s,* "May you receive his words about it!"
Cf. PT §611b: *sḏm n ḥr n sww n=k rdi.n=f šms kw nṯrw,* "Listen to Horus: it will not be dangerous for you, for he has made the gods follow you." This sentence in P.W551 di-

---

531 For *ḥtm,* "to provide," see *Wb.* III 196, 9–197, 9.

532 Faulkner, *Ancient Egyptian Pyramid Texts*, p. 118; Allen, *The Ancient Egyptian Pyramid Texts*, p. 80.

verges from its older PT parallel in meaning, but not in sound.[533] The scribe of the present manuscript may have played with the sound of the original *n sww n=k,* resulting in the very different sense of *nis.n=k,* "(Listen to Horus,) whom you have summoned." Notably, the Saite tomb of Mutirdis 104a, 4–5, parallels P.W551.
Some discrepancies with the parallel texts should be noted:

1. The omission of the phonetic complement □ of *ḥtp,* , is paralleled by PT §611a from the pyramid of Merenre.
2. Cf. the phonetic complements of *sḏm,* , in PT §611b.
3. Cf. the phonetic complements of *šms,* , in PT §611b.

7, 24–25

Y Cf. the variation in Mutirdis 104a, 5: *rs ir=k rdi n=k ḥr ip=f tw ꜣḫ.n=f im=k sꜥr n=k ḥr nṯrw is rdit.n=f n=k st,* "Awaken yourself. Horus causes for you that he may claim you. He has power through you. Horus has caused the gods to ascend to you, indeed, he has given it to you."
The phrase *ꜣḫ.n=f im=k* also occurs in line 11 of this column. Faulkner translates this phrase in PT §612b as "It will go well with him through you," while Allen offers a more literal interpretation: "(Horus) has become *akh* through you."[534]
Cf. the latter clause in PT §613a: *siꜥr.n n=k ḥr nṯrw rdi.n=f n=k sn,* "Horus has elevated the gods to you: he has given them to you."
Some discrepancies with the parallel texts should be noted:

1. *rs* is written in PT §612a and in BM 23, 20.
2. Note the determinative of *ip,* , in PT §612a.
3. *ꜣḫ,* , does not have determinatives in PT §612b.
4. This spelling of *sḥḏ,* , corresponds to the pyramid of Merenre.

7, 25

Z In this manuscript, *nbt,* , modifies the relative form of *iṯt*. PT §613b closely corresponds: *di.n ṯw ḥr m-ḥꜣt nṯrw rdi.n=f iṯt=k ṯw nbt*. However, Sethe translates *nbt* as "lady," probably following the inscription from the pyramid of Teti, which spells the term .[535] On the contrary, Faulkner and Allen read *nb* as the nominal adjective "all," and follow Gunn's suggestion of understanding *ṯwt* as the independent pronoun in its possessive sense.[536] Cf. Mutirdis 104a, 6–7: *rdi.n ṯw ḥr m-ḥꜣt nṯrw rdit.n=f iṯt=k twt rꜥ*.

---

533 For the discussion of word play, see section 1.5.1, above.

534 Faulkner, *Ancient Egyptian Pyramid Texts*, p. 118; Allen, *The Ancient Egyptian Pyramid Texts*, p. 80, respectively.

535 Faulkner, *Ancient Egyptian Pyramid Texts*, p. 119.

536 Faulkner, *ibid.*, reads "all that belongs to you," while Allen, *The Ancient Egyptian Pyramid Texts*, p. 80, translates the phrase as "all that is yours."

Cf. the more extended versions of the latter clause in PT §613c: *mr.n sw ḥr ir=k n wp.n=f ir=k sʿnḫ.n ṯw ḥr m rn=k pw n ʿnḏti,* "Horus has bound himself to you and cannot separate from you. Horus has caused you to live, in your name of Andjety." Cf. the erroneous use of *im* in Mutirdis 104a, 7: *mr.n s ḥr im=k wp r=k sʿnḫ tw ḥr m rn=k n ʿnḏti*. Cf. the 2nd person dependent pronoun in BM 23, 22: *mr.n sw ḥr ir=k nn wp.n ḥr ir=k sʿnḫ.n kw ḥr m rn=k n ʿnḏti*.

Some orthographic features and discrepancies should be noted:

1. *rdi* is written with  (X8) in PT §613b.
2. *iṯt* is written  in PT §613b.
3. *mr* is written 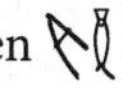 in PT §613c.
4. This spelling of *wp,* , corresponds with PT §613c in the pyramid of Teti.
5. This spelling of *ʿnḏti,* , corresponds with PT §614a in the pyramid of Merenre.[537]

7, 26

AA The remaining traces confirm a correspondence with PT §614c and BM 23, 22. The subject of *d* is omitted from P.W551, as well as the PT and BM parallels: *d n=k s imim=k nr n=k ḫftw=k nb*. Cf. Mutirdis 104a, 8: *m-ʿ=k nrw n=k ḫftw=k nbw*.

This spelling of *imim,* 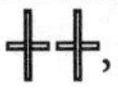, corresponds with PT §614c in the pyramid of Merenre.[538] The following *imim* in P.W551 is superfluous.

7, 26–27

BB The 3rd person singular feminine suffix pronoun of *rn* refers to the eye of Horus. Cf. the very similar PT §614d: *mḥ.n kw ḥr tm.ti m irt=f m rn=s pw n wȝḥt-nṯr*. Horus is omitted from the variant of the spell in the pyramid of Teti. Cf. Mutirdis 104a, 8–9: *mḥ.n ṯw ḥr im.tw m irt=f m rn=swy n wȝḥt*. Cf. BM 23, 22–23: *mḥ.n kw ḥr ḥtm.ti im irt=f m rn=s pwy n mḏ*. PT §614d has the epithet *wȝḥt-nṯr,* while Mutirdis 104a, 8–9 simply has 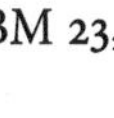, *wȝḥt*. However, the remaining traces do not appear to be similar to this group. Cf. the unusual 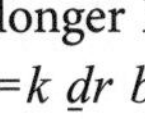, *mḏ,* in BM 23, 23.

The broken portion of this line may be reconstructed on the basis of PT §615a: *i.ḫmʿ.n n=k ḥr nṯrw,* "Horus has collected the gods for you," and Mutirdis 104a, 9 and BM 23, 23: *iḫm n=k ḥr nṯrw*.

Cf. the longer PT §615b–d: *n biȝ.n=sn ir=k ḏr bw šm.n=k im ip.n n=k ḥr nṯrw n biȝ. n=sn ir=k ḏr bw mḥ.n=k im,* "They cannot be away from you in any place in which you have gone. Horus has allotted the gods to you and they cannot be away from you in any place in which you became immersed." Cf. BM 23, 23: *n biȝ im=sn r=k ḏr bw nb mḥ.n=k im*. The parallels have a shorter writing of *biȝ* than what the traces in this

537 For *ʿnḏti*, "God of Busiris," see *Wb.* I 207, 12.

538 For *imim*, "to be strong," see Faulkner, *Ancient Egyptian Pyramid Texts*, p. 58, n. 1.

manuscript indicate. Cf. PT §615:  and BM 23, 23: . *mḥ* has a more extended spelling in PT §615d: .

7, 27–28

CC Cf. PT §616a–d: *ink.n n=k nbt-ḥwt ꜥt=k nbt m rn=s pw n sš3t nbt ḳdw swḏ3.n(=s) n=k sn rdi.tw n mwt=k nwt m rn=s n ḏrwt,*[539] "Nephthys has collected for you all your limbs in this name of hers of Seshat, Lady of Builders. (She) has made them hale for you. You have been given to your mother Nut, in her name of Coffin." The abbreviated writing of Seshat is similar to its rendering in PT §616b from the pyramid of Merenre: . *ḏrwt* has a more common determinative (O20) in PT §616d: . The pyramid of Teti offers a different name in place of *ḏrwt*: ... *m rn=s n ḳrs*.
Cf. Mutirdis 104a, 9–10: *ink.n n=k nbt-ḥwt ꜥtw=k nbw m rn=s pwy n sš3t nbt ḳdw wḏ3. n=s tw di=s tw n mwt=k nwt nḏr=s im=k m rn=s pwy n ḏrt*. Cf. BM 23, 24: *ink.n n=k nbt-ḥwt ꜥt=k m rn=s pw n sš3t nbt ḳdw sw3ḏ n=k mwt=k nwt ꜥt=s ḥr=k m rn=s pw n ḏrt*. The word following Nut in P.W551, which begins with ... and acts as the direct object of *di*, is likely *ꜥt*, as in the BM version.

7, 28–29

DD Cf. PT §616e: *ink.n=s ṯw m rn=s n ḳrs*. Mutirdis 104a, 10 corresponds to the PT variant adding a demonstrative *pwy* after *rn=s*. Cf. BM 23, 24: *ink.n=s kw m rn=s pw ḳrs*. The phonetic *s*, , and  determinative (Q6) of *ḳrs* remain in P.W551.
The damaged text may be reconstructed on the basis of PT §§616f–17a: *i.siꜥ.ti n=s m rn=s n iꜥ iꜥb.n n=k ḥr ꜥtw=k ni rdi.n=f snw=k,* "You have been raised to her in her name of the tomb's superstructure. Horus has gathered your limbs for you, he will not let you suffer." Cf. Mutirdis 104a, 10–11: *sꜥr.n=s tw m rn=s pwy n iꜥ iꜥb n=k nṯrw ꜥwt=k nbt nn rdit.n=f snwy=k*. BM 23, 25 is similar to Mutirdis: *sꜥr.n=s kw m rn=s pw n iꜥ ꜥwt=k nbt n rdi.n=f snwy=k*.

7, 30

EE For a possible reconstruction see PT §617b–c and Mutirdis 104a, 11–12: *dmḏ.n=f kw/tw ni ẖnn.ti im=k sꜥḥꜥ.n ṯw ḥr m nwtwtw,*[540] "He has joined you and nothing in you can be disturbed. Horus has made you stand: Do not stumble!" Cf. the dependent pronouns in BM 23, 26: *dmḏ.n=f tw n ẖnw im=k sꜥḥꜥ.n kw ḥr m nwtwtw*.

7, 30–31

FF The remaining traces point to a reconstruction of the address "Osiris of Padikakem," standard to this papyrus. Only the top of the red  is visible.

539 For *ḏrwt*, "coffin," see *Wb.* V 601, 3.

540 For *nwtwtw*, a substantive attested already in the PT, see *Wb.* II 224, 16.

The damaged portion may be reconstructed on the basis of PT §618a–b: *wṯs ỉb=k ỉr=f ꜥꜣ ỉb=k wn r=k nḏ.n ṯw ḥr nỉ ḏd.n nḏ=f ṯw,* "Lift up your heart towards him, may your heart be great (i.e., rejoice). Open your mouth, for Horus has protected you and his protection of you cannot fail."[541] Cf. BM 23, 27: *ṯs ỉb=k ỉr=f ꜥꜣ ḥꜣt=k ỉr=f wn r=k nḏ.n kw ḥr n ḏd n nḏ=f ṯ(w).* See also Mutirdis 104a, 13: *wṯs ỉb=k ỉr=f ꜥꜣ ỉb=k rf wn r=k nḏ.n ṯw ḥr m ḏdw n nḏt=f tw.*

7, 31–32

GG Cf. PT §619a–b: *hy wsỉr NN pw ṯwt nṯr sḫm nỉ nṯr mỉt=k rdỉ.n n=k ḥr msw=f wṯs=sn ṯw,* "O, Osiris NN! You are the god who has control. There is no god like you. Horus has given to you his children, that they may raise you." Mutirdis 104a, 14 is somewhat ambiguous: *NN twt ḥr nṯr ꜥꜣ sḫm ꜥꜣ n nṯr mỉtt=k rdỉ n=k ḥr msw=f wṯs=sn tw,* "NN, you are Horus, the Great God, whose power is great. There is no god like you. Horus gives his children to you that they may raise you." BM 23, 27–28 is closer to the present manuscript: *hy wsỉr ḫnty-ỉmntyw tw(t) nṯr ꜥnḫ wꜥ.ti nn nṯr mr=k rdỉ n=k ḥr msw=f wṯs=sn kw.*
Note the determinative (O1) for *mr,* , in BM 23, 28.

7, 32

HH The *m* preceding *šms* is omitted from PT §620a and Mutirdis 104a, 15.
Some discrepancies with the parallel texts should be noted:

1. *šms,* , has phonetic complements in PT §620a.
2. *sḫm,* ( ), does not have a (A24) in PT §620a.
3. *fꜣi,* , is written with the determinative (Q4) in PT §620b.

7, 32–33

II Cf. the suffix pronouns in PT §§620b–21a and Mutirdis 104a, 15–6: *fꜣi.n ṯw ḥr m rn=f n ḥnw wṯs.n=f tw m rn=k pwy n skr ꜥnḫ.ti nmnm=k rꜥ nb,* "Horus has raised you in his name of the *Henw*-Bark, he has lifted you up in this your name of Sokar. Live that you may move about every day." BM 23, 28 omits the demonstrative *pwy.* *ꜥnḫ* is a stative used in the exclamatory sense.[542]
The following orthographic peculiarities and discrepancies with the parallel texts should be noted:

1. *ḥnw* is written in PT §620b and in BM 23, 27.
2. is written in place of *tw* following *ꜣḫ* in PT §621b.

---

541 For the reading of *n ḏd.n nḏ=f* as a *sḏm.n=f* verb with a nominal *sḏm=f* subject, see Faulkner, *Ancient Egyptian Pyramid Texts*, p. 119, n. 9.

542 Gardiner, *Egyptian Grammar*, §313.

3. The reading of as "Sokar" is questionable, as (G5) stands in place of (G10), expected in the name of Sokar. The spelling in PT §620c supports the reading. However, the phonetic in BM 23, 28 points to the variation "Sokar-Horus."

7, 33–34

JJ The (N18) of *3ḫt*, , is written on the following line. *3ḫt-prrt-rꜥ/itn-im=s*, "Horizon from which Re Comes Forth," is a PT epithet of the deceased, applied here to Osiris.[543]

The verbs in the latter phrase are stative forms used in the exclamatory sense, despite the distinction between *ti* and *tw* endings.

Cf. the gemination of *pr* in PT §621b–c: *3ḫ.ti m rn=k n 3ḫt prrt rꜥ im=s w3š.ti spd.ti b3.ti sḫm.ti n ḏt ḏt*. Mutirdis 104a, 16 slightly alters the statements: *3ḫ.tw m rn=k pwy n 3ḫt-pḫr-rꜥ im=s sw3š ṯw spd.ti b3.ṯw 3ḫ.ṯw sḫm.ṯw n ḏt*, "You are a spirit in this your name of Horizon in which Re turns. Be strong, be effective, be a *ba*, be glorified, be powerful forever."

The distinction between the stroke (Z1) and the determinative (N17) in the two *ḏt* words, and , suggests two diverse readings of "body" and "eternity," respectively.

Some discrepancies with the parallel texts should be noted:

1. The determinative (D54) of *pr*, , is omitted from BM 23, 28.
2. *w3š* is spelled in PT §621c and in BM 23, 28.
3. *spd* has a more extended phonetic spelling in PT §621c: .
4. *sḫm* is written in PT §621c and in BM 23, 28.

543 Leitz et al., eds., *Lexikon* I, p. 52.

3.2.8. *sꜣḫw* III, SPELL 8 *Lines 7, 34–45*[544]

From the beginning, this spell uses prospective and imperative verb forms, commanding Osiris to stand up and, despite death, seize the authority of his kingship. The close connection of Re and Osiris is emphasized, as the former summons (*nỉs*) the latter. Comparable to spell 4, above, at this point in the solar cycle, Osiris is invited to receive the standard formula of offerings, following his union with Re.[545]

TRANSLITERATION

sꜣḫ
ḏd mdw
ḫr (7, 35) *wr ḥr gs=f*
ꜥḥꜥ nṯr
sḫm=f ḥnꜥ=f
wrrt=f tp=f
mr wrrt rꜥ
pr=f m ꜣḫt
nḏ ḥr=f ỉn ḥr m ꜣḫt
36. *hy wsỉr ḫnty-ỉmnt(tyw) wsỉr n Pꜣ-dỉt-kꜣ-km*
ṯs.tỉ
šsp n=k sꜥḥ ỉr.n=k psḏt ꜥꜣt
wn 37. *n=k ḥr nst gb*
m st rdỉ.n rꜥ ḫnty-psḏt
ỉṯt n=k sḫm
ḫnp n=k wrrt
*hy wsỉr ḫnty-ỉmnt(tyw) wsỉr n Pꜣ-dỉt-*38.*-kꜣ-km*
nfr.w(y) nn
wr.w(y) nn ỉr n=k ỉt=k gb
rdỉ.n=f n=k nst=f
wḏ=k mdt n štꜣw-swt
sšm.tw 39. *špsw=sn*
šms tw ꜣḫw nb(w) m rn=sn pw n štꜣw-swt
hy wsỉr ḫnty-ỉmnt(tyw) wsỉr n Pꜣ-dỉt-kꜣ-km
(7, 40) *nḏm ỉb=k*
ꜥꜣ ḥꜣt=k
nṯw tm n ḥr ỉm sp=f
nỉs tw rꜥ m rn=k pw n snḏ-n=f-ꜣḫw-nb
41. *šꜥt=k pw r ỉbw nṯrw mr šꜥt rꜥ*
pr=f m ꜣḫt
mr šꜥt ḥr nb-pꜥt

544 See section 1.7.3, above.

545 See the discussion of the Osiris-Re conjunction in text notes for line 1, 43.

hy wsir ḫnty-imnt(tyw) wsir n P3-dit-k3-km
42. *sšt3-irw=f inpw is ḥr ẖt=f*
šsp.n=k ḥr=k r s3b
ṯs
wsir ḫnty-imnt(tyw) wsir n P3-43.-dit-k3-km
ʿḥʿ ḥms r ḫ3=k m t r ḫ3=k m ḥnḳt r ḫ3=k m iw3 r ḫ3=k m 3pdw r ḫ3=k ḫt
nbt nfr(t) wʿb(t) im
44. *hy wsir ḫnty-imnt(tyw) wsir n P3-dit-k3-km*
gm tw rʿ ʿḥʿw ḥ(nʿ)=k mwt=k nwt
sšm=s kw m w3wt (7, 45) *3ḫt*
ir n=k mnw=k im
nfr.tw ḥn(ʿ) k3=k n ḏt ḏt

TRANSLATION

Glorification spell.
Words spoken:
"The Great One (7, 35) has fallen upon his side.
May the god stand up,
his power being with him
and his *Wereret* (on) his head,
as the *Wereret* of Re.[A]
He comes forth from the horizon,
as he is greeted by Horus in the Horizon (Horemakhet).
36. O, Osiris, Foremost of the West(erners), Osiris of Padikakem.
Raise yourself!
Receive for yourself the dignity which the Great Ennead has made for you,
that you may be 37. upon the throne of Geb,
in the place which Re, Foremost of the Ennead, has given.
Seize for yourself the power,
take for yourself the *Wereret*! [B]
O, Osiris, Foremost of the West(erners), Osiris of Padi-38.-kakem.
How good is this,
how great is this which your father, Geb, has done for you!
He gave to you his throne,
that you may command words to Those whose Seats are Secret,
so that their august ones may 39. be guided,
so that all the spirits may follow you in these names of theirs,
"Those whose Seats are Secret." [C]
O, Osiris, Foremost of the West(erners), Osiris of Padikakem.
(7, 40) May your heart be sweet,
may your heart be great,
for you belong to him (from) whose actions (you) will not be far.
Re summons you in this name of yours of He whom All the Spirits Fear.[D]

41. This terror of you is in the hearts of the gods as the terror of Re,
when he goes forth from the horizon;
like the terror of Horus, Lord of Humanity.[E]

O, Osiris, Foremost of the West(erners), Osiris of Padikakem.
42. He whose Form is Secret, like Anubis upon his belly.
You have received your face of a jackal.
Rise! [F]

Osiris, Foremost of the West(erners), Osiris of Pa- 43.-(di)kakem.
Stand up and sit down to your 1000 of bread, to your 1000 of beer, to your 1000 of ox, to your 1000 of fowl, to your 1000 of every good and pure thing, therein.[G]

44. O, Osiris, Foremost of the West(erners), Osiris of Padikakem.
May Re find you standing w(ith) your mother Nut,
that she may lead you on the two paths of the (7, 45) horizon.
Make for yourself your monument there,
perfect with your *ka* forever and ever."

TEXT NOTES

As this spell focuses on the cyclical union of Re and Osiris resulting in rebirth, the great fallen god is requested to stand up. The assertion that Osiris' *Wereret* crown is the *Wereret* of Re initially links the two gods. The appropriation of the *Wereret* crown implies that the deceased god has attained the *ꜣḫ*-status and equates him with the authority of Re as his nocturnal counterpart.[546] The nightly union of the two gods is further implied when Osiris is addressed with an epithet of Re, "He whom All the Spirits Fear."[547]

Similarly, the somewhat awkward statement *nṯw tm n ḥr ỉm sp=f,* "You (=Osiris) belong to him (from) whose actions (you) will not be far," emphasizes the same point. This clause is challenging due to the ambiguous meaning of *sp* and the dual determinatives of *tm*. The use of the 2nd person singular suffix pronoun of *ḥr* in the parallel PT 677 (§2024b) clarifies the translation of this line: *nṯw tm ḥr=k ỉm sp=f,* "You belong to him from whose event you will not be far." The enigmatic *sp,* "event, action," which is simply written 𓊗 in BM 24, 15, refers to the daily solar cycle of Re, mentioned in the following clause: "when he (=Re) goes forth from the horizon."[548] However, the confusion caused by the 𓅆 determinative (G7) and 𓂜 (D35) after *tm* allows the consideration of a different rendering of this line: *nṯw tm n ḥr=k ỉm sp=f,* "You belong to Atum, not being far removed from his deed." The lack of determinatives for *tm,* 𓏏𓍃𓅓, in PT §2024b supports the possibility of interpreting the group as the name of the god Atum and *sp=f,* "his deed," as that of creation. Nevertheless,

---

546 Goebs, *Crowns*, pp. 35–47. See also Gutbub, in *Mélanges Maspero* I, p. 34, who points to the association of this crown with the morning rites and with the justification of Osiris, reinforcing the solar-Osirian unity.

547 For the epithet *snḏ-n=f-ꜣḫw-nbw*, attested since the OK, see Leitz et al., eds., *Lexikon* VI, p. 403.

548 Allen, *The Ancient Egyptian Pyramid Texts*, p. 277, n. 59.

the presence of the  determinative (D35) in P.W551 suggests understanding *tm* as a relative form of the negative verb.[549]

7, 34–35

A This line corresponds with the beginning of PT 677 (§§2018–28c)[550] and text 104b in the tomb of Mutirdis.[551] Further examples of this spell are found in P.Louvre 2129, N 38–42.[552]

Cf. PT §2018a: *ḏd mdw ḫr wr ḥr gs=f ꜥḥꜥ nṯr is*. Here, *ꜥḥꜥ* should be taken as a participle, with the particle *is*, omitted from P.W551, translated as "like." Cf. the slight variation in Mutirdis 104b, 17: *ḫr wr ḥr gs=f dit ꜥḥꜥ nṯr*.

PT §§2019a–b repeats the first two lines of the spell, replacing *wr* with NN. The PT spell parallel continues in §2019b: *sḫm=f ḥnꜥ=f wrrt=f tp=f mi wrrt rꜥ*.[553] Cf. Mutirdis 104b, 17–18: *sḫm=f m-ꜥ=f wrrt=f tp=f mi wrrt n rꜥ*. P.W551 uses the common substitution *mr* for *mi* in the parallel texts.[554] BM 24, 3 corresponds to this line of P.W551, but omits the suffix pronoun after the first *wrrt*.

Some discrepancies with the parallel texts should be noted:

1. *sḫm*, , has the full phonetic spelling in PT §2018b.
2. PT §2018b consistently uses the  determinative (S2) for *wrrt*, , while P.W551 and BM 24, 3 have the  determinative (F51), possibly confusing the original *Wereret* crown with the uraeus snake.[555]
3. *tp=f*, , lacks a determinative in PT §2018b.
4. Re has phonetic complements in BM 24, 3: .

7, 36–37

B PT §§2020a–21a addresses the king: *hꜣ NN pw ṯs ṯw šsp n=k sꜥḥ=k i.ir.n n=k psḏty wn=k ḥr nst wsir m st ḫnty-imntyw*, "O, NN, raise yourself! Receive for yourself your dignity which the Dual Ennead has made for you, that you may be upon the throne of Osiris, in the place of the Foremost of the Westerners." Mutirdis 104b, 19 corresponds to the PT parallel. See also the first clause in BM 24, 5–7: *ṯs.ti šsp=k sꜥḥ ir.n=k psḏt ꜥꜣt wn.n=k ḥr nst gb (w)ṯs tw rꜥ ḫnty-psḏt*. The epithet *ḫnty-psḏt*, "Foremost of the Ennead," is commonly used for the god Re.[556] Osiris, as the father of Horus(=king), is here re-

549 Faulkner, *Ancient Egyptian Pyramid Texts*, p. 291, n. 4.

550 The translation of the subsequent spells is based on Allen, *The Ancient Egyptian Pyramid Texts*, p. 277.

551 The translation of the subsequent spells is based on Assmann, *Mutirdis*, pp. 94ff.

552 Assmann, *Mutirdis*, p. 94, n. 100.

553 For *wrrt* with the  determinative (V1), "coil on the crown, i.e., of uraeus," see *Wb.* I 333, 14.

554 Wilson, *Ptolemaic Lexikon*, p. 409.

555 *Wb.* I 333, 13; Wilson, *Ptolemaic Lexikon*, p. 244.

556 Leitz et al., eds., *Lexikon* V, pp. 812–13.

placed by Geb, as the father of Osiris(=deceased), because the deceased is a private individual rather than a king, as in the PT.

Cf. the suffix pronouns in PT §2021b and Mutirdis 104b, 20: *iṯt n=k sẖm=f šsp n=k wrrt=f. šsp* was restored in the largely damaged PT §2021b by Sethe.[557] Cf. BM 24, 7–8: *iṯt n=k sẖm=k ẖnp n=k wrrt=f.*

Some discrepancies with the parallel texts should be noted:

1. *sʿḥ* is written in PT §2020b.
2. *psḏt* is expressed with eighteen signs, , in PT §2020b, while BM 24, 6 has . Note that the *psḏt,* “Ennead,” of PT was also replaced by *psḏt ʿꜣt,* “Great Ennead,” in line 2 of the present column.
3. *wn* is written in PT §2021a.
4. *nst* is written with (F20) in PT §2021a, , and in BM 24, 6.
5. *iṯt,* , has no determinatives in PT §2021b.
6. *sẖm,* , has phonetic complements in PT §2021b.

7, 37–39

c Cf. PT §2022a–b: *hꜣ NN nfr.w nn wr.w nn ir.n n=k it=k wsir di.n=f n=k nst=f.* The text of P.W551 was again consciously altered for a non-royal deceased. Mutirdis 104b, 20–21 follows the same principle: *hꜣ wsir NN nfr.wy nn ir n=k it=k gb rdit n=k nst=f.*

Cf. PT §2023a and BM 24, 9–11: *wḏ=k mdw n štꜣw-swt sšm=k špsw=sn.*[558] The scribe of the present manuscript makes *sšm* a passive verb. Cf. Mutirdis 104b, 21: *wḏ=k mdw n štꜣw-swt sšm špsw wsir ḫnty-imntyw*. The parallel with Mutirdis 104b ends here. The epithet *štꜣw-swt* is omitted from the partly destroyed PT §2024a: *šms ṯw ꜣḫw* [*nb m rn=sn pw*]. Faulkner offers the following reconstruction of this phrase: “[All] the spirits follow you [whoever they may be (?)],” while Allen translates: “[All] the *akh*s will follow you [in their identity of the dead].”[559] The plural *ꜣḫw* is written here. Cf. the consistent use of three ooo determinatives (N33) indicating the plurality of *ꜣḫw,* , in PT §2023b.

Some discrepancies with the parallel texts should be noted:

1. PT §2022a and BM 24, 9 have the more usual spelling of *nn*: .
2. *di* is written in PT §2022b.
3. *wḏ,* , lacks phonetic complements in PT §2023a.
4. *swt* is spelled in PT §2023a.
5. *špsw* is spelled in PT §2023a.

557 Sethe, *Übersetzung und Kommentar* II, p. 489.

558 For the epithet *štꜣ-swt*, “He whose Seats are Secret,” as a name of Osiris, see Leitz et al., eds., *Lexikon* VII, p. 136.

559 Faulkner, *Ancient Egyptian Pyramid Texts*, p. 291, n. 3, and Allen, *The Ancient Egyptian Pyramid Texts*, p. 277, respectively.

7, 39–40

D The omission of (D28) in the name of Padikakem, , continues until the end of this column.

The phrase *nḏm ib=k,* "May your heart be sweet," expresses a wish for Osiris' joy, with *nḏm,* , written without determinatives in PT §2024a. In the clause *ʿꜣ ḥꜣt=k,* "may your heart be great," an idiom for pride, *ʿꜣ* is written in PT §2024a. On the contrary, cf. the extended in BM 24, 13.

Some discrepancies with the parallel texts should be noted:

1. *ḥr,* , is more fully spelled out in PT §2024b.
2. *nis* is spelled with the expected determinative in PT §2025a: .
3. The abbreviated *rʿ,* , is paralleled by PT §2025a. BM 24, 15 includes the determinative (G7) for Re.
4. BM 24, 15 uses (D26) for *p* of the demonstrative *pw*.
5. PT §2025a has an unusual spelling of *snḏ*: .

7, 41

E PT §2025b does not specify to whom the "hearts" belong: *šʿt=k r ibw mi šʿt rʿ pr=f m ꜣḫt.* Cf. BM 24, 15–16: *šʿt=k ẖr ibw mr šʿt rʿ pr=f m sp.* The phrase *mr šʿt ḥr nb-pʿt* is omitted from PT §2025b. The epithet *nb-pʿt,* "Lord of Humanity," is primarily used for Horus and Osiris.[560]

Some discrepancies with the parallel texts should be noted:

1. *šʿt* is consistently written with a determinative in PT §2025b: .
2. The plurality of *ibw* is indicated by I I I in BM 24, 16.
3. *mr* stands for *mi,* , as is written in PT §2025b.
4. Re is spelled phonetically in BM 24, 26: .
5. *pr* does not have the determinative (D54) in BM 24, 16.
6. *ꜣḫt,* , has (N18) in place of (N27) in PT §2025b.

7, 42

F The deceased is being likened to Anubis here,[561] with the enclitic particle *is* used in its comparative sense.[562] *inpw,* , is spelled as a logogram in PT §2026a.

Faulkner emends the original *irw=f* into *irw=k,* "your form," in PT §2026a.[563]

---

560 Leitz et al., eds., *Lexikon* III, p. 629.

561 For the epithet describing Anubis and the deceased, *sštꜣ-irw=f,* "He whose Form is Secret," see Leitz et al., eds., *Lexikon* VI, p. 646.

562 *Wb.* I 130, 9.

563 Faulkner, *Ancient Egyptian Pyramid Texts*, p. 291, n. 5

Cf. the second clause of this line in the parallel of PT §2026b: *šsp n=k ḥr=k n s3b ṯs ṯw*, "You have received your face of a jackal! Raise yourself!" Cf. the prospective form of *šsp* in BM 24, 18-9: *šsp=k ḥr=k m s3b ṯs=ṯ.*
Some features of P.W551 and discrepancies with the parallels should be noted:

1. *ḫt* is spelled 𓐍𓏏 in BM 24, 18.
2. The 𓂋 following *ḥr=k* must be a mistake for the genitive *n*.
3. *s3b* has phonetic complements in PT §2026b: 𓊃 .

7, 42–43

G PT §2027a–b does not repeat the preposition *r*: *ꜥḥꜥ ḥms r ḫ3=k m t ḫ3=k m ḥnḳt ḫ3=k m iw3 ḫ3=k m 3pd ḫ3=k m ḫt nbt ꜥnḫt nṯr im.*
Cf. BM 24, 20–21: *ḥms r ḫ3wy=k m t ḥnḳt ḫ3wy=k m iw3 3pd r ḫ3wy=k m ḫt nbt nfr(t) ꜥnḫ(t) nṯr im.*
Some discrepancies with the parallel texts should be noted:

1. Note the dot at the end of line 7, 43, indicating the division of the name Padikakem.
2. *ꜥḥꜥ* is written 𓂝𓊢𓂝 in PT §2026b and 𓊢 in BM 24, 19.
3. *ḥms* is written in PT §2027a and only (A7) in BM 24, 20.
4. *t* shows an abbreviated writing in PT §2027a: .
5. *iw3* is spelled (F1) in PT §2027a and BM 24, 20.

7, 44–45

H The scribe of P.W551 has interpreted *wꜥb* as a modifier of *ḫwt nbt nfrt*, "all good and pure things," from the previous line, although the PT and BM clearly intend *wꜥb* as the imperative "Become pure!" Cf. PT §2028a–b: *hy NN pw wꜥb gm ṯw rꜥ ꜥḥꜥ.ti ḥnꜥ mwt=k nwt sšm=s ṯ(w) m w3wt 3ḫt*, "O, this NN, become pure, so that Re may find you standing with your mother Nut, and that she may lead you on the two paths of the horizon." BM 24, 22–23 is closer to the PT parallel: *wꜥb gm ti rꜥ ꜥḥꜥw s3.n mwt=k nwt sšm=sn kw m w3wt 3ḫt*. Note the plural suffix pronoun of *sšm* in BM 24, 23.
Cf. the very similar subsequent clause in PT §2028c: *ir=k imn=k im nfrw ḥnꜥ k3=k n ḏt ḏt.*
The following orthographic features of P.W551 and discrepancies with the parallels should be noted:

1. *gm* has an abbreviated spelling in PT §2028a and BM 24, 22.
2. *rꜥ*, 𓂋𓂝, is phonetically spelled without a determinative here. Cf. 𓇳 (N5) in PT §2028a and BM 24, 22.
3. The abbreviated *ḥnꜥ*, , includes the erroneous in P.W551. Cf. in PT §2028a.
4. An extra is written in *sšm*, . Cf. in PT §2028b.

5. A superficial following *sšm=s kw* likely stems from the frequent variation of the 2nd person singular dependent pronouns *kw* and *tw*.
6. The plural *w3wt* is written in PT §2028b and in BM 24, 23.
7. *3ḫt* is spelled in BM 24, 23.
8. This spelling of *mnw,* , is paralleled by BM 24, 23. Cf. for *mnw* in PT §2028c.
9. *k3,* , lacks the determinative (G7) in PT §2028c.

3.2.9. *s3ḫw* III, SPELL 9 — *Lines 8, 1–9*[564]

Much like in many earlier spells, no specific speaker is indicated for Spell 9. This spell not only calls on Osiris to arise and regain his powerful status, but also explicitly states that he has already done so and is safe and fully supported. As the new king of the Netherworld, Osiris is said to be more glorified or effective (*3ḫ*) than the Glorified Gods (*nṯrw-3ḫw*).[565] He is assured that having again seized his insignia of authority, he will not be opposed. Accordingly, he is commanded to perform all the actions necessary for resurrection (reassembling his dismembered body, raising himself, and accepting offerings), which were previously done by his immediate family.

TRANSLITERATION

(8, 1) *grḥ*
s3ḫ
ḏd mdw
ṯs w3(!) wsir ḫnty-imntyw wsir n P3-dit-k3-km
wn ti
ꜥ3 pḥty=k
ḥms=k ḫnt (nṯrw)
2. *ir=k nw(y) ir.n=k m ḥwt sr im iwnw*
hy wsir ḫnty-imnt(yw) wsir n P3-dit-k3-km
šsp.n=k sꜥḥ=k
nn dr rdwy=k 3. *m pt*
nn ḫsf=k m t3
ntf is 3ḫ ms nwt snḳ nbt-ḥwt
di=sn (n=)k ꜥḥꜥ=k ḥr-ḫt t3
ir=k wn=k ir n=k m-b3ḥ
4. *3ḫw=k r nṯrw 3ḫw*
in=sn st
šm=k r p gm=k ḫsf=k im

564 See section 1.7.3, above.
565 Leitz et al., eds., *Lexikon* IV, p. 454.

iw=k r-iw nḫn gm=k ḫsf=k im
iw ir.n=k (8, 5) *irt gb*
wsir ḫnty-imntyw wsir n P3-dit-k3-km
n ṯw(t) is ḥr nst=f ꜥḥꜥ
wsir ḫnty-imntyw wsir n P3-dit-k3- 6.*-km m ḏb3 m sm3*
n ḫsf=k m bw nbt šm=k im
nn dr rdwy=k m bw nbt šm=k im
n dr rdwy=k m 7. *m*(!) *bw nbt mry=k im*
hy hy ṯs tw wsir ḫnty-imntyw wsir n P3-dit-k3-km
šsp n=k tp=k
inḳ.n n=k 8. *ḳsw=k*
s3ḳ n=k ꜥwt=k
wḫ3 n=k t3 ir iwf=k
šsp n=k t=k pn i.ḫm ḫsḏd=f
ḥnḳt=k i.ḫm(t) ꜥm(3)
ꜥḥꜥ=k r ꜥ3wy 9. *ḫsf rḫywt*
pr n=k ḫnty-mnwt=f
nḏr=f ꜥ=k
šd=f kw r pt
r bw wꜥb mr=k im

TRANSLATION

(8, 1) Pause.
Glorification spell.
Words spoken:

"Raise yourself, Osiris, Foremost of the Westerners, Osiris of Padikakem.
Hurry!
You, Great of Strength,
may you sit before (the gods)!
2. May you do this which you have done in the Mansion of the Prince who is in Heliopolis! [A]
O, Osiris, Foremost of the West(erners), Osiris of Padikakem.
You have taken possession of your insignia,
and your feet shall not be repelled 3. from the sky.
You shall not be opposed on earth,
for you are, indeed, an *akh*, whom Nut bore, whom Nephthys suckled.[B]
They caused (for) you that you arise from the land,
that you may do that which you did for yourself formerly,
4. and that you may be more glorified than the glorified gods.
May they bring it! [C]
Should you go to Pe that you may find your enemy there,
or should you come to Nekhen that you may find your enemy there,
you will do (8, 5) that which Geb did,

Osiris, Foremost of the Westerners, Osiris of Padikakem,
for you are indeed upon his throne.[D]
Arise, Osiris, Foremost of the Westerners, Osiris of Padika-6.-kem adorned as a wild bull.
You will not be opposed in any place where you go.
Your feet shall not be repelled from any place that you go.
Your feet shall not be repelled from 7. any place in which you desire to be.[E]
O! O! Raise yourself! Osiris, Foremost of the Westerners, Osiris of Padikakem,
seize for yourself your head,
collect for yourself 8. your bones,
gather for yourself your limbs,
shake off the earth from your flesh, for yourself.[F]
Take for yourself this bread of yours, which does not know its destruction,
and your beer which does not know (of) becoming sour.[G]
As you stand at the two doors 9. which keep out the common folk,
Khentymenwtef will come to you,
and he will grasp your arm,
that he might take you to the sky,
to the pure place in which you desire to be."[H]

TEXT NOTES

Before reestablishing Osiris on his throne, spell 9 calls on the resurrected god to take his place before the gods and perform his role associated with the Mansion of the Prince who is in Heliopolis (*ḥwt sr ỉm ỉwnw*). The variant of this spell from the Teti pyramid replaces *ḥwt sr* with *ḥwt sḫmw,* interpreted as "the Mast Enclosure."[566] While this temple is associated with the justification of Osiris, references to it, as well as its location, are intimately connected with Re, accentuating the underlying theme of the solar-Osirian unity.[567]

8, 1–2

A This line corresponds to the beginning of PT 365 (§§622–25).[568] Cf. the slight differences in PT §622a–b, which calls on the deceased king to do that which Osiris has done: *ḏd mdw ṯs ṯw NN pw wn ṯw ꜥꜣ pḥty ḥms=k ḫnt nṯrw ỉr=k nw ỉr.n wsỉr m ḥwt sr ỉmt ỉwnw.* The plural demonstrative *nwy,* spelled  in PT §622b, which modifies the relative *ỉr.n=k,* is used nominally here.[569]

566 Allen, *The Ancient Egyptian Pyramid Texts*, p. 81. Faulkner, *Ancient Egyptian Pyramid Texts*, p. 120, n. 1, reads *ḥwt sḫmw* as "Mansion of the 'Wand' or 'Mast.'" For *ḥwt sr*, "mansion of the prince," see Wilson, *Ptolemaic Lexikon*, p. 632.

567 Gutbub, in *Mélanges Maspero* I, pp. 38–40.

568 The translation of the subsequent spells is based on Allen, *The Ancient Egyptian Pyramid Texts*, p. 81.

569 *Wb.* II 216, 2–17; Wilson, *Ptolemaic Lexikon*, p. 498.

There are some notable orthographic peculiarities and discrepancies with the parallel texts:

1. *s3ḫ* is written  in BM 25, 1.
2. Similarly, *ḏd mdw* is abbreviated to  in BM 25, 1.
3.  (V4), following *ṯs,* is a corrupt writing of  (U33), which stands in place of the dependent pronoun *ṯw*.[570]
4. *ḫnty,* 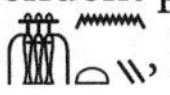, has a more extended spelling, while *imntyw,* , lacks phonetic complements in BM 25, 2.
5. This spelling of *wni,* , omitting the  determinative (D54), corresponds to PT §622a in the pyramid of Pepi.[571]
6.  stands for the dependent pronoun *ṯw,* written  in BM 25, 2.
7. *pḥty* is spelled  in BM 25, 3 and 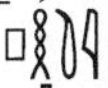 in PT §622a.
8. The  determinative (Q1) for *ḥmst,* , occurs in PT §622b of the pyramid of Neferkare.[572]
9. *ḫnt* is written  in PT §622b and  in BM 25, 3.
10. The expected *nṯrw,* , is not written after *ḫnt* here or in BM 25, 3.
11. *ḥwt sr* is spelled phonetically in PT §622b:  and  in BM 25, 4.
12. *im* is spelled 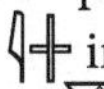 in PT §622b.
13. *iwnw* is spelled  here.[573] PT §622b and BM 25, 4 show the more typical spelling:  and , respectively.

8, 2–3

B PT §§622d–23b: *ni ḏr rd=k m pt ni ḫsf=k m t3 n ṯwt is 3ḫ ms nwt snḳw* [*nbt-ḥwt*] *dmd=sn ṯw,* "Your foot has no limit in the sky and you cannot be barred in the world, for you are an *akh*, whom Nut bore and [Nephthys] suckled, as they joined you." The PT spell was reinterpreted by later scribes of P.W551 and BM. Both later versions alter the original *ḏr,* , "limit," to the similar sounding *dr,* "to repel," and *dmd=sn ṯw,* "they joined you," to the similar *di=sn (n=)k,* "they caused for you." The scribe of BM 25, 6–7 prefers here the original negation *n(i)* of the PT parallel.
ntf must to be a mistake for the 2nd person independent pronoun *ntk/ṯwt,* as suggested by the parallels of PT §623a and BM 25, 7.
Some discrepancies with the parallel texts should be noted:

1. *imntyw,* , has a more extended spelling in BM 25, 5.
2. *šsp* has phonetic complements in BM 25, 5: .
3. The (Y1) and  (A24) are consistently omitted in *ḫsf* in PT §622d. Cf. *ḫsf,* 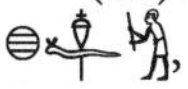, in BM 25, 6.

570 For the occasional similarity of these two signs in hieratic, see Verhoeven, *Untersuchungen zur späthieratischen Buchschrift*, pp. 192 and 194.

571 *Wb.* I 313, 10–34, 14.

572 For this spelling of *ḥmst,* "to sit, dwell," see *Wb.* III 96, 13–98, 22.

573 *Wb.* I 54, 5.

4. *tꜣ*, , has no determinatives in PT §622d.
5. *ꜣḫ*, , is regularly abbreviated in PT §623a.
6. Nut, , does not have the expected determinative (G7) in any of the parallels.
7. *snḳ*, , has the typical determinative (D27) in PT §623a.

8, 3–4

C There is a small but clearly intentional gap between lines 3 and 4.
Cf. PT §623c: *ꜥḥꜥ=k ḥr nḫt=k ir=k wnt=k ir=k m-bꜣḥ,* "When you stand up in your forcefulness, you shall do what you used to do formerly."[574] Cf. *wnn=k* in BM 25, 9.
The group , paralleled by BM 25, 8, is understood as *ḥr-ḫt,* "behind, to, after, on."[575] Otherwise this phrase may be understood following PT §623c: , *ꜥḥꜥ=k ḥr nḫt=k*.
Cf. PT §624a: *ꜣḫ=k ir ꜣḫw nbw,* "be more *akh* than all the *akhs*," and BM 25, 9: *ꜣḫ=k r ꜣḫ=sn. ꜣḫw* is spelled in PT §624a. Cf. Faulkner's rendering of a phrase in CT 45, I 194e: *mk ṯw ir=k ꜣḫ.ti bꜣ.ti r nṯrw rsw šmw,* "You are more spirit-like and more soul-like than the southern or northern gods."[576]
The clause *in=sn st* is omitted from the PT parallel. The 3rd person plural suffix pronoun refers to the gods, while the 3rd person singular dependent pronoun designates *ꜣḫ* as the state of being glorified.[577]

8, 4–5

D The rendering of *ḫsf=k im* as "your enemy" is based on the determinative (A24), not present in the PT parallel. However, Allen's translation clarifies the original meaning of this portion in PT §§624b–25a: *šm=k ir p gm=k ḫsf=k im iwt=k ir nḫn gm=k ḫsf=k im ir=k irt wsir n ṯwt is ḥr nst=f,* "Should you go to Pe you will find your welcome there, should you return to Nekhen you will find your welcome there, and you shall do what Osiris did, for you are the one on his throne."[578] Cf. the abbreviated version of BM 25, 9–11: (*i*)*st šm=k r nḫn gm=k s ḫsf=k.* Here again the later spells were intentionally altered for a private individual, replacing the original Osiris with Geb, the father of Osiris, with whom the deceased was associated at this time. Osiris is addressed with the 2nd person singular independent pronoun *ṯwt* preceded by the preposition *n*, occasionally found before a clause with an independent pronoun as subject.[579]

---

574 For the use of *m-bꜣḥ* as an adverb, see Wilson, *Ptolemaic Lexikon*, p. 302; Gardiner, *Egyptian Grammar*, §205, 2.

575 *Wb.* III 347, 13–14.

576 Faulkner, *Ancient Egyptian Coffin Texts* I, p. 40, n. 16.

577 See section 2.2, above.

578 Faulkner, *Ancient Egyptian Pyramid Texts*, p. 120, n. 3, similarly suggests a less hostile meaning, referring to the gods of Pe and Nekhen: "You shall go to Pe and find him whom you will meet there."

579 Gardiner, *Egyptian Grammar*, §§64; 154 and 164.10.

Some grammatical and orthographic features, as well as discrepancies from the parallel texts, should be mentioned:

1. The phonetic complement for *gm*, , is omitted in PT §624b.
2. The presence of *t* in the verb *iwt*, , in PT §624c supports the reading of *šm* and *iw* as prospective forms.
3. The construction *r-iw* before *nḫn* likely stands for the LP preposition *r-ir*. Otherwise, it should be understood as a mistake.
4. The particle *iw* preceding *ir.n=k* acts as the *i*-prefix of the emphatic form.[580]
5. The dot following the determinative (G7) of Geb likely indicates the continuation of the clause below.
6. *nst* is written in P.W551.[581] Cf. the more typical spelling in PT §625a and in BM 25, 12.

8, 5–7

E PT §625b–d addresses the deceased as an already glorified spirit: *ꜥḥꜥ ꜣḫ pn* [*ꜥꜣ*] *pḥty ḏbꜣ m smꜣ* [*wr*] *ni ḫsf=k m bw nb šm=k im ni dr rd=k m bw nb mry=k im*, “Stand up this *akh*, [great] of strength and adorned as the [great] wild bull! You will not be opposed in any place where you go. Your foot will not be repelled in any place where you wish (to be).” The phrase *nn dr rdwy=k m bw nbt šm=k im* is omitted from PT §625c. The use of the negation *nn* in place of *n* in P.W551 is paralleled by BM 25, 15–16.

There are some notable orthographic peculiarities and discrepancies with the parallel texts:

1. *ꜥḥꜥ* is spelled with phonetic complements in PT §625b: .
2. BM 25, 13 omits from *imntyw*, .
3. *ḏbꜣ* is spelled phonetically in PT §625b from the pyramids of Teti and Neferkare: , while the pyramids of Pepi and Merenre have only ().
4. *smꜣ* has a number of different spellings in the various versions of PT §625b: .
5. *ḫsf* shows a phonetic spelling in PT §625c: .[582]
6. *mr* has phonetic complements in PT §625d of the pyramid of Teti: . The other pyramids have a more extended spelling: ().
7. *im*, , does not have the determinative (Y1) in BM 25, 16.

8, 7–8

F Line 8, 7 corresponds to the beginning of the parallel PT 373 (§§654–55).[583] Cf. the beginning of PT §654a: *ḏd mdw ihy ihy ṯs ṯw NN pn*.

---

580 Edel, *Altägyptische Grammatik*, § 449.

581 *Wb.* II 321, 6–323, 15 has no examples of this spelling.

582 For the spelling of *ḫsf* in P.W551 and BM 25, 16, see *Wb.* III 335, 6–336, 12.

583 The translation of the subsequent spells is based on Allen, *The Ancient Egyptian Pyramid Texts*, p. 83.

There are some notable orthographic discrepancies with the parallel texts:

1. The vocative has a more extended spelling in PT §654a: .
2. The determinative (D54) of *ṯs,* , is omitted in BM 25, 17.[584]
3. *šsp,* (), does not have determinatives in PT §654b and BM 25, 18.
4. The determinative of *tp,* , is omitted from PT §654b or BM 25, 18.
5. *ink̇,* , has the determinative (D32) in PT §754b.[585]
6. *s3k̇,* or , is written with phonetic complements in PT §654c.[586]
7. *ꜥwt* is written in BM 25, 19 and all versions of PT §654c.
8. *t3,* , lacks determinatives in PT §654c.
9. *iwf* is written in PT §654c.

8, 8

G is understood as *ẖsḏd,* "to become bad (of bread),"[587] on the basis of its phonetic spelling in the parallel of PT §655a: . Otherwise, the lack of the phonetic complement may allow the reading of this word as *sḏ,* "to break."[588]
Cf. the very similar PT §655a: *šsp n=k t=k (pn) i.ẖm ẖsḏ ḥnk̇t=k i.ẖm ꜥm3.* The demonstrative, *pn,* appears only in the pyramid of Neferkare in PT §655. Note the lack of suffix pronouns for *ẖsḏd* and *ꜥm3* in the PT version.[589] The 3rd person singular feminine suffix pronoun of *ꜥm3* in P.W551 refers back to *ḥnk̇t.*
This line also corresponds to CT 751, VI 380m: *di n=k t=k n ḥw3=sn ḥnk̇t=k n ẖsḏdw.* See also CT 327, IV 163g–h: *t=f pw i.ẖm ẖsḏdw ḥnk̇t=f pw i.ẖm ꜥw3.*
There are some orthographic peculiarities and discrepancies with the parallel texts:

1. The PT parallels omit the plural strokes for *t*: .
2. The phonetic complement is written below the determinative of the 2nd *iẖm,* .
3. *ꜥm3* is spelled in BM 25, 21 and in PT §655a.

8, 8–9

I The parallel of PT §654b has for *ꜥ3wy,* implying a multiple rather than a dual number of doors that bar the common folk (*rḫyt,* spelled in the pyramid of Neferkare). This line also corresponds to CT 68, I 289e–f: *ꜥḥꜥ=k r=k r ꜥ3wy ẖsfw rḫyt.*
PT §655c–d offers a different explanation of the journey with Khentymenwtef (spelled without the determinative [A53] in PT §655c): *šd=f ṯw ir pt ḥr it=k gb,* "that he might

584 For this spelling of *ṯs,* see *Wb.* V 405, 1–407, 15.

585 For *ink̇,* "to embrace, grasp, collect," see *Wb.* I 100, 19–101, 7.

586 For the spelling of *s3k̇* in P.W551, see *Wb.* IV 25.

587 *Wb.* III 339, 4.

588 *Wb.* IV 373, 8–375, 3.

589 For *ꜥm3,* "to become sour (of beer)," see *Wb.* I, 185 1.

take you to the sky, away from you father Geb." Following this point PT 373 and P.W551 diverge.

Some orthographic peculiarities and discrepancies with the parallel texts should be mentioned:

1.  is mistakenly spelled above following *pr*.
2. *nḏr* is spelled  in PT §655c.
3. PT §655c phonetically spells *pt* , while BM 25, 24 has .
4. *bw* is abbreviated in BM 25, 24: .
5. *mr,* 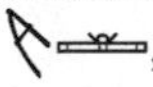, has a determinative in BM 25, 25.
6. The determinative (Y1) is omitted from *im,* , in BM 25, 25.

3.2.10. *sꜣḫw* III, SPELL 10 — SPOKEN IN CONJUNCTION WITH A SACRIFICE OF A GOAT *Lines 8, 9–21*

No specific speaker is indicated for this spell. The opening of the spell declares the completed resurrection of the deceased Osiris, emphasizing the support that was offered by Horus and Geb. The speech of Isis and other gods addresses Osiris, asserting his protection and hoping for the slaughter of his enemies, or symbols thereof. Appropriately, as the end of the spell indicates, the recitation is to coincide with a slaughter and consequent offering of the animals that represent Seth and his gang.

TRANSLITERATION

sꜣḫ
ḏd mdw
rs (8, 10) *wr*
nhs wr
ṯs.n s(*w*) *wsir ḥr gs=f*
msḏ-ḳdt
n-mr=f-bꜣgi
ꜥḥꜥw nṯr
sḫm.n(!)*.ti m ḏt=f*
s-11.-*sꜥḥꜥ sw ḥr*
wṯs=f sw im nḏit
nḏ.n sw sꜣ=f m-ꜥ stš
nḏ.n sw ḥr
dr.n=f twꜣw=f
s-12.-*snb.n=f ihꜣ im iwꜥ=f*
ꜥꜣ=f(!) *in ḥr d n=f rdwy=f in gb*
šmꜣi stš tp-ꜥ irt-ḥr
ii ḥr ḫtm 13. *m ḥkꜣw=f*
ḏnḏn.n=f ḫftw=f

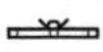

ꜥḥꜥ.n wsir ḫnty-imntyw wsir n P3-dit-k3-km
is ꜥpr-m-3ḫw=f
14. *ḥtm iwꜥ=f*
wn=f
i.n 3st i.n msw=f nṯrw
myn r=ṯn 3ḫw=f 8 ipw ḫns ḳbhw
imst ḥp dw3-(8, 15)-*mwt=f ḳbḥ-snw=f ḥ3ḳw ir-m-ꜥw3 m3-it=f ir-rn=f-ḏs=f nṯr-bi3tyw*
wsir ḫnty-imntyw wsir n P3-dit-k3-km
16. *mḫr=s pw ꜥb n pt wꜥbt m 3ḫt*
sw wꜥb ḳsw=k k3=s(*n*)
ꜥnḫ.n=f m bw pwy imim
hy hy msw=f ipw 17. *nn*
rdit.n rꜥ m gs=f dpt
m msḏ m3 sw swt
stp=ṯn s3=ṯn ḥr it=ṯn wsir
irt=ṯn n=f hnw
18. *wḏ=ṯ*(*n*) *n=f s3-t3*
di.t(*w*) *n=f ḫftw=f ḫr=f iḫ*
di=ṯn n(!)*=f sbiw=f m ꜥḏw ꜥ3w*
m sip.n im=f m hh
m3ꜥ 19. *hrw=k wsir ḫnty-imntyw wsir n P3-dit-k3-km*
ḫr rꜥ nb-pt
ḫr nṯrw nb(*w*)*-itrty*
ḏd mdw
is in n=k twt m (8, 20) *ḥr m3ꜥ m wi3*
irw m dḫs wꜥ ib di m ꜥḥ n 3sbt r kmt
s3ḫ pw r ꜥnḫw nb grḥ 21. *pr m rꜥ*

TRANSLATION

Glorification spell.
Words spoken:
"The Great One awakens,
(8, 10) The Great One wakes up.
Osiris raised himself from his side
the One who Hates Sleep,
One who does not Love Weariness.[A]
The god stands,
being powerful of his body.
11. Horus has lifted him up,
he raised him in Nedit.[B]
His son protects him from Seth.
Horus protects him,

he repels his enemies.[C]
12. He cures the mourning in his heir.
His arm is given(!) by Horus, his two legs are given to him by Geb.
Seth wanders before the eye of Horus.
Horus comes provided 13. with his magic,
he cuts his enemies.[D]
Osiris, Foremost of the Westerners, Osiris of Padikakem stands up,
like the One who is Equipped with his Spirits,
14. who is provided with his heir,
as he exists.[E]
So says Isis, so say his children, the gods:
'Come, you, these eight spirits of his, who traverse *Kebehu*:
Imsety, Hapy, Dua-(8, 15)-mutef, Kebehsenuef, He who Plunders,
He who Acts by Force, He who Sees his Father, He who Makes
his Own Name, the Miraculous God.' [F]
Osiris, Foremost of the Westerners, Osiris of Padikakem.
16. Its lower part is the east of heaven, the pure one in the horizon.
He is pure of bones (as) (th)ey say:
'He has lived in this place of lamentation.' [G]
O! O! These are his children,
17. whom Re placed on his side of the boat,
hating that Seth might see him.
May your protection be upon your father, Osiris,
as you made for him the exaltation! [H]
18. You commanded for him protection of the land,
and his enemies were placed under him for him.
May you give to him his rebels in the great slaughter,
as those who are among them are assigned to the fire.[I]
Your voice is 19. justified, Osiris, Foremost of the Westerners, Osiris of Padikakem,
in the presence of Re, the Lord of Heaven,
(and) in the presence of the gods, Lords of the Two Conclaves." [J]
Words spoken:
"Now, the image was brought to you in (8, 20) the face of the one who guides the *wiꜣ*-bark.
One goat is made as a slaughter-offering, and placed in the oven of Asbet for Egypt.
This is a glorification for every star of the night 21. who comes forth as Re." [K]

TEXT NOTES

The description of the god's rebirth involves an account of Osiris raising himself on his side. Since the dead were generally placed on their left side during burial, the suggestion of rising from one's side implied resurrection. Similarly, the epithet of Osiris and the deceased, *msd-ḳdt,* "One who Hates Sleep,"[590] refers to his triumph over death.[591] The following epithet, *n-mr=f-b3gi,* "One who does not Love Weariness," equally accurately describes Osiris. The parallel CT 349, IV 383e–f slightly alters the latter title to *msḏ-ḳdt bwt=f-b3gi,* "One who Hates Sleep, whose Abomination is Weariness." *Stundenwachen* XV, 39–40 offers yet another version of the same idea: *msḏ=k ipḏ(sic) ḳdt n mr.n=k kkw,* "What you hate is sleep, and you do not love darkness."[592]

The subsequent clauses clarify that Osiris stands up with the help of Horus, who is said to raise his father in Nedit. PT 532 (§1256a–b) identifies Nedit as the place where Seth scattered the severed parts of Osiris: *gm.n=sn n wsir ndi.n sw sn=f stš r t3 m ndit,* "They found Osiris after his brother Seth threw him down in Nedit."[593] This geographical designation presents a remarkable instance of the use of paronomasia in religious texts, as the term Nedit is connected with the verb *ndi,* "to cast, throw down (on the ground)."[594]

The reading of the initial part of line 8, 12: "He cures the mourning in his heir. His arm is given by Horus…" is questionable and likely contains an error. The scribe may have easily confused the common writing of 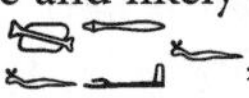, (*iwꜥ=f ꜥ3=f*) "his eldest (heir)," with 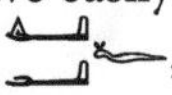, (*di ꜥ=f*) "his arm is given." Since either reading points to a scribal mistake (the extra suffix pronoun for *ꜥ3* or the erroneous spelling of *di*), it is best to follow the much more clearly written parallels here. BM 26, 8–9 and P.Sekowski 12, 5 have the phonetic *iwf=f dit ꜥ=f:*  and , respectively. Since 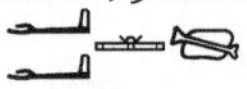 in the following line 8, 14 is similarly ambiguous, the scribe of the present manuscript is either using the wrong determinative for *ꜥt,* "limbs," or, more probably, is punning on the word *iwꜥ,* "heir."[595] Nevertheless, the parallel P.Sekowski 12, 8 refers to the deceased Osiris as *ḫtm m ꜥt(=f),* "(one) who is provided with (his) limb(s)."

As Osiris rises, Isis and the gods summon eight spirits, whose number likely stems from the GR epithet *3ḫw=sn-ḫmntyw.*[596] The four sons of Horus are listed first. The subsequent epithets *ir-m-ꜥw3,* "He who Acts by Force,"[597] as well as *ḥ3ḳw,* "He who Plunders,"[598] appear along with the names of the four sons of Horus as early as the CT[599] and play a protective role in the *Stundenwachen* ritual.[600] Despite its violent connotations, *ꜥw3,* "to rob, robber," in the next epithet is frequently used in the name of a deity protecting Osiris.[601] The epithets

590 Leitz et al., eds., *Lexikon* III, p. 446.

591 *Wb.* V 79, 7; *Wb.* II 154, 6.

592 Cf. the translation of Junker, *Stundenwachen*, p. 89: "Was du hassest, ist der Schlaf, und du liebst die Finsternis nicht."

593 Allen, *The Ancient Egyptian Pyramid Texts*, p. 165.

594 *Wb.* II 367, 12–13. For further discussion of word play, see section 1.5.1, above.

595 For further discussion of punning, see section 1.5.1, above.

596 Leitz et al., eds., *Lexikon* I, p. 45.

597 Leitz et al., eds., *Lexikon* I, pp. 444–45.

598 Leitz et al., eds., *Lexikon* V, pp. 26–27.

599 See spells 404 and 405, Faulkner, *Ancient Egyptian Coffin Texts* II, pp. 49 and 55.

600 See hours 5–8 of the day, Junker, *Stundenwachen*, pp. 3–5 and 51–61.

601 *Wb.* I 171, 3–12. Wilson, *Ptolemaic Lexikon*, p. 141.

m33-it=f, "He who Sees his Father,"[602] and *ir-rn=f-ḏs=f,* "He who Makes his Own Name,"[603] also appear together with the four sons of Horus in CT spells 404, 405, and 1126.[604] Notably, a variant reading of the latter epithet *irr-n=f-ḏs=f,* "He who Acts on his Own Behalf," was proposed by Faulkner.[605]

Towards the end of the spell the resurrected Osiris is again alluded to as the giant solar-Osirian deity, reaching to "the east of heaven." He is called "the pure one (*wꜥbt*) in the horizon." The term *wꜥbt,* typically translated "pure," presents another phonetic word play with the GR meaning of *wꜥbt,* "heaven," and a visual pun on *ḳbḥw,* "sky, heaven."[606]

The instructions of this spell direct the speaker to coincide the recitation with the sacrifice of a goat in the "oven of Asbet." The epithet *3sbt,* "Flaming One,"[607] probably refers to Isis in CT 227, III 260e.[608] However, Asbet, the protective goddess of the fourth hour of the day, may be specifically intended here.[609] Various Ptolemaic temples portray Asbet as the guardian of Osiris, while the Book of Overthrowing Apophis depicts her as a protector against the enemy of Re: *nsrt 3sbt ḥr tk3 sẖr=tn ḏw-ḳd m ds(w)=tn,* "Flame of Asbet, who has authority over the torches. May you destroy the One of Evil Form (=Apophis) with your knives."[610] As such, the flames of the fiery goddess guard Osiris and Re from their enemies, represented in this spell as sacrificial animals.

8, 9–10

A The beginning of this spell on line 8, 9 follows a small intentional gap.[611] This passage parallels a liturgy in P.Sekowski 12, 2–13, 3.[612] The text also corresponds to P.Berlin 3057 (B), col. 1, P.BM 102525, sheets 4–5 and P.BM 102524 (BMI), P.Salt 1821 (A) (BMII), P.BM 10317, B27 (BMIII), and parts of the *Stundenwachen* ritual, XVII–XVIII.[613]

P.Sekowski 12, 2–3 is somewhat different: *s3ẖw rs wr ṯs.n s(w) wsir ḥr rdwy=f,* "Glorification: The Great One awakens, Osiris raised himself to his feet." Cf. also BMI and BMII: *s3ẖw rs wr nhs wr ṯs.n sw wsir ḥr rdwy=f st,* "Glorification: The Great One

602 Leitz et al., eds., *Lexikon* III, pp. 199–200.

603 Leitz et al., eds., *Lexikon* I, pp. 471–72.

604 Faulkner, *Ancient Egyptian Coffin Texts* II, pp. 49 and 55; *ibid.*, III, p. 166, respectively.

605 Faulkner, *Ancient Egyptian Coffin Texts* II, p. 52, n. 43.

606 *Wb.* I 284, 10, and V 30, 1–6, respectively. For a further discussion of word play, see section 1.5.1, above.

607 Wilson, *Ptolemaic Lexikon*, p. 21.

608 Faulkner, *Ancient Egyptian Pyramid Texts*, p. 110, n. 2, distinguishes between *3zbt,* "Flaming one," and *3sbt,* "(the goddess) Asbet," although he does not offer a translation for the latter word. See also *Wb.* I 20, 19; Leitz et al., eds., *Lexikon* I, p. 80.

609 For a detailed discussion of Asbet, see Gutbub, in *Mélanges Maspero* I, pp. 37–41, who points to Asbet's connection with the fiery Nesret on p. 38.

610 P.Bremner-Rhind 22, 22; see Faulkner, *Bremner-Rhind*, p. 45; Faulkner, *JEA* 23 (1937): 168.

611 See section 1.7.3, above.

612 The translation of the subsequent spells is based on Szczudlowska, *ZÄS* 98 (1970): 50–80.

613 Szczudlowska, *ZÄS* 98 (1970): 52, n. 12. All of the above are based on Szczudlowska's publication.

awakens, the Great One wakes up. Osiris has risen to his feet." This variant suggests a possibility of emending the present text to the reflexive *ṯs.n sw wsir,* "Osiris raised himself."

The parallel with a part of PT 247 (§260) and CT 349, IV 383, omits the initial statements. Cf. PT §260a–b: *NN pi ṯs ṯw ḥr gs=k ir wḏ msḏ-ḳdd sb3gy,* "NN, raise yourself from your side! Do (my) command, One who Hates Sleep but were made weary."[614] Thus, the original causative *sb3gy,* "caused to be weary, slack," was emended by later scribes to *n mr=f b3gy,* "who does not love weariness." Cf. CT IV 383c: *N ṯs ṯw ḥr gs=k ir wḏ(=i),* "N, raise yourself from your side and do (my) command."[615]

Some orthographic peculiarities and discrepancies with the parallels should be noted:

1.  has no determinatives in BM 26, 1.
2. *ḏd mdw,* , has an abbreviated spelling in BM 26, 1.
3. The determinative for *rs,* 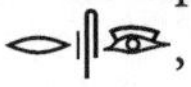, is written on the following line. The superfluous stroke after  is not paralleled in any of the texts.
4. The superfluous signs in *nhs,* , are not present in BM 26, 2.
5. *ṯs,* 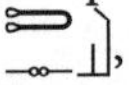, does not have the  determinative (D54) in BM 26, 2.
6. The spelling of *msḏ,*  with , typical for the GR era, corresponds to BM 26, 3.[616]
7. *b3gi,* 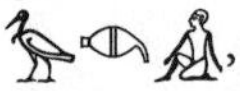, is unusually spelled with  (R6).[617] Cf. the phonetic spelling of *b3gi* in PT §260b:  and CT IV 383f:  / .

8, 10–11

B The phrase *ꜥḥꜥ nṯr sḫm.n(!).ti m ḏt=f* has an erroneous *n* following the stative *sḫm*. This clause in the original spell in PT §260b and CT IV 383g is much shorter: *ꜥḥꜥ im ndit*. Cf. BM 26, 4–5: *ꜥḥꜥ nṯr st sḫm nṯr m ḏt.f.* The PT and CT parallels diverge from the present manuscript following this clause.

The following orthographic peculiarities and discrepancies from the parallels should be mentioned:

1. *sḫm,* , has the  determinative (G7) in BM 26, 4.
2. Nedit has a GR spelling in P.W551: 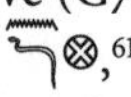,[618] while PT §260b and CT IV 383g spell , and 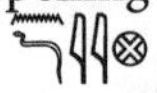 is found in BM 26, 6.
3. The *s,* , at the end of line 8, 10 is repeated as the causative for *sꜥḥꜥ,* .
4. The  determinative (A7) of *sꜥḥꜥ* must be a mistake, as the parallels of PT §260b and CT IV 383g lack determinatives, while BM 26, 5 has .

614 Cf. Allen, *The Ancient Egyptian Pyramid Texts*, p. 41.

615 Cf. Faulkner, *Ancient Egyptian Coffin Texts* I, p. 283, n. 6.

616 *Wb.* II 154, 1–9.

617 Möller, *Hieratische Paläographie* III, p. 49 (516 *bis*).

618 *Wb.* II 367, 15.

8, 11

c P.Sekowski 12, 3 names Osiris' son in the first clause: *nḏ n sw sꜣ=f ḥr m-ʿ stš nḏ.n sw ḥr dr.n=f twꜣw=f.* BM 26, 6–7 corresponds to P.Sekowski: *nḏ sw sꜣ=f ḥr*. Cf. the 2nd person suffix pronoun in *Stundenwachen*, 36: *nḏ.n sꜣ=k ḥr*.
There are some notable orthographic peculiarities and comparisons with the parallel texts:

1. The scribe of BM 26, 5 regularly writes  for Horus.
2. *sꜣ*, , lacks the  determinative (G7) in BM 26, 6.
3. *nḏ* is written  in P.Sekowski 12, 3.
4. The determinative (Y1) for *dr*, 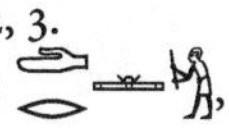, is paralleled by BMII 1. Cf. the  determinative (D40) in BM 26, 7.
5. The  (V4) of *twꜣw*, , is somewhat destroyed but visible. Cf. the  determinative (A24) in P.Sekowski 12, 3.
6. The *s*, , at the end of line 8, 11 belongs to the *snb* of the following line.

8, 12–13

d Cf. P.Sekowski 12, 5–6: *snb iḥꜣ im iwf=f di ʿ=f in ḥr di n=f rdwy=f in gb šmꜣ stš tp-ʿwy ḥr ii ḥr ḥtm m ḥkꜣw=f*, "He removed his enemies and he heals the pain which was in his flesh. His arm is given to him by Horus. His feet are given to him by Geb. Seth wanders before Horus. Horus has come provided with his magic." *ḥtm*,[619] spelled in the GR manner in P.W551: , is used as a perfect passive participle. However, Szczudlowska suggests an alternate reading with *ḥtm* as a stative and *ii* as a perfective active participle, translating the passage, "Seth wanders before Horus who has come (and) Horus is provided with his magic."[620] Cf. also BM 26, 8–10: *snb iḥꜣ im iwf di ʿ=f in ḥr di n=f rdwy=f in gb šmꜣ in stš tp-ʿ ḥr ii ḥtm m ḥkꜣw=f.* P.W551 clearly carries a somewhat different sense, accenting the mourning of Horus rather than the pain that Osiris experienced. The lack of a preposition after *ḏnḏn* suggests reading it as "to cut" rather than "to be angry."[621] The 3rd person suffix pronoun of *ḏnḏn* refers to Horus. However, cf. P.Sekowski 12, 7–8: *dndn.n=f ḫftw=f ẖr=f nšni iry stš r wsir*, "He has directed his fury (against) his enemies. He has appeased the rage which Seth had prepared against Osiris."
These orthographic features and discrepancies with the parallel texts should be mentioned:

1. *snb*, , has no determinatives in P.Sekowski 12, 4 and BM 26, 8.
2. *rdwy*, , has the  determinative (F51) in all parallel texts.
3. *šmꜣi* is written  in all parallel texts except for BM 26, 10: .

619 *Wb.* III 196, 9–197, 9.
620 Szczudlowska, *ZÄS* 98 (1970): 73.
621 See *Wb.* V 472, 9–10 and *Wb.* V 471, 21–472, 5, respectively.

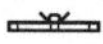

4. Seth is written  in all parallel texts except for BM 26, 10, which uses  (A13).
5. The  (N31) determinative of *irt-ḥr* is paralleled by BMII, 2.[622]
6. *ḥḳ3w* has the  determinative (A2) in P.Sekowski 12, 6 and lacks determinatives in BM 26, 11: .
7. *dndn* is written 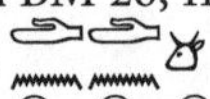 P.Sekowski 12, 6.
8. *ḫftw* is spelled . Cf. P.Sekowski 12, 6: 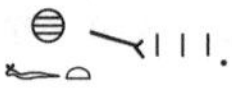. This word is written in red ink in BM 26, 11.

8, 13–14

E Cf. P.Sekowski 12, 8: *ꜥḥꜥ wsir ḥr rdwy=f is ꜥpr 3ḫw=f,* "Osiris rises to his feet. Indeed, he is equipped with his magical protection." Note the singular *3ḫ=f* in BM 26, 12.
These discrepancies with the parallel texts should be mentioned:

1. *imntyw,* , has no phonetic complements in BM 26, 12.
2. *ꜥpr,* , lacks the determinative (Y1) in BM 26, 12.
3. *ḫtm* has a more usual spelling in P.Sekowski 12, 8:  and in BM 26, 13: .

8, 14–15

F Cf. P.Sekowski 12, 9: *i.n=sn nṯrw ḏd in 3st,* "So said the gods. Isis said."
Szczudlowska also understands the group 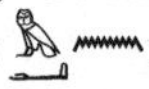 in P.Sekowski 13, 1 as an imperative *my,* but suggests that is a mistake for : *my rf ṯn 3ḫw 4 ipw ḫns ḳbḥw,* "Come then, you, these four blessed spirits who traverse *Kebehu.*"[623] However, is commonly included in the spelling of the imperative *my,* emphasized in P.W551 by the preposition *r,* , and the 2nd person plural suffix pronoun *ṯn,* .[624] Cf.  in BM 26, 14.
The 3rd person singular suffix pronoun of *3ḫw* is paralleled only by BMI, 14. The text of P.Sekowski diverges from the present manuscript following the names of the four sons of Horus.
There are some notable orthographic peculiarities and discrepancies with the parallel texts:

1.  and  are added above the line following , *ms*. Cf.  in BM 26, 13.
2. *ḫns* has the  determinative (D54) in all parallels except BM 26, 14.
3. *ḳbḥw* is written 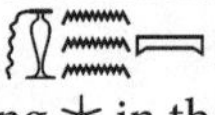 in P.Sekowski 13, 2.
4. The dot following  in the name of Duamutef must indicate a continuation of the name on the next line. *mwt* is written  in P.Sekowski 13, 2 and BM 26, 15, but has the  determinative (G7) in BMI and BMII.

622 *Wb.* I 107, 12.

623 Szczudlowska, *ZÄS* 98 (1970): 56, n. a.

624 Gardiner, *Egyptian Grammar*, § 337.3. For the spelling of this 2nd person plural suffix pronoun, see Daumas, *Valeurs phonétiques* II, p. 313.

5. *snw* in the name of Kebehsenuef is written 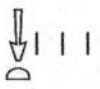 in all parallels. The  determinative (G7) is paralleled by BMI 4.
6. The name of *ḥ3ḳw* is written  in BM 26, 16.
7. *m3* in the name of *m3-it=f* is spelled  (U1). Cf.  in BM 26, 16.

8, 16

G The 3rd person singular feminine suffix pronoun of *mẖr* refers to *Kebehu.*
The second clause is introduced by the pronominal performative *sw,* followed by *wꜥb.*[625]
Note the word play in the sounds of *ḳsw* and *k3=s,* where the *s* of *k3=s* stands for the 3rd person plural suffix pronoun *sn,* referring back to Isis and the gods mentioned in line 14.[626]
The reading of , *ꜥnḫ.n=f,* is questionable, as the hieratic group may also stand for , *ḥn(ꜥ)=f,* "with him." Cf. BM 26, 19: *ksw=f k3s ꜥnḫ(?)=f m bw pwy nḫ(?)=ṯn.*
wꜥbt is a late term for "heaven." The writing of , a late term for "lamentation," is unusual due to the hieroglyphic shape of the first . Thus, the entire group may be a duplication of  in hieroglyphic and hieratic. The lack of a determinative suggests a possibility of reading *im,* "therein." [627]

8, 16–17

H The 2nd person plural suffix pronoun of *stp* refers back to Isis and the gods. The 3rd person singular suffix pronoun following the preposition *n* refers to Osiris.
Cf. the "children of his children" in BM 26, 20–23: *hy hy msw msw=f pwy nn irt n rꜥ m gs=f dpt m msḏ m3n sw sṯẖ stp=ṯn s3=ṯn ḥr it=ṯn wsir.* Assmann translates the clause *m msḏ m3n sw sṯẖ,* "weil er nicht wollte (es haßte), daß Seth ihn sehen könnte." [628]
These orthographic discrepancies with the parallel texts should be noted:

1. The  determinative (G7) for Osiris is consistently omitted from BM 26, 23.
2. The determinative of *hnw,* , is written on line 8, 18. Cf.  (A8) in BM 26, 23.

8, 18

I The particle *iẖ* is used in the prospective *iẖ+sḏm=f* construction. *sip* is used in the sense of assigning the rebels to a slaughter or fire.[629]
There are some notable orthographic discrepancies with the parallel texts:

1. *ẖft(=f) ẖr=f,* , is written in red ink in BM 26, 24.

625 Černý and Groll, *Late Egyptian Grammar*, pp. 33–34, 2.6.1–2.
626 For further discussion of word play, see section 1.5.1, above.
627 For *imim,* a LP term for "lamentation" and variant of *im,* see *Wb.* I 82, 22.
628 Assmann, *Totenliturgien* I, p. 270 and n. 148.
629 Wilson, *Ptolemaic Lexikon*, p. 798.

2. The following should be understood as a mistake for , *n*.
3. *im*, , has a phonetic complement in BM 26, 25.

8, 19

J *itrty* in the GR epithet *nbw-itrty*, "Lords of the Two Conclaves/ Shrines," is a name of Osiris' bark.[630] Cf. *nṯrw nb m itrty* in BM 26, 27.

8, 20–21

k The clause *pr m rʿ* is omitted from BM 26.
Some orthographic features and discrepancies with the parallels should be noted:

1. *dḫs* is spelled in BM 26, 29.[631]
2. Asbet appears as in BM 26, 30.
3. *kmt* is written , without the ⊗ determinative (O49), in BM 26, 30.
4. *ʿnḫw*, a LP and GR term for "stars," is spelled in BM 26, 30.[632]
5. Note the dot at the end of the line. The sign preceding the dot is repeated on the following line.

3.2.11. *s3ḫw* III, SPELL 11 — SPOKEN BY THE LECTOR PRIEST

Lines 8, 21–30[633]

This spell opens with a speech of Horus, who indicates that the protected Osiris has been resurrected. In the context of the solar cycle, Osiris' epithet "Chief of the District" (*ḥry-tp-sp3t*) equates the reborn Osiris with Re. Order is established as Seth and his gang are defeated. Just as Osiris is in his rightful place, surrounded and praised by Horus and the court, the deceased Padikakem is proclaimed to be justified. The spell closes with instructions for its recitation during sacrifice and presentation of offerings.

TRANSLITERATION

s3ḫ
ḏd mdw in ẖry-ḥbt
i.n ḥr n nṯrw m=ṯn
rs.n twty wsir
nḏ.n sw m-ʿ iry r=f 22. *rdi.n ʿḥʿ=f m nṯr*
gm n=f ḏw=f r=s(n)

630 See *Wb.* I 148, 1–10, and Leitz et al., eds., *Lexikon* III, p. 806, respectively.
631 For the GR term *ṯḫs*, often spelled with a , "to slaughter, disassemble," see *Wb.* V 328, 4–7.
632 *Wb.* I 204, 6.
633 See section 1.7.3, above.

hy wsir ḫnty-imntyw wsir n P3-dit-k3-km
ii.k(w) i it
n=k 23. *s3=k ḥr*
mk ḏ3ḏ3t
nḏ n ḥr=k m hrw=k pn nfr wbn im=f ḥr sp3t m ḥtpw ḏf3w
dit pt ḳm3 t3
24. *m rn=k n ḥry-tp-sp3t*
n rdi iry sbiw
m3ʿ.n=f r=k
in n=k swt pfy ḥ3w imyw šwt=f
(8, 25) *ḳm3 ḳ3s*
sni=sn ⌜*r*⌝ *rdwy k3=k*
ḫrw ḥʿʿ m-ḫnw ḥʿ
i3wt m r itrty
wsir 26. *ḥtp ḥr iḫt=f*
ḫnm sw m⌜*sw*⌝*=f nṯrw*
swt ḫr m-ḫnw ḫbt=f
sm3iw=f m s3 sbiw
27. … …*=ṯn* … ⌜*sw*⌝ *ḥr ḏ3ḏ3t r gs wsir š*…
nṯr im … *ḥknw*
⌜*ḳnbtyw*⌝ *m ḥy-s3-t3*
28. … … … … … … … … … … [*wsir P3-dit-k3-km*]
m3ʿ ḫrw=k
29. *ḫr i*… … … *im ḫrt-*⌜*nṯr*⌝
ḏd mdw
s… … ⌜*sri 4*⌝ … *di šm=sn*
iw=sn m bḥn (8, 30) *tp=sn m m3ʿ wšn=sn n wsir*
di m sbi n sḏt
wn m3ʿ ipw is ḥtp ib ipf
wḏḥ pw tp-t3 n nsw ḏt

TRANSLATION

Glorification spell.
Words spoken by the lector priest:
"Horus speaks to the gods among you:
'As the forms of Osiris have awakened,
those who protect him from those who act against him 22. have caused him to become a god,
he having found his evil against th(em).
O, Osiris, Foremost of the Westerners, Osiris of Padikakem.
I have come, father!
To you belongs 23. your son, Horus.' A

Behold, the court.
Hail to you on this your good day, on which you shine therein it upon the districts with offerings and provisions
which heaven gives and earth creates,
24. in your name of Chief of the District.[B]
The making of a rebellion is not allowed,
he having offered on your behalf.
This naked Seth is brought to you among his gang
(8, 25) who are cast down and bound.[C]
May they kiss the two feet of your *ka*!
The rejoicing voice is in the palace,
and praising is at the entrance to the two conclaves.[D]
Osiris is 26. satisfied with his belongings.
The gods unite him with his off⸢spring⸣.
Seth has fallen into his place of execution,
his companions following the rebel.[E]
27. … your … him Horus (and) the court are at the side of Osiris …,
the god who is in (is) praising,
and the ⸢courtiers⸣ are rejoicing.[F]
28. …. … … … … … … … … [Osiris of Padikakem],
true of your voice.[G]
29. … … … who are in the ⸢nec⸣ropolis." [H]
Words spoken.
… … ⸢four geese⸣ causing that they go,
as they are sacrificing (8, 30) their head(s) in presenting their offerings to Osiris,
being presented as a burnt offering.
This is indeed, the offering, which satisfies this heart.
This is the command of the king on earth, forever.[I]

TEXT NOTES

8, 21–23

A The phrase *ꜥḥꜥ m nṯr* is reminiscent of a more familiar *ꜥḥꜥ m nswt*, "to become king."[634]
The clause *gm n=f ḏw=f r=sn* should be understood as "the one who met his opponent (i.e., Seth)."
The sign below 𓈖, *n*, of *rdi.n* is likely a mistake for the 3rd person singular masculine suffix pronoun *f*.

634 *Wb.* I 219, 5.

8, 23–24

B The epithet *ḥry-tp-spꜣt,* "Chief of the District," appears to be an abbreviation of one of the many primarily late epithets, such as *ḥry-tp-spꜣt-ỉmnt, ḥry-tp-spꜣt-ỉgrt, ḥry-tp-spꜣwt=f,* as well as the NK title *ḥr-tp-spꜣt.*[635]
Cf. *Stundenwachen* XV, 43–33: *ỉn=sn n=f ḥtpw ḏfꜣw rdỉ pt ḳmꜣ tꜣ,* "They bring to him offerings and provisions which heaven gives and the earth creates."[636]
Two orthographic discrepancies with the parallel texts should be noted:

1. *hrw* is spelled in BM 27, 7.
2. *pt* is spelled in BM 27, 9.

8, 24–25

C The 3rd person masculine singular suffix pronoun of *mꜣꜥ* refers to Horus. Cf. the preposition in BM 27, 10–11: *mꜣ.n=f n=k.*
 is understood here as *ỉmyw šwt,* "among the gang, group."[637] However, cf. Szczudlowska's reading of this group in P.Sekowski 19, 6–7, as *ỉmyw-ḫt:*[638] *ỉn=ỉ n=k sbỉ pfy ḫꜣw ỉmyw-ḫt=f smꜣ ḳꜣs s(w),* "I have captured for you that naked rebel who goes after him (*sic*). I have slain and chained him."[639]
These orthographic peculiarities and discrepancies with the parallel texts should be noted:

1. *ỉmyw* is more abbreviated in BM 27, 12: .
2. The determinative (Aa2) of *ḳmꜣ,* , must be a scribal error. Cf. the more usual determinative in BM 27, 12: .
3. The determinative (A24) also appears for *ḳꜣs* in BM 27, 12–13: . Cf. in P.Sekowski 19, 7.

8, 25

D Cf. P.Sekowski 19, 7–8 and BM 27, 13–15: *snỉ=sn r rdwy kꜣ=k ḫrw ḥꜥꜥ m-ẖnw ḥꜥ ỉꜣw ḳꜣ m r ỉtrty,* "May they kiss the two feet of your *ka*! The rejoicing voice is in the palace, and the exalted praising is at the entrance to the two conclaves." Note the phonetic complements for *rdwy* in P.Sekowski 19, 7: .

635 Leitz et al, eds., *Lexikon* V, p. 454.

636 Junker, *Stundenwachen*, p. 89. For the expression *dỉt pt ḳmꜣ tꜣ*, "that which heaven gives and the earth creates," see *Wb.* V 35, 8.

637 Wilson, *Ptolemaic Lexikon*, p. 996–97; *Wb.* IV 426, 5.

638 Szczudlowska, *ZÄS* 98 (1970): 77.

639 Note that Szczudlowska supplies 1st person singular suffix pronouns in the last clause. For *ḳꜣs*, "to bind, tie up," see Wilson, *Ptolemaic Lexikon*, p. 1047; *Wb.* V 13, 1–7.

8, 25–26

E Cf. P.Sekowski 19, 9–20,1: *wsir ḥtp ḥr ẖwt=f ẖnm sw msw=f nṯrw stš ẖw m ẖbt=f smꜣw=f m sꜣ ꜣḳr,* "Osiris is content with his affairs, as his children, the gods have united him. Seth has fallen in his place of slaughter and his companions are under the guardians of Aker." The phonetic similarity between *sꜣ,* , "guardian," of P.Sekowski and *sꜣ,* , "back, following," in the present manuscript points to a possibly intentional pun of the two words.[640] The *sbiw* at the end of this clause must refer to Seth, implying that his companions are next to fall.

Some orthographic peculiarities and discrepancies from the parallel texts should be noted:

1. *ḥtp* is more abbreviated in P.Sekowski 19, 8: .
2. *ỉẖt* shows a GR spelling here: .[641] The scribe of BM 27, 15 abbreviates this term even further: .
3. *stš* is spelled in P.Sekowski 20, 1.
4. Szczudlowska transcribes the determinative for *ẖr* as , although this group in hieratic is similar to the determinative (A15), typical for *ẖr*.
5. *ẖnw* is spelled in BM 27, 17.
6. (A8) should be understood as the equivalent of (A31) for the phonetic *ẖb*.[642] Cf. the more conventional determinative (O1) in P.Sekowski 20, 1 and most parallels. BM 27, 17 has .
7. *smꜣiw* is spelled in all parallels except for BM 27, 17 which has only the (A14).
8. *sꜣ* is spelled in BM 27, 18.

8, 27

F Cf. P.Sekowski 20, 2–4: *nḏm ib=tn ḥr nṯrw ḏꜣḏꜣt r gs wsir š(s)t im=s ḥr rdit ḥknw ḳrtyw m iꜣw sp 2,* "Be happy, Horus and the gods of the court beside (the sanctuary of)[643] Osiris! Those who are in it are rejoicing. The inhabitants of the Netherworld are in great adoration." The remaining (O38) and allow the reading of *ḳnbtyw* following *ḥknw* in parallel to B 3, 15.[644] BM 27, 18–21 seems to correspond to the remaining traces: *nḏm ib=tn ḥr msw m ḏꜣḏꜣt irw wsir št im rdi ḥknw ḳrtyw m hy-sꜣ-tꜣ*. Notably, the group *r gs* occurs only in the B and BM parallels.

The expression *hy-sꜣ-tꜣ,* "jubilation, rejoicing," is frequently attested in the GR period.[645]

---

640 For a discussion of word play, see section 1.5.1, above.

641 *Wb.* I 124.

642 For *ẖbt,* "place of execution," see *Wb.* II 252, 9–14.

643 Szczudlowska omits *r gs,* "beside," from the transcription and supplies "sanctuary" in the translation.

644 Szczudlowska, *ZÄS* 98 (1970): 77, n. 20, 3.

645 *Wb.* II 483, 12.

8, 28

G This line is largely broken and its apparent parallel appears only in BM 27, 21–24: *pḫꜣ-ib rꜥ nb m rkḥ.tw ḫftw=k m ꜥḥ ḥr ḫt mꜣꜥ ḫrw=k.*

8, 29

H The text in the lacuna may be reconstructed on the basis of BM 27, 24–26: *wsir ḫnty-imntyw ḫr mꜣꜥ ḫrw=k ḫr it=k gb ḫr ḏꜣḏꜣt im ḫrt-nṯr.*

8, 29–30

I The phonetic complement *d* for *ḏd*, , is indicated with a dot here. Traces of (G39) for *ꜣpd* and IIII are visible. Cf. the instructions for reciting spell 11 of *sꜣḫw* III in BM 27, 26–27: *ḏd mdw st in n=k ꜣpd 4 rdi šm=sn iw=sn m bḥn,* and in P.Sekowski 20, 4: *ḏd mdw ḥr sri 4.t,* "Words to be recited upon four geese."

The group transliterated here as *m mꜣꜥ wšn=sn* may also be read as *m šw snḏ=sn n* ..., "for lack of their respect for ...." Notably, *wšn* is spelled in BM 27, 28. Cf. P.Sekowski 20, 4–5: *rdit šm=sn m-bꜣḥ nw 4 wšr=sn m-ḫt,* "that they go four times before and after they are placed as sacrifice."

The expression *wn mꜣꜥ pw* also occurs in medical texts, such as P.Ebers 63, 3.[646]

3.2.12. *sꜣḫw* III, SPELL 12 — SPOKEN BY THE LECTOR PRIEST

Lines 8, 31–9,1[647]

This spell describes the success of various gods in the resurrection of Osiris. He has been reassembled, raised, and rejuvenated by Isis, Nephthys, Khnum, and others, as Nut is again represented as the vehicle for his rebirth. While Horus was the first to establish the correct order of succession, the mention of his children maintains this order. The process of mummification and, in particular, the wrapping and purification of the body is noted as necessary for Osiris' rejuvenation. An integral part of Osiris' protection is also the repelling of Seth and other enemies, who are equated with sacrificial animals. Within this context, the spell again concludes with an instruction that the recitation be accompanied by an offering of fowl.

TRANSLITERATION

31. *sꜣḫ*
ḏd mdw in ḫry-ḥbt
wsir ḫnty-imntyw wsir n Pꜣ-dit-kꜣ-km
sꜣḳ.n kw ꜣst

646 Vernus, in *GM* 170 (1999): 105, n. 22.

647 See section 1.7.3, above.

ink.n kw nbt-ḥwt
ḥ-32.-ngg=sn ḥr-ẖt=k m nw ḥr nw m-ḥꜣt wḏꜥ
pẖr=s(n) tp=k r rsw
ẖw=sn kw mḥ=k
hy wsir 33. ḫnty-imntyw wsir n Pꜣ-dit-kꜣ-km
nṯr ṯs.n kw ẖnm
sꜥḥꜥ.n kw ḥpḥp
mꜣ=sn nṯr pn im=k
nḏr 34.=sn kw ḥr ḏbꜥw=sn
snẖn=sn kw
r šm=k r wꜣḏ-wr
hy wsir ḫnty-imntyw wsir n Pꜣ-dit-kꜣ-km
twt=s(n) ẖꜣt (8, 35) sbꜣ-wꜥ
sḫm-šps
pr m nwt
rwi n=k ḥr pw nṯrw šmsw.n kw m nb=sn
rnn.n kw mwt=k 36. nwt
ms=s tw m nḫn
hy wsir ḫnty-imntyw wsir n Pꜣ-dit-kꜣ-km
in n=k ḥr msw=f
išs smꜣ m rn=k ḥnꜥ 37. nw ẖt=f
mꜣꜥ=sn nb=sn im=k
mr=sn kw swꜣḏ.n kw
hy wsir n ḫnty-imntyw wsir Pꜣ-dit-kꜣ-km
nw 38.=sn nḏ nꜣy ḥꜣ kꜣ=k
di=sn n=k ḫftw=k ẖr=k
hy wsir ḫnty-imntyw wsir n Pꜣ-dit-kꜣ-km
ꜥb.n=k ḥr imy-spdt sꜣ-spdt
39. pr im=k
hy wsir n ḫnty-imntyw wsir n Pꜣ-dit-kꜣ-km
ḥw=f n=k swt m-m ḫnt m rn=f pwy n kꜣ-pt
sgrḥ (8, 40) n=f ḳsw n swt m biꜣ iḫmw-sk
hy wsir n ḫnty-imntyw wsir n Pꜣ-dit-kꜣ-km
ḥw n=k inp
ḳn r ḫftw 41.=k
sšm=k r sw m ḫnt nṯr
mrt=k
nḏ ḥr=k in rkḥw
di ḫftw=k m ꜥẖ ḥr nsrt
mꜣꜥ ḫrw=k
42. wsir ḫnty-imntyw wsir n Pꜣ-dit-kꜣ-km
mꜣꜥ ḫrw=k ẖr ḥr m ḫnt-ꜥꜣw
wnn=f pẖr m sꜣ=k
ḥw=f n=k smꜣw šwt stš

(9, 1) *ḏd mdw*
is in n=k srt pꜣ(!) 4
r di(t) šm=sn iw=sn m mꜣʿw tpw=sn n wsir ḫnty-imntyw wsir n Pꜣ-dit-kꜣ-km
di m-sbi n sḏt
mꜣʿ ip(w) ḥr sꜣṯw nt(!)

TRANSLATION

31. Glorification spell.
Words spoken by the lector priest:
"Osiris, Foremost of the Westerners, Osiris of Padikakem.
Isis has pulled you together,
Nephthys has embraced you.
32. May they rejoice behind you always before the Judged One (=Seth),
as (th)ey surround your head against the south,
they protect you to your north.[A]
O, Osiris, 33. Foremost of the Westerners, Osiris of Padikakem.
The god, Khnum, raised you,
Hepwy caused that you stand,
that they may see this god in you.[B]
They grasped 34. you with their fingers,
and they rejuvenated you,
so that you may go to the Great Green.[C]
O, Osiris, Foremost of the Westerners, Osiris of Padikakem.
Th(ey) have assembled the corpse (8, 35) of the Unique Star,
Noble Power,
One who Came Forth from Nut.
This Horus and the gods, who follow you, give way to you as their lord.
Your mother, Nut, has nursed you,
36. she bore you as a youth.[D]
O, Osiris, Foremost of the Westerners, Osiris of Padikakem.
Horus brings for you his children.
Who unites with your name, 37. wrapping his body?
May they make proper their lord within you!
Their binding of you is rejuvenation for you.[E]
O, Osiris, of (*sic*) Foremost of the Westerners, Osiris Padikakem.
May they 38. wrap that protection behind your *ka*,
as they place for you your enemies under you.[F]
O, Osiris, Foremost of the Westerners, Osiris of Padikakem.
Horus, He who is in Sothis, the Effective Son, purifies for you,
39. having come forth from you.[G]
O, Osiris, Foremost of the Westerners, Osiris of Padikakem.
He strikes for you Seth in Henet, in this name of his of Bull of Heaven.
He pacified (8, 40) the bones of Seth in the heaven of the circumpolar stars.[H]

O, Osiris, Foremost of the Westerners, Osiris of Padikakem.
Anubis strikes for you,
harming your enemies,
41. that you may be guided to him before the god,
(with) those whom you bound.
Hail to you by the Burning Ones,
who place your enemies in the oven upon the fire,
that you may be justified.[I]
42. Osiris, Foremost of the Westerners, Osiris of Padikakem.
You are justified by Horus as the Foremost of the Great Ones,
so that he may follow after you.
He strikes for you the companions and the gang of Seth.[J]
(9, 1) Words spoken.
"Now, the 4 geese are brought to you,
in order to be caused to go as they are sacrificing their heads for
Osiris, Foremost of the Westerners, Osiris of Padikakem,
being presented as a burnt offering.
This is an offering (which is made) upon the ground.[K]

TEXT NOTES

Isis and Nephthys reassemble and protect Osiris in the beginning of this spell. The unusual choice of words in the phrase *ḥngg=sn ḥr-ḫt=k m nw ḥr nw m-ḥ3t wḏ*ʿ, "May they rejoice behind you always, before the Judged One," may be due to an attempt at alliteration, with most words beginning with "*ḥ*."[648] *ḥngg,* 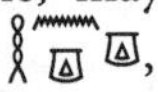, the phonetic  of which is written on the previous line 8, 31, is a LP variant of *ḥ3g3g* (*ḥr*), "to rejoice (about)."[649] This term is perhaps a pun on the GR *ngg,* which describes the noise made by a sistrum and is thus associated with joy, particularly of goddesses.[650] *ngg* also occurs in PT 668 (§1959a) in reference to the screeching of a falcon.[651] Further instances of word play in this spell occur in the epithets of Horus, *imy-spd,* "He who is in Sothis," and *s3-spd,* "Effective Son,"[652] which are clearly puns on each other.[653]

Paronomasia again plays an important role in the name of Henet, the place where Horus strikes Seth down. The ⊗ determinative (O49) of *ḥnt,* , points to reading this word as a place name and could be understood as *pr-ḥnt,* the Serapeum in the 10th nome of Lower Egypt.[654] Notably, *ḥnt,* "crocodile," is also a LP and GR term equated with Seth.[655] Having

648 For further discussion of word play, see section 1.5.1, above.

649 Szczudlowska, *ZÄS* 98 (1970): 76, n. 19; *Wb.* III 34, 18; *ibid.*, 35, 3; *ibid.*, 121, 9.

650 Wilson, *Ptolemaic Lexikon*, p. 553; *Wb.* II 350, 9–12. See section 1.5.1, above.

651 Allen, *The Ancient Egyptian Pyramid Texts*, p. 265.

652 Leitz et al, eds., *Lexikon* I, p. 251.

653 Leitz et al, eds., *Lexikon* VI, p. 92. See section 1.5.1, above.

654 Brugsch, *Dictionnaire géographique de l'ancienne Égypte*, p. 498.

655 Wilson, *Ptolemaic Lexikon*, p. 660; *Wb.* III 121, 14.

gained another victory over Seth, Horus pacifies "the bones of Seth in the heaven (*bỉ3*) of the circumpolar stars." The choice of *bỉ3,* understood as the GR term for "heaven,"[656] likely stems from *bỉ3,* "iron (associated with Seth)."[657] This notion is supported by PT 21 (§14a), which describes Horus performing the OM ceremony on Osiris with an instrument made of "metal that came from Seth" (*bỉ3 pr m stš*).[658]

8, 31–32

A This spell is paralleled by P.Sekowski 18, 2–19, 4. The text also corresponds to P.Berlin 3057 (B), col. 1; P.BM 102525, cols. 4–5 and P.BM 102524 (BMI); P.Salt 1821 (A) (BMII), P.BM 10317, B27 (BMIII) and parts of the *Stundenwachen* ritual.[659] Cf. P.Sekowski 18, 9: *s3ḳ.n kw 3st ỉnḳ.n k(w) nbt-ḥwt. s3ḳ* is spelled  in P.Sekowski 18, 9 and all other parallels.

Cf. P.Sekowski 19, 1: *ḥ3g3g=sn ḥr ḫt=k m nw ḥr nw r mḥtt s3w,* "They rejoice when you pass the water on the north of Sais." Unlike the other parallels of this passage, P.Sekowski 19, 1 and the present manuscript do not have the  determinative (D54) for *ḫt,* , suggesting that this word is the compound preposition *ḥr-ḫt,* "behind, after."[660] Szczudlowska translates *ḥr-ḫt=k* as "on your passing."

The suggestion of Szczudlowska is followed here in understanding  as the equivalent of the LP and GR expression *m nw r nw,* "always."[661] The first *nw* has the phonetic complement  in every parallel text. The  is omitted from all the parallels. The second *nw* is spelled with the  determinative in P.Sekowski 19, 1 and its parallels, likely originating from the LP and GR *nw,* "waters of the underworld," frequently spelled with  (U19).[662]

 (Aa21) replaces the name of Seth in the CT.[663] Sethe translated the sign as "der Gerichtete."[664] Nonetheless, due to a lack of a determinative,  may also be read as *wḏꜥ,* "judgment."

More orthographic features and discrepancies with the parallels should be noted:

1. The  determinative (W7)[665] replaces the more typical  determinative (D32) for *ỉnḳ,* 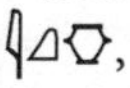, of P.W551,[666] which is written without a determinative in all the parallels.

656 Wilson, *Ptolemaic Lexikon*, p. 306; *Wb.* I 439, 9.

657 Wainwright, *JEA* 18 (1932): 13–14.

658 Allen, *The Ancient Egyptian Pyramid Texts*, p. 252.

659 The transliteration and translation of this and subsequent spells of P.Sekowski and its parallels is based on Szczudlowska, *ZÄS* 98 (1970): 50–80.

660 *Wb.* III 347, 13–15.

661 Szczudlowska, *ZÄS* 98 (1970): 76. For *nw*, "time," see *Wb.* II 219, 7 and 15.

662 *Wb.* II 221, 11.

663 te Velde, *Seth*, p. 30, n. 7; Kees, *MVAG* 29 (1924): 83.

664 Sethe, *ZÄS* 58 (1923): 76, n. 38

665 Möller, *Hieratische Paläographie* III, p. 505.

666 *Wb.* I 100, 19–22.

2. The presence of in *ḥngg* is paralleled only by BMII 2, 19. Note its  determinative (A2) in all the parallels.
3. The preposition *ḥr,* , is written with a phonetic complement *r*.[667]
4. Note the dot at the end of line 8, 32.

8, 33

B *nṯr* is omitted before *ṯs* in all parallels. Cf. BM 28, 6: *ṯs.n=k tw*. Furthermore, the phrase *mꜣ=sn nṯr pn im=k* is omitted from all parallel texts, except BM 28, 7: *mꜣ=sn nṯr=sn im=k.*
ḥpḥp is a NK and GR name of a god. Cf. *ḥpwy*, the "the god of fans." [668]
There are some notable orthographic peculiarities and discrepancies with the parallel texts:

1. *ṯs* is spelled  in P.Sekowski 19, 2.
2. None of the parallels have the determinative (Y1) for *ẖnm,* and the  determinative (G7) is omitted from Khnum in BM 28, 6.
3. This spelling of *sꜥḥꜥ,* , corresponds to P.Sekowski 19, 2 and BM 28, 7.
4. The and of the 3rd person plural suffix pronoun of *mꜣꜣ* are reversed.
5. *nṯr,* 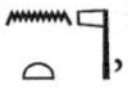, is written with phonetic complements in BM 28, 7.

8, 34

C Cf. the very similar P.Sekowski 19, 2–3: *nḏri=sn tw ḥr ḏbꜥw=sn nẖn=sn tw r šm=k r wꜣḏ-wr*(?), "They grasp you with their fingers. They have rejuvenated you, so that you may go to the Great Green(?)." Although P.Sekowski spells ,[669] it is difficult to agree with Szczudlowska's reading of this group as an administrative building. , *š n wꜣḏ-wr* in BMII 20 points to a more probable reading of this as a general geographical indication of a body of water.[670] Notably, the term *wꜣḏ-wr* appears as an epithet of Osiris, who is said to be the sovereign and lord of the *wꜣḏ-wr*.[671]
Some orthographic features and discrepancies with the parallels should be noted:

1. The beginning of *nḏr,* , is written in line 8, 33. This term is spelled  in all parallel texts except for BM 28, 8.
2. The  following 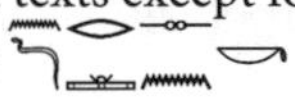 must be understood as a mistake for *w* here.
3. The plurality of *ḏbꜥw* is indicated by in all parallels except BM 28, 8.
4. The and of the 3rd person plural suffix pronoun of *ḏbꜥw* are reversed.

667 *Wb.* III 131.
668 See *Wb.* III 3, and Leitz et al., eds., *Lexikon* V, pp. 123–24, respectively.
669 Szczudlowska, *ZÄS* 98 (1970): 59.
670 Szczudlowska, *ZÄS* 98 (1970): 76.
671 Vandersleyen, *Ouadj our*, p. 44.

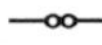

8, 34–36

D Cf. P.Sekowski 19, 4: *ꜣtt.n k(w) mwt=k nwt ms=s tw m nḫn,* "Your mother Nut created you, she bore you as a youth."
The following orthographic peculiarities and differences from the parallel texts should be noted:

1. Only ★ (N14) is written for *sbꜣ* in BM 28, 10.
2. *pr,* , lacks a determinative in BM 28, 10.
3. Nut does not have a determinative (G7) here.
4. The following is superfluous.
5. indicate plurality of *nṯrw,* , in BM 28, 11.
6. *šms,* , lacks a determinative in BM 28, 11.
7. *mwt,* , erroneously has I I I.
8. Nut is written in BM 28, 12.
9. Note the dot at the end of line 8, 35.

8, 36–37

E Cf. the suffix pronouns in BM 28, 14–16: *smꜣ.n=k ḥnꜥ nw ẖt=f mꜣꜥ=sn nb=sn im=k mr=sn kw swꜣḏ=sn kw.*
There are some notable orthographic peculiarities and discrepancies with the parallel texts:

1. The and of the 3rd person plural suffix pronoun of *mr* are reversed. The following the suffix is superfluous.
2. The preposition is written before *ḫnty-imntyw* rather than before the name Padikakem in line 8, 37.

8, 37–38

F The 3rd person plural suffix pronoun of *nw* refers to the children of Horus. The plurality of the demonstrative *nꜣy* points to the protective significance of the mummy bandages mentioned in the previous line. Correspondingly, the preposition *ḥꜣ,* "behind, around," is generally used in a protective sense, fitting the context.[672]

8, 38–39

G Cf. the somewhat similar phrase of P.Sekowski 18, 2–4: *ꜥb=f n=k ḥꜥw=k m ḥr im spdt sꜣ spd,* "May he offer to you your members as Horus who is in Sothis, the Effective Son." Cf. a similar phrase in PT 366 (§632d): *ḥr spd pr im=k m ḥr im spdt,* and PT 593 (§1636b): *ḥr spd pr im=k m rn=f n ḥr-im-spdt.*

672 Wilson, *Ptolemaic Lexikon,* p. 610; *Wb.* III 8, 12ff.

There are some notable orthographic discrepancies with the parallel texts:

1. *spdt* is spelled  in P.Sekowski 18, 3, while the other parallels have 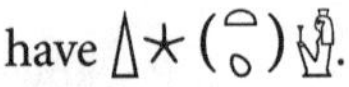.
2. *s3,* , has the  determinative (G7) in all parallels except BM 28, 19.
3. *spd* is spelled phonetically in every parallel: .

8, 39–40

H The 3rd person singular masculine suffix pronoun refers to Horus.
Cf. a similar phrase in CT 838, VII 40n: … *stẖ ḥnt is ḥw n=k sw m rn=f n iḥ-pt,* "… Seth of Henet. Smite him in his name of Bull of the Sky."[673] The transliteration of the group  is questionable. It may be read *k3-n-pt,* "Bull of Heaven," which is often written without the genitive , or as the OK epithet of the protector and guide of the deceased, *iḥ-pt,* "Cattle of Heaven."[674]
Cf. Szczudlowska's rendering of P.Sekowski 18, 5–6: *nḥm.n(sic) ḳsw n stš m bi3 iẖ-mw-sk,* "Save the bones for (him)! Seth will not be thunderbolt of the Imperishable." Szczudlowska considers a variant reading *ḳsw n stš* and refers to Plutarch's statement concerning the bones of Seth being of iron (*bi3*). She discounts the possibility of translating *ḳsw n stš* as the object and *m bi3 iẖmw-sk* as an adverbial expression, because *bi3,* in this case, would have to be read as "firmament," a late term which typically has a different determinative.[675] However, the lack of a determinative for *bi3,*  in the present manuscript, as well as the lack of a suffix pronoun after *ḳsw n* support reading *ḳsw n stš* as the object of *sgrḥ*. See also B 3, 7 and BMII 2, 18: *nḥm n=f….*
The following orthographic discrepancies with the parallel texts should be mentioned:

1. *bi3* is written  in P.Sekowski 18, 5-6.
2.  (E21) stands for Seth in P.Sekowski 18, 5; the name is spelled phonetically in all other parallels: 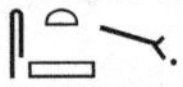.
3. *iẖmw-sk* has a more extended spelling in P.Sekowski 18, 6: .

8, 40–41

I *sšm* is used as a passive *sḏmw=f.*[676]
Cf. the epithet *rkḥw-ddw-sḏt-m-ʿẖw,* "Burning Ones who Place the Fire in the Oven."[677]
Some orthographic discrepancies with the parallel texts should be noted:

1. *ẖnt* is spelled 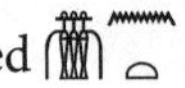 in BM 28, 24.

673 Faulkner, *Ancient Egyptian Coffin Texts* III, p. 26.
674 Leitz et al, eds., *Lexikon* VII, p. 255, and *ibid.*, I, p. 540, respectively.
675 Szczudlowska, *ZÄS* 98 (1970): 58 and 76.
676 Gardiner, *Egyptian Grammar*, §§419–23. For the expression *sšm r*, "to lead to," see *Wb.* IV 285, 12.
677 Leitz et al, eds., *Lexikon* IV, p. 729. For *rkḥw*, "The Burning Ones," see Leitz, *ibid.*, IV, p. 729.

2. The LP  determinative for *mr,* 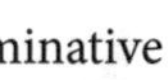, supports the reading "to bind." [678]
3. *ḫrw,* 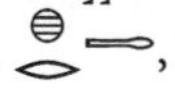, shows phonetic complements in BM 28, 26.

8, 42

J *ḫnt-ʿ3w* should be understood as the epithet *ḫnt-psḏt-ʿ3t,* "Foremost of the Great Ennead." [679] The epithet is written  in BM 28, 28.
wnn is here written for the prospective 2nd tense, *wn=f.*

9, 1

K Cf. lines 8, 29–30 of the present manuscript: *ḏd mdw s… …(sri 4) di šm=sn iw=sn m bḥn tp=sn m m3ʿ wšn=sn n wsir di m sbi n sḏt wn m3ʿ ipw is ḥtp ib*. Cf. Szczudlowska's translation of the slightly different P.Sekowski 20, 4–5: *ḏd mdw ḥr srw 4 rdit šm=sn m-b3ḥ sp 4 wšr=sn m-ḫt,* "Words to be recited upon four geese to cause that they go four times before (and) after they are put as sacrifice." [680]
Some orthographic peculiarities of this line should be noted:

1.  is understood here as an extension of the determinative of *srt,* rather than the definite article.
2. The and of the 3rd person plural suffix pronoun are reversed after *šm* and *iw*.
3. *imntyw* is consistently spelled with two *t*s in this column: .
4.  is a GR spelling of *s3ṯ.w,* "ground." [681] The  following this group is likely superfluous.

678 Möller, *Hieratische Paläographie* III, p. 19.
679 Leitz et al., eds., *Lexikon* V, p. 814.
680 Szczudlowska, *ZÄS* 98 (1970): 63 and 77.
681 *Wb.* III 423, 8–12.

3.2.13. *s3ḫw* III, SPELL 13 — SPOKEN BY THE LECTOR PRIEST

Lines 9, 2–11[682]

In this spell, Isis reminds Osiris of the role of Horus as his true heir and avenger. In this context, the cattle captured and sacrificed by Horus symbolize the destruction of Seth. Osiris is protected not only by his immediate heir, Horus, but also by various other gods, including the children of Horus and Khnum. The end of the spell again instructs its recitation to be made in conjunction with the slaughter and presentation of offerings.

TRANSLITERATION

2. *s3ḫ*
ḏd mdw in ḫry-ḥbt
rs=ṯn m ḥtp
nṯrw ipw b3w mnḫw ḏ3ḏ3t ḥ3 wsir
hy sp 2 msw ḥr nb-ʿnḫ-m-3ḫt rdit n rʿ m 3. *s3w wsir*
ss=sn b3w ḫftw=f
di=ṯn sḫm wsir ḫnty-imntyw wsir n P3-dit-k3-km ḫr nṯrw
šʿt=f m irty sbi
4. *hy wsir ḫnty-imntyw wsir n P3-dit-k3-km*
ip.n kw s3=k ḥr sḫm-m-ḏt=f
hy wsir ḫnty-imntyw wsir n P3-dit-k3-km
sḥʿ.n kw snt (9, 5)*=k 3st*
s3ḫ kw nbt-ḥwt
wsir i in 3st
mṯn s3=k ḥr ʿḥʿ m swt=k
rtḥ=f n=k sm3w stš
ḥw=f n=k k3
6. *k3s*(!)*=f n=k sm3*
spḥ=f ʿr
ṯs=f n=k smn(w)
hy wsir ḫnty-imntyw wsir n P3-dit-k3-km
nḏm s3=k ʿ3 ḥ3ty=k
7. *in n=k ḥr msw=f*
st ḥw=sn n=k ḫftw=k ipw
pḏ n=k sw ḫr=k
ḥw.n ḥr 3pdw rf m ḫbt
m s3.n tn inp
8. *hy wsir ḫnty-imntyw wsir n P3-dit-k3-km*
in.n n=k ḏḥwty ḫftiw=k pw
ḫnty=k ḥr=f
ʿ3 pḥty=k r=f m rn=f pfy n k3

682 See section 1.7.3, above.

9. *nḏ ḥr=k in iry-nwḥ wsir ḫnty-imntyw wsir n P3-dit-k3-km*
iry sbḥ n ḫftw=k ẖr=k
i.nḏ ḥr=k m ꜥnḫ (9, 10) *m ḥtp*
ẖnm m-ḫt=k

ḏd mdw
st ḳ3s k3 n ḫryt ꜥr 3pd
dr nmt
st wḏ di=sn r bik im
wn-m3ꜥ pw
is ḥtp 11. *ib ipw w3ḥ tp t3 n nsw ḏt*

TRANSLATION

2. Glorification spell.
Words spoken by the lector priest:
"May you awaken in peace!
These gods, beneficent *ba*s, and the council are around Osiris.
O! O! Re has placed the children of Horus, the Lord of Life in the Horizon, as the 3. protection of Osiris,
that they may burn the *ba*s of his enemies.[A]
May you cause that Osiris, Foremost of the Westerners, Osiris of Padikakem has power with the gods,
and that terror of him may be in the eyes of the rebels.[B]
4. O, Osiris, Foremost of the Westerners, Osiris of Padikakem.
Your son, Horus, Powerful in his Body, has recognized you.
O, Osiris, Foremost of the Westerners, Osiris of Padikakem.
Your sister, Isis, (9, 5) praised you,
as Nephthys glorified you." [C]
Osiris, utterance by Isis:
"Now, your son, Horus, is standing in your places.
He has caught for you the confederates of Seth.
He has smitten for you the bulls.
6. He has bound for you the wild bulls.
He lassoed the goat.
He tied for you the geese.[D]
O, Osiris, Foremost of the Westerners, Osiris of Padikakem.
May your son be happy and your heart proud!
7. Horus brings for you his children.
Now, they strike for you these enemies of yours,
stretching him(!) for you under you.
Horus strikes the birds, indeed, on the slaughtering block,
as Anubis protects you.[E]
8. O, Osiris, Foremost of the Westerners, Osiris of Padikakem.
Thoth brought to you these enemies of yours,

your slaughter being upon him(!),
your strength being greater than his in that his name of Bull.[F]
9. Hail to you by the two guardians, who clothe Osiris, Foremost of the Westerners, Osiris of Padikakem.
May the shouting of your enemies be made under you!
Hail to you in life, (9, 10) in peace!
Khnum is behind you." [G]

Words spoken:
"Now, bound are the offering bull, goat, and fowl,
which were presented to the slaughtering place.
Now, their transfer to the Falcon, therein, has been commanded.
It is the truth.
Now, that which satisfies 11. the heart is an offering upon land for the king, forever." [H]

TEXT NOTES

The protection and acceptance of Osiris by various gods is expressed by their position *ḥꜣ*, "around," the resurrected god. The preposition , *ḥꜣ*,[683] presents a possible word play on *ḥꜣ*, "to mourn."[684] In this case, the phrase *ḥꜣ wsir*, "around Osiris," also points to the well-attested epithet of Isis and Nephthys *ḥꜣt-wsir*, "Mourners of Osiris," and the GR *ḥꜣyty*, "Two Mourners."[685] In turn, Horus, the other principal guardian of Osiris, is identified by the weighty epithets *nb-ꜥnḫ-m-ꜣḫt*, "Lord of Life in the Horizon,"[686] and *sḫm-n-ḏt*, "Powerful of Body."[687]

The sacrificial animals symbolizing the enemies of Osiris include bulls, wild bulls, goat, geese, and other fowl that are caught, smitten, bound, and lassoed. For instance, the term *spḥ*, "to lasso," applied in this case to a goat, not only indicates triumph, but also implies an act of punishment in the capture of evil-doers.[688] This theme is further elaborated upon in PT 580 (§1544a–c): *ḥw.n(=i) n=k ḥw ṯw m iḥ smꜣ.n(=i) n=k smꜣ ṯw m smꜣ ngꜣ.n(=i) n=k ngꜣ ṯw m ngꜣ*, "I have struck for you as an ox the one who struck you, I have killed for you as a wild bull the one who killed you, I have broken down for you as a longhorned bull the one who broke you down."[689]

683 *Wb.* III 8, 12.
684 *Wb.* III 7, 1–5. For further discussion of word play, see section 1.5.1, above.
685 Wilson, *Ptolemaic Lexikon*, p. 611.
686 Leitz et al., eds., *Lexikon* III, p. 599.
687 The GR epithet *sḫm-n-ḏt* may also refer to both Osiris and Horus Behdety; see Leitz et al., eds., *Lexikon* VI, p. 549.
688 *Wb.* IV 105, 6; Zandee, *Death as an Enemy*, p. 233.
689 Allen, *The Ancient Egyptian Pyramid Texts*, p. 185.

9, 2–3

A *ḫry-ḥbt,* regularly spelled  in this column, is written with red ink in BM 29, 1.
Some orthographic peculiarities and discrepancies with the parallel texts should be noted:

1. *ḥtp,* , consistently lacks determinatives in BM 29.
2. *ḥ3* is written with a phonetic complement in BM 29, 3: .
3. Osiris is always spelled  in BM 29.
4. *ꜥnḫ* is written 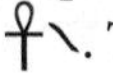. The first sign may also be understood as  (V28) standing for *ꜥnḫ.*[690]
5. *3ḫt* has a more extended spelling of  in BM 29, 4.
6. Re, 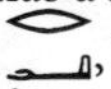, has no  determinative (G7) here. Cf.  in BM 29, 4.
7. The  is a phonetic complement for *s3,* , of line 9, 3.[691] Cf.  (V16) for *s3w* in BM 29, 5.

9, 3

B The construction *sḫm ḥr* should be understood in the sense of "to have power with (someone)."[692] The phonetic complement  of *sḫm,* , was added slightly above the line. Cf. the full phonetic spelling in BM 29, 6.
There are notable orthographic peculiarities and discrepancies with the parallels:

1. *nṯrw* is spelled  in BM 29, 7.
2. *šꜥt* has the (Y1) determinative in BM 29, 7: .[693]
3. *sbi* is written  in BM 29, 7.

9, 4–5

C Cf. the initial verb in BM 29, 8–9: *ink n=k tw s3=k ḥr sḫm m ḏt=f.*
These orthographic peculiarities and discrepancies with the parallel texts should be noted:

1. is unusually placed above the : , in the first occurrence of Padikakem in line 9, 4.
2. The  determinative (G7) of *sḫm,* , is paralleled in BM 29, 9.

---

690 Zivie-Coche, in P. der Manuelian, ed., *Studies in Honor of William Kelly Simpson*, pp. 869–70.

691 For the spelling of *s3w*, "to guard," with the pintail duck (G39), see *Wb.* III 416, 12–417, 21.

692 *Wb.* IV 248, 18.

693 *šꜥt*, "terror, fear," is a synonym of *nr* in the PT; see Wilson, *Ptolemaic Lexikon*, p. 526.

9, 5–6

D The below the determinative (Y1) of  was likely originally a  of *ḳ3s=f,* "he has bound," thus paralleling the *sḏm=f* construction of the preceding and subsequent verbs.[694] This rendering makes more sense in the context than , *ḳ3,* "to exalt, raise."

Cf. the *sḏm.n=f* form of *rtḥ* in BM 29, 11: *rtḥ.n=f n=k sm3w šwt stš*. BM 29, 14 includes birds, as well as goats, in the process of lassoing: *spḥ=f n=k 3pd ʿr.*[695]

Some discrepancies with the parallel texts should be noted:

1. Isis, following *snt=k,* is written  in BM 29, 10.
2. Isis, following *i in,* is written  in BM 29, 11.
3. *s3=k,* , lacks the  determinative (G7) in BM 29, 11.
4. *ʿhʿ* is written  in BM 29, 11.
5. *sm3w* is written  in BM 29, 12.
6.  stands for *k3* in BM 29, 13.
7. *sm3* is written  in BM 29, 13.

9, 6–7

E The singular dependent pronoun *sw* after *pḏ n=k* refers to Seth.

Some orthographic peculiarities and discrepancies with the parallel texts should be noted:

1. The  (M17) following *nḏm,* , is superfluous.
2. *ḥ3t* is written 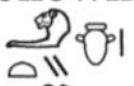 in BM 29, 15.
3. The particle *st,* , is written with  (U33).
4. *ẖr,* 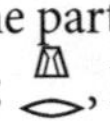, lacks the determinative (Y1) in BM 29, 17.
5. BM 29, 17 uses the  determinative (D40) in the spelling of *ḥw,* 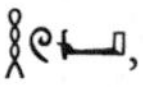, in place of the  determinative (A24) in P.W551.
6. The  (T30 and O26) determinative for *ẖbt* is typical to the GR period.[696]

9, 8

F The reading of  as *ḥnty,* "to slaughter,"[697] is uncertain. Although  frequently stands for the phonetic *ḥn,*[698] this first group may also be transcribed as  (W2), while the following group may be  (O11), 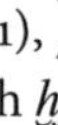 (U39), or 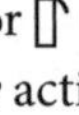 (V36).[699] The context suggests a noun or a verb in the relative form, with *ẖftw=k pw* acting as the direct semantic object.

694 For *ḳ3s*, "to bind," see *Wb.* V 13, 1–7.

695 For *ʿr*, "goat," see *Wb.* I 208, 10.

696 *Wb.* III 252, 9–14.

697 *Wb.* III 122, 11–14.

698 Daumas, *Valeurs phonétiques* III, p. 777.

699 Möller, *Hieratische Paläographie* III, 348, 405, and 590, respectively.

Cf. BM 29, 20: … *ḫftw=k pw ḫpš=k ḥr=f ꜥ3 pḥty=k r=f. pḥty* is written in BM 29, 20. The 3rd person singular masculine suffix pronoun of *ḥr,* "upon," refers to the collective of the enemies of Osiris. The preposition *r* and the 3rd person singular masculine suffix pronoun may also be understood as the enclitic particle *rf.*
Note the dot at the end of this line.

9, 9–10

G , *iry,* is a perfect passive/prospective participle. The group may also be understood as the epithets *iry-nwḥ,* "Those who Pertain to the Winding," or *s3w-nwḥ,* "Those who Guard the Winding."[700] Cf. the epithet *iryw-nw-ddw-sbḥw,* "Guardians of Those who Shout Out."[701]
These discrepancies with the parallel texts should be noted:

1. *iry* is spelled in BM 29, 21.
2. (F51) consistently indicates plurality of *ḫftw,* , in BM 29, 22.
3. *ꜥnḫ* is written in BM 29, 23.

9, 10–11

H The presentation of the bull, goat, and fowl is expressed with the passive *sḏmw=f* form of *wḏ,* "to command," preceded by the particle *isṯ*. This construction, *isṯ+sḏmw=f,* describes a situation or concomitant fact belonging to the past and is frequently impersonal.[702]
Cf. BM 29, 25–27: *k3 3pd dr st di wḏ di=sn r bik ipw w3ḥ ipw tp t3 nsw ḏt. bik,* "Falcon," is here an epithet of the deceased, but at other times may refer to various gods.[703] The phrase *tp t3,* "upon land," likely refers to the lifetime of the king, i.e., the time during which the king is on Earth, as opposed to the Netherworld.
Note the use of (W2) in place of the expected (W22) for , *dr,* "to present."[704]

---

700 For *nwḥ,* "to bind," see *Wb.* II 223, 14. Neither of the latter variants is found in Leitz et al., eds., *Lexikon.*

701 Leitz et al., eds., *Lexikon* I, p. 418.

702 Gardiner, *Egyptian Grammar,* §422.1.

703 Leitz et al., eds., *Lexikon* II, pp. 758–61.

704 For *dr,* "to present," with the determinative (W22), see *Wb.* V 476, 1–25.

3.2.14. *s3ḫw* III, SPELL 14 — SPOKEN BY THE LECTOR PRIEST

Lines 9, 11–19[705]

The beginning of this spell records the speech of Horus and continues the theme that equates sacrificial animals with Seth. The Two Kites, Isis and Nephthys, awaken Osiris by playing the *sr*-drum.[706] The second portion of the spell does not specify the speaker, but reiterates the significance of music and offerings that accompany the recitation of this spell in revivifying the deceased Osiris.

TRANSLITERATION

s3ḫ
ḏd mdw in ẖry-ḥbt
    nḏ ḥr=k it wsir i.n ḥr
    mk nṯr ii.k(wi) i n=k s3=k ḥr
    in(=i) n=k ḫftw=k
        12. *ipw rdit n=k psḏt ẖr=k*
    ḥw(=i) n=k sw
    ḥw.n(=i) iḥ m rn=f pw n iḥ
    smn r=f m rn=f n smn
    iḥ=k pw
        nis=k št ḥr s3=f nmi 13.*=k ḥr=f*
    ḥw n=k sw n itm m rn=f pw n iḥ
    ng3 n=k sw n itm m rn=f pw n ng3
    pḏt n=k sw itm m rn=f pw n pḏt
    14. *šsr n=k sw itm m ḏbʿw=f pfy*
        tšr.n=f
            ḥnmmt im=f
                m rn=f pfy šsr
    in(=i) n=k sw m sʿḥ
        mtn m ḫḫ=f ḳḳ=f
            (9, 15) *dp=f tp n ḫt=k nbt*
    n=k iwʿ=k
        (*i*) *n=i*
    ink iwʿ=k ḥr nst=k
    hy wsir ḫnty-imnt(yw) wsir n P3-dit-k3-km
        stp.n ḥr ḫpš n 16. *ḫftw=k*
        dr.n ḥr sn=f ḥ3=f

---

705 See section 1.7.3, above.

706 *Wb.* IV 191, 6–9; for *srw m sr*, "to play the drum," see *Wb.* IV 191, 11. See also Wilson, *Ptolemaic Lexikon*, pp. 881–82.

hy wsir ḫnty-imntyw wsir n P3-dit-k3-km
sḥr.n ḥr k3w=sn r=sn
nḏ ḥr=k
17. *ʿḥʿ.ṯ(w) m nṯr*
ḥn(t).ṯw ḫftw=k ḫr
ḏd mdw
st ḏrty srt m sr m srs.n nṯry nt nṯr im ḥr ḥʿʿ sp 18. *4*
ḫft tḫs k3 pwy n ḫryt ʿr=s
wp.n 3pd pḫr n ḫ3yt
ḥw stp šs3-ḫpš ib(w)=sn r bw nt imnt im
19. *di rs m bw mtr*

TRANSLATION

Glorification spell.
Words spoken by the lector priest:
"Hail to you, (my) father, Osiris," says Horus;
"Now, god, I have come," says to you your son, Horus.
"(I) have brought for you these enemies of yours,
12. whom the Ennead placed for you, under you.[A]
(I) beat him for you,
(I) beat the bull in this his name of Bull.
Be firm against him in his name of Goose!
He is your bull,
on whose back you have summoned (*sic*) the pool when you traveled 13. on it.[B]
Atum beat him for you in this his name of Bull.
Atum killed him for you in this his name of Longhorn Cattle.
Atum stretched him for you in this his name of Stretched One.[C]
14. Atum killed him for you with those fingers of his,
and he has slaughtered,
the sun-folk being with him
in his name of Sacrificial Bull.[D]
(I) brought him to you as a *sʿḥ*,
whose throat is marked so that he may be eaten,
(9, 15) his taste being the best of all your things.[E]
To you belongs your inheritance,
so I (say),
I am your heir upon your throne.[F]
O, Osiris, Foremost of the West(erners), Osiris of Padikakem.
Horus has cut off the strong arm of 16. your enemies.
Horus has repelled his double from him.
O, Osiris, Foremost of the Westerners, Osiris of Padikakem.
Horus removed their *kas* from them.

Hail to you!
17. May you stand as a god,
as you destroy your fallen enemies." G
Words spoken:
"Now, the Two Kites, who play the *sr*-drum, and cause to awaken the holy place of the god therein, are rejoicing," Four times.
18. "before slaughtering this offering bull, its goat,
and dividing the fowl and the offerings on the offering table,
so that the chosen one, Skilled of Arm, may strike their heart(s) at the place of the West therein,
19. causing awakening at the right place." H

TEXT NOTES

Much of this spell is devoted to the defeat of the enemies, as epitomized by the slaughter of sacrificial animals. This is followed by a short but important reference to drumming as a symbolic means of assisting Osirian rebirth in religious and mortuary rituals.

Continuing the theme from previous spells, Horus details the capture and sacrifice of various animals by himself and Atum. Line 9, 13 specifies the actions of Atum, presenting a deliberate play on the sounds of each pair: *ḥw,* "to strike," and *iḥ,* "bull;" *ngꜣ,* "to kill, cut up,"[707] and the more familiar *ngꜣ,* "longhorn cattle;" *pḏt,* "to stretch," and *pḏt,* "Stretched One."[708] The latter *pḏt* is clearly used as an epithet of cattle; "Stretched One"[709] fitting with the notion of executing the enemies of Osiris. Faulkner translates this term in PT 580 (§1545a) as "stretched bull,"[710] interpreting it as a reference to the stretching of the legs of the bull before slaughtering.[711]

In the second portion of the spell, Isis and Nephthys help to revivify Osiris by playing the *sr*-drum, frequently depicted in funerary scenes. The epithet of the two goddesses — *ḏrty,* "Two Kites"[712] — possibly intends a pun on the common expression *ḏr sr,* "to strike a drum."[713] Notably, due to the lack of metal pieces that jingle on the known Egyptian drums, the term *sr* should perhaps be translated specifically as "frame drum."[714] The association of *sr*-drums with lamenting women and the *Stundenwachen* ritual, evident on LP coffins, papyri, as well as in Dendera and Edfu,[715] suggests that loud sounds must have been deemed

707 *Wb.* II 348, 16–19; Wilson, *Ptolemaic Lexikon*, p. 553.

708 For further discussion of word play, see section 1.5.1, above.

709 Leitz et al., eds., *Lexikon* III, p. 184; *Wb.* I 569, 6. Assmann, *Totenliturgien* I, p. 459, translates this epithet as "Ausgespannter."

710 Faulkner, *Ancient Egyptian Pyramid Texts*, p. 235.

711 Faulkner, *Ancient Egyptian Coffin Texts* III, pp. 15–16, n. 7.

712 Leitz et al., eds., *Lexikon* VII, p. 632.

713 *Wb.* V 595, 2. For further discussion of word play, see section 1.5.1, above.

714 von Lieven, in K. Ryholt, ed., *Carlsberg Papyri* 7, p. 22.

715 See the forthcoming publication of Andrea Kucharek, *Die Klagelieder von Isis und Nephthys*, p. 11, nn. 57–59, and p. 12. von Lieven, in K. Ryholt, ed., *Carlsberg Papyri* 7, pp. 23–29.

beneficial to awakening the deceased, while the rhythms of such drums offered protection from the enemies of Osiris.[716]

9, 11–12

A This text is paralleled by P.Malcolm (=P.BM 10081) (BM), col. 30, 1–29, published by Assmann.[717] This text also occurs in CT 839, VII 42–43f.[718]
The possibility of translating the clause *ỉn n=k ẖftw=k* with *ỉn* in a participial form should also be considered: "(Horus) who brought for you your enemies." Cf. the very similar BM 30, 33: *mk wy ỉỉ.kwỉ ỉn(=ỉ) n=k sꜣ=k ḥr ỉn(=ỉ) n=k ẖftw=k ỉpw.*[719] See also CT VII 42l–o: *[m]k (wỉ) ỉỉ.k(wỉ) ỉt=ỉ wsỉr ỉnk sꜣ=k ỉnk ḥr ỉỉ.n[=ỉ ỉn=ỉ n=k ẖftw]=k pw,* "[Lo]ok, [I] have come, O my father Osiris, for I am your son, I am Horus. [I] have come [that I may bring to you] this [foe] of yours." The 3rd person dependent pronoun allows *rdỉ* to be read as a *sḏm=f* form in CT VII 42p: *rdỉ … =k sw ps[ḏt] ẖr=k.*
Some orthographic peculiarities and discrepancies with the parallel texts should be noted:

1. The expected 1st person singular ending of the stative *ỉỉ* is abbreviated to *k*. Note the  determinative (G7) following *ỉỉ*.
2. The group  may also be understood as the 1st person independent pronoun *ỉnk*.[720]
3. The  determinative (G7) is placed after the group *sꜣ=k ḥr* in BM 30, 2.

9, 12–13

B The 3rd person dependent pronoun *sw* refers to the enemy of Osiris.
Cf. BM 30, 5–6: *ḥw(=ỉ) n=k sw (m) ỉḥ m rn=f pw n ỉḥ.* This clause is not in CT 839.
The reading of 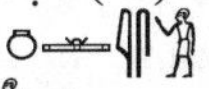 as *nis* does not make sense here. *nmtỉ,* , of BM 30, 8 has the same  determinative (A26) as *nis* in P.W551, which may explain the scribe's confusion. Cf. the more logical BM 30, 7–8: *smn r=f m rn=f pw n smn ỉḥ=k pw nmỉ=k št ḥr sꜣ=f nmtỉ=k ḥr=f,* "Be firm against him in this his name of Goose! He is your bull, on whose back you have traversed the lake."
Some orthographic peculiarities and discrepancies with the parallel texts should be noted:

---

716 von Lieven, in K. Ryholt, ed., *Carlsberg Papyri* 7, pp. 29–38; Darnell, *SAK* 22 (1995): 57, n. 58; Manassa, in B. Rothöhler and A. Manisali, eds., *Mythos & Ritual*, pp. 119–20 and nn. 45–46, points out that loud sounds were prohibited from certain Osirian sanctuaries on some occasions.

717 The translation of the subsequent texts of BM is based on Assmann, *Totenliturgien* I, pp. 463–65.

718 The translation of the subsequent CT spells is based on Faulkner, *Ancient Egyptian Coffin Texts* III, p. 27. Cf. Assmann, *Totenliturgien* I, pp. 459–60.

719 Cf. the translation by Assmann, *Totenliturgien* I, p. 463: "Siehe, ich bin gekommen!, sagt dir dein Sohn Horus. Ich bringe dir diese deine Feinde."

720 *Wb.* I 101, 13.

1. *ḫr* is written  in BM 30, 5.
2. (P11), *mni,* acts as a phonetic complement for *smn,* .
3. The  determinative (G38) points to the reading of 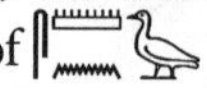 as *smn,* "goose." [721]

9, 13

C The 3rd person singular masculine suffix pronouns of *rn* refer back to the enemy. Cf. the demonstrative pronouns in BM, 30, 8–12: *ḥw n=k sw itm m rn=f pw n iḥ ngꜣ n=k sw itm m rn=f pfy n ngꜣ pr n=k sw itm m rn=f pw n pḏ*. This line also corresponds to CT VII 42s–43a, which addresses Osiris in the 2nd person: [...] ⸢*ngꜣ n=k sw itm m rn=f pw*⸣ *n ngꜣ* ⸢*pḏ n*⸣*=k* ⸢*sw itm*⸣ *m rn=k pw n* ⸢*pḏw*⸣.
Some orthographic peculiarities and discrepancies with the parallel texts should be noted:

1. The s following *hw n=k sw* and *ngꜣ n=k sw* are superfluous.
2. Note the determinative (Y1) for *pw,* 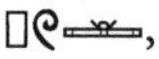, preceding *n iḥ*.
3. *pḏt* is written 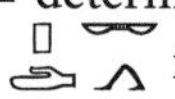 in BM 30, 10.

9, 14

D Cf. the stick as Atum's weapon in BM 30, 12–13: *šsr n=k sw itm m mdw=f.* This clause is replaced in CT VII 43b with: *di.n n=k sw itm m* ⸢*ḏw*⸣. *šsr* is understood as "to kill, slay," [722] but the term may also be used in the sense of "to lash" [723] as part of the process of subduing and slaughtering of the similar sounding *sšr,* "sacrificial bull." [724] Cf. BM 30, 13–14 and CT VII 43c: *šsr=f ḥnmmt im=f m rn=f pw n šsr*. Faulkner translates *šsr* in the passive sense, "he will be bound, the sun-folk being with him...," while Assmann points out the uncertainty of this reading.[725] *ḥnmmt* may be defined as "deities or heavenly spirits particularly connected with the idea of renaissance or resurrection." [726]
Some orthographic peculiarities and discrepancies with the parallel texts should be noted:

1. The verb *šsr* is spelled phonetically in CT VII 43c: .
2. The determinative (T11) of 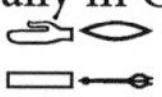 points to a confusion between *dšr,* "red, to be red," and *šsr,* "to slaughter."
3. *ḥnmmt* lacks phonetic complements in CT VII 43c: .[727]

---

721 *Wb.* IV 136, 2–4.

722 Wilson, *Ptolemaic Lexikon*, p. 1033; *Wb.* IV 547, 5–7.

723 Faulkner, *Ancient Egyptian Coffin Texts* III, pp. 15–16, n. 7; see also PT 580 (§§1544–45).

724 Wilson, *Ptolemaic Lexikon*, p. 1032; *Wb.* IV 547, 8–9.

725 Faulkner, *Ancient Egyptian Coffin Texts* III, p. 27, and Assmann, *Totenliturgien* I, p. 459, respectively.

726 Serrano, *SAK* 27 (1999): 368.

727 Faulkner, *Ancient Egyptian Coffin Texts* III, pp. 27–28, n. 12.

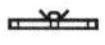

4. Note the  determinative (G7) for *rn=f.*
5. The epithet *sšr* lacks phonetic complements in CT VII 43c: .

9, 14–15

E This sentence is somewhat cryptic. The context suggests that the 3rd person singular dependent pronoun *sw* as well as the following clause refer to the enemy (Seth), who generally does not wear a seal on his neck. Nevertheless, the meaning is clarified by the use of *sꜥḥ* in reference to the neck of a bull in a festival of Min.[728] Beside the obvious mortuary connotations of the similarly written *sꜥḥ,* "mummy," the verb *sꜥḥ,* "to reward, present" may create an intentional pun here.[729] Thus, another reading could be: "(I) brought him to you as a reward." Notably, Assmann appears to understand *sw* as a reference to Atum in BM 30, 14–15: *ỉn(=ỉ) n=k sw m sꜥḥ mtnw=f m ḫḫ=f,* "Ich bringe ihn dir als *sꜥḥ* mit einem Siegel um seinen Hals."[730]
The phrase *mtn m ḫḫ=f* likely means "whose throat is slashed." The basic definition of *mtn* is "to mark, inscribe,"[731] but the GR *mtn,* "knife," invokes the idea of cutting and thereby marking the throat of the sacrificial bull.[732] Cf. Faulkner's rendering of CT VII 43d–e: *ỉn.n(=ỉ) n=k sw m ỉḥ mtw m ḫḫ=f,* "I bring him to you as a bull with a duct(?) in his neck," who suggests that *mt,* "vessel, duct" refers to the windpipe, which is to be strangled.[733]
Yet another notable term in this line is *ḳḳ,* "to eat," which is a later variant of *wnm.*[734] Wilson points to the likely confusion between the old writing of *wnm* with two  (X7) and  (N29) of *ḳḳ* in GR times.[735] Cf. the determinative for this term in CT VII 43e: .
Two discrepancies with the parallel texts should be noted:

1. *dp* is spelled with phonetic complements in BM 30, 16: 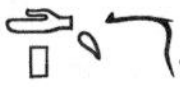.[736]
2. *ḫt,* 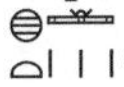, is replaced with *išt,* 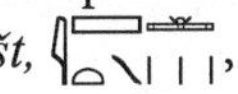, in BM 30, 16.

9, 15

F Note the alliterative play on sounds in the words *dp* and *tp* in the beginning of this clause.[737]

728 *Wb.* IV 50, 6.
729 *Wb.* II 50, 8–15. For further discussion of word play, see section 1.5.1, above.
730 Assmann, *Totenliturgien* I, p. 646.
731 *Wb.* II 170, 11–12.
732 Wilson, *Ptolemaic Lexikon*, p. 476; *Wb.* II 171, 7.
733 Faulkner, *Ancient Egyptian Coffin Texts* III, pp. 27–28, n. 13.
734 *Wb.* V 71, 10.
735 Wilson, *Ptolemaic Lexikon*, p. 1069.
736 Werning, in *LingAeg* (2004): 183–204.
737 For this spelling of *dp*, "taste," see *Wb.* V 444, 16–445, 9. For further discussion of word play, see section 1.5.1, above.

Cf. the 3rd person singular suffix pronoun of "inheritance" in BM 30, 17–18: *n=k ỉwʿ=f ỉn=ỉ ink ỉwʿ(!)=k ḥr nst=k.*[738] The  determinative (A1) of the second *ỉwʿ*, , in CT VII 43f supports its reading as a noun: *ỉwʿ=f(!) n=ỉ ink ỉwʿ=k ḥr nst=k,* "His(!) inheritance belongs to me, I am your heir upon your throne." Alternatively, the term in CT may be understood as a participle: *ink ỉʿr=k ḥr nst=k,* "I am the one whom you raised upon your throne."

Two discrepancies with the parallel texts should be noted:

1. *ink* has a more typical spelling  in CT VII 43f, while BM 30, 17 parallels P.W551.
2. *nst* is spelled 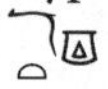 in CT VII 43f and 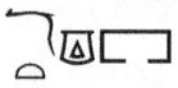 in BM 30, 18.

9, 15–17

G The first statement also occurs in PT 372 (§653a): *stp.n ḥr ḫpšw ḫftw=k,* but PT §653b does not correspond: *in.n n=k sn ḥr šʿw,* "(Horus) brought them to you cut up."[739] Cf. the suffix pronouns in PT §653c: *sḥr.n ḥr kꜣ=sn ir=sn.*

Some orthographic peculiarities and discrepancies with the parallel texts should be noted:

1. The first *imnt* is written  (R13) here.
2. The and of the 3rd person plural suffix pronoun of *kꜣw* are reversed here.
3. *nḏ,* , lacks phonetic complements in BM 30, 22.
4.  is written for *ṯw* following *ʿḥʿ* and *ḥn(t)*[740] in BM 30, 22.
5. The plurality of *ḫftw* is indicated by repetition in BM 30, 22–23: 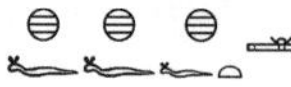.

9, 17–19

H *nṯry* is here taken to mean "holy place," although this term may also be understood as "divinity, holiness," or as a description of the deceased.[741]

, *sšꜣ ḫpš,* is reminiscent of the epithet of a protective deity *šsꜣ-ʿ,* "Skilled of Arm."[742]

The reading of 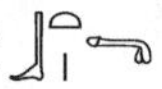 as *bw mtr* is questionable.  (D52), without phonetic complements, may also be read as *ʿꜣ,* "donkey, (as an epithet of) Seth," or *mt,* "man." The possibility of reading *mt,* "death," should be considered, although the *Wb.* has no examples of this word spelled with .

738 Cf. the translation of Assmann, *Totenliturgien* I, p. 464: "'Dir gehört sein Erbe/Fleischstück' sage ich, ich bin dein Erbe auf deinem Thron".

739 Cf. the translation of Allen, *The Ancient Egyptian Pyramid Texts*, p. 83: "Horus has selected your opponents' forelegs and Horus has fetched them to you cut up."

740 For *ḥnt,* "to destroy, kill," see Wilson, *Ptolemaic Lexikon*, p. 659; *Wb.* III 122, (12–13).

741 *Wb.* II 364, 26; *Wb.* II 363, 1–364, 18; and *Wb.* II 364, 8 and 15, respectively.

742 Leitz et al., eds., *Lexikon* VII, p. 112.

Some orthographic peculiarities and discrepancies with the parallel texts should be noted:

1. The sign above  is understood as  (M36) of *ḏrty*, 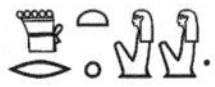.
2. *srt* is written  in BM 30, 24.
3. *nṯry* is spelled  here.[743]
4. *ỉm* lacks determinatives in BM 30, 25: .
5. *ḥ*ˁˁ is spelled  in BM 30, 25.
6. *tḫs* is spelled  in BM 30, 26.[744]
7. *k3* is spelled  in BM 30, 26. Cf. the demonstrative *pn* in BM 30, 26.

3.2.15. *s3ḫw* III, SPELL 15 — SPOKEN BY THE LECTOR PRIEST

Lines 9, 19–44[745]

The beginning of this spell implies the finality of Osiris' situation by pointing out that "there is no going forth from Pe / Abydos." This spell is intended to be recited before a number of potent protective female deities (or images thereof), who are likely the possessors of the series of enigmatic feminine epithets in the beginning of the spell. Further gods, known as the Sharp-Eyed ones, are called upon to avenge Osiris.[746] Osiris is also protected by Re and other gods of the hourly guard, who are responsible for repelling his enemies and preventing them from attacking again. Interestingly, both strength (*ỉm ˁ=sn,* "what is in their arms") and utterances (*ỉm r=sn,* "what is in their mouth") are employed by these gods. A direct address to Seth follows, demanding his retreat, while calling attention to the numerous guardians of Osiris. The end of the spell finally addresses Osiris himself, describing his victory and the support of his powerful family. His funerary equipment is then safeguarded, as Mut secures the support of the mummy bandages, while the limbs of the deceased are strengthened by the offerings. In the last two lines of the spell, the deceased himself makes a statement of his newly acquired, effective state.

TRANSLITERATION

s3ḫ
ḏd mdw in ḫry-ḥbt
  nhm m pt
  sdd m t3
    hrw smsw pw smsw-pr-nfr
  wḥˁ=tn (9, 20) *ˁḥˁ=ṯn pwy n nw*
    m hrw wḥˁ ṯssw m 3bḏw

743 For this sign, see Daumas, *Valeurs phonétiques* III, p. 508.

744 For *tḫs*, "slaughter, killing," see *Wb.* V 328, 4–7.

745 See section 1.7.3, above.

746 For this GR epithet, see Leitz et al., eds., *Lexikon* III, p. 470.

hy nṯr-stt ṯs wty
nn pr m p
wꜥty
ỉwtt-21.-*snwt=s*
ḥḏt-ꜥfn twi-nn
nn pr m ꜣbḏw
ꜣw-šwty nẖꜣẖꜣ-mnḏwy
ỉn rk ḥr n ỉt=f wsir
ẖrw pfy n smꜣꜥ ẖrw=f
rdit.n 22. *rꜥ n sꜣw(!)=f pwy nty m ꜣbḏw*
rdit.n=f ḏdw ỉw
ṯs n=f tp=f ỉw
smn n=f nḥbt
ỉw nḥm 23.=*f m-ꜥ ẖftw=f*
ꜣd r=f m-ẖnw kkw
hy hy nṯrw iptnw mds-irty
ỉmy šwt wsir
nḏḥḏḥ 24. *ḳd-kꜣ n-rdi-n=f-nbi=f ẖnty-hh dšr-irty*
ẖnt-ḥwt-ins pr-m-ẖt mꜣ-m-ḥr=f
(9, 25) *ỉi.n=f m rꜥ*
rdit tn rꜥ m sꜣ wsir
msḏ mꜣꜣ irt.n sw stš
wṯs=ṯn nṯr(w) ỉmy(w)-wnwt=sn
sꜣw=ṯn ỉmy(w)-26.-*wšꜣw*
ḥw=ṯn n=f swt n smꜣw=f
ỉm ẖpr ḥꜥḏꜣ m snw sp
ḥꜣ.n sby pfy ḏw m ꜥḳ r ꜥt 27. *ḏsr nt wsir im=s*
ỉw ꜣḫw 8 *iptw ỉḳrw m sꜣ nṯr pwy špsy*
nḏ ḥr ẖftw n=sn
ntrw m 28. *s…*
bḥn=sn kw im ꜥ=sn
sẖr=sn kw im r=sn
ḥꜣ=k sbiw ẖsi
29. … *m ỉi* … *ḥꜣt twy nt wsir*
nṯr im=s
ỉw … *r kw*
d=f bin=k pfy
ḥr ḏd n=k
mꜣ.n=k (9, 30) … … … … *iw* … *pfy* … *sꜣw=f*
ḥr … *m ẖbt twy ḏw* … … … *nṯrw*
31. *tw* … … *nṯr-ꜥꜣ iry r=k ḥꜣ=k*
stš pwy … *nwt m ỉi r ḥꜥ twy nt wsir im=sy*
32. *kꜣ it=f ḏḥwty*
irw=f pw mꜣꜥ n isds

snty pr=sn r=k
    pr ẖt r=k m pt
33. *dšr r=k m tꜣ*
    dr.n s(t) sꜣ=k m pt ḫr rꜥ
sswnw=sn kꜣ=k m tꜣ ḫr gb
    ḥw=sn sḏb=k is
        34. *ḫr kꜣw ḥry-tp-ꜥnḫw*
            m wḏt n rꜥ nṯr-ꜥꜣ
iry rk ḥꜣ=k
sbiw ẖsi-ḳd dšrt m ꜥḳ (9, 35) *wꜥbt nty wsir im=s*
šnm ḫnty-nṯry ꜥḥꜥ m ḫsf=k ḥnꜥ snt wr(t)-fꜣw
    nt siꜣkb ḥr sn=s 36. *wsir*
dr n=s sꜣ=k ḥtmyw kꜣ=k
nn pr=k m ẖbt=k twy
    ḏw ẖr sꜣw gb ḏt
        m wḏt.n 37. *ḏꜣḏꜣt-ꜥꜣt-m-ẖrt-nṯr*
iry r=k is šd mḏꜣt tn
    ẖft wn nḫbt wꜣḏyt ḥnꜥ snt wrt-38.-fꜣw
        m wnwt=sn m s(ꜣ) nṯr pn is irp nmst 2-t m ḏrt n wꜥ nb im=sn
            imn pr-r=f ẖt sšt
            39. *wsir pw*
            ꜣst ẖr tp=f
            nbt-ḥwt ḥr rdwy=f
(9, 40) *im wrt ꜥš sp 2*
    mwt dr ṯꜣm m-ꜥ iry r=i
41. *ḫꜣwt wrt ii=n*
    nn nni
    nn gꜣḥ ꜥtw=k iptn
42. *grḥ*
    nwt ṯs wy
    ink sꜣ pfy dr wrḏtyw m-ꜥ iry r=i
    43. *pd-ẖr-rdwy=f pẖr ḥꜣ=i*
    ḫꜣḫ snw
    nn ḥm wrḏ 44. *ꜥwt=i iptn*

TRANSLATION

Glorification spell,
words spoken by the lector priest:
    "Roaring is in the sky,
    quaking is on the land.
        It is the voice of the Elder, the Elder of the *pr-nfr*.[A]
    May you release (9, 20) your position at the (right) time,
        on the day of loosening the knot in Abydos.

O, Divinely Fragranced One who ties the bandages,
  there is no going forth from Pe.[B]
The Sole One,
the One Without 21. her Second,
that one White of Head-Cloth,
  there is no going forth from Abydos.
One Tall of Plumes, Full of Breasts,
the one whom Horus has, indeed, brought to his father, Osiris,
  (on) this day of making his voice justified.[C]
Re has given 22. this sons(!) of his, who is in Abydos.
He has given the vertebra,
  so that his head may be tied for him,
  that his neck may be made firm for him,
    which he seized 23. from his enemies,
      who have raged against him in the darkness.[D]
O! O! Gods who are reckoned as the Sharp-Eyed,
Those who are in the Suite of Osiris:
  Nedjehdjeh, 24. He who Fashioned the Bull, He whose Flame was not Placed, He who is before the Fire, Red-Eyed One, Foremost of the Mansion of the Red Linen, He who Comes out After, He who Sees with his Face! [E]
(9, 25) He has come as Re.
Re has placed you as the protector of Osiris,
  who hates seeing that which Seth did.
May you rise, god(s), Those who are in Their Hours!
May you protect Those who are in 26. the Darkness,
  as you strike for him Seth and his companions.
Do not let wrongdoing occur the second time
  from that evil rebel entering into the sacred 27. chamber of Osiris, who is in it.[F]
These eight excellent spirits are protecting this noble god.
The enemy(?) hails to them,
  as the gods are 28. … …
They restrain with their arm(s),
they overthrow you with what is in their mouth.
Retreat, wretched wrongdoer! [G]
29. … … come … this tomb of Osiris,
  the god therein it.
… … you.
He placed that Evil One of yours,
  saying to you:
    'You have seen (9, 30) … … … that … … his son,
    Horus … in this evil place of slaughter … … … gods.[H]
    31. … … … Great God who acted against you, retreat!
    This Seth, … Nut is coming to this palace of Osiris, who is in it.' [I]

32. His father and Thoth will say:
'This image of his is the true one of *Isdes*'.
The two sisters, they went to you,
as the fire came forth to you in the sky.[J]
33. The Red Ones were against you on earth,
but your son has driven (th)em away from the sky in the presence of Re.
Your *ka* has destroyed them on earth in the presence of Geb,
for they have repelled your obstacle, indeed,
34. in the presence of the *ka*s of the Chief of the Living,
according to the command of Re, the Great God.
The one who acted against you, retreat! [K]
O, the Rebel, the One Wretched of Character, the Red One, is the one who entered (9, 35) the *wꜥbt* of Osiris, who is in it.
Khnum, the Foremost of the Holy Palace, is standing before you with the sister, Great of Splendor,
who causes to be mourned her brother, 36. Osiris.[L]
Your son repels for her the destroyers of your *ka*.
There is no going forth from this slaughtering place of yours,
the evil being under the protection of Geb, forever,
according to the command of 37. the Great Court in the Necropolis.[M]
Make for yourself, indeed, the reading of this document,
in the presence of Nekhbet and Wadjet, with the sister, Great of 38. Splendor,
at the time (when) they are behind this god with two jugs of wine in the hand of each one of them:
'The Hidden One, He who Came Forth for Himself is behind the window.[N]
39. It is Osiris.
Isis is at his head,
Nephthys is at his feet.' [O]
(9, 40) Those who are on the West Side of Thebes, call twice:
'Mut, prevent the bandages from acting against me!' [P]
41. Offering table, we say:
'There exists no weakness,
there exists no weariness in these limbs of yours!'" [Q]
42. Pause.
"Nut is the one who raised me.
I am that son who prevents the weary from acting against me.[R]
43. The One who Spreads out Under his Two Feet, who encircles my head.
The sisters hurry,
there is indeed, no weariness 44. (in) these limbs of mine.'" [S]

TEXT NOTES

One of the groups in charge of protecting Osiris in this spell are the *mds-irty,* "Sharp-Eyed,"[747] gods. Their name probably derives from the *mds*-guardians of the gates in the Underworld. These eight guardian deities who follow Osiris are also described by the well-attested epithet *imyw-šwt/ḫt-wsir,* "Those in the Suite of Osiris."[748] Their specific epithets are listed in lines 9, 23–24. After the first relatively short epithet *nḏḥḏḥ,*[749] all consequent epithets of the Sharp-Eyed deities are based on considerably longer appellations primarily known from the BD. The first three deities appear in the *Stundenwachen* ritual as protectors of Osiris during hours 9–11 of the day.[750] Their titles, *ḳd-k3, nn-rdi-n=f-nbi=f,* and *ḫnty-hh=f,*[751] appear to originate from *k3-n-rdi-n=f-nbi=f-ḫnty-hwt=f,* "Bull to whom the Fire is not Given before his Flame."[752] This long epithet, attested in the CT and BD, was separated into three distinct ones and slightly altered by the later scribes. *ḳd-k3,* "He who Fashioned the Bull," became popular in the GR period as an epithet of a protective deity.[753] , *ḳd,* may in fact be a corruption of *3ḳdḳd,* which is typically part of the seven following epithets.[754]

Similarly, the epithet *dšr-irty-imy/ḫnty-ḥwt-ins,* "Red-Eyed One in the/Foremost of the Mansion of the Red Linen,"[755] primarily attested in the earlier BD, was divided into two epithets in P.W551: *dšr-irty,* "Red-Eyed One," and *ḫnty-ḥwt-ins,* "Foremost of the Mansion of the Red Linen."[756] In the context of the protective role of the deities, *ins,* "red linen," was attributed with the power of restoring the faculty of sight.[757] The epithet *pr-m-ḫt-m33-m-ḥr=f,* "He who Comes out After and Sees with his Face,"[758] was also separated into two: *pr-m-ḫt* and *m33-m-ḥr=f.*[759] The  determinative (G7) between each of the above eight epithets supports a distinct reading of each.

9, 19

A Although the transitive use of *sdd,* "to shake, tremble," with *m* becomes popular in the GR period,[760] a parallel phrase occurs in the NK papyrus BM 9997 3, 12: *nh3m m*

747 Wilson, *Ptolemaic Lexikon*, pp. 480–81.
748 Leitz et al., eds., *Lexikon* I, p. 276.
749 For *nḏḥḏḥ,* see Leitz et al., eds., *Lexikon* IV, pp. 604–5.
750 Junker, *Stundenwachen*, pp. 4–5 and 62–64.
751 See Leitz et al., eds., *Lexikon* VII, pp. 230–31; *ibid.*, III, pp. 495–96; and *ibid.*, V, p. 827, respectively.
752 Leitz et al., eds., *Lexikon* VII, p. 261.
753 Leitz et al., eds., *Lexikon* VII, pp. 230–31; *Wb.* V 80, 15.
754 Leitz et al., eds., *Lexikon* I, p. 82.
755 Leitz et al., eds., *Lexikon* VII, p. 571.
756 Leitz et al., eds., *Lexikon* VII, p. 571; *ibid.*, V, p. 829.
757 Smith, *Liturgy of Opening the Mouth for Breathing*, p. 16; Smith, *Mortuary Texts of Papyrus BM 10507*, pp. 92–94.
758 Leitz et al., eds., *Lexikon* III, p. 78.
759 Leitz et al., eds., *Lexikon* III, pp. 78 and 202.
760 *Wb.* IV 367, 9.

pt sdd m t3, "Roaring in heaven. Quaking on earth."[761]  (F33) provides a phonetic complement for *sdd,* , here. Cf. the more extended spelling of *sdd* in BM 31, 2: .

smsw, "Elder," is a widely attested epithet of Horus, among other deities.[762] *pr-nfr* is the term for the "place of mummification."[763]

9, 20

B The ⊗ determinative (O49) supports the reading of  as *3bḏw,* "Abydos," rather than *i3btt,* "east."[764]

Cf. a similar phrase in PT 358 (§593): *NN wtwt šw wḥꜥ ṯswt=k in nbwi nw,* "NN, Shu's first born, your ties have been loosened by the Two Lords of Nu."[765]

The reading of  as *stt* is questionable. The  determinative (Aa2) frequently occurs with *st/ḥs* words. It may be understood as the epithet *st,* "Shooting One," or as *st,* "Blazing One (the name of the guard of the 10th gate in the Book of Gates)."[766] Otherwise, the group may be read as *ḥsty,* "Favored One."[767]

9, 20–21

C These statements contain a number of feminine epithets. *wꜥty,* "Sole One," refers to either Isis or Nut.[768] The series of feminine epithets continues with the epithet of Isis, among other goddesses, *iwtt-snwt=s,* "One Without her Second/Equal."[769] *ḥḏt-ꜥfn,* "White of Head-Cloth," occurs in the PT as an epithet attributed to various goddesses.[770] *3wt-šwty,* "Long of Plumes," belongs to Nekhbet,[771] while *nḫ3ḫ3t-mnḏwi,* "Full-Breasted One," is attested for Nut, Nekhbet, and others.[772]

A number of PT examples clarify this series of epithets, suggesting that they may all be addressing Nut. Cf. PT 412 (§729a–b): *mwt=k sm3t wrt ḥrt-ib nḫb ḥḏt ꜥfnt 3wt šwti*

761 For P.BM 9997, see Leitz, *Magical and Medical Papyri*, p. 9 and plate 3.

762 Leitz et al., eds., *Lexikon* VI, pp. 347–49.

763 *Wb.* I 517, 11. For a discussion of the term *pr-nfr*, interpreting *nfr* as the space associated with "creation, rejuvenation, or end and beginning," see Frandsen, in J. Osing and E. Nielsen, eds., *The Heritage of Ancient Egypt*, pp. 49–62.

764 For this spelling of Abydos, see *Wb.* I 9, 1.

765 Allen, *The Ancient Egyptian Pyramid Texts*, p. 74. For the group *wḥꜥ ṯst*, "to remove a knot," see *Wb.* I 348, 8.

766 Leitz et al., eds., *Lexikon* VI, p. 679, and *ibid.*, VI, p. 684, respectively.

767 Leitz et al., eds., *Lexikon* V, pp. 474–75.

768 Leitz et al., eds., *Lexikon* II, p. 286.

769 Leitz et al., eds., *Lexikon* I, p. 169.

770 Leitz et al., eds., *Lexikon* V, p. 604.

771 Leitz et al., eds., *Lexikon* I, p. 6.

772 Leitz et al., eds., *Lexikon* IV, p. 297. For *mnḏ*, "breast," see *Wb.* II 92, 11–93, 8. For *nḫ3ḫ3*, "to be full (of breasts)," see *Wb.* II 306, 10.

nẖ3ẖ3t mnḏwt, "Your mother is the great wild cow in the midst of Nekheb, with white head-cloth, wide plumage, and dangling breasts."[773] Cf. also PT 582 (§1566a–b): *in mwt nt NN sm3t wrt 3w šwti sšpt ˁfnt ng3g3t mnḏwt,* "It is the mother of NN, the great wild cow with long plumage, dazzling head-cloth, and dangling breasts;" PT 675 (§2003a–b): *mwt=k sm3t wrt ḥrt-ib nḫb ḥḏt ˁfnt 3wt šn nẖ3t* [*mnḏwi*], "Your mother is the great wild cow in the midst of Nekheb, with white head-cloth, long hair, and dangling [breasts];" and PT 703 (§2204a–b): *mwt=k tw ḥwrt wrt ḥḏt ˁfnt ḥrt-ib nḫb wb3t šwt nẖ3ẖ3t mnḏwi,* "Your mother is the great Impoverishing Uraeus, with white head-cloth in the midst of Nekheb, open plumage, and dangling breasts."[774] This string of epithets also occurs in the CT, such as CT 517, VI 106h.

The expression *twi-nn,* "that there," is typical of the NK and GR period.[775]

There are two orthographic peculiarities and discrepancies with the parallel texts:

1. *mnḏwt* is spelled with phonetic complements in BM 31, 5: .
2. The reading of , *rk,* is questionable, due to the narrowness of the top sign.

A more cursive script is used following line 9, 21, although the content of the passage is not interrupted.

9, 21–23

D Note the inconsistency of the number of *s3w,* "sons," and the demonstrative *pwy* referring back to it. Consequently, the plurality of *s3w* is likely a mistake here. Cf. BM 31, 6–7: *rdit.n rˁ n s3=f pw nty m 3bḏw rdit.n=f r ḏdwt … ṯs n=f tp=f r smn n=f nḥbt=f r nḥm n=f.*

The enemies of Osiris are identified as those who *3d r,* "rage against," him.[776] Accordingly, *3d,* "Furious One," is a well-attested epithet of Seth and Sobek.[777] Thus, the phrase *3d r=f m-ẖnw kkw* may also be read: *3d rf m-ẖnw kkw,* "The Furious One is, indeed, in the darkness."

Some orthographic features and discrepancies with the parallels should be noted:

1. *3bḏw* is spelled here. Cf. in BM 31, 6.[778]
2. *ṯs* is written in BM 31, 7.
3. *tp,* , lacks the determinative (F51) in BM 31, 7.
4. *smn* is spelled in BM 31, 7.
5. *nḥbt* is spelled in BM 31, 7.

773 Allen, *The Ancient Egyptian Pyramid Texts*, p. 87.

774 Allen, *The Ancient Egyptian Pyramid Texts*, pp. 186, 276, and 303, respectively.

775 *Wb.* V 251, 10.

776 *Wb.* I 24, 15.

777 Leitz et al., eds., *Lexikon* I, p. 90.

778 For the spelling of Abydos as , see *Wb.* I 9, 1. For the epithet of various gods, including the sun god as well as the deceased, *nty-m-3bḏw*, "He who is in Abydos," see Leitz et al., eds., *Lexikon* IV, p. 367.

6. *nḥm* is spelled in BM 31, 7.
7. *ḫft*, , is written with in BM 31, 7.
8. The dot following *kkw*, , likely indicates the end of a clause.

9, 23–24

E Some orthographic peculiarities and discrepancies with the parallel texts should be noted:

1. *ipw* is spelled in BM 31, 8.
2. The spelling of the first part of in line 9, 23 is likely a confusion with the similar and familiar *ḥḏ-tꜣ*, "morning."
3. *n-rdi-n=f-nbi=f*, , lacks the determinative (G7) in BM 31, 9.
4. *hh* is written with phonetic complements in BM 31, 9: .
5. stands for *ḫnty-ḥwt-ins* in BM 31, 10.
6. *ḫt*, , is written without a determinative in BM 31, 10.

9, 25–26

F Although the phrase *sꜣ wsir*, "Son of Osiris," is written , it implies the common GR epithet , *sꜣ-wsir*, "Protector of Osiris,"[779] spelled more suitably in BM 31, 11 as .
irt is used as a relative form here, with a redundant dependent pronoun *sw*. Cf. the GR epithet of the Sharp-Eyed deities, *msḏ-mꜣꜣ-sbi*, "One who Hates Seeing the Enemy."[780]
imyw-wnwt=sn, "Those who are in their Hours," is a GR epithet of the red-eyed gods, and the deceased,[781] who offer their protection to the *imyw-wšꜣw*, "Those who are in the Darkness," a Kushite and GR epithet of the deities that guard Osiris and the deceased.[782]
The 3rd person singular feminine suffix pronoun of *im* refers to *ꜥt*, "chamber."
Cf. the latter part of this clause in BM 31, 12–14: *ḥw=ṯn n=f swt ḫsf=ṯn n=f smꜣw=f im ḫpr ḥꜥ m snwt sp ḥꜣ=k sbiw pfy ḏw m ꜥḳ r ꜥt ḏsr.n=ṯn wsir im=s*.
The following orthographic discrepancies should be noted:

1. *wnwt* is spelled in BM 31, 11.
2. *sp* is written in BM 31, 13.
3. *ḥꜣ* is spelled in BM 31, 13.

779 Leitz et al., eds., *Lexikon* VI, pp. 116–17.
780 Leitz et al., eds., *Lexikon* III, p. 446.
781 Leitz et al., eds., *Lexikon* I, p. 264.
782 Leitz et al., eds., *Lexikon* I, p. 265.

9, 27–28

G For a possible reconstruction of the destroyed portion of line 9, 28, see BM 31, 15: *nḏ ḥr=tn nṯrw m ssn r=sn bḥn=sn kw*. The remainder of the line in BM 31 corresponds to P.W551.

Some orthographic peculiarities and discrepancies with the parallels should be noted:

1. , *3ḫw*, "spirits" is spelled with the  determinative (A52).[783]
2. The number 8 is spelled  in BM 31, 14.
3. *iḳrw* is spelled phonetically as *iḫrw*, , in BM 31, 14.
4.  (Z6) likely represents an enemy of Osiris, such as Seth or his companions. It may, perhaps, be an error.
5. Note the lack of the  determinative (G7) for *nṯrw*, present in BM 31, 15: .
6. *sbiw* is written  in BM 31, 16.

9, 29–30

H Much of these two lines is destroyed. Cf. BM 31, 16–18: *m s3 r ḥꜥt nt wsir … im=s iw inp ꜥḥꜥ ir=k d=f bin=k pfy ḥr ḏd n=k m33 imnw nt nṯr ꜥ3 … grḥ pf s3=f ḥr … ti m ḫbt=k twy ḏw m s3*.

The plural strokes of *s3w*, , are likely a mistake, since the name of Horus follows.

The term *ḫbt*, "place of slaughter," written in its late form here and in BM 31, 18: , refers specifically to the place of Seth's punishment, according to Zandee.[784]

9, 31

I Cf. BM 31, 19–20: *ntrw ꜥb m wḏw … nṯr ꜥ3 irt ir=k ḥ3=k nbi pfy pw s3 nwt m s3 r ḥꜥ twy nt … sy*.

The lacuna following *stš pwy* most probably contained *s3*, "son," for *s3 nwt*, "Son of Nut," a well-attested epithet of Seth.[785]

9, 32

J *k3* is a parenthetic phrase for "(he) will say," which, according to Wilson, "is used in constructions to give names or epithets of places or persons."[786]

---

783 *Wb.* I 16, 2. For this writing of (G25), see Verhoeven, *Untersuchungen zur späthieratischen Buchschrift*, p. 141.

784 For this spelling, see *Wb.* III 252, 9–14. Zandee, *Death as an Enemy*, pp. 16 and 170.

785 Leitz et al., eds., *Lexikon* VI, pp. 82–83.

786 Gardiner, *Egyptian Grammar*, §436; Wilson, *Ptolemaic Lexikon*, p. 1079, respectively.

isds, a LP identification of *isdn,* is a name of Thoth and Anubis, among others. The holder of this epithet is generally connected with kingship and the correct inheritance of the throne.[787]
Some orthographic peculiarities and discrepancies with the parallel texts should be noted:

1.  stands for *irw* in BM 31, 20.
2. | | | are mistakenly placed before the suffix pronoun of *pr* in P.W551.
3. *pt* is written  here, while BM 31, 21 abbreviates the word to .

Following this line is an intentional gap, followed by a less cursive text written in the first hand of the manuscript.

9, 33–34

K The triumph over the "Red One," *dšr* (i.e., Seth), is further described here.[788] The term *sswn,* "to destroy, destruction," may also be understood as "punishment."[789]
The basic meaning of *sḏb* is "obstacle, impurity."[790] However, Kees points to the use of *ḥw sḏb* in a curse formula in the Admonitions and Merikare, translating the group "to curse, damn."[791] Faulkner reads this phrase in CT 427, V 273c as "an obstacle is smitten down."[792] PT 537 (§1299a–b) clarifies the term further: *rḏ=k r=k n rʿ ḥw=f n=k sḏb ir=(k)*…, "When you will make your speech to Re, he will strike for you (any) obstruction against (you)…"[793] Zandee agrees with the more powerful interpretation as a punishment for the enemies of the god.[794]
The triumphant Osiris is now referred to by the epithet *ḥry-tp-ʿnḫw,* "Chief of the Living."[795]
Cf. the last phrase, calling the defeated Seth to retreat, with line 9, 31: … *nṯr ʿ3 iry r=k ḥ3=k.*
There are notable orthographic peculiarities and discrepancies with the parallels:

1. Although *dšrt* generally carries negative connotations, the  determinative (G37) is not attested for this word in *Wb.* V. Cf. the determinative for *dšrt* in BM 31, 21: 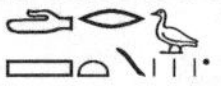.
2. BM 31, 22 consistently omits determinatives for *dr*: .

787 *Wb.* I 134, 10–12; Leitz et al., eds., *Lexikon* I, pp. 560–61.

788 Leitz et al., eds., *Lexikon* VII, pp. 570–71.

789 Wilson, *Ptolemaic Lexikon,* p. 919; *Wb.* VI 273, 7–15; and Zandee, *Death as an Enemy,* p. 284, respectively.

790 Wilson, *Ptolemaic Lexikon,* p. 977; *Wb.* IV 381, 7–382, 15.

791 Kees, *ZÄS* 63 (1928): 75–76.

792 Faulkner, *Ancient Egyptian Coffin Texts* II, p. 71, n. 6.

793 Allen, *The Ancient Egyptian Pyramid Texts,* p. 116.

794 Zandee, *Death as an Enemy,* pp. 249–50.

795 Leitz et al., eds., *Lexikon* V, p. 390.

3. BM 31, 22 consistently omits the determinative for *sꜣ*: .
4. Re, , is written with phonetic complements in BM 31, 22.
5. *kꜣ*, , lacks the determinative (G7) in BM 31, 22.
6. *sḏb* is spelled in BM 31, 22.
7. *nṯr*, , lacks the determinative (G7) in BM 31, 23.

9, 34–36

L Osiris is protected by Khnum, whose epithet *ḫnty-nṯry* is reminiscent of the GR epithet *ḫnm-m-nṯry*, "Khnum in the *Netjeri*,"[796] and by his sister, *wrt-fꜣw*, "Great of Splendor."[797]
Seth is referred to by the GR epithet *ḫsy-ḳd*, "The One Wretched of Character."[798]
Some orthographic peculiarities and discrepancies with the parallel texts should be noted:

1. *nty*, , following *wꜥbt* stands for the genitive *nt*.
2. *wꜥbt* is written in BM 31, 24.
3. Considering the variation of *š* and *ḫ* in Late Egyptian, must be understood as the name of Khnum.
4. *ꜥḥꜥ* is spelled in BM 31, 25.
5. *ḫsf* is written in BM 31, 25.
6. is mistakenly written instead of the dependent pronoun *sw* after *ḫsf*.
7. *snt* is simply written in BM 31, 25.
8. *fꜣw* is frequently spelled .[799] Cf. in BM 31, 25.
9. stands for the feminine relative adjective *ntt*, referring to the sister (Isis).
10. *siꜣkb*, , has the determinative (A28) in BM 31, 25.[800]

9, 36–37

M The phrase "the evil being under the protection of Geb" signifies that Geb controls the evil-doers and protects Osiris from evil, as has been determined by the Great Court in the Necropolis, *ḏꜣḏꜣt-ꜥꜣt-imyt-ḫrt-nṯr*.[801]
Some orthographic peculiarities and discrepancies with the parallel texts should be noted:

796 Leitz et al., eds., *Lexikon* VI, p. 29. For *nṯry*, "holy palace," see *Wb.* II 364, 26.
797 For this GR epithet of Isis, as well as other goddesses, see Leitz et al., eds., *Lexikon* II, p. 487.
798 Leitz et al., eds., *Lexikon* VI, p. 54.
799 *Wb.* I 575, 3–15. Cf. text notes for lines 5, 41–43, above.
800 For the construction *iꜣkb ḥr*, "to mourn for," see *Wb.* I 34, 8.
801 Leitz et al., eds., *Lexikon* VII, p. 598.

1. *ḥtmtyw* has an abbreviated spelling in BM 31, 26.[802]
2. Note the determinative (O1) of *ẖbt*, , omitted from BM 31, 26.
3. *ẖr*, , lacks the determinative (Y1) in BM 31, 26.

9, 37–38

N Cf. the 3rd person masculine suffix pronoun in BM 31, 27: *irt ir=f is šd mḏ3t tn,* which implies that this BM line addresses the lector priest, rather than the deceased.

The determinative (A5) of *imn*, , suggests that this is a verbal form, rather than a name of the god Amun. Thus, the epithet *imn,* "Hidden One," clearly refers to Osiris here, although it can denote other deities as well.[803] Due to the unusual spelling of *pr*, , with a stroke, the reading of the unattested epithet *pr-r=f,* "He who Came Forth for Himself," is questionable.

sšd is a "window (of appearance; or in a temple)."[804] This word is followed by the demonstrative *pn* in BM 31, 29.

Some orthographic peculiarities and discrepancies with the parallel texts should be noted:

1. *nẖbt* is spelled here; BM 31, 28 has a similar .[805]
2. *w3ḏyt*, , is also more abbreviated in BM 31, 28.
3. *wnwt*, , lacks the determinative (N5) in BM 31, 28.
4. *nmst*, "jug," is spelled here.[806] Cf. in BM 31, 29.
5. *wꜥ* is written with a stroke here. Cf. *wꜥ*, , in BM 31, 39.

9, 39

O The clause *wsir pw* is omitted from BM 31, 29.

Some discrepancies with the parallel texts should be noted:

1. *tp*, , omits the determinative (F51) in BM 31, 30.
2. Nephthys, , does not have the determinative (G7) in BM 31, 30.
3. *rdwy*, , also omits the determinative (F51) in BM 31, 30.

9, 40

P The epithet *imy-wrt,* "Those who are on the West Side of Thebes," refers to the dead.[807]

---

802 For *ḥtmyw*, "destroyers," see Wilson, *Ptolemaic Lexikon*, p. 689.

803 Leitz, et al., eds., *Lexikon* I, pp. 339-41.

804 *Wb.* IV 301, 14-302, 7.

805 For this spelling of *nẖbt*, see *Wb.* III 309, 7-9.

806 For this spelling of *nmst*, see *Wb.* II 269, 7-8; Daumas, *Valeurs phonétiques* IV, p. 790.

807 *Wb.* I 73, 9-12; Leitz, et al., eds., *Lexikon* I, p. 232.

9, 41

Q Cf. BM 31, 32: *ḫꜣwt wrt ỉỉ=n sp 2 nn nnỉ nn gꜣḥ ʿtw=k ỉpn.*
Some discrepancies with the parallel texts should be noted:

1. *ỉỉ* is written  in BM 31, 32.
2. *gꜣḥ* is more abbreviated in BM 31, 32: .[808]

9, 42

R Cf. the demonstrative in BM 31, 33: *nwt ṯs wy ỉnk sꜣ pwy dr wrd m-ʿ ỉr(y) r=ỉ.* BM omits *grḥ*, "pause."
Some discrepancies with the parallel texts should be noted:

1. Nut is written  in BM 31, 32.
2. *ṯs* is more extended in BM 31, 32–33: 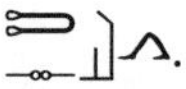.
3. *wrd* is written  in BM 31, 33.

9, 43–44

S Cf. BM 31, 33–34: *pḏ-ḫr-rdwy=f pḫr ḥꜣ pt=ỉ ḫꜣḫ tꜣ n snw*. BM omits the enclitic particle *ḥm.*[809]

808 For *gꜣḥ*, "to be weak," see *Wb.* V 155, 8–10.

809 Wilson, *Ptolemaic Lexikon*, p. 643; Gardiner, *Egyptian Grammar*, §253.

3.2.16. *s3ḫw* III, SPELL 16 — SPOKEN BY THE LECTOR PRIEST

Lines 10, 1–21[810]

The last spell of *s3ḫw* III is meant to be recited by the lector priest, who speaks of Thoth's triumph over the enemies of Osiris. Numerous other deities ensure the victory by once again associating sacrificial animals, such as *šsr,* "sacrificial bull,"[811] with the fate of the enemies of Osiris. The end of the spell seems to be an instruction for a vignette, which does not, in fact, appear on the papyrus.[812] The use of the phrase *twt nb,* "form, statue of the lord (=king, in this context),"[813] suggests that if the king (or the deceased) was not present, his images were to be used in the ritual.

TRANSLITERATION

(10, 1) *s3ḫ*
ḏd mdw in ḥry-ḥbt
wsir ḫnty-(imn)tyw wsir n 2. *P3-dit-k3-km*
in.n n=k ḏḥwty ḫftw=k
ḥw r 3. *ʿwy=f*
ḳm3 iw rdwy=f
wdn=f sw m ḫnt nṯrw 4. *mrt=k*
hy wsir ḫnty-imntyw wsir n P3-dit-k3-(10, 5)*-km*
w3s n=k ḫftw=k pfy m mni fdw 6. *nt ds*
i.nḏ ḥr=k in iry=k
*nwḥ wsir ḫnty-*7.*-imntyw wsir n P3-dit-k3-km*
dy sbḥ.n 8. *ḫftw=k ḫr=k*
*hy wsir ḫnty-imntyw wsir n P3-dit-k3-*9.*-km*
dn.n ḥr sm3w nt b=k
sgrḥ.n=f (10, 10) *n=k ʿb sbiw=k*
*hy wsir ḫnty-imntyw wsir P3-dit-k3-*11.*-km*
siʿr n=k inp is ḫpš n stš
fdḳ.n 12. *ḥr*
hy wsir ḫnty-imntyw wsir P3-dit-k3-km
wḏʿ n=k (i)t=k 13. *itm tpw sbiw=k*
i.nḏ ḥr=k
ʿḥʿ tw m ḫnm-nṯr
ʿnḫ 14. *m-ḫt=k*
ḏd mdw ḫft spḥw šsr pfy
sḏr (10, 15)*=f w3w r ʿrwt ʿ3t*
ḥḏ=s n wpt-rnpt ḥb

810 See section 1.7.3, above
811 Wilson, *Ptolemaic Lexikon*, p. 1032; *Wb.* IV 454, 2–3.
812 For *sšm*, "cult image," see *Wb.* IV, 291, 6–16.
813 *Wb.* V 256, 1–2.

ḥnʿ rdit sbḥw 16.*=f*
r sḏm nṯr ḫrw=f
st ir sšm pn r gs nṯrt tn 17. *špst ḥr msw*
msw m-ḫnt ʿ3t 3ḫ-šps 18. *nṯr ipw ʿḥʿ ḥ3=f sp 2*
m iwf=f m ʿwy=sn
wn m3ʿ
19. *is ḥtp ipw*
w3ḥ pw nsw tp t3
ist rʿ ḥr (10, 20) *inp nsw ḏs=f ʿḥʿ*
ir nsw m ḥʿ=f
ir.tw p3 21. *twt nb*
iw=f pw nfr

TRANSLATION

(10, 1) Glorification spell.
Words spoken by the lector priest:
"Osiris, Foremost (of the West)erners, Osiris of 2. Padikakem.
Thoth has brought for you your enemies,
who succumbed to 3. his two arms,
who were thrown to his two feet.
He placed him in front of the gods 4. whom you love.[A]
O, Osiris, Foremost of the Westerners, Osiris of Padika-(10, 5)-kem.
Those enemies of yours are overturned for you at the four mooring posts of 6. flint.[B]
Hail to you by your two guardians,
who clothe Osiris, Foremost 7. of the Westerners, Osiris of Padikakem,
who cause that your enemies 8. cry out under you.[C]
O, Osiris, Foremost of the Westerners, Osiris of Padika-9.-kem.
Horus has cut your associates of Seth.
He pacified (10, 10) for you the foe and your enemies.[D]
O, Osiris, Foremost of the Westerners, Osiris Padika-11.-kem.
Anubis has, indeed, presented to you the foreleg of Seth,
which Horus has 12. severed.[E]
O, Osiris, Foremost of the Westerners, Osiris of Padikakem.
Your father, Atum, has cut off for you 13. the heads of your enemies.
Hail to you!
Stand up as the one united with the god,
for life is 14. behind you!" [F]
Words spoken while lassoing that sacrificial bull
as he spends the night (10, 15) far from the great gate,
when it is illuminated in the New Year's festival,
causing that he cry out
16. so that the god may hear his voice.[G]

"Now, indeed, this image is to be made before this Noble Goddess, and 17. the offspring of Horus.[H]

The offspring who are before the Great One, Noble Spirit, and this god 18. are standing behind him," Twice.

"as his flesh is in their arms.[I]

(It) is the truth.

19. Now, as for this offering,

it is the offering of the king upon earth

while Re, Horus, (10, 20) Anubis and the king himself are present.[J]

As for the king in his palace,

one makes 21. an image of the lord."

It has come (to an end) well.[K]

TEXT NOTES

The last spell confirms the victory over the enemies of Osiris as they are "overturned at the four mooring posts of flint." Mooring is at times used as a euphemism for death, with the PT frequently alluding to the lamenting and nurturing qualities of the mooring post. Nevertheless, the term *mni,* "mooring post," also appears as an instrument of torture for the enemies of Osiris.[814] A similar idea is conveyed in PT 461 (§872b): *ḥw n=k mnit wrt sḏb…*, "The great Mooring Post will strike away obstruction for you…"[815] The notion of security invoked by the mooring post is further illustrated in the tomb of Ramses VI: *msẖtyw pw n stš wnn=f m pt mḥtt w3w n mnitwy n dsw m nwḥ n ḏʿm,* "The Foreleg of Seth (i.e., the Great Bear Constellation), it is in the northern sky, tied to two mooring posts of flint by a chain of white gold (i.e., electrum)."[816] A further association of the mooring posts with protection of Osiris comes from their connection with Isis, and possibly Nephthys, established in PT 666A (§1927e): *nis ṯw mnit m 3st is* …, "The Mooring-Post shall call you as Isis…."[817] The choice of flint as the material of the posts connects them to the sphere of the divine through this stone's attributes of danger and, thus, protection.[818] As one of the first stones employed in Egypt, flint was used to fashion both weapons and tools since predynastic times,[819] and evokes protective connotations. The number four, in turn, represents the four sides of the universe, hence alluding to the all-encompasing protection of the resurrected god.

814 Zandee, *Death as an Enemy*, pp. 225–26.

815 Allen, *The Ancient Egyptian Pyramid Texts*, p. 224.

816 Graves-Brown, in K. Piquette and S. Love, eds., *Current Research in Egyptology 2003*, p. 63; Piankoff, *Le Livre du jour et de la nuit*, pp. 24 and 95.

817 Allen, *The Ancient Egyptian Pyramid Texts*, p. 323.

818 Graves-Brown, in K. Piquette and S. Love, eds., *Current Research in Egyptology 2003*, p. 57.

819 Lucas and Harris, *Ancient Egyptian Materials and Industries*, pp. 411–12.

10, 1–4

A The expected *imntyw* is omitted from line 10, 1.
The construction *ḥw r*+direct object, "to succumb,"[820] points to Thoth's triumph over the enemies of Osiris. The perfect passive participle of *ḳmꜣ* is used in the *ḳmꜣ r*+direct object construction, "to throw something to/on,"[821] paralleling the previous clause.
Cf. a similar phrase to a portion of this clause in P.Louvre 3129, D15–16: *in=f n=k stš ẖsi m ntt ḥw r ꜥwy=f ḳmꜣ pꜣ rdwy=f,* "He brings to you the wretched Seth as the one who succumbed to his two arms, who was thrown (to) his two feet."[822] Cf. BM 32, 3: *in.n n=k ḏḥwty … … … ḳmꜣ=f r rdwy=f.*
sw must be a mistake for the plural dependent pronoun, referring to *ḫftw=k.*
Some orthographic peculiarities and discrepancies with the parallel texts should be noted:

1. *ḳmꜣ* is written  in BM 32, 3.
2. *ntrw* is spelled  here, with the phonetic ҁ indicating plurality.
3. *mrt,*  has the unusual  determinative (A4),[823] paralleled by BM 32, 4: .

10, 5–6

B The verb *wꜣs,* "to make fall, overturn," is transitive here.[824]
ḫftw is spelled  in BM 32, 5.

10, 6–8

C Cf. col. 9, 9: *nḏ ḥr=k in iry nwḥ wsir ḫnty-imntyw n Pꜣ-dit-kꜣ-km iry sbḥ n ḫftw=k ẖr=k,* "Hail to you by the two guardians, who clothe Osiris, Foremost of the Westerners, Osiris of Padikakem. May the shouting of your enemies be made under you!" 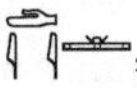, *dy,* written  in BM 32, 7, is most likely an imperfect active participle of the verb (*w*)*d,* a synonym of *rdi.*[825] Cf. the epithet *iryw-nw-ddw-sbḥw,* "Guardians of Those who Shout Out."[826]
Some discrepancies with the parallel texts should be noted:

1. *iry* is written with phonetic complements in BM 32, 6: .
2. *ẖr,* , lacks the 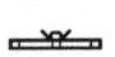 determinative (Y1) in BM 32, 8.

---

820 *Wb.* III 46, 5 and 17.
821 *Wb.* V 33, 8–16.
822 Urk. VI, 39, 17–18.
823 Möller, *Hieratische Paläographie* III, p. 2.
824 *Wb.* I 260, 9–261, 1; Wilson, *Ptolemaic Lexikon*, p. 199.
825 *Wb.* I 385, 1; Gardiner, *Egyptian Grammar*, §357.
826 Leitz et al., eds., *Lexikon* I, p. 418.

10, 8–10

D The enemies of Osiris are here referred to by the Saite and GR epithet *smꜣyt b*, "Associates of Seth."[827] The GR term *b*, , describes Seth.[828] The 2nd person singular suffix pronoun and refer to the epithet in its entirety.
Cf. the accomplices rather than *ꜥb*, "foe," in the second clause in BM 32, 10: *sgrḥ.n=f n=k smꜣw sbiw=k*.
Some orthographic peculiarities and discrepancies with the parallel texts should be noted:

1. The determinative (F18) of *dn*, , must be understood as a mistake for the somewhat similar hieratic writing of (T30).
2. *sgrḥ*, , generally has the determinative (D41).
3. The reading of as *ꜥb*, "foe," is uncertain, as no example of this word spelled with (W10) is attested.[829]
4. *sbiw* is spelled in BM 32, 10.

10, 11–12

E The term *fdḳ*, "to divide, sever," is frequently used for cutting off the forelegs of bulls and enemies of Osiris, whom the slaughtered cattle symbolizes.[830]
Some discrepancies with the parallel texts should be noted:

1. The dot at the end of line 10, 10 likely indicates the continuation of the name Padikakem on the following line.
2. The name of Seth is written in red ink in BM 32, 11.
3. *fdḳ* is written in BM 32, 12.

10, 12–14

F The determinative (G7) after *ẖnm* refers to the epithet *ẖnm-nṯr* as a whole and should not be read as the name of Khnum. Thus, the wish implies the vindication of the deceased and his ensuing unification with Osiris. In support of this, *ẖnm* is spelled without determinatives: , while *nṯr* does have the determinative (G7): in BM 32, 14. Cf. the slight variation in BM 32, 12–15: *wḏꜥ n=k (i)t=k itm tpw b=k nḏ ḥr=k ꜥḥꜥ ti m ẖnm-nṯr m ꜥnḫ m-ḫt=k*.
Some discrepancies with the parallel texts should be noted:

---

827 Leitz et al., eds., *Lexikon* VI, p. 318.
828 *Wb.* I 410, 9.
829 *Wb.* I 174, 13. For the reading of (W10) as the phonetic *ꜥb*, see Daumas, *Valeurs phonétiques* IV, p. 778.
830 *Wb.* I 583, 6–15; Wilson, *Ptolemaic Lexikon*, p. 391.

1. The name of Atum is written in BM 32, 12.
2. *ꜥḥꜥ* is spelled without phonetic complements, , in BM 32, 13.
3. stands for the 2nd person singular dependent pronoun *tw* in BM 32, 13.
4. *ẖt* is simply spelled in BM 32, 14.

10, 14–16

G The lack of a determinative in the verb *sḏr,* , allows for an alternate reading of this group as *ḏsr,* "to be sacred, calm."[831] Wilson points to the GR revival of the archaic sense of *ḏsr* as "clearing and purifying in preparation for a ritual," which may be applicable here.[832] The 3rd person singular masculine suffix pronoun of *sḏr* refers to the sacrificial bull. Cf. in BM 32, 15.
Cf. BM 32, 15–17: *sḏr=f wꜣ=f r ꜥrwt ꜥꜣt ḥḏ=s n wpt-rnpt ḥnꜥ rdi sbḥ=f r sḏm nṯrw.*
wpt-rnpt, "new year," refers to the first day of the year, I *ꜣẖt* 1, as well as the feast associated with it.[833]
Some orthographic peculiarities and discrepancies with the parallel texts should be noted:

1. *ḏd mdw* shows an abbreviated spelling in BM 32, 14: .
2. *wꜣw* is spelled in BM 32, 15.
3. The determinative for *ꜥrwt,* , should be understood as (O32), erroneously missing the strokes on top.

10, 16–17

H Cf. BM 32, 16–18, omitted from P.W551: *r sḏm nṯrw r nfr n sbiw=f ẖr in tw … m nis=f dẖs m ꜥwt im im=f.*

10, 17–18

I The epithet *ꜥꜣt,* "Great One," is said of Nut among other goddesses.[834]
BM 32, 20 provides an intentional gap between the two *msws*.

10, 18–21

J Cf. col. 9, 10–11 of the present manuscript: *wn-mꜣꜥt pw is ḥtp ib ipw wꜣḥ tp tꜣ n nsw ḏt.*
Cf. slight variations in the latter clause in BM 32, 23–25: *rꜥ ḥr inp nsw ḏs=f ꜥḥꜥ ir nsw m*

831 *Wb.* V 609, 12–614.

832 Wilson, *Ptolemaic Lexikon*, pp. 1247–48.

833 Spalinger, *Private Feast Lists of Ancient Egypt*, p. 32; Depuydt, *Civil Calendar and Lunar Calendar in Ancient Egypt*, p. 50.

834 Leitz et al., eds., *Lexikon* II, p. 54.

ḥʿ=f ỉrt m pꜣ ỉrw nb ʿ(nḫ) w(ḏꜣ) s(nb).[835] *ḥʿ*, , written with (W11) instead of the similar determinative (O11), is a LP and GR term for "palace (to which tribute is brought)."[836]

nfr is spelled here.[837] Cf. the end of *sꜣḫw* III in BM 32, 26: *ỉw=f pw.*

835 Cf. the translation of Schott, *MDAIK* 14 (1956): 183: "Re, Horus, Anubis und der König selbst sollen gegenwärtig sein. Ist aber der König in seinem Palast, vollziehe man (das Ritual) mit einer Statue des Herrn-Leben, Heil und Gesundheit."

836 *Wb.* III 39, 17.

837 *Wb.* I 253.

Appendix — Index of Epithets

1. EPITHETS OF OSIRIS AS A SOLAR DEITY

The significance of the theme of the solar-Osirian unity is apparent throughout the texts of P.W551. Osiris acted as the nocturnal counterpart of Re, who symbolically died every evening. In turn, the solar deity joined Osiris in his nightly journey through the Netherworld in order to be reborn in the morning. In this context, the cyclical occasion of the union of these two gods may be understood as the moment of creation and, thus, the instance when rebirth took place. Naturally, the idea of creation alludes to both sexuality and fertility. As such, the union of Re and Osiris was at times described in explicitly sexual terms, resulting in the rebirth of both deities, as well as the cyclical regeneration of the universe. Numerous examples associate the solar-Osirian unity with Heliopolis, the chief cult place of Re and the location where Osiris was resurrected. The two joined gods formed a giant solar-Osirian deity who filled heaven and earth — or the universe. Consequently, the fusion of the two gods represented a unification of the sun and moon, with Osiris identified as the latter. These two celestial bodies were symbolized by the two eyes of the giant god, as embodied in the Night and Day barks.

A selection of epithets of Osiris as a solar deity is presented below. Their significance is discussed in detail in the appropriate text notes. The following list refers to each epithet's mention in the papyrus by column and line number.

ꜣḫt-pr-rꜥ-ỉm=s	Horizon from which Re Comes Forth … 7, 33–34
ỉwny	Heliopolitan … 3, 16
ỉwn-ḥꜥꜥ	Rejoicing Pillar … 1, 43
bꜣ-nk	Copulating *Ba* … 2, 18
bnw	*Benu* bird … 1, 43; 1, 45
mry-rꜥ	Beloved one of Re … 1, 15
šn-wr-sk	… 7,7
šn-wr-dbn-ḥꜣw-nbw	*šn-wr* who Encircles the Islands … 7, 6–7
sḥḏ-tꜣ-n-nṯrw-m-ỉwt=f	He who Illuminates the Land for the Gods by his Coming … 3, 51
kꜣ-kꜣw	Bull of Bulls … 6, 7

2. FURTHER EPITHETS OF OSIRIS

This list excludes familial epithets such as Brother, Husband, One who Came Forth from Nut/Geb, etc.

ꜣḫ-ỉmy-ḏndrw	Spirit who is in the *ḏndrw*-Bark … 7, 11
ꜣḫ-šps	Noble Spirit … 10, 17
ꜥnḏti	Andjety … 7, 25
ꜥšꜣt-m-mrwt-wꜥt	One Rich of Love for the Sole One. … 4, 26
ỉmn	Hidden One … 9, 38
ỉn-wnnt-nbt-m-r-ꜥwy=f	One who Brings Everything that Exists by the Action of his Hands … 3, 3
ỉry-tꜣ	Protector of the Land … 4, 21
ỉty	Sovereign … 2, 10; 4, 6
wr	Great One … 7, 35; 8, 9; 8, 10
wḥm-ꜥnḫ	Repeater of Life … 6, 11
pꜣy-wꜥ	Unique One … 2, 14
ꜥpr-m-ꜣḫw=f	One who is Equipped with his Spirits … 8, 13
pr-r=f	He who Came Forth for Himself … 9, 38
mꜣr	Miserable One … 4, 5
mnḫ-sḫry-di.n-nṯrw	Beneficent of the Counsels which the Gods Give … 2, 14
mr-ỉnb-ḥḏ	One who Loves Memphis … 3, 16
mr-nṯr	Canal of the God … 7, 10
mr-ḥmwt	One whom Women Love … 1, 37
mrtyw	Beloved One … 4, 20
mrt-ḥmwt	One who Loves Women … 4, 20
msḏ-ḳdt	One who Hates Sleep … 8, 10
n-mr=f-bꜣgi	One who does not Love Weariness … 8, 10
nb	Lord … 3, 8; 3, 11; 3, 12
nb-sꜣwt	Lord of Asyut … 7, 9–10
nḫn-ḫy	Young Child … 4, 11
nṯr-ỉm-ḥnw	God who is in the *Henw*-Bark … 7, 33
nṯr-šps	Noble God … 5, 55; 9, 27
rnpy	Rejuvenated One … 5, 33
ḥꜥpy	Inundation … 3, 24
ḥw-ḳy-m-ẖnw=f	One who Strikes the Insect(?) inside him(self) … 4, 31
ḥwn-nfr	Beautiful Youth … 1, 16; 3, 37
ḥp-ꜥnḫ	Living Apis … 3, 2
ḥry-tp	Chief … 5, 43
ḥry-tp-spꜣt	Chief of the District … 8, 24
ḥtp-m-ỉrw=f	One whose Form is at Rest. … 4, 29
ḫnty-ỉmntyw	Foremost of the Westerners … *passim.*
ḫrp-šps	Noble Leader … 6, 19
sꜣḥ	Orion … 6, 40

sbꜣ-wꜥ	Unique Star ... 8, 35
sn-irw=f	One who Changes his Forms ... 4, 36
snḏ-n=f-ꜣḫw-nb	He whom All the Spirits Fear ... 7, 40
sḫm-spd	Powerful and Effective One ... 5, 53
sḫm-šps	Noble Power ... 8, 35
sštꜣ-irw=f	He whose Form is Secret ... 7, 42
sḏr-ḥr-psd=f-mi-ḫt-ḥḏ	One who Rests upon his Back like a Damaged Tree ... 4, 30
šps-prw-m-ḏfꜣw	One with whose Provisions the Temples are Made Splendid ... 3, 48
šn-m-nbw-tp=f-m-ḫsbd	Golden Child, whose Head is of Lapis-lazuli ... 2, 2
ṯꜣi-nfr	Good Husband ... 4, 4
km-wr	... 7, 6
ḳnw	Brave One ... 4, 5

3. EPITHETS OF OTHER DEITIES

This list includes epithets of deities other than Osiris. Their precise identifications are discussed in the appropriate text notes.

ꜣw-šwty	Tall of Plumes ... 9, 21
ꜣḫty	Two *Akhs* ... 6, 3
iwtt-sn-nwt=s	One Without her Second ... 9, 20–21
imy-wrt	Those who are on the West Side of Thebes ... 9, 40
imy-spdt	He who is in Sothis ... 8, 38
imyw-wnwt=sn	Those who are in their Hours ... 9, 25
imyw-wšꜣw	Those who are in the Darkness ... 9, 26
imyw-šwt-wsir	Those in the Suite of Osiris ... 9, 23
imyw-tꜣ-ꜥnḫ	Those who are in the Land of Life ... 2, 21
ir-m-ꜥwꜣ	He who Acts by Force ... 8, 15
ir-rn=f-ḏs=f	He who Makes his Own Name ... 8, 15
wꜥty	Sole One ... 4, 26; 9, 20
wnp	Stabbed One ... 5, 44
wnp-ḥr	One whom Horus Stabbed ... 5, 44
wr(w)	Great One(s) ... 6, 4; 6, 33; 7, 34; 8, 9; 8, 10; 10, 17
wr(t)-fꜣw	Great of Splendor ... 9, 35; 9, 37–38
wḏꜥ	Judged One ... 8, 32
pfy	That One ... 3, 42; 5, 9; 5, 14
pr-m-ḫt	He who Comes out After ... 9, 24
pd-ẖr-rdwy=f	One who Spreads out Under his Two Feet ... 9, 43
mꜣ-m-ḥr=f	He who Sees with his Face ... 9, 24
mꜣ-it=f	He who Sees his Father ... 8, 15
mds-irty	Sharp-Eyed Ones ... 9, 23

n-rdi-n=f-nbỉ=f	He whose Flame was not Placed … 9, 24
nb-ꜥnḫ-m-ꜣḫt	Lord of Life in the Horizon … 9, 2
nb-iwꜥ	Possessor of Inheritance … 2, 22
nb-pꜥt	Lord of Humanity … 7, 41
nb-pt	Lord of Heaven … 8, 19
nbw-ỉtrty	Lords of the Two Conclaves … 8, 19
nbt-nsr	Mistress of Flame … 3, 45
nbt-ḳdw	Lady of Builders … 7, 28
nbd	Evil One … 2, 48; 3, 13; 3, 52; 9, 29
nḫꜣḫꜣ-mnḏwy	Full of Breasts … 9, 21
nṯr-ꜥꜣ	Great God … 5, 42; 9, 31; 9, 34
nṯrwy-ꜥꜣw-m-pt	Great Gods in Heaven … 6, 18
nṯr-biꜣtyw	Miraculous God … 8, 15
nṯr-stt	Divinely Fragranced One … 9, 20
nḏḥḏḥ	Nedjehdjeh … 9, 23
rkḥw	Burning Ones … 8, 41
ḥꜣḳw	He who Plunders … 8, 15
ḥrt	Heaven … 7, 1
ḥry-tp-ꜥnḫw	Chief of the Living … 9, 34
ḥḏt-ꜥfn	One White of Head-Cloth … 9, 21
ḫnty-imntt	Foremost of the West … 5, 43
ḫnty-psḏt-ꜥꜣt	Foremost of the Great Ennead … 6, 21; 6, 28
ḫnty-ꜥꜣt	Foremost of the Great One…6, 46
ḫnty-nṯry	Foremost of the Holy Palace … 9, 35
ḫnty-ḥwt-ins	Foremost of the Mansion of the Red Linen … 9, 24
ḫnty-hh	He who is before the Fire … 9, 24
ẖnm-wr	Great Well … 6, 44
ẖsi-ḳd	One Wretched of Character … 9, 34
sꜣ-nḏ-it(=f)	Son who Protects (his) Father … 7, 11
sꜣ-spdt	Effective Son … 8, 38
sꜣt-wrt-imy-ḳdm	Oldest Daughter who is in Qedem … 6, 8
smꜣr-nb-pt	He who Makes Wretched the Lord of Heaven … 5, 3
smsw	Elder … 9, 19
smsw-pr-nfr	Elder of the *pr-nfr* … 9, 19
snwty	*Senwt*-Shrines … 7, 15
snty=k-wr(ty)-ꜥꜣ(ty)=k	Two Great and Mighty Sisters … 6, 14
sḫm-m-ḏt=f	Powerful in his Body … 9, 4
sšpt	Luminous Ones … 6, 39
šntꜣyt	Shentayt … 5, 23
šsꜣ-ḫpš	Skilled of Arm … 9, 18
št-pt	… 6, 42; 7,1
štꜣw-swt	Those whose Seats are Secret … 7, 38–39
kꜣ	Bull … 9, 8
kꜣ-pt	Bull of Heaven … 8, 39

ḳd-kꜣ	He who Fashioned the Bull … 9, 24
dšr	Red One … 9, 33; 9, 34
dšr-ỉrty	Red-Eyed One … 9, 24
ḏrwt	Coffin … 7, 28–29
ḏrty	Two Kites … 9, 17

Bibliography

Allen, James. *The Inflection of the Verb in the Pyramid Texts,* BAe 2 (Malibu: Undena, 1984).

——. "Funerary Texts and their Meaning," in S. D'Auria, P. Lacovara, C. Roehrig, eds., *Mummies and Magic: The Funerary Arts of Ancient Egypt* (Boston: Museum of Fine Arts, 1988), pp. 38–49.

——. *The Ancient Egyptian Pyramid Texts,* P. der Manuelian, ed., Writings from the Ancient World 23 (Atlanta: Society of Biblical Literature, 2005).

Allen, Thomas George. *Occurrences of Pyramid Texts, with Cross Indexes of these and other Egyptian Mortuary Texts,* SAOC 27 (Chicago: University of Chicago, 1950).

Alliot, Maurice. *Le culte d'Horus à Edfou au temps des Ptolémées,* vol. 1, BdE 20/1 (Cairo: IFAO, 1949).

Altenmüller, Hartwig. *Die Texte zum Begräbnisritual in den Pyramiden des Alten Reiches,* ÄgAb 24 (Wiesbaden: Harrassowitz, 1972).

——. "Stundenwachen," in *LÄ* IV (1986): cols. 104–6.

Assmann, Jan. *Liturgische Lieder an den Sonnengott. Untersuchungen zur altägyptischen Hymnik I,* MÄS 19 (Berlin: Hessling, 1969).

——. "Neith spricht als Mutter und Sarg," *MDAIK* 28 (1972): 127–39.

——. "Verklärung," in *LÄ* II (1975): cols. 998–1006.

——. *Das Grab der Mutirdis. Grabung im Asasif 1963–1970,* vol. 6, AV 13 (Mainz: DAIK, 1977).

——. "Fest des Augenblicks – Verheissung der Dauer. Die Kontroverse der ägyptischen Harfnerlieder," in J. Assmann, E. Feucht, and R. Grieshammer, eds., *Fragen an die altägyptische Literatur: Studien zum Gedenken an Eberhard Otto* (Wiesbaden: Dr. Reichert, 1977), pp. 55–84.

——. "Harfnerlied und Horussöhne," *JEA* 65 (1979): 56–77.

——. *Re und Amun: die Krise des polytheistischen Weltbilds im Ägypten der 18.-20. Dynastie,* OBO 51 (Freiburg, Schweiz: Universitätsverlag; Göttingen: Vandenhoeck & Ruprecht, 1983).

——. "Egyptian Mortuary Liturgies," in S. Groll, ed., *Studies in Egyptology Presented to Miriam Lichtheim* (Jerusalem: Magnes, Hebrew University, 1990), pp. 1–45.
——. "Altägyptische Kultkommentare," in J. Assmann and B. Gladigow, eds., *Text und Kommentar. Archäologie der literarischen Kommunikation* IV (Munich: Fink, 1995), pp. 93–109.
——. *Images et rites de la mort dans l'Égypte ancienne: L'apport des liturgies funéraires* (Paris: Cybèle, 2000).
——. *Altägyptische Totenliturgien. Totenliturgien in den Sargtexten des Mittleren Reiches*, vol. 1. Supplemente zu den Schriften der Heidelberger Akademie der Wissenschaften, Philosophisch-Historische Klasse 14 (Heidelberg: Universitätsverlag C. Winter, 2002).
——. "Das Leichensekret des Osiris: Zur kultischen Bedeutung des Wassers im alten Ägypten," in N. Grimal, A. Kamel, and C. May-Sheikholeslami, eds., *Hommages Fayza Haikal*, BdE 138 (Cairo: IFAO, 2003), pp. 5–6.
——. *Altägyptische Totenliturgien. Totenliturgien und Totensprüche in Grabinschriften des Neuen Reiches*, vol. 2. Supplemente zu den Schriften der Heidelberger Akademie der Wissenschaften, Philosophisch-Historische Klasse 17 (Heidelberg: Universitätsverlag C. Winter, 2005).

Badawy, Alexander. "Zwei Denkmäler des grossen Gaugrafen von Memphis Amenophis *ḥwjj*," *ASAE* 44 (1944): 181–224.
——. "The Spiritualization of Kagemni," *ZÄS* 108 (1981): 85–93.

Baines, John. "Bnbn. Mythological and Linguistic Notes," *Orientalia* 39 (1970): 389–404.

Bakir, Abd el-Mohsen. *The Cairo Calendar no. 86637* (Cairo: General Organization for Government Printing Offices, 1966).

Bakry, Hassan. "A Late-Period Statuette," *ASAE* 60 (1968): 1–6.

El-Banna, Essam. "À propos des aspects Héliopolitains d'Osiris," *BIFAO* 89 (1989): 101–26.

Barguet, Paul. *Le papyrus N. 3176 (S) du Musée du Louvre*, BdE 37 (Cairo: IFAO, 1962).
——. *Les textes des sarcophages Égyptiens du Moyen Empire* (Paris: Les Éditions du CERF, 1986).

Barta, Winfried. *Aufbau und Bedeutung der altägyptischen Opferformel* (Glückstadt: Augustin, 1968).
——. *Die Bedeutung der Pyramidentexte für den verstorbenen Konig*, MÄS 39 (München, Berlin: Deutscher Kunstverlag, 1981).

Bedier, Shafia. *Die Rolle des Gottes Geb in den äyptischen Tempelinschriften der griechisch-römischen Zeit*, HÄB 41 (Hildesheim: Gerstenberg, 1995).

Bellion, Madeleine. *Egypte ancienne: catalogue des manuscrits hiéroglyphiques et hiératiques et des dessins, sur papyrus, cuir ou tissu, publiés au signalés* (Paris: Bellion, 1987).

Belluccio, Adriana. "Le myth du Phénix à la lumière de la consubstantialité royale du père et du fils," in T. di Netro, G. Zaccone, eds., *Sesto Congresso Internazionale di Egittologia. Atti.* vol. 2 (Turin: Stabilimento Poligrafico S.p.A., 1993), pp. 21–40.

Billing, Nils. *Nut: The Goddess of Life in Text and Iconography*, USE 5 (Uppsala: Uppsala University, 2002).

Borghouts, Joris. "Akhu and Hekau: Two Basic Notions of Ancient Egyptian Magic, and the Concept of the divine Creative Word," in A. Roccati and A. Siliotti, eds., *La Magia in Egitto ai Tempi dei Faraoni* (Milan: Rassegna Internazionale di Cinematografia Archeologica Arte e Natura Libri, 1987), pp. 29–46.

Brand, Peter. "Use of the term *ꜣḫ* in the reign of Seti I," GM 168 (1999): 23–33.

Breasted, James Henry. *Development of Religion and Thought in Ancient Egypt: Lectures Delivered on the Morse Foundation at Union Theological Seminary.* The Morse Lectures (New York: Scribner's Sons, 1912).

Van den Broek, Roloff. *The myth of the Phoenix, according to Classical and Early Christian Traditions*, ÉPRO 24 (Leiden: Brill, 1972).

Brugsch, Heinrich Karl. *Dictionnaire géographique de l'ancienne Égypte, contenant par ordre alphabétique la nomenclature comparée des noms propres géographiques qui se rencontrent sur les monuments et dans les papyrus, notamment les noms des préfectures et de leurs chefs-lieux, des temples et sanctuaires* (Leipzig: Hinrichs, 1879–80).

———. *Thesaurus inscriptionum Aegyptiaerum. Altägyptische Inschriften* (Leipzig: Hinrichs, 1883–91).

de Buck, Adrian. *The Egyptian Coffin Texts.* 7 vols., OIP 34, 49, 64, 67, 73, 81, 87 (Chicago: University of Chicago, 1935–61).

Budde, Dagmar. "'Die den Himmel durchsticht und sich mit den Sternen vereint:' Zur Bedeutung und Funktion der Doppelfederkrone in der Götterikonographie," *SAK* 30 (2002): 57–102.

Caminos, Ricardo. *The Chronicle of Prince Osorkon*, AnOr 37 (Rome: Pontificum Institutum Biblicum, 1958).

———. "Another Hieratic Manuscript from the Library of Pwerem, Son of Kiki (pB.M. 10288)," *JEA* 58 (1972): 205–24.

Cassonnet, Patricia. *Études de néo-égyptien. Les temps seconds: i-sḏm.f et i-iri.f sḏm; entre syntaxe et sémantique*. (Cybèle: Paris, 2000).

Cauville, Sylvie. "Les mystères d'Osiris à Dendera: Interprétation des chapelles osiriennes," *BSFE* 112 (1988): 23–36.

——. *Le temple de Dendara: les chapelles osiriennes*, 3 vols., BdE 117–19 (Cairo: IFAO, 1997)

——. *Dendara: les fêtes d'Hathor* (Leuven, Stirling: Uitgeverij Peeters, 2002).

Černý, Jaroslav. "Philological and Etymological Notes," *ASAE* 51 (1951): 445–46.

——. *Paper & Books in Ancient Egypt* (Chicago: Ares, 1977 [1952]).

Černý, Jaroslav and Groll, Sarah Israelit. *A Late Egyptian Grammar*, Studia Pohl: Series maior 4 (Rome: Biblical Institute, 1993).

Chassinat, Emile. *Le mystère d'Osiris au mois de Khoiak*, vol. 1. (Cairo: IFAO, 1966).

Coenen, Marc and Verrept, Bert. "The Mortuary Liturgies in the Funerary Papyrus Baltimore Walters Art Museum 10.551," *GM* 202 (2004): 97–102.

Coulon, Laurent. "Le sanctuaire de Chentayt à Karnak," in Z. Hawass, ed., *Egyptology at the Dawn of the 21st Century: Proceedings of the Eighth International Congress of Egyptologists, Cairo 2000*, vol. 1 (Cairo, New York: American University in Cairo, 2003), pp. 138–46.

——. "Trauerrituale im Grab des Osiris in Karnak," in J. Assmann, F. Maciejewski, and A. Michaels, eds., *Der Abschied von den Toten: Trauerrituale im Kulturvergleich*, (Göttingen: Wallstein, 2005), pp. 326–41.

Crum, Walter. *A Coptic Dictionary* (Oxford: Clarendon, 2000 [1939]).

Cruz-Uribe, Eugene. "Opening of the Mouth as Temple Ritual," in E. Teeter and J. Larson, eds., *Gold of Praise: Studies on Ancient Egypt in Honor of Edward Wente*, SAOC 58 (Chicago: University of Chicago, 1999), pp. 69–73.

Darnell, John. "Hathor returns to Medamûd," *SAK* 22 (1995): 47–94.

——. "The Apotropaic Goddess in the Eye," *SAK* 24 (1997): 35–48.

——. *The Enigmatic Netherworld Books of the Solar-Osirian Unity: Cryptographic Compositions in the Tombs of Tutankhamun, Ramesses VI and Ramesses IX*, OBO 198 (Fribourg: Academic Press; Göttingen: Vandenhoeck & Ruprecht, 2004).

Daressy, Georges. "Inscriptions du tombeau de Psametik a Saqqarah," *RdT* 17 (1895): 17–25.

——. "Notes et remarques," *RdT* 20 (1898): 72–86.

——. *Textes et dessins magiques* (Cairo: IFAO, 1903).

Daumas, François. *Valeurs phonétiques des signes hiéroglyphiques d'époque gréco-romaine*, 4 vols. (Montpellier: Publications de la recherche – Université de Montpellier, 1988–95).

——. "Lapis-lazuli et régénération des dieux," in S. Aufrère, ed., *L'univers Minéral dans la pensée Égyptienne*, BdE 105 (Cairo: IFAO, 1991), pp. 463–82.

Davies, Norman de Garis. "Tehuti: Owner of Tomb 110 at Thebes," in S.R.K. Glanville, ed., *Studies presented to F.Ll. Griffith*. Egypt Exploration Society (London: Humphrey Milford, Oxford University, Amen House, 1932), pp. 279–90.

Dawson, Warren. "Studies in the Egyptian Medical Texts – V," *JEA* 21 (1935): 30–40.

Demarée, Robert. The *ꜣḫ iḳr n rꜥ*- Stelae: On Ancestor Worship in Ancient Egypt, EgUit 3 (Leiden: Terra BV, 1983).

Depauw, Mark and Smith, Mark. "Visions of Ecstasy: Cultic Revelry before the Goddess Ai/ Nehemanit. Ostraca Faculteit Letteren (K.U.Leuven) dem. 1–2," in F. Hoffmann and H. J. Thissen, eds., *Res Severa Verum Gaudium: Festschrift für Karl-Theodor Zauzich zum 65. Geburtstag am 8. Juni 2004*, Studia Demotica 6 (Leuven; Dudley: Uitgeverij Peeters, 2004), pp. 67–93.

Depuydt, Leo. *Civil Calendar and Lunar Calendar in Ancient Egypt*, OLA 77, (Leuven: Uitgeverij Peeters, 1997).

——. "The Hieroglyphic Representation of the Moon's Absence (*psḏntyw*)," in L. Lesko, ed., *Ancient Egyptian and Mediterranean Studies in Memory of William A. Ward*, (Providence: Department of Egyptology, Brown University, 1998), pp. 71–89.

Derchain, Philippe. "La pêche de l'œil et le mystères d'Osiris a Dendara," *RdE* 15 (1963): 11–25.

——. *Le papyrus Salt 825 (BM10051), rituel pour la conservation de la vie en Égypte*, Mémoires de la Classe des lettres 58 (Brussels: Palais des Académies, 1965).

Derchain-Urtel, Maria-Theresia. "Wortspiele zu 'Ort' und 'Bewegung' in Edfu und Dendera," in *Mélanges Adolph Gutbub*. (Montpellier: Université de Montpellier, 1984), pp. 55–61.

——. "Das *snḏ*-Zeichen und seine Verwendung in griechisch-römischer Zeit," in M. Minas and J. Zeidler, eds., *Aspekte spätägyptischer Kultur: Festschrift für Erich Winter zum 65. Geburtstag*, AT 7 (Mainz am Rhein: von Zabern, 1994), pp. 77–80.

Desroches-Noblecourt, Christiane. "Une Coutume Égyptienne Méconnue," *BIFAO* 45 (1947): 185–232.

Dorman, Peter. *The Tombs of Senenmut: The Architecture and Decoration of Tombs 71 and 353*, Metropolitan Museum of Art Egyptian Expedition 24 (New York: Metropolitan Museum of Art, 1991).

Drioton, Étienne. *Rapport sur les fouilles de Médamoud (1925). Les Inscriptions.* Part III, vol. 2. (Cairo: Imprimerie de l'IFAO, 1926).

DuQuesne, Terence. "Effective in Heaven and on Earth," in J. Assmann and M. Bommas, eds., *Ägyptische Mysterien?* (München: Fink, 2002), pp. 37–46.

——. "The spiritual and the sexual in ancient Egypt," in *DiscEg* 61 (2005): 7–24.

——. "The Osiris-Re Conjunction with particular Reference to the Book of the Dead," in B. Backes, I. Munro and S. Stöhr, eds., *Totenbuch-Forschungen. Gesammelte Beiträge des 2. Internationalen Totenbuch-Symposiums Bonn, 25. bis 29. September 2005*, (Wiesbaden: Harrassowitz, 2006), pp. 23–33.

Edel, Elmar. *Altägyptische Grammatik*, AnOr 34 (Rome: Pontificium Insitutum Biblicum, 1955).

——. *Neue Deutungen Keilschriftlicher Umschreibungen ägyptischer Wörter und Personennamen* (Vienna: Österreichische Akademie der Wissenschaften, 1980).

Egberts, Arno. "Action, Speech, and Interpretation: Some Reflections on the Classification of Ancient Egyptian Liturgical Texts," in C. Eyre, ed., *Seventh International Congress of Egyptologists*, OLA 82 (Leuven: Uitgeverij Peeters, 1998), pp. 358–63.

El-Naggar, Salah. "Étude préliminaire d'un ciel voûté de l'hypogée de Bakenrenef (L.24) à Saqqara," *EVO* 9 (1986): 15–38.

Englund, Gertie. *Akh - une notion religieuse dans l' Égypte pharaonique*, Uppsala Studies in Ancient Mediterranean and Near Eastern Civilizations 11 (Stockholm: Almquist & Wiksell, 1978).

——. "The Border and the Yonder Side," in E. Teeter and J. Larson, eds., *Gold of Praise: Studies on Ancient Egypt in Honor of Edward Wente*, SAOC 58 (Chicago: University of Chicago, 1999), pp. 101–9.

Engsheden, Åke. *La reconstitution du verbe en égyptien de tradition 400–30 avant J.-C*, USE 3 (Uppsala: Uppsala University, 2003).

Erman, Adolf. *Die Märchen des Papyrus Westcar II: Glossar, Palaeographische Bemerkungen und Feststellung des Textes*, Mittheilungen aus den Orientalischen Sammlungen der Königlichen Museen zu Berlin 4 (Berlin: Spemann, 1890).

Eyre, Christopher. *The Cannibal Hymn: A Cultural and Literary Study* (Liverpool: Liverpool University, 2002).

Fairman, Herbert W. "Notes on the Alphabetic Signs Employed in the Hieroglyphic Inscriptions of the Temple of Edfu," *ASAE* 43 (1943): 193–310.

——. "An Introduction to the Study of Ptolemaic Signs and their Values," *BIFAO* 43 (1945): 51–138.

Farid, Adel. "Two Demotic Annuity Contracts," in S. Bedier, K. Daoud, Z. Hawass, eds., *Studies in Honor of Ali Radwan*, vol. 1, ASAE Supplement 34 (Cairo: Conseil Suprême des Antiquités de l'Égypte, 2005), pp. 323–46.

Faulkner, Raymond. *The Papyrus Bremner-Rhind (British Museum 10188)*, BAe 3 (Brussels: Édition de la Fondation Égyptologique Reine Élisabeth, 1933).

——. "The Lamentations of Isis and Nephthys," in *Mélanges Maspero* I, Mémoires publiés par les membres de l'IFAO 66 (Cairo: IFAO, 1934), pp. 337–348.

——. "The Bremner-Rhind Papyrus—I," *JEA* 22 (1936): 121–40.

——. "The Bremner-Rhind Papyrus—II," *JEA* 23 (1937): 10–16.

——. *The Ancient Egyptian Coffin Texts: Spells 1–354*, vol. 1 (Warminster: Aris & Philips Ltd, 1973).

——. *The Ancient Egyptian Coffin Texts: Spells 355–787*, vol. 2 (Warminster: Aris & Philips Ltd, 1977).

——. *The Ancient Egyptian Coffin Texts: Spells 788–1185 & Index*, vol. 3 (Warminster: Aris & Philips Ltd, 1978).

——. *Ancient Egyptian Pyramid Texts* (Oxford: Clarendon Press, 1998 [1969]).

Foster, John. "Wordplay in *The Eloquent Peasant*: The Eighth Complaint," *BES* 10 (1989–1990): 61–76.

Fóti, László. "Hermes Trismégiste et la mythologie égyptienne," *StudAeg* 12 (1989): 9–29.

Frandsen, Paul John. "On the Root of *nfr* and a 'Clever' Remark on Embalming," in J. Osing and E. Nielsen, eds., *The Heritage of Ancient Egypt: Studies in Honor of Erik Iversen*, (Copenhagen: Carsten Niebuhr Institute of Ancient Near Eastern Studies, University of Copenhagen: Museum Tusculanum, 1992), pp. 49–62.

——. "On Fear of Death and the Three *bwts* Connected with Hathor," in E. Teeter and J. Larson, eds., *Gold of Praise: Studies on Ancient Egypt in Honor of Edward F. Wente*, SAOC 58 (Chicago: University of Chicago, 1999), pp. 131–48.

Friedman, Florence. "Review of Gertie Englund, *Akh - une notion religieuse dans l'Égypte pharaonique*," *JARCE* 19 (1982): 145–47.

——. "The Root Meaning of *ꜣḫ*: Effectiveness or Luminosity," Serapis 8 (1985): 39–46.

Gabra, Sami. *Rapport sur les Fouilles d'Hermoupolis Ouest (Touna el-Gebel)* (Cairo: IFAO, 1941).

Gardiner, Alan. *Late Egyptian Stories*. BAe 1 (Brussels: Édition de la Fondation Égyptologique Reine Élisabeth, 1932).

——. "The House of Life," *JEA* 24 (1938): 157–79.

——. *Egyptian Grammar: Being an Introduction to the Study of Hieroglyphs*, 3rd ed. (Oxford: Griffith Institute, Ashmolean Museum, 1994).

Gauthier, Henri. "Les statues thébaines de la déesse Sakhmet," *ASAE* 19 (1920): 177–207.

Gee, John. "Ba Sending and its Implications," in Z. Hawass, ed., *Egyptology at the Dawn of the Twenty-first Century: Proceedings of the Eighth International Congress of Egyptologists, Cairo, 2000*, vol. 2, (Cairo, New York: American University in Cairo, 2003), pp. 230–37.

Germond, Philippe. *Sekhmet et la protection du monde*, AH 9 (Geneva: Éditions de Belles-Lettres, 1981).

Gestermann, Louise. *Die Überlieferung ausgewählter Texte altägyptischer Totenliteratur („Sargtexte") in spätzeitlichen Grabanlagen*, 2 vols., ÄA 68 (Wiesbaden: Harrassowitz, 2005).

Gillam, Robyn. *Performance and Drama in Ancient Egypt* (London: Duckworth & Co. Ltd., 2005).

Goebs, Katja. *Crowns in Egyptian Funerary Literature: Royalty, Rebirth, and Destruction*. (Oxford: Griffith Institute, 2008).

Goelet, Ogden. *The Egyptian Book of the Dead: The Book of Going Forth by Day*. Translated by R. Faulkner (San Francisco: Chronicle Books, 1994).

Goldwasser, Orly. "The Allure of the Holy Glyphs: A Psycholinguistic Perspective on the Egyptian Script," *GM* 123 (1991): 37–50.

Goyon, Jean-Claude. "Le cérémonial de glorification d'Osiris du papyrus du Louvre I. 3079," *BIFAO* 65 (1967): 89–156.

——. "Cérémonial pour faire sortir Sokaris," *RdE* 20 (1968): 63–96.

——. *Rituels funéraires de l'ancienne Égypte*, Littératures anciennes du Proche-Orient 4 (Paris: Les Editions de Cerf, 1972).

——. *Confirmation du pouvoir royal au nouvel an: Brooklyn Museum papyrus 47.218.50*, 2 vols., BdE 52; Wilbour Monographs 7 (Cairo: IFAO; New York: The Brooklyn Museum, 1972–74).

——. "La littérature funéraire tardive," in *Textes et Langages de l'Égypte pharaonique. Hommage à Jean-François Champollion*, BdE 64/3 (Cairo: IFAO, 1974), pp. 73–81.

——. "La fête de Sokaris à Edfou: à la lumière d'un texte liturgique remontant au nouvel empire," *BIFAO* 78 (1978): 415–38.

——. *Le Papyrus d'Imouthès, fils de Psintaês au Metropolitan Museum of Art de New-York* (New York: Metropolitan Museum of Art, 1999).

Graefe, Erhart. "Noch einmal Osiris-Lunus," *JEA* 65 (1979): 171–73.

——. *Das Grab des Padihorresnet, Obervermögensverwalter der Gottesgemahlin des Amun (Thebanisches Grab Nr. 196)*, 2 vols., MonAeg 9 (Brussels: Fondation Égyptologique Reine Élisabeth; Turnhout: Brepols, 2003).

Graindorge, Catherine. "La quête de la lumière au mois de khoiak: Une histoire d'oies," *JEA* 82 (1996) : 83–105.

Grapow, Hermann. *Religiöse Urkunden: Ausgewählte Texte des Totenbuches*, Urk. 5 (Leipzig: Hinrichs, 1915–17).

———. *Sprachliche und schriftliche Formung ägyptischer Texte*, LÄS 7 (Glückstadt, Hamburg, New York: Augustin, 1936).

Graves-Brown, Carolyn. "The Spitting Goddess and the Stony Eye: Divinity and Flint in Pharaonic Egypt," in K. Piquette and S. Love, eds., *Current Research in Egyptology 2003. Proceedings of the Fourth Annual Symposium which took place at the Institute of Archaeology, University College London 18–19 January 2003* (Oxford: Oxbow Books, 2005), pp. 57–70.

Green, Michael. "Some notes on the words *wšbt* and *šbt*," GM 41 (1980): 43–50.

Griffiths, John Gwyn. "Osiris and the moon in Iconography," *JEA* 62 (1976): 153–59.

———. "The striding bronze figure of Osiris-l'aḥ at Lyon," *JEA* 65 (1979): 174–75.

———. *The Origins of Osiris and his Cult* (Leiden: Brill, 1980).

Guglielmi, Waltraud. "Lachen und Weinen in Ethik, Kult und Mythus der Ägypter," *CdE* 55/109 (1980): 69–86.

———. "Zu einigen Literarischen Funktionen des Wortspiels," in F. Junge, ed., *Studien zu Sprache und Religion Ägyptens: Zu Ehren von Wolfhart Westendorf*, vol. 1, (Göttingen: Hubert & Co., 1984), pp. 491–506.

———. "Die ägyptische Liebespoesie," in A. Loprieno, ed., *Ancient Egyptian Literature: History and Forms*, PAe 10 (Leiden, New York, Köln: Brill, 1996), pp. 335–47.

Gutbub, Adolph. "Un Emprunt aux textes des pyramides dans l'hymne à Hathor, dame de l'ivresse," in *Mélanges Maspero I*, 4th fascicle, Mémoires publiés par les membres de l'IFAO 66 (Cairo: IFAO, 1961), pp. 31–72.

Haikal, Fayza. *Two Hieratic Funerary Papyri of Nesmin*, vol. 1: *Introduction, Transcriptions and Plates*, BAe 14 (Brussels: Fondation Égyptologique Reine Élisabeth, 1970).

———. *Two Hieratic Funerary Papyri of Nesmin*, vol. 2: *Translation and Commentary*, BAe 15 (Brussels: Fondation Égyptologique Reine Élisabeth, 1972).

Hannig, Rainer. *Die Sprache der Pharaonen. Grosses Handwörterbuch. Ägyptisch–Deutsch (2800–950 v.Chr.)*, Kulturgeschichte der antiken Welt 64 (Mainz: von Zabern, 1995).

Hartwig, Melinda. *Tomb Painting and Identity in Ancient Thebes, 1419–1372 BCE*, MonAeg 10. (Brussels: Fondation Égyptologique Reine Élisabeth; Turnhout: Brepols, 2004).

Hayes, William C. *Royal Sarcophagi of the XVIII Dynasty*, Princeton Monographs in Art and Archaeology: Quarto Series 19 (Princeton: Princeton University, 1935).

———. *The Scepter of Egypt: A Background for the Study of the Egyptian Antiquities in the Metropolitan Museum of Art*, vol. 2, 2nd ed. (New York: The Museum: Abrams, Inc., 1990).

Hays, Harold. "*hꜣ snḏ* 'Oh, be fearful!'," GM 204 (2005): 51–56.

Hegenbarth, Ina. "'O seht, ich gehe hinter meinem *ꜣḫ.t*-Auge...' – Einige Überlegungen zu den Barken des mittleren Registers der zweiten Stunde des Amduat," SAK 30 (2002): 169–85.

Herbin, François-René. "Un hymne à la lune croissante," *BIFAO* 82 (1982): 237–82.

———. "Une liturgie des rites décadaires de Djemê, Papyrus Vienne 3865," *RdE* 35 (1984): 105–26.

———. *Le livre de parcourir l'éternité*, OLA 58 (Leuven: Uitgeverij Peeters, 1994).

———. "La renaissance d'Osiris au temple d'Opet (P. Vatican Inv. 38608)," *RdE* 54 (2003): 67–129.

———. "Un texte de glorification," *SAK* 32 (2004): 171–204.

Hoch, James. *Middle Egyptian Grammar*, SSEA 15 (Mississauga: Benben, 1997).

Hodge, Carleton T., "Ritual and Writing: An Inquiry into the Origin of Egyptian Script," in S. Noegel and A. Kaye, eds., *Afroasiatic Linguistics, Semitics, and Egyptology: Selected Writings of Carleton T. Hodge* (Bethesda: CDL, 2004), pp. 199–220.

Hornung, Erik. *Das Amduat. Die Schrift des verborgenen Raumes.* 2 vols. Die Kurzfassung. Nachtrag, ÄgAb 7, 13 (Weisbaden: Harrassowitz, 1963).

———. *Das Buch der Anbetung des Re im Westen (Sonnenlitanei) nach den Versionen des Neuen Reiches,* 2 vols., AH 2–3 (Geneva: Éditions de Belles-Lettres, 1976).

———. "Vom Sinn der Mumifizierung," *WdO* 14 (1983): 167–75.

———. *Unterweltsbücher der Ägypter* (Zurich: Artemis, 1992).

Iversen, Eric. "The Inscription of Herwerre' at Serâbit-al-Kâdem," in F. Junge, ed., *Studien zu Sprache und Religion Ägyptens: Zu Ehren von Wolfhart Westendorf*, vol. 1, (Göttingen: Hubert & Co., 1984), pp. 507–19.

Jansen-Winkeln, Karl. *Text und Sprache in der 3. Zwischenzeit: Vorarbeiten zu einer spätmittelägyptischen Grammatik*, ÄAT 26 (Wiesbaden: Harrassowitz, 1994).

———. "'Horizont' und 'Verklärtheit:' Zur Bedeutung der Wurzel *ꜣḫ*," SAK 23 (1996): 201–215.

Jasnow, Richard and Zauzich, Karl-Theodor. *The Ancient Egyptian Book of Thoth: A Demotic Discourse on Knowledge and Pendant to the Classical Hermetica.* vol. 1, (Wiesbaden: Harrassowitz, 2005).

Johnson, Janet. *The Demotic Verbal System*, SAOC 38 (Chicago: University of Chicago, 1976).

Junge, Friedrich. *Neuägyptisch: Einführung in die Grammatik*, (Wiesbaden: Harrassowitz, 1996).

Junker, Hermann. *Die Stundenwachen in den Osirismysterien, nach den Inschriften von Dendera, Edfu und Philä dargestellt*, DAWW 54/1 (Vienna: Hölder, 1910).

Kahl, Jochem. *Siut-Theben: Zur Wertschätzung von Traditionen im alten Ägypten*, PÄe 13 (Leiden, Boston, Köln: Brill, 1999).

Kákosy, László. "Temples and Funerary Beliefs in the Graeco-Roman Epoch," in *L'Égyptologie en 1979. Axes prioritaires de recherches*, vol. 1, Colloques internationaux du Centre National de la Recherche Scientifique 595 (Paris: Éditions du Centre National de la Recherche Scientifique, 1982), pp. 117–27.

Kees, Hermann. "Zur Ersetzung des Seth durch Thot und andere Götter," *MVAG* 29 (1924): 83–90.

———. "Textkritische Kleinigkeiten," *ZÄS* 63 (1928): 75–78.

———. *Totenglauben und Jenseitsvorstellungen der alten Ägypter* (Berlin: Akademie, 1956).

Kitchen, Kenneth. "The Festival Calendar of Ramses II at Abydos: A Preliminary Report," in G. Posener, ed., *Actes XXIXe Congrès des Orientalistes, l'Égyptologie, 1973* (Paris: L'Asiathèque, 1975), pp. 65–69.

———. *Catalogue of the Egyptian Collection in the National Museum, Rio de Janeiro*, 2 vols. (Warminster, Rio de Janiero: Museu Nacional, Universidade Federal de Rio de Janeiro, Departamento de Antropologia, Setor de Arqueologia, 1990).

Klotz, David. *Adoration of the Ram: Five Hymns to Amun-Re from Hibis Temple*, YES 6 (New Haven: Yale Egyptological Seminar, 2006).

Koemoth, Pierre. *Osiris et les arbres. Contribution à l'étude des arbres sacrés de l'Égypte ancienne*, AegLeo 3 (Liège: CIPL, 1994).

Koenig, Yvan. *Le Papyrus Boulaq 6: Transcription, traduction et commentaire*, BdE 87 (Cairo: IFAO, 1981)

Kuentz, Charles and Desroches-Noblecourt, Christiane. *Le petit temple d'Abou Simbel*, vol. 1., Markaz Tasjīl al-Āthār al-Miṣrīyah. Mémoires 1 (Cairo: Centre de documentation et d'étude sur l'ancienne Égypte, 1968).

Kucharek, Andrea. *Die Klagelieder von Isis und Nephthys*, Forthcoming publication.

LeBlanc, Christian. "L'école du temple (ât-sebait) et le per-ankh (maison de vie). A propos de récentes découvertes effectuées dans le contexte du Ramesseum," *Memnonia* 15 (2005): 93–101.

Lefebvre, Gustave. "Un couvercle de sarcophage de Tounah," *ASAE* 23 (1923): 229–45.

——. *Le Tombeau de Petosiris*, 3 vols. (Cairo: IFAO, 1923–24).

Leitz, Christian. *Tagewählerei: Das Buch ḥꜣt nḥḥ pḥ.wy ḏt und verwandte Texte*, ÄgAb 55 (Wiesbaden: Harrasowitz, 1994).

——. *Magical and Medical Papyri of the New Kingdom*, Hieratic Papyri in the British Museum VII. (London: British Museum, Cambridge University, 1999).

——. *Lexikon der ägyptischen Götter und Götterbezeichnungen*, 7 vols., OLA 110–16 (Leuven: Uitgevertij Peeters, 2002).

Lepsius, Richard. *Das Todtenbuch der Ägypter nach dem hieroglyphischen Papyrus in Turin*, (Leipzig: Wigand, 1842).

——. *Denkmaeler aus Aegypten und Aethiopien: Nach den Zeichnungen der von seiner Majestät den Koenige von Preussen Friedrich Wilhelm IV nach diesen Ländern gesendeten und in den Jahren 1842–1845 ausgeführten wissenschaftlichen Expedition auf Befehl Seiner Majestät*, vol. 2 (Berlin: Nicolai, 1849).

Lesko, Leonard. *The Ancient Egyptian Book of Two Ways*, (Berkeley, Los Angeles, London: University of California, 1972).

Lichtheim, Miriam. *Ancient Egyptian Literature*, vol. 1 (Berkeley, London, Los Angeles: University of California, 1975).

——. *Ancient Egyptian Literature*, vol. 2 (Berkeley, London, Los Angeles: University of California, 1976).

——. *Ancient Egyptian Literature*, vol. 3 (Berkeley, London, Los Angeles: University of California, 1980).

von Lieven, Alexandra. "Religiöse Texte aus der Tempelbibliothek von Tebtynis – Gattungen und Funktionen," in S. Lippert and M. Schentuleit, eds., *Tebtynis und Soknopaiu Nesos. Leben im römerzeitlichen Fajum. Akten des Internationalen Symposions vom 11. bis 13. Dezember 2003 in Sommerhausen bei Würzburg* (Wiesbaden: Harrassowitz, 2005), pp. 57–70.

——. "Eine Punktierte Osirisliturgie," in K. Ryholt, ed., *The Carlsberg Papyri 7: Hieratic Texts from the Collection*, (Copenhagen: Carsten Niebuhr Institute of Ancient Near Eastern Studies, University of Copenhagen: Museum Tusculanum, 2006), pp. 9–38.

Lloyd, Allan. "The Inscriptions of Udjahorresnet: A Collaborator's Testament," *JEA* 68 (1982): 166–80.

Loprieno, Antonio. "'Puns and Word Play in Ancient Egyptian," in S. Noegel, ed., *Puns and Pundits. Word Play in the Hebrew Bible and Ancient Near Eastern Literature* (Bethesda: CDL, 2000), pp. 3–20.

Lucas, Alfred and Harris, John R. *Ancient Egyptian Materials and Industries.* (Mineola: Dover Inc., 1999).

Lustman, Jacqueline. *Étude Grammaticale du Papyrus Bremner-Rhind* (Paris: Lustman, 1999).

der Manuelian, Peter. *Living in the Past: Studies in Archaism of the Egyptian Twenty-Sixth Dynasty*, SIE (London: Kegan Paul International Ltd, 1994).

Manassa, Colleen. *The Great Karnak Inscription of Merneptah: Grand Strategy in the 13th Century BC*, YES 5 (New Haven: Yale Egyptological Seminar, 2003).

——. *The Late Egyptian Underworld: Sarcophagi and Texts*, ÄAT 72, 1 (Wiesbaden: Harrassowitz, 2007).

——. "Sounds of the Netherworld," in B. Rothöhler and A. Manisali, eds., *Mythos & Ritual, Festschrift für Jan Assmann zum 70. Geburtstag*, Religionswissenschaft 5 (Münster: LIT, 2008), pp. 109–35.

Maspero, Gaston. *Sarcophages des époques persane et ptolémaïque*, vol. 2, Mathaf al-Miṣrī. Catalogue général des antiquités égyptiennes du Musée du Caire 72 (Cairo: IFAO, 1939).

Mathieu, Bernard. *La poésie amoureuse de l'Égypte ancienne: recherches sur un genre littéraire au nouvel empire*, BdE 115 (Cairo: IFAO, 1996).

Meeks, Dimitri. *Année lexicographique*, vol. 1 (Paris: Meeks, 1980 [1977]).

——. *Année lexicographique*, vol. 2 (Paris: Meeks, 1981 [1978]).

——. *Année lexicographique*, vol. 3 (Paris: Meeks, 1982 [1979]).

——. *Mythes et légendes du Delta d'après le papyrus Brooklyn 47.218.84*, MIFAO 125 (Cairo: IFAO, 2006).

Mendel, Daniela. *Die kosmogonischen Inschriften in der Barkenkapelle des Chonstempels von Karnak*, MRE 9 (Brussels: Fondation Égyptologique Reine Élisabeth; Turnhout: Brepols, 2003).

Meuli, Karl. *Gesammelte Schriften*, vol. 1 (Basel/Stuttgart: Schwabe & Co., 1975).

Möller, Georg. *Ueber die in einem späthieratischen Papyrus des Berliner Museums erhaltenen Pyramidentexte* (Berlin: Druck von B. Paul, 1900).

——. *Hieratische Paläographie*, 3 vols. (Osnabrück: Zeller, 1965).

Morenz, Ludwig. "Neues zum *pr-anx* - Zwei Überlegungen zu einem institutionellen Zentrum der sakralen Schriftlichkeitskultur Altägyptens," *GM* 181 (2001): 77–81.

Morenz, Siegfried. "Wortspiele in Ägypten," in *Festschrift Johannes Jahn, zum XXII. November MCMLVII*, (Leipzig: Seemann), pp. 23–32.

——. "Das Problem des Werdens zu Osiris in der griechisch-römischen Zeit Ägyptens," in P. Derchain, ed., *Religions en Égypte Hellénistique et Romaine. Colloque de Strasbourg 16–18 mai 1967*. Université de Strassburg. Centre de recherches d'histoire des religions. Bibliothèque des Centres d'Études Supérieures spécialisés (Paris: Universitaires de France, 1969), pp. 75–91.

Moret, Alexandre. "Légende d'Osiris à l'époque thébaine d'après l'hymne à Osiris du Louvre," *BIFAO* 30 (1931): 725–50.

Münster, Maria. *Untersuchungen zur Göttin Isis vom Alten Reich bis zum Ende des Neuen Reiches*, MÄS 11, (Berlin: Hessling, 1968).

Naville, Édouard. *The Temple of Deir el Bahari*, vol. 4, Memoir of the EEF 19 (London, Boston: EEF, 1898).

Niwínski, Andrzej. "The Solar-Osirian Unity as Principle of the Theology of the 'State of Amun' in Thebes in the 21st Dynasty," *JEOL* 30 (1987–88): 89–106.

Nordh, Katarina. *Aspects of Ancient Egyptian Curses and Blessings: Conceptual Background and Transmission*, Acta Universitatis Upsaliensis. Boreas 26 (Uppsala, Stockholm: Gotab, 1996).

Ogdon, Jorge. "A New Dramatic Argument in the Coffin Texts (Spells 30–37)," in *L'Égyptologie en 1979. Axes prioritaires de recherches*, vol. 2, Colloques internationaux du Centre National de la Recherche Scientifique 595 (Paris: Éditions du Centre National de la Recherche Scientifique, 1982), pp. 37–43.

——. "Studies in Ancient Egyptian Magical Thought, V. A New Look at the Terminology for 'Spell' and Related Terms in Magical Texts," *DiscEg* 40 (1998): 137–45.

Ockinga, Boyo. "The Burden of Khaakheperre'sonbu," *JEA* 69 (1983): 88–95.

Onstine, Suzanne. "The Relationship between Osiris and Re in the Book of Caverns," *JSSEA* 25 (1998 [1995]): 66–77.

Otto, Eberhard. *Das ägyptische Mundöffnungsritual*, 2 vols., ÄgAb 3 (Wiesbaden: Harrassowitz, 1960).

——. "Ach," in *LÄ* I (1975): cols. 49–52.

Le Page Renouf, Peter. "On Some Religious Texts of the Early Egyptian Period Preserved in Hieratic Papyri in the British Museum," *TSBA* 9 (1893): 295–306.

Parker, Richard. *The Calendars of Ancient Egypt* (Chicago: University of Chicago, 1950).

Parkinson, Richard and Quirke, Stephen. *Papyrus*, Egyptian Bookshelf (London: British Museum, 1995).

Patane, Massimo. "Quelques aspects des Textes des Pyramides à la basse époque," *DiscEg* 24 (1992): 43–46.

Piankoff, Alexandre. *Le livre des portes*, vol. 1, MIFAO 74, (Cairo: Imprimerie de l'IFAO, 1939).

———. *Le Livre du jour et de la nuit, avec un chapitre sur l'écriture énigmatique, par Etienne Drioton*, BdE 3 (Cairo: IFAO, 1942).

———. "Le livre des Quererts. Seconde Division," in *BIFAO* 42 (1944): 1–62.

———. "Le livre des Quererts. Sixième division," *BIFAO* 43 (1945): 1–50.

Piccione, Peter. "Mehen, Mysteries, and Resurrection from the Coiled Serpent," *JARCE* 27 (1990): 43–52.

———. "Sportive Fencing as a Ritual for Destroying the Enemies of Horus," in E. Teeter and J. Larson, eds., *Gold of Praise: Studies on Ancient Egypt in Honor of Edward Wente*, SAOC 58 (Chicago: University of Chicago, 1999), pp. 335–49.

Porter, Bertha and Moss, Rosalind. *Topographical Bibliography of Ancient Egyptian Hieroglyphic Texts, Reliefs, and Paintings*, 7 vols. (Oxford: Clarendon; New York: Oxford University, 1927).

Quack, Joachim. "Fragmente des Mundöffnungsrituals aus Tebtynis," in K. Ryholt, ed., *The Carlsberg Papyri 7: Hieratic Texts from the Collection* (Copenhagen: Carsten Niebuhr Institute of Near Eastern Studies, University of Copenhagen, 2006), pp. 69–150.

Quirke, Stephen. "Archive," in A. Loprieno, ed., *Ancient Egyptian Literature: History and Forms*, PAe 10 (Leiden, New York, Köln: Brill, 1996), pp. 379–401.

Quaegebeur, Jan. "La Designation *(pꜣ-)ḥry-tp*: Phritob," in G. Dreyer, G. Fecht, and J. Osing, eds., *Form und Mass: Beiträge zur Literatur, Sprache und Kunst des alten Ägypten. Festschrift für Gerhard Fecht*, ÄAT 12 (Weisbaden: Harassowitz, 1987), pp. 368–94.

Ranke, Hermann. *Die ägyptischen Personennamen*, 2 vols. (Glückstadt: Augustin, 1935).

Riggs, Christina. *The Beautiful Burial in Roman Egypt : Art, Identity, and Funerary Religion*, (Oxford, New York: Oxford University, 2005).

Ritner, Robert. "A Uterine Amulet in the Oriental Institute Collection," *JNES* 43 (1984): 209–21.

———. *The Mechanics of Ancient Egyptian Magical Practice*, SAOC 54 (Chicago: University of Chicago, 1993).

Rössler-Köhler, Ursula. *Kapitel 17 des Ägyptischen Totenbuches: Untersuchungen zur Textgeschichte und Funktion eines Textes der altägyptischen Totenliteratur*, GOF 10, (Wiesbaden: Harrassowitz, 1979).

——. "Zum Problem der Spatien in altägyptischen Texten: Versuch einer Systematik von Spatientypen," *ASAE* 70 (1984–85): 383–408.

Roth, Ann Macy. "The Social Aspects of Death," in S. D'Auria, P. Lacovara, and C. Roehrig, eds., *Mummies and Magic: The Funerary Arts of Ancient Egypt* (Boston: Museum of Fine Arts, 1988), pp. 52–59.

——. "The *psš-kf* and the 'Opening of the Mouth' Ceremony: A Ritual of Birth and Rebirth," JEA 78 (1992): 113–47.

——. "Fingers, Stars, and the 'Opening of the Mouth': The Nature and Function of the *nṯri*-blades," JEA 79 (1993): 57–79.

el Sabban, Sherif. *Temple Festival Calendars of Ancient Egypt*, Liverpool Monographs in Archaeology and Oriental Studies (Liverpool: Liverpool University, 2000).

Sauneron, Serge. *Villes et légendes d'Égypte*, BdE 90 (Cairo: IFAO, 1983).

Schott, Siegfried. *Urkunden Mythologischen Inhalts*, Urk 6 (Leipzig: Hinrichs, 1929).

——. *Mythe und Mythenbildung im alten Ägypten*, UGAÄ 15 (Leipzig: Hinrichs, 1945).

——. "Totenbuchspruch 175 in einem Ritual zur Vernichtung von Feinden," *MDAIK* 14 (1956): 181–89.

Schott, Siegfried and Schott, Erika. *Bücher und Bibliotheken im Alten Ägypten: Verzeichnis der Buch- und Spruchtitel und der Termini technici* (Wiesbaden: Harrassowitz, 1990).

Schneider, Hans. "Bringing the Ba to the Body," in C. Berger, G. Clerc, and N. Grimal, eds., *Hommages à Jean Leclant*, vol. 4, BdE 106/4 (Cairo: IFAO, 1994), pp. 355–62.

Seeber, Christine. *Untersuchungen zur Darstellung des Totengerichts im Alten Ägypten*, MÄS 35, (Munich and Berlin: Deutscher Kunstverlag, 1976).

Serrano, José. "Origin and Basic Meaning of the Word *ḥnmmt* (the so-called "sun-folk")," SAK 27 (1999): 353–68.

Servajean, Frédéric. *Les formules des transformations du Livre des Morts: à la lumière d'une théorie de la performativité. XVIIIe–XXe dynasties*, BdE 137 (Cairo: IFAO, 2003).

Sethe, Kurt. *Urkunden der 18. Dynasty. Historisch-biographische Urkunden von Zeitgenossen der Hatschepsowet*, Urk. 4/7 (Leipzig: Hinrichs, 1906).

——. *Die altägyptischen Pyramidentexte*, 2 vols. (Leipzig: Hinrichs, 1908–10).

——. "Die Sprüche für das Kennen der Seelen der heiligen Orte," *ZÄS* 58 (1923): 1–24; 57–78.

——. *Urkunden des Alten Reichs*, Urk.1 (Leipzig: Hinrichs: 1933).

——. *Übersetzung und Kommentar zu den altägyptischen Pyramidentexten*, 2 vols. (Hamburg: Augustin, 1935).

Silverman, David. "CT Spell 902 and its Later Usages in the NK," in *L'Égyptologie en 1979. Axes prioritaires de recherches*, vol. 1, Colloques internationaux du Centre National de la Recherche Scientifique 595 (Paris: Éditions du Centre National de la Recherche Scientifique, 1982), pp. 67–70.

Simpson, William Kelly. *The Mastabas of Qar and Idu: G 7101 and 7102* (Boston: Museum of Fine Arts, 1976).

Smith, Mark. "On Some Orthographies of the Verbs *mꜣ*, 'see', and *mn*, 'endure', in Demotic and other Egyptian Texts," in H. Thissen and K. Zauzich, eds., *Grammata Demotika. Festschrift für Erich Lüddeckens zum 15. Juni 1983* (Würzburg: Gisela Zauzich, 1984), pp. 193–210.

——. *The Mortuary Texts of Papyrus BM 10507*. Demotic Mortuary Papyri in the British Museum 3 (London: British Museum, 1987).

——. *The Liturgy of Opening the Mouth for Breathing* (Oxford: Griffith Institute Ashmolean Museum, 1993).

——. *Papyrus Harkness (MMA 31.9.7)* (Oxford: Griffith Institute, 2005).

——. "Osiris NN or Osiris of NN?" in B. Backes, I. Munro, and S. Stöhr, eds., *Totenbuch-Forschungen: Gesammelte Beiträge des 2. Internationalen Totenbuch-Symposiums Bonn, 25. bis 29. September 2005* (Wiesbaden: Harrassowitz, 2006).

——. "Democratization of the Afterlife," in J. Dieleman, W. Wendrich, eds., UCLA Encyclopedia of Egyptology (UC Los Angeles, 2009). Http://escholarship.org/uc/item/70g428wj.

Spalinger, Anthony. "Parallelism of Thought," in C. Berger, G. Clerc, and N. Grimal, eds., *Hommages à Jean Leclant*, BdE 106/4 (Cairo: IFAO, 1993), pp. 363–77.

——. "The Feast of *tḫy*," in SAK 20 (1993): 289–303.

——. "A Religious Calendar Year in the Mut Temple at Karnak," *RdE* 44 (1993): 161–84.

——. "A Chronological Analysis of the Feast of *tḫy*," SAK 20 (1993): 289–303.

——. "From Esna to Ebers: An Attempt at Calendrical Archeology," in P. der Manuelian, ed., *Studies in Honor of William Kelly Simpson*, vol. 2. (Boston: Museum of Fine Arts, 1996), pp. 755–63.

——. *The Private Feast Lists of Ancient Egypt* (Wiesbaden: Harrassowitz, 1996).

Szczudlowska, Albertina. "Liturgical Text Preserved on Sękowski Papyrus," *ZÄS* 98 (1970): 50–80.

Tait, John. "Guidelines and Borders in Demotic Papyri," in M. Bierbrier, ed., *Papyrus, Structure and Usage* (London: British Museum, 1986), pp. 63–89.

Tylor, Joseph and Griffith, Francis. *The Tomb of Paheri at el-Kab*, Memoir of the EEF 11 (London: EEF, 1894).

Valdesogo Martín, María R. "Les cheveux des pleureuses dans le rituel funéraire Égyptien. Le geste *nwn*," in Z. Hawass, ed., *Egyptology at the Dawn of the Twenty-first Century: Proceedings of the Eighth International Congress of Egyptologists,* Cairo, 2000, vol. 2, (Cairo, New York: American University in Cairo, 2003), pp. 548–57.

Vandersleyen, Claude. *Ouadj our = w3ḏ wr: un autre aspect de la vallée du Nil,* Etude 7 (Brussels: Connaissance de l'Egypte Ancienne, 1999).

van Dijk, Jacobus. "The Symbolism of the Memphite Djed-Pillar," *OMRO* 66 (1986): 7–17.

te Velde, Herman. *Seth: God of Confusion*, PAe 6 (Leiden: Brill, 1977).

Verhoeven, Ursula. *Das Saitische Totenbuch der Iahtesnacht: P.Colon. Aeg 10207*, vol. 2, (Bonn: Habelt, 1993).

——. *Untersuchungen zur späthieratischen Buchschrift*, OLA 99 (Leuven: Uitgeverij Peeters, 2001).

Vernus, Pascal. *Athribis: textes et documents relatifs à la géographie, aux cultes, et à l'histoire d'une ville du delta égyptien à l'époque pharaonique*, BdE 74 (Cairo: IFAO, 1978).

——. "*Omina* calendériques et comptabilité d'offrandes," in *RdE* 33 (1982): 89–124.

——. "Écriture du rêve et écriture hiéroglyphique," *Littoral* 7/8 (1983) : 27–32.

——. *Chants d'amour de l'Égypte antique: présentation traduction et notes*, La Salamandre (Paris: Imprimerie nationale Editions, 1992).

——. "La position linguistique des textes des sarcophages," in H. Willems, ed., *The World of the Coffin Texts*, EgUit 9 (Leiden: Nederlands Instituut voor het Nabije Oosten, 1996), pp. 143–96.

——. "Une formulation de l'autobiographie et les expressions avec *wn* et *m3ʿ*," in GM 170 (1999): 101–5.

Wainwright, Gerald. "Iron in Egypt," *JEA* 18 (1932): 3–15.

van Walsem, Rene. "Month Names and Feasts at Deir el Medina," in R. Demarée and J. Janssen, eds., *Gleanings from Deir el Medina*, EgUit 1 (Leiden: Nederlands Instituut voor het Nabije Oosten, 1982), pp. 215–44.

Waterfield, Robin. *The Histories. Herodotus.* Oxford World's Classics (Oxford: Oxford University, 1998).

Watterson, Barbara. "The Use of Alliteration in Ptolemaic," in J. Ruffle, G. Gaballa, K. Kitchen, eds., *Glimpses of Ancient Egypt: Studies in Honour of H.W. Fairman* (Warminster: Orbis Aegyptiorum Speculum, 1979), pp. 167–69.

Wente, Edward F. "Mysticism in Pharaonic Egypt?" *JNES* 41 (1982): 161–79.

Werning, Daniel A. "The Sound Values of the Signs Gardiner D1 (Head) and T8 (Dagger)," *LingAeg* (2004): 183–204.

Westendorf, Wolfhart. "Beiträge aus und zu den medizinischen Texten," *ZÄS* 92 (1966): 128–54.

Willems, Harco. "The Embalmer Embalmed: Remarks on the Meaning of the Decoration of some Middle Kingdom Coffins," in J. van Dijk, ed., *Essays on Ancient Egypt in Honour of Herman te Velde* (Gronigen: STYX, 1997), pp. 343–72.

———. "The Social and Ritual Context of a Mortuary Liturgy of the Middle Kingdom (CT Spells 30–41)," in H. Willems, ed., *Social Aspects of Funerary Culture in the Egyptian Old and Middle Kingdoms. Proceedings of the International Symposium held at Leiden University 6–7 June, 1996*, OLA 103 (Leuven: Uitgeverij Peeters, 2001), pp. 253–372.

Wilson, John Albert. "Funeral Services of the Egyptian Old Kingdom," *JNES* 3 (1944): 209–10.

Wilson, Penelope. *A Ptolemaic Lexikon: A Lexicographical Study of the Texts in the Temple of Edfu*, OLA 78 (Leuven: Uitgeverij Peeters, 1997).

Winter, Erich. "Nochmals zum senut-Fest," *ZÄS* 96 (1970): 151–52.

de Wit, Constant. *Les inscriptions du temple d'Opet, à Karnak*, vol. 3, BAe 11–13 (Brussels: Édition de la Fondation Égyptologique Reine Élisabeth, 1958–68).

Yoyotte, Jean. "Religion de l'Egypte ancienne," *AEPHE* 86 (1977–78): 163–72.

———. "Religion de l'Égypte ancienne," *AEPHE* 88 (1979–80): 193–99

Žabkar, Louis. *A Study of the Ba Concept in Ancient Egyptian Texts*, SAOC 34 (Chicago: University of Chicago, 1968).

———. "A Hymn to Osiris Pantocrator at Philae," *ZÄS* 108 (1981): 141–71.

Zandee, Jan. *Death as an Enemy According to Ancient Egyptian Conceptions*, Studies in the History of Religions 5 (Leiden: Brill, 1960).

———. "Das Schöpferwort im alten Ägypten," in T. van Baaren et al., eds., *Verbum: Essays on Some Aspects of the Religious Function of Words, Dedicated to Dr. H. W. Obbink*, Studia Theologica Rheno-Traiectina 6, (Utrecht: Kemink, 1964), pp. 33–66.

Zivie-Coche, Christiane. "Miscellanea Ptolemaica," in P. der Manuelian, ed., *Studies in Honor of William Kelly Simpson*, vol. 2 (Boston: Museum of Fine Arts, 1996), pp. 869–74.

Indices

INDEX OF WORDS AND PHRASES DISCUSSED

The following list refers to each term's location in the papyrus by column and line number.

TEXTS CITED

This list includes only the texts that are extensively cited as parallels to P.W551. Their occurrences are referred to by page number.

GENERAL INDEX

The following list refers to the term's location by page number.

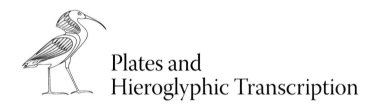

Plates and Hieroglyphic Transcription

Text passages written in red in P.W551 are indicated by a light gray background in the hieroglyphic transcription.

PLATE 1

W.551 COLUMN 1

W.551 COLUMN 1

32
33
34
35
36
37
38
39
40
41
42
43
44
45
46
47
48
49
50
51

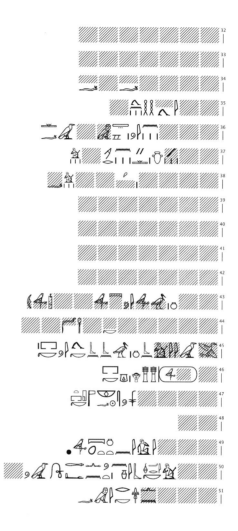

PLATE 2

W.551 COLUMN 2

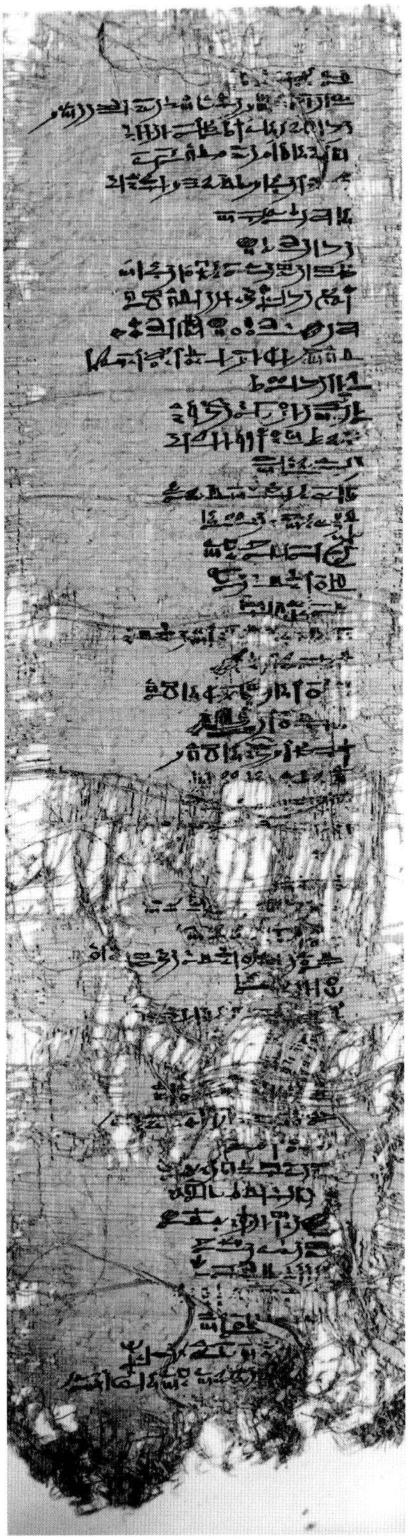

W.551 COLUMN 2

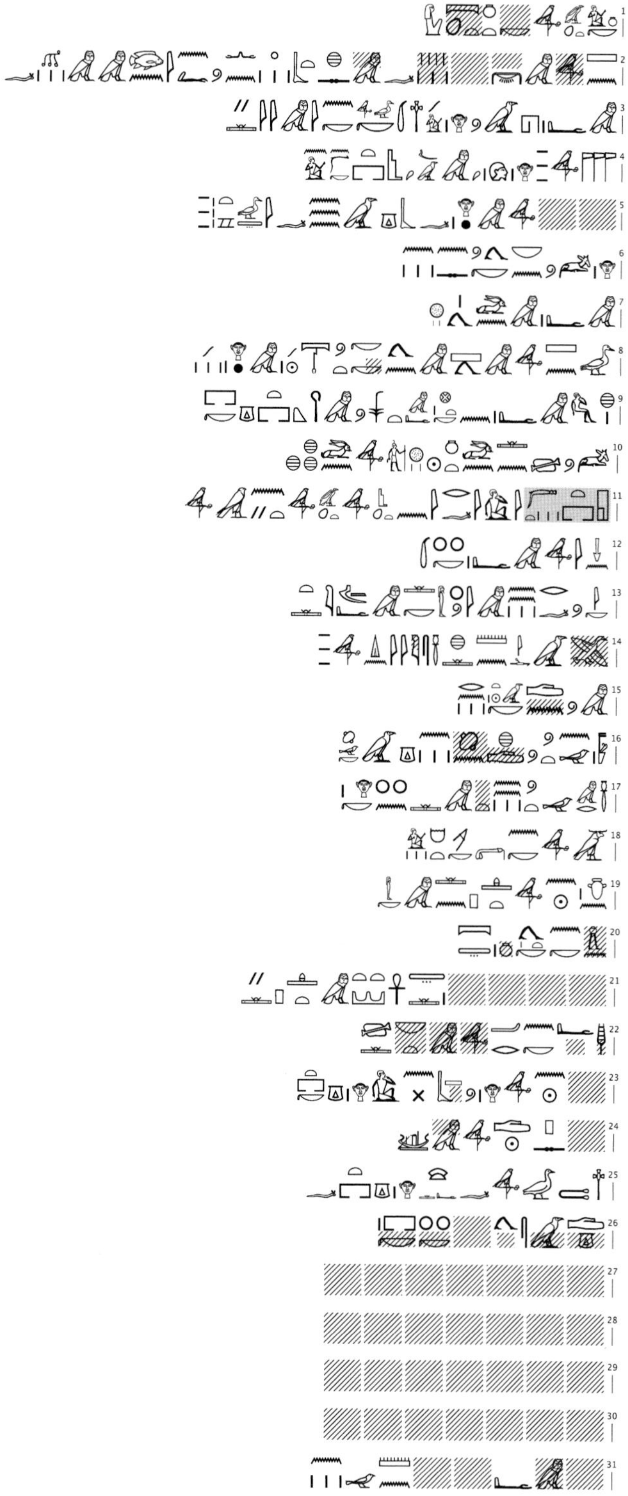

32
33
34
35
36
37
38
39
40
41
42
43
44
45
46
47
48
49

PLATE 3

W.551 COLUMN 3

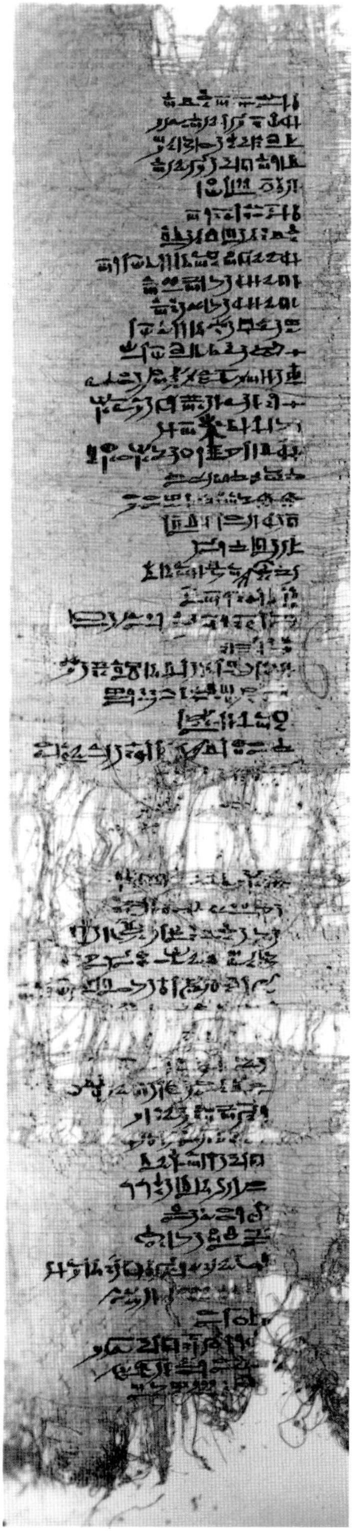

W.551 COLUMN 3

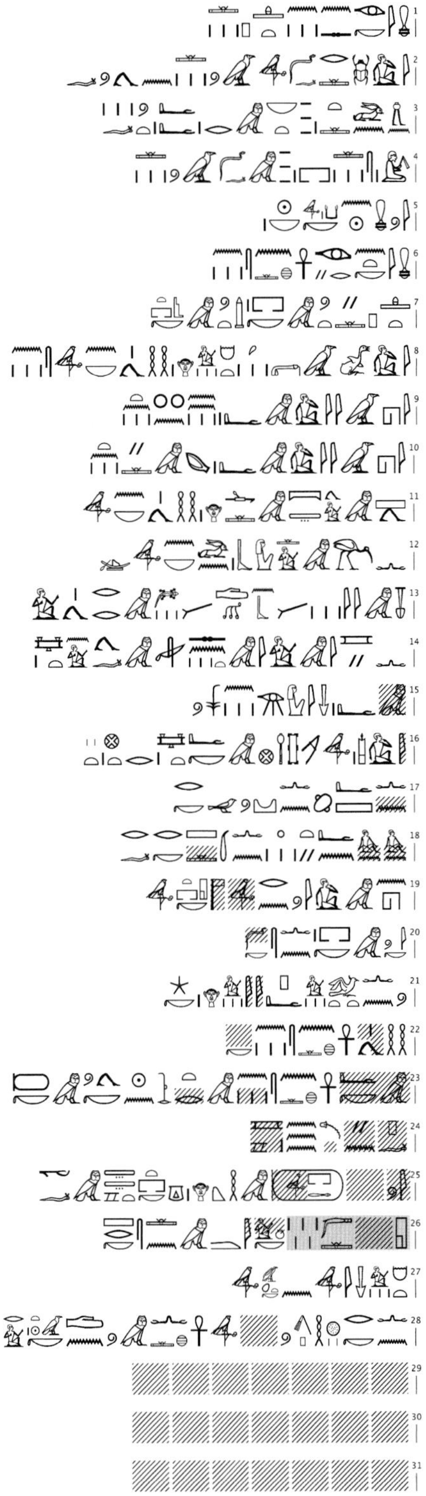

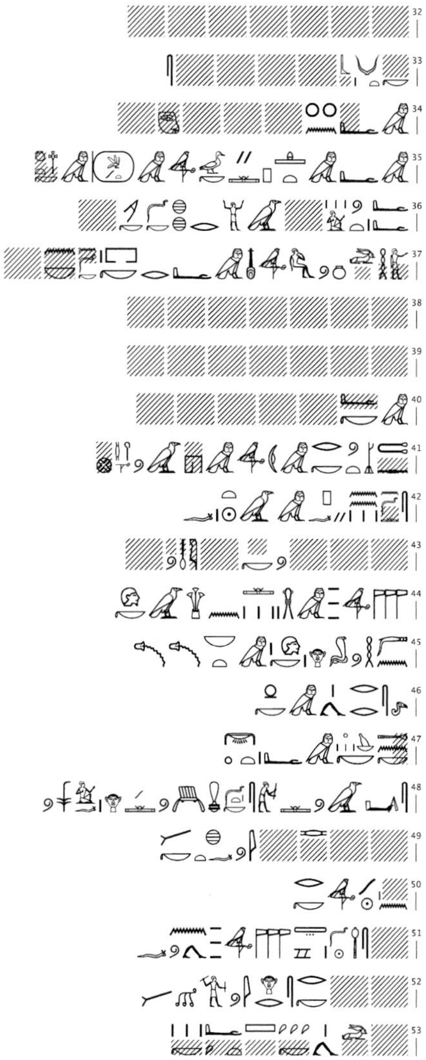
32
33
34
35
36
37
38
39
40
41
42
43
44
45
46
47
48
49
50
51
52
53

PLATE 4

W.551 COLUMN 4

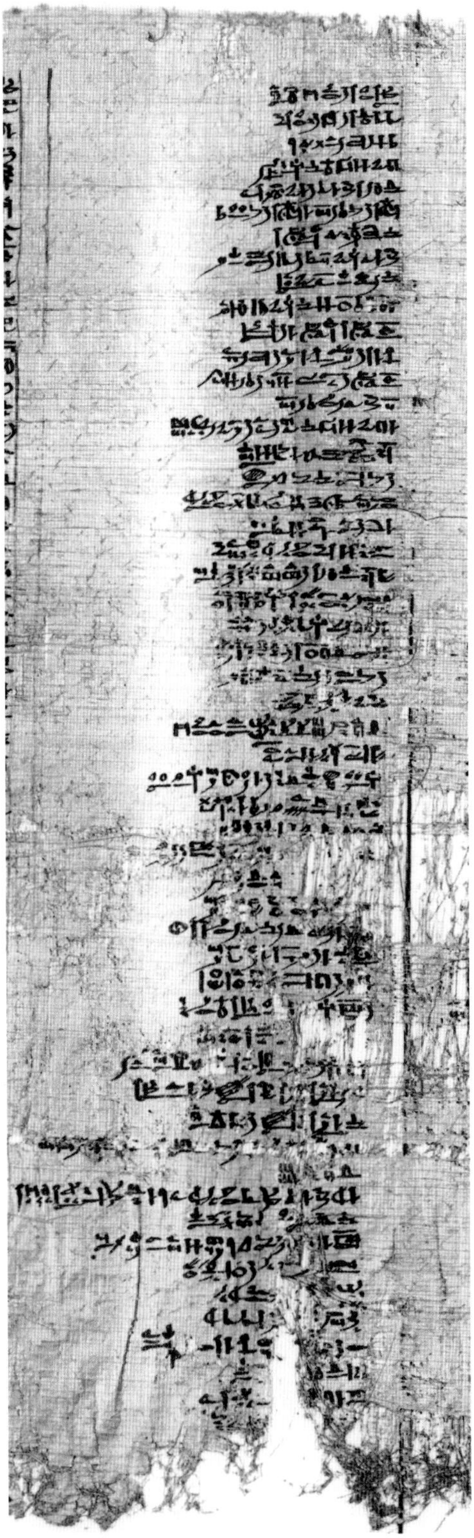

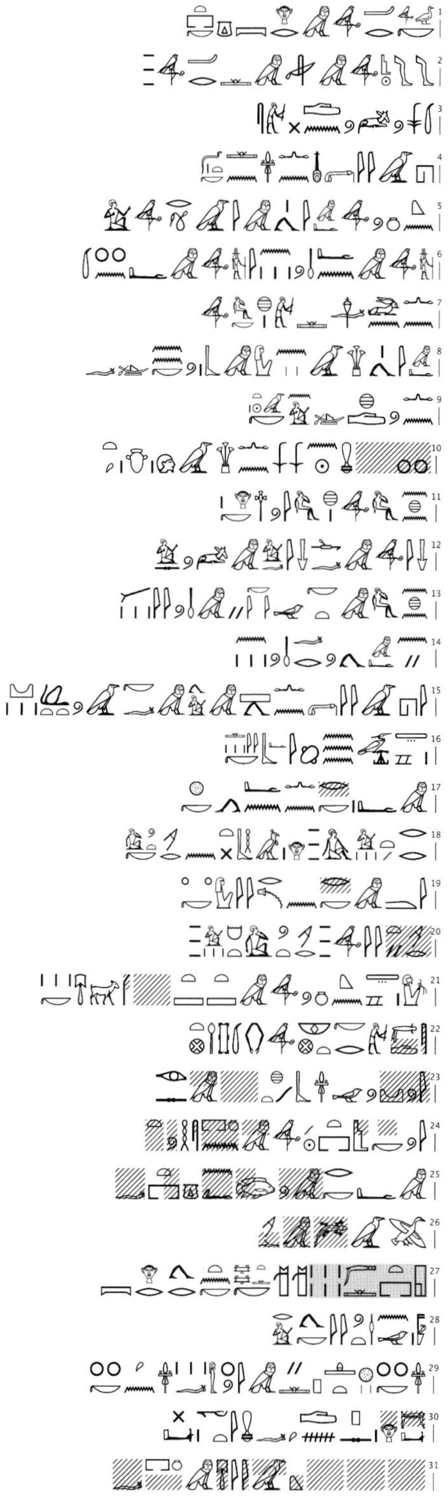

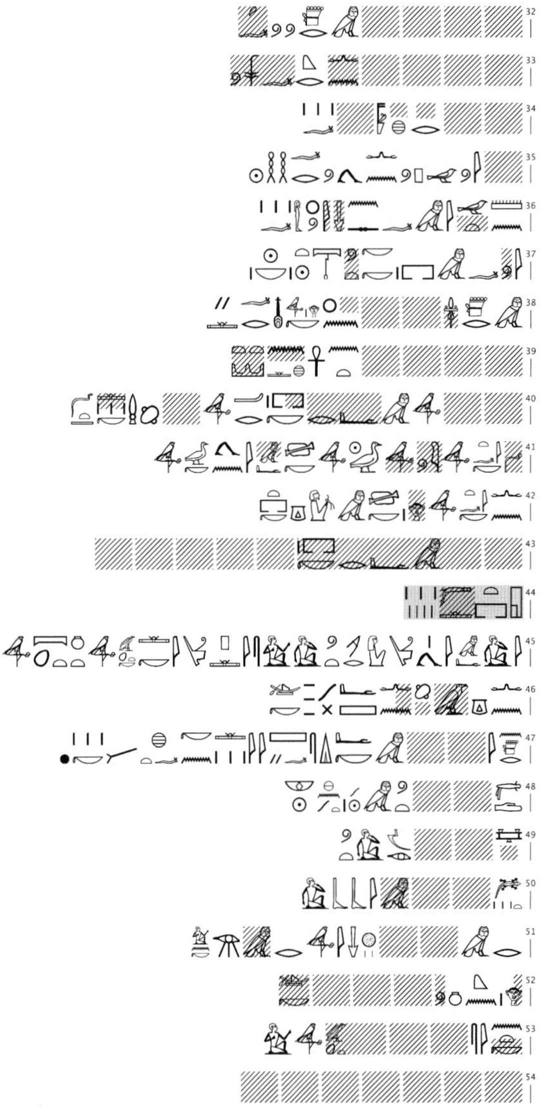
32
33
34
35
36
37
38
39
40
41
42
43
44
45
46
47
48
49
50
51
52
53
54

PLATE 5

W.551 COLUMN 5

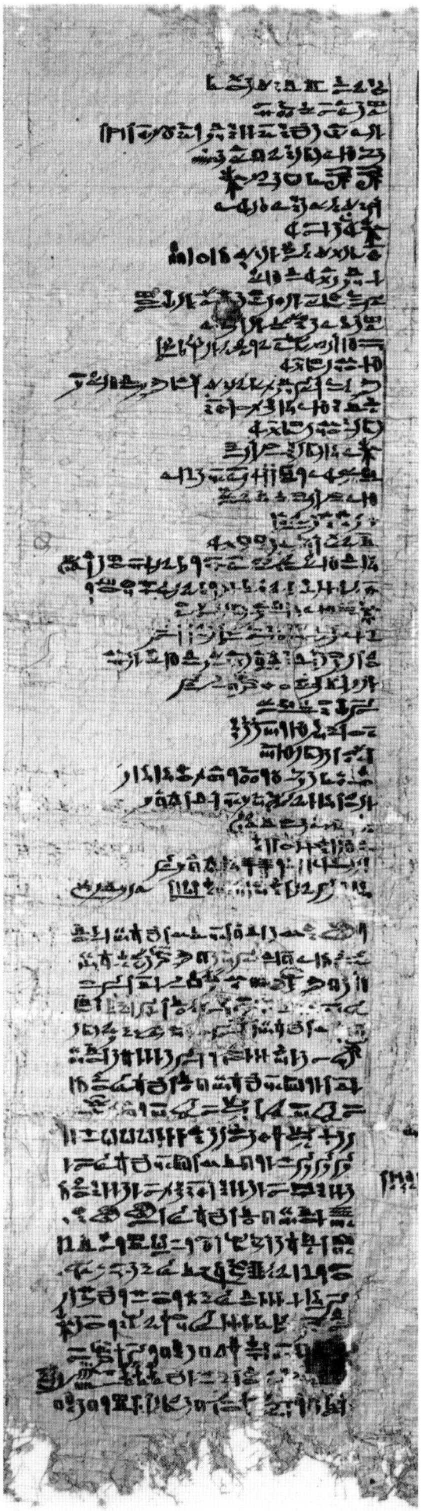

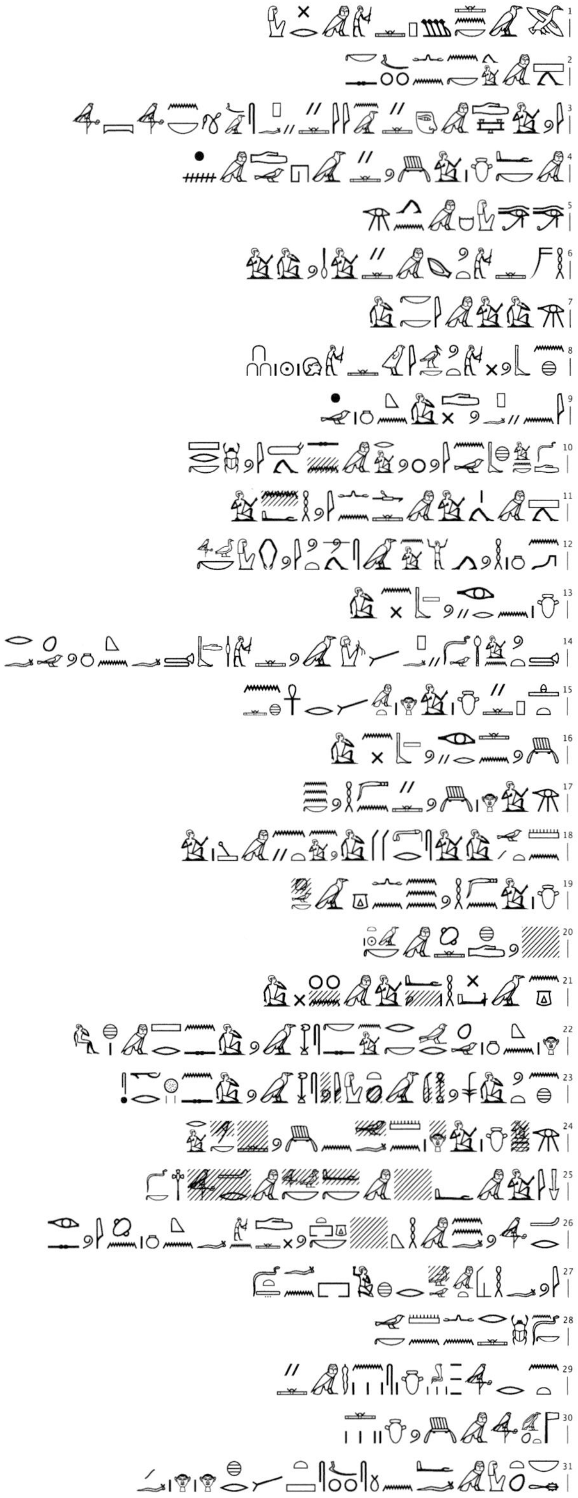

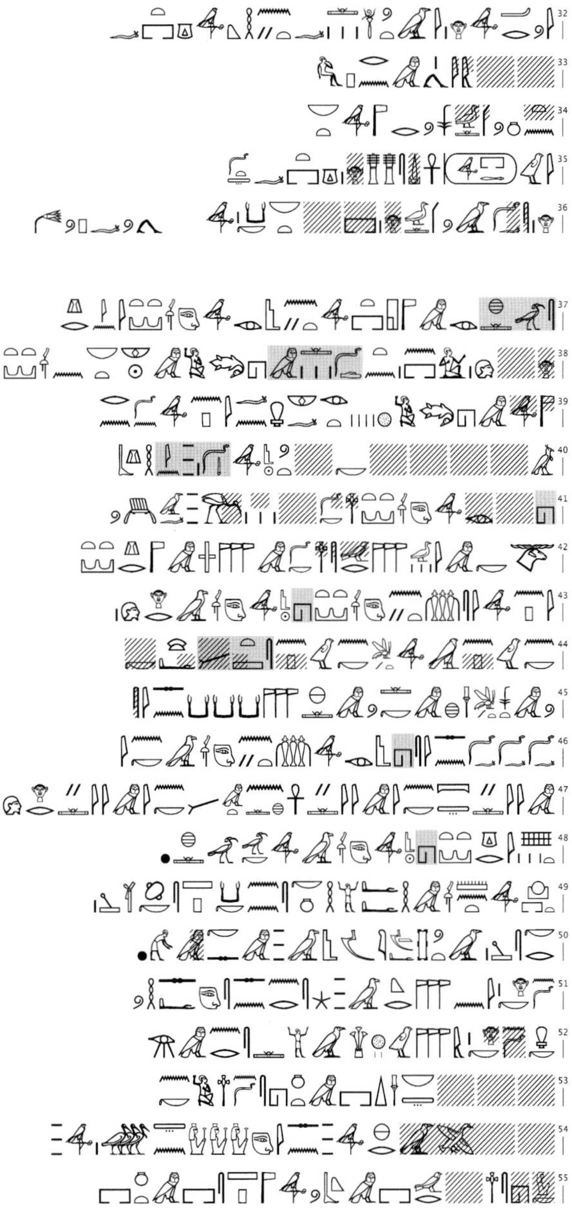

PLATE 6

W.551 COLUMN 6

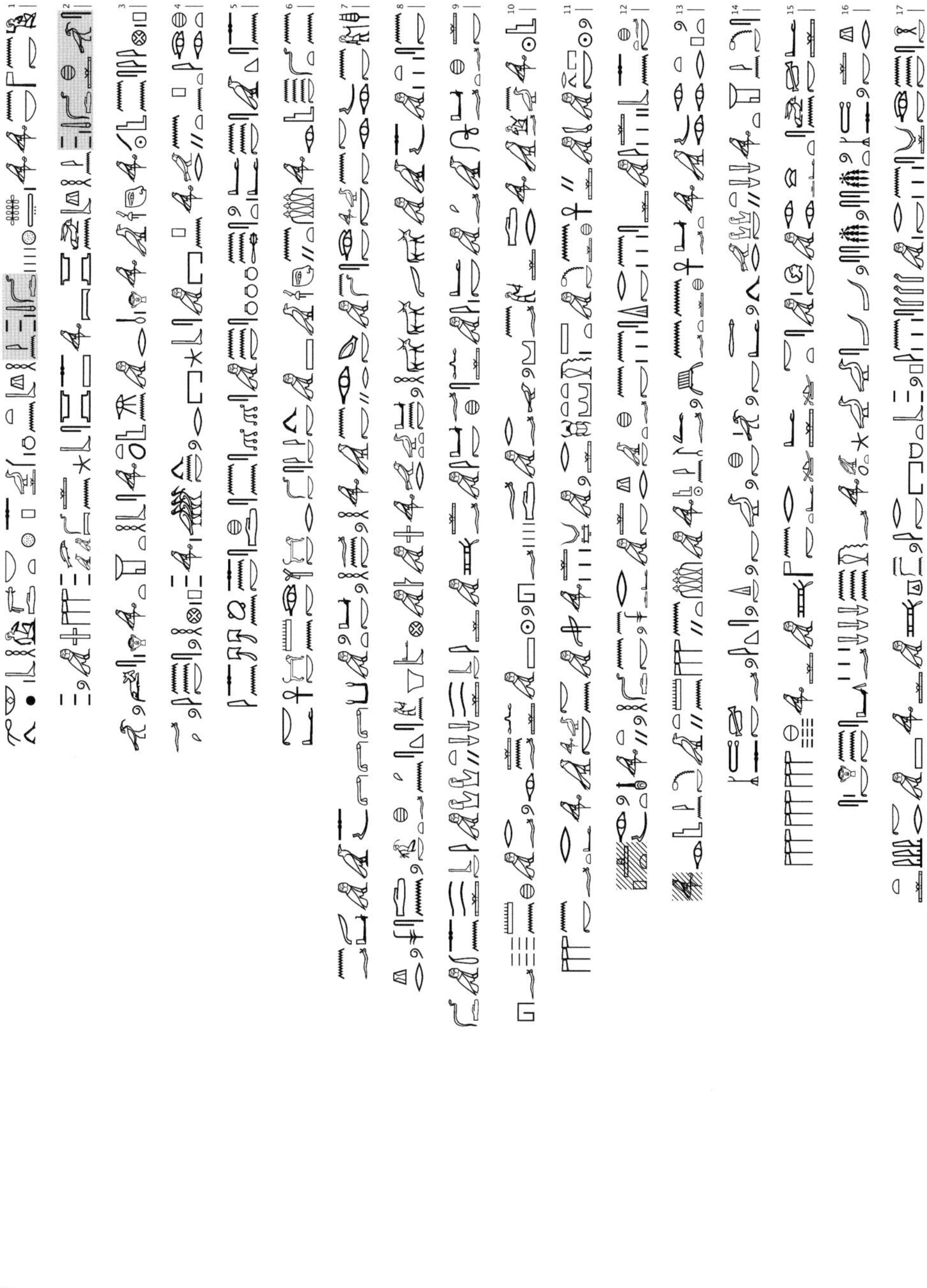

W.551 COLUMN 6

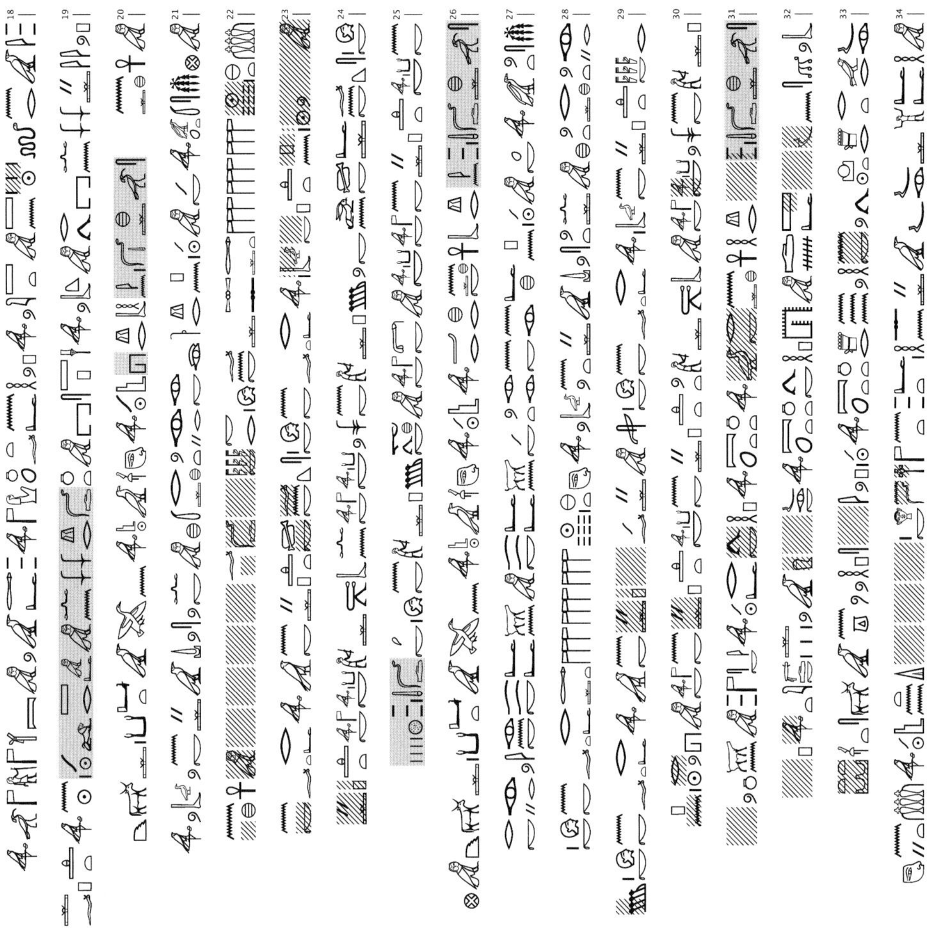

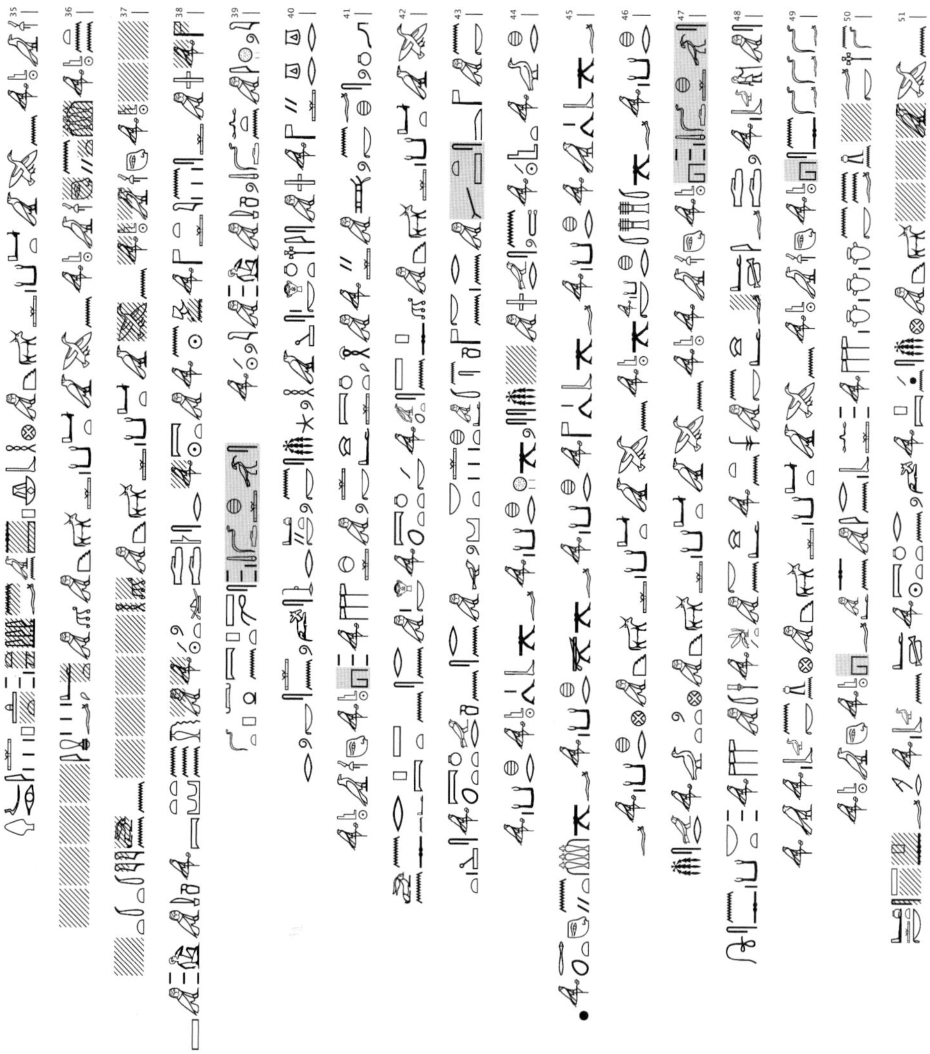

PLATE 7 W.551 COLUMN 7

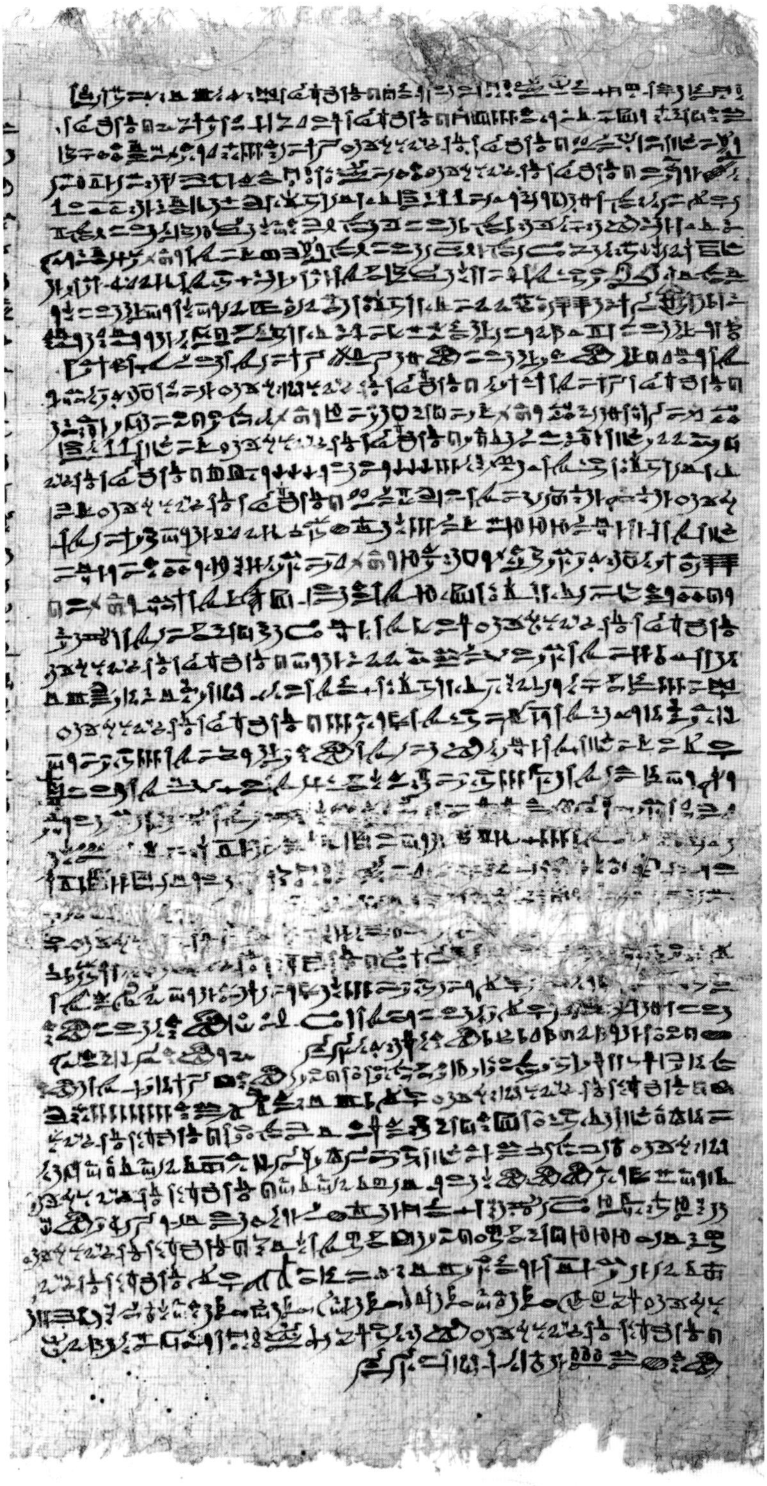

W.551
COLUMN 7

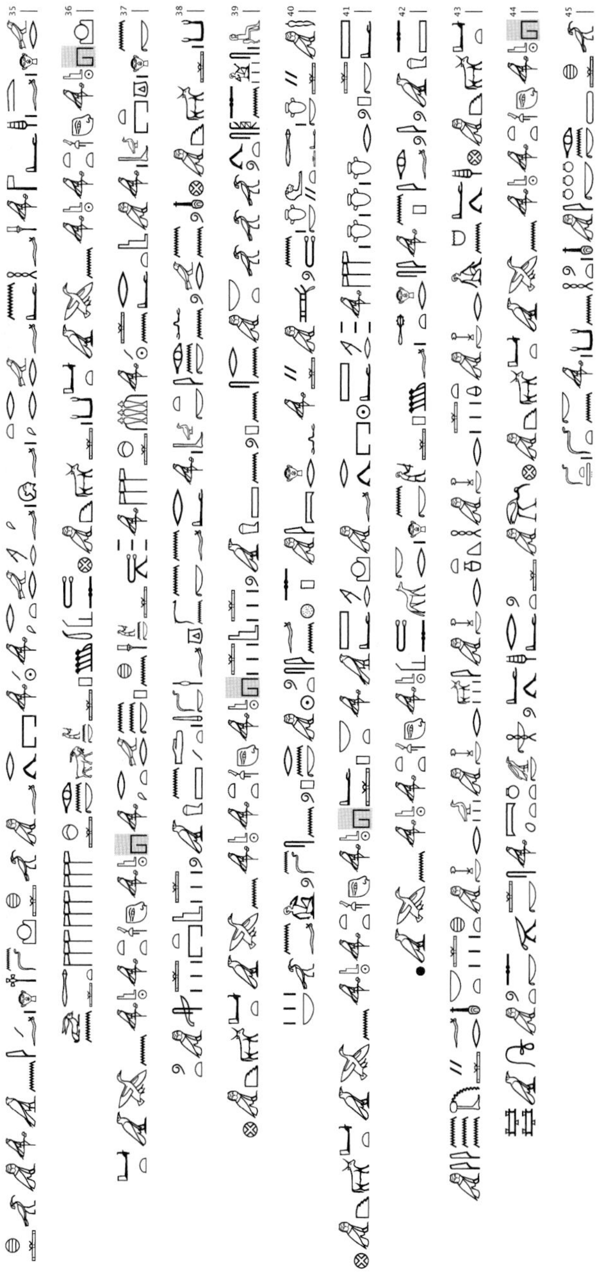

PLATE 8 W.551 COLUMN 8

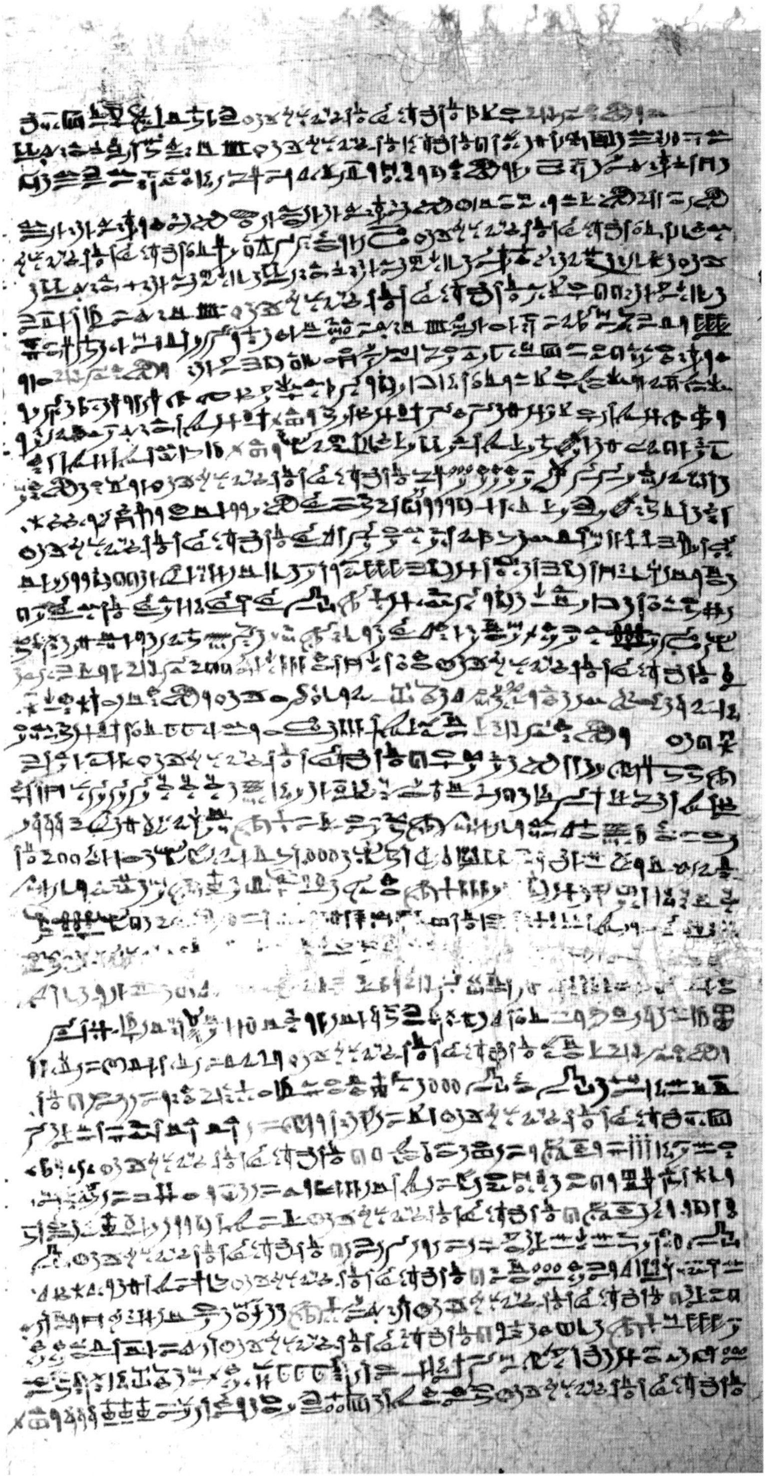

W.551
COLUMN 8

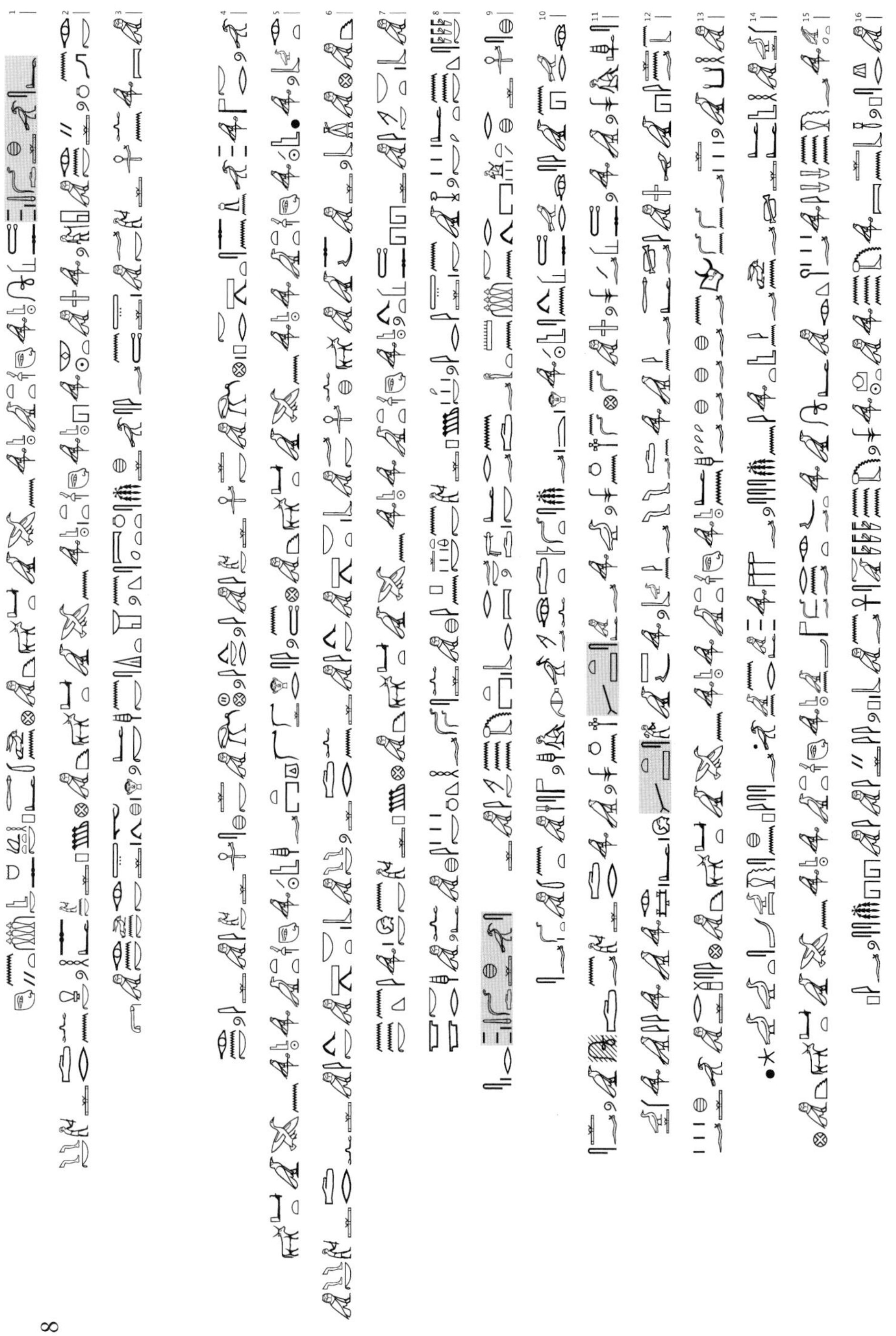

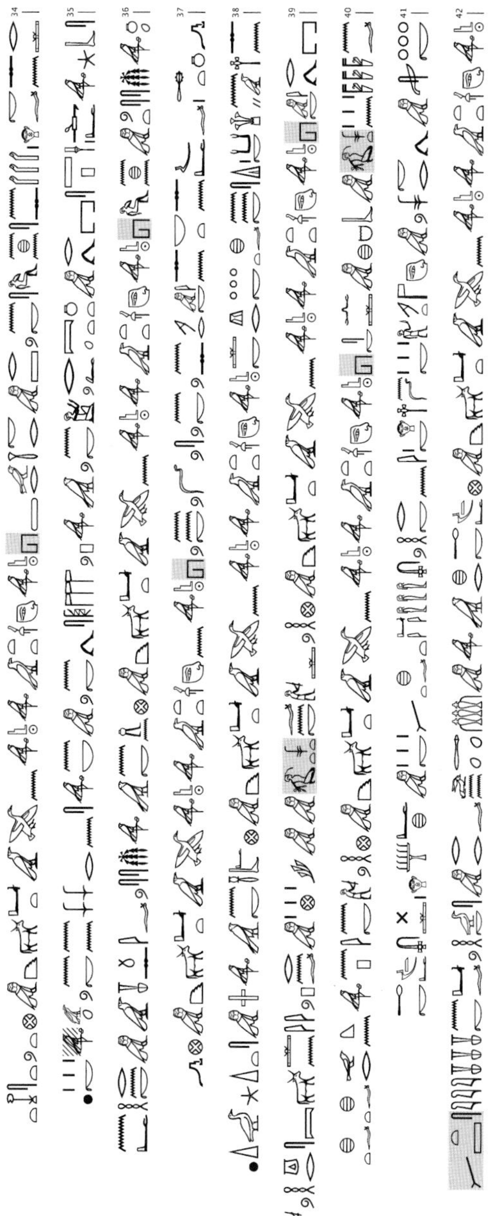
34
35
36
37
38
39
40
41
42

PLATE 9 W.551 COLUMN 9

W.551 COLUMN 9

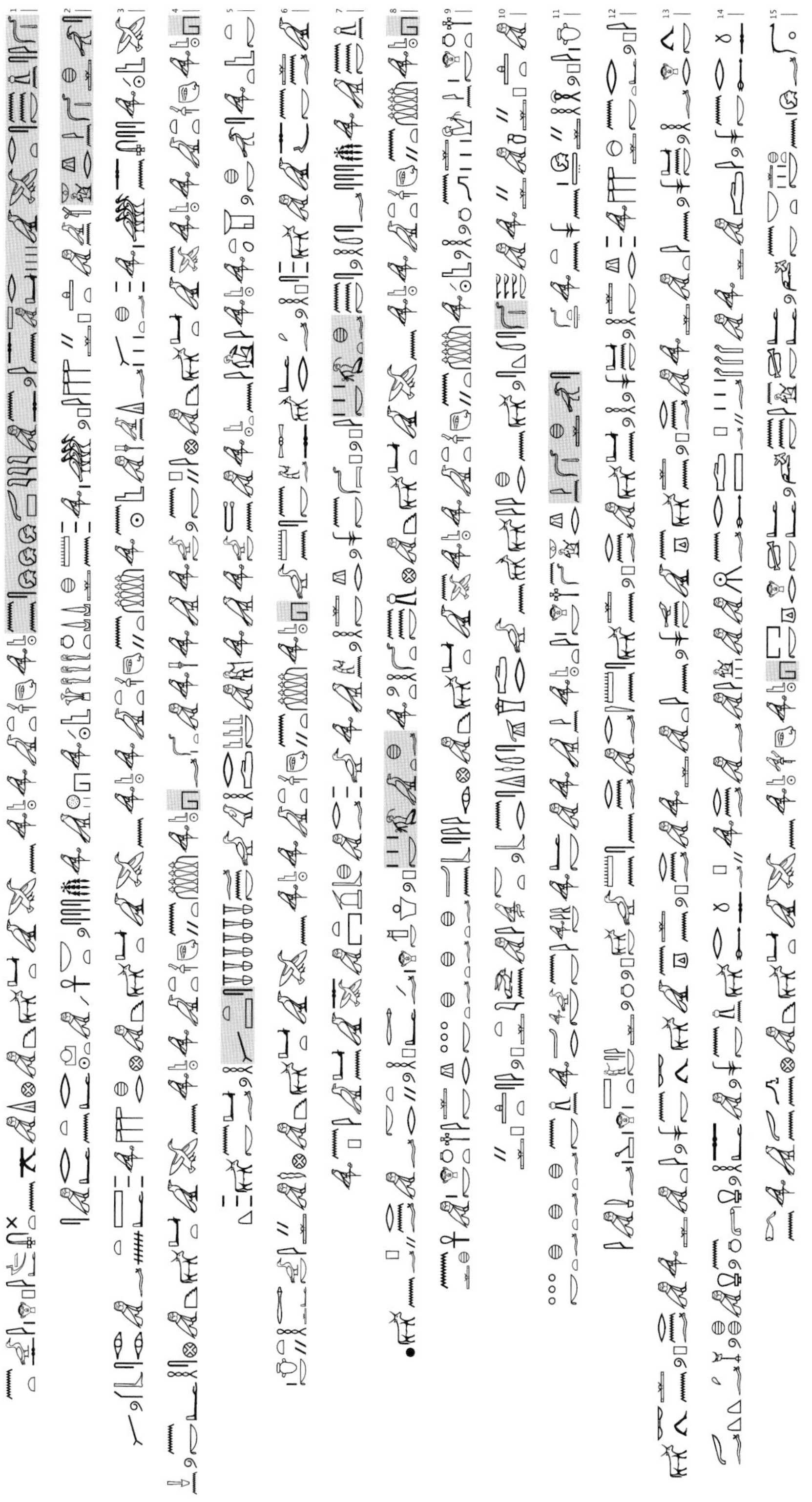

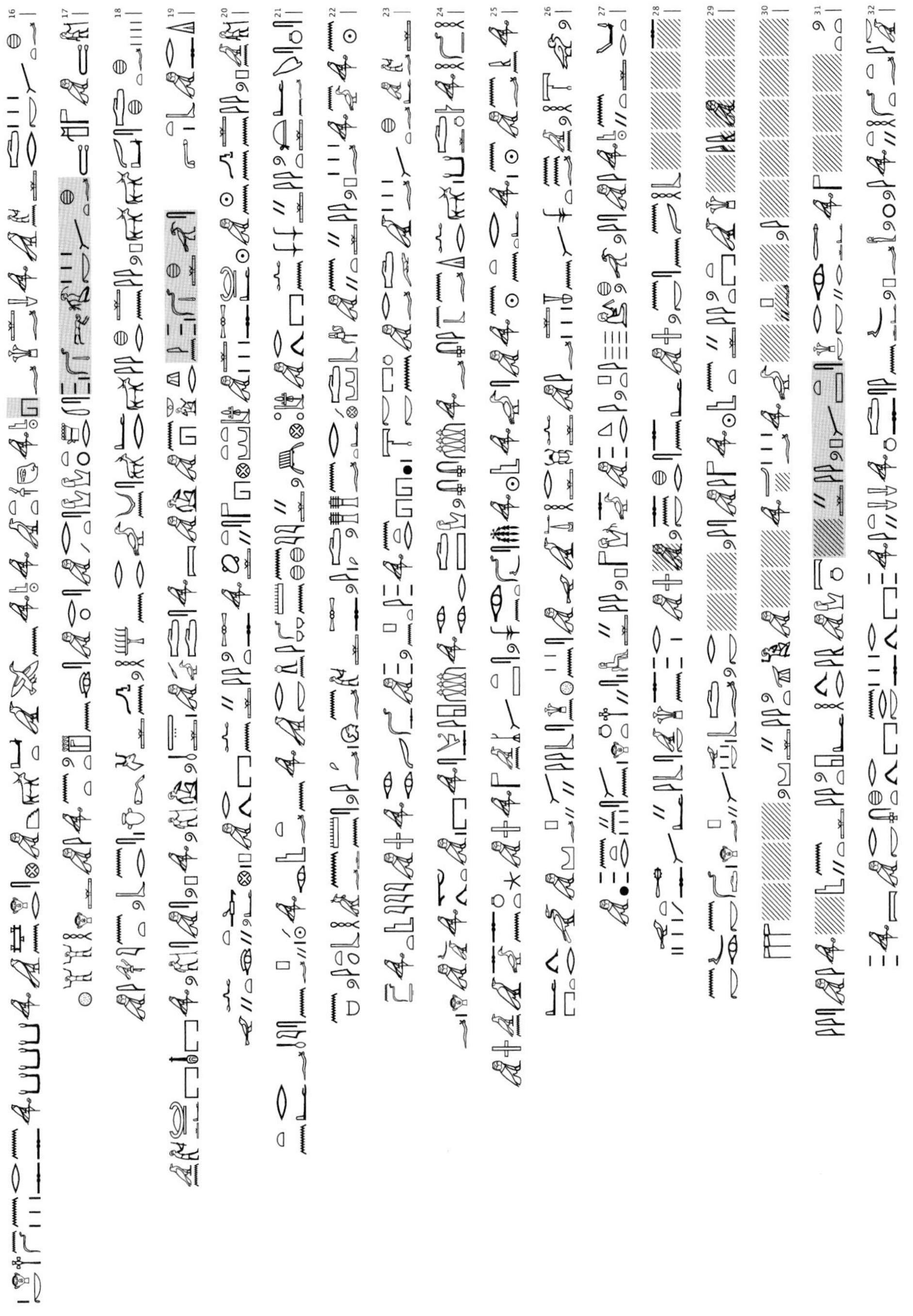

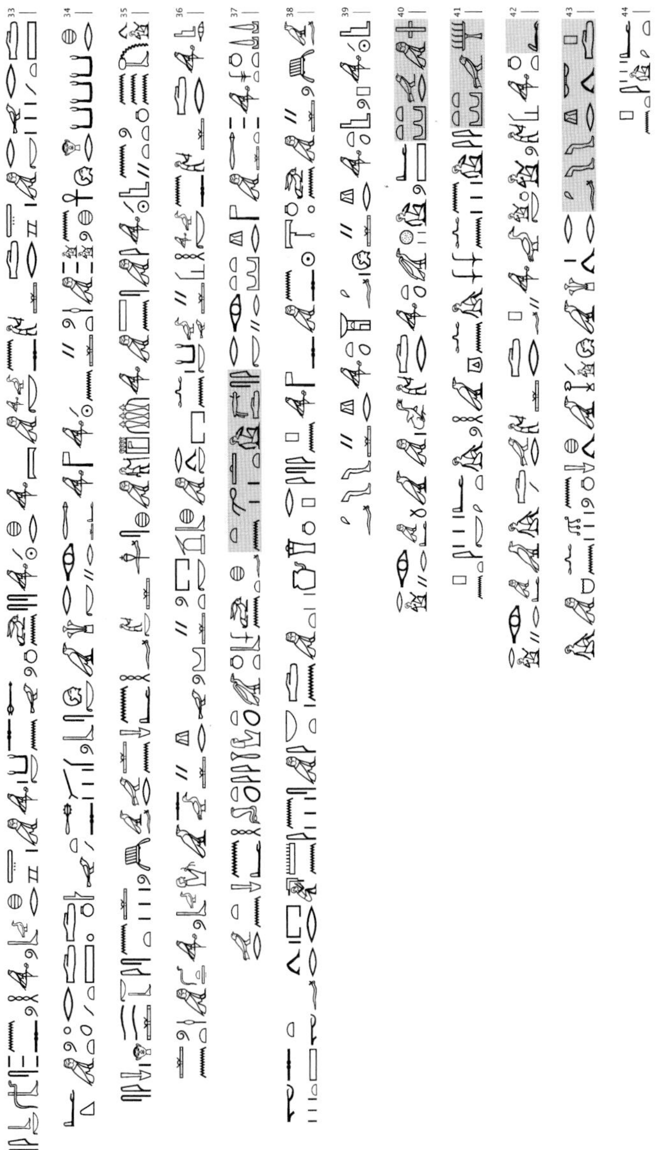

PLATE 10 — W.551 COLUMN 10

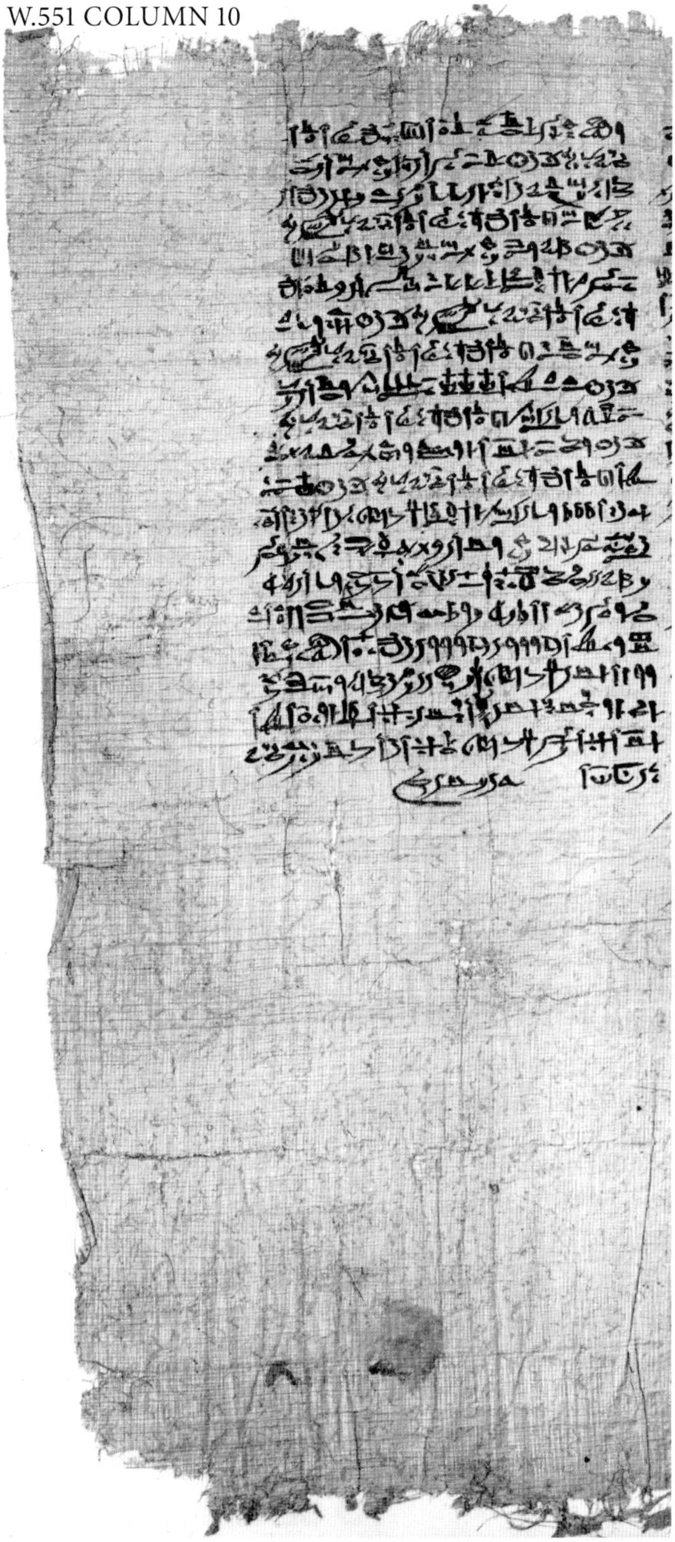

W.551 COLUMN 10

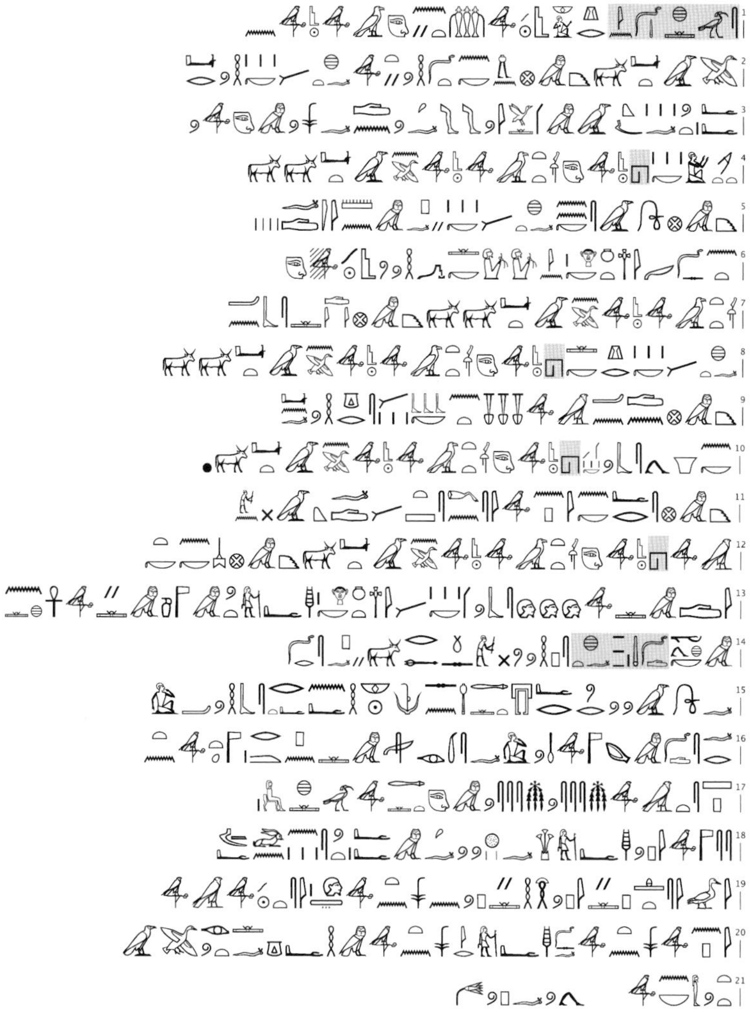